The Grammar of Criminal Law

The Grammar of Criminal Law

Volume Two: International Criminal Law

GEORGE P. FLETCHER

OXFORD
UNIVERSITY PRESS

OXFORD
UNIVERSITY PRESS

Oxford University Press is a department of the University of Oxford. It furthers the University's objective of excellence in research, scholarship, and education by publishing worldwide. Oxford is a registered trademark of Oxford University Press in the UK and certain other countries.

Published in the United States of America by Oxford University Press
198 Madison Avenue, New York, NY 10016, United States of America.

CIP data is on file at the Library of Congress
ISBN 978-0-19-090357-2

Note to Readers

This publication is designed to provide accurate and authoritative information in regard to the subject matter covered. It is based upon sources believed to be accurate and reliable and is intended to be current as of the time it was written. It is sold with the understanding that the publisher is not engaged in rendering legal, accounting, or other professional services. If legal advice or other expert assistance is required, the services of a competent professional person should be sought. Also, to confirm that the information has not been affected or changed by recent developments, traditional legal research techniques should be used, including checking primary sources where appropriate.

(Based on the Declaration of Principles jointly adopted by a Committee of the American Bar Association and a Committee of Publishers and Associations.)

To my father, Nicholas Fletcher (1896–1960),
who taught me to think with an international perspective

Contents

Preface

This volume of the *Grammar* has been a long time coming. The political events of the last 14 years have been so intense that it was hard to foresee a lasting impact of the Rome Statute and the International Criminal Court. As of this writing, in early 2019, the United States seems to be indifferent to the international cooperation necessary to deal sensibly with climate change, immigration, the avoidance of armed conflict, and the control over nuclear proliferation. We have become, temporarily, a country of American nationalists, ever more disdained by the leading powers of Europe.

But this, too, shall pass. The United States will soon discover that the United Nations and our European and Asian allies are essential to our own prosperity. My hope is that this book, along with the many fine authors cited in the notes, will contribute to reinvigorated international cooperation.

Allow me to add a few personal notes. My father, Nicholas Fletcher, to whom this volume is dedicated, was born under the name Fleischer Miklós in Szécsény, Hungary. He came from a family of large landowners and, as a result, joined the Austro-Hungarian army with privileged status as an einjähriger Freiwilliger (roughly, one-year volunteer). He was taken prisoner by the Russians and, after being released, returned to Hungary, confronted political chaos after, and then left to make his way to the United States. I am proud to say that he entered the country, illegally, by swimming the Rio Grande at the now famous juncture of Nogales and El Paso. As cousin Paul put it recently, he was a "well-to-do wetback."

His subsequent life embodies the American dream. He had no skills when he started working in Chicago, but he learned how to paint houses and work in construction. During World War II, he imported leather goods from his brother Géza who decided to immigrate to Argentina.

My childhood was one of linguistic cacophony. Greek in the streets, English at school, Hungarian at home, and then Spanish in the third grade in Glendale. Finally, at my father's suggestion, I learned German in high school and Russian in college. Along the way, I picked up some French and Modern Hebrew. With the mélange of different languages, it was impossible not to develop an international perspective on law and politics.

Fortunately, my students at Columbia Law School confirmed the importance of having learned these languages. I feel grateful to the many students in the fall of 2018 who sought to learn criminal law in my classes. They came from Germany, Italy, China, Singapore, the Netherlands, Brazil, Turkey, and, yes, even the United States.

I particularly appreciate the research assistance in this volume of David C. Kellam. Allow me as well to express my thanks to co-teachers on topics related to criminal law, Rabbi Saul Berman (biblical jurisprudence) and Michel Paradis (jurisprudence of war).

Introduction

International Criminal Law—Basic Concepts

1. The Influence of Scholars

To understand the international legal order in the field of criminal law, we need to ask three elementary questions. What is international law? What is criminal law? And what happens to these two fields when they are joined together?

International law is about the legal obligations that arise between and among states. That is the beginning of a long and complicated story. By referring to a state's entity, we mean a collection of people on a territory with a sovereign—a government—that can act in the name of the people. The club of states is like other clubs. The extant members decide whether if you are a revolutionary state, you are invited to join. The states need not be democratic and, of course, if we look back to the origins of international law, very few of the participants were democratic. Hugo Grotius and Samuel Puffendorf are thought to be the writers who created the first conceptualization of the field. That is not to say that there was no international law before Grotius, only that his master work, *De Jure Belli et Pacis*, formulated the field in writing, much as Edward Cooke and William Blackstone formulated the common law for the study of English and American students.

That there are students who read these books, of course, is critical for its transmission to the field from generation to generation. The implication is that the generative books lie at the foundation of the field.

We can talk about the sources of international law in several different senses. The source of ideas used in transmitting the field is, as noted, the books. As we shall see, however, sources can mean, as well, the books that have made it authoritative. These other sources can include treaties, either bilateral or multilateral, customary practices regarded as obligatory and, finally, the decision of courts adjudicating disputes under these sources. Then

The Grammar of Criminal Law: Volume Two: International Criminal Law. George P. Fletcher.

the process continues with additional books and articles for succeeding generations interpreting the hierarchy of treaties, customary law, scholarly interpretation, and judicial application.

With the rise of Parliament, we encounter the situation we face today in international criminal law after the enactment of the Rome Statute.[1] The first question was whether Parliament could change the common law. Can the Rome Statute—or the Statute of the International Court of Justice—change the law derived from the founders, Grotius and Puffendorf? We assume that these treaties can have that effect, but it is worth taking a step to realize the analogy with the development of English law.

Three points are important as the analysis takes on this complexity. First, we have introduced a jurisprudential or philosophical moment, and it should be obvious that we could not proceed successfully without this self-reflective theoretical perspective; secondly, at the metalevel, we have the same problem of authority as we had on the basic level, namely do we follow the treaties, the scholarly authorities, or the judges? Third, the answer to that last question depends largely on where you are situated in the legal culture. If you are a student, you will likely want to read the books; if you are judge, you will be interested in what fellow judges think; and the legislators might have a different focus altogether: they might be interested in their political parties or their constituents.

Karl Llewellyn, a professor and the author of the Uniform Commercial Code, coined the concept of "situation sense."[2] A lawyer must know to whom he is talking to and adjust his presentation accordingly. Writing a brief differs from negotiating and writing a legal opinion, or a legislative history differs from deciding a case. For these purposes, scholars are not lawyers. We enjoy the illusion that we are speaking truth for truth's sake. At least this is the purpose of our writing.

In his famous speech to graduating law students, published in the *Harvard Law Review*, Oliver Wendell Holmes Jr. argued in favor of the bad man's view of the law.[3] This is in line with Llewellyn's view: the lawyer should be interested in predicting what the courts will do so that he can give his client the best possible advice. Yet Holmes was also a wise and experienced jurist.

[1] Rome Statute for the International Criminal Court, July 17, 1998, 2187 U.N.T.S. 3; U.N. Diplomatic Conference of Plenipotentiaries on the Establishment of an International Court, U.N. Doc. A/Conf.183/9 [hereinafter Rome Statute].

[2] *See* K. Llewellyn, The Common Law Tradition (1960).

[3] O.W. Holmes, *The Path of the Law*, 10 Harv. L. Rev. 457 (1897).

He recognized the importance of the theory of the law and in a magnificent aphorism concluded: "To an imagination of any scope the most far-reaching form of power is not money, it is the command of ideas. . . . Read the works of the great German jurists, and see how much more the world is governed today by Kant than by Bonaparte."[4]

Holmes's genius is recognizing the distinctive roles of lawyers, and of course, the principle applies to international lawyers as well. One function is to advise clients about what the courts will do in fact. Another function is to cultivate the great ideas not only of his legal system but of the great legal systems around the world.

The year 1897 is significant. Napoleon had commanded a commission to draft French Code Civil in 1804. The product has had influence in private law all over the world. The Code is written in elegant French. The great writer Stendhal is said to have read 10 paragraphs of the Code the very night before retiring.

But Germans did not follow the French example. They deliberately withdrew to academic discourse to cultivate the implication of Kant's principal works written in 1785 and 1795. In 1896, the year before Holmes's lecture, they finalized a draft of their own civil code *Das Bürgerliches Gesetzbuch*, which was adopted in the year 1900 and, with amendments, remains valid to this day. The German Criminal Code was developed later and has been recodified several times. Thus, we return to the influence of scholars over the development of the law.

2. The Concept of *Dogmatik*

Holmes relied on the word "theory" to capture the humanistic dimension of the law. "Theory" is the apt translation of the German word *Dogmatik*, the ideas that were developed in the flourishing academic period between 1804 to 1896. The *Dogmatik* of the criminal law developed later, and indeed it was not fully developed until the twentieth century.

As the French Code Civil has an impact around the world, the German contribution in the *Dogmatik* has had a comparable influence.

All over Latin America, China, Japan, Greece, and Turkey, you find many civil codes based on the French mode but explanatory material in both civil

[4] *Id.*

and criminal law always based on the German *Dogmatik*. As I have found many times lecturing around the world to scholars of criminal law, the use of the German *Dogmatik* provides a lingua franca that transcends the diversity of language, religion, and national culture.

We should acknowledge the pretentious side of scholars' generating a *Dogmatik*. The concept of "dogma" is not attractive in the secular or liberally religious countries of the West because it has the connotation of required beliefs dictated from above. A person who is "dogmatic" holds fixed beliefs not subject to reasoned argument. A common translation in legal English is "doctrine" and no one wants to be called "doctrinaire." With Holmes, I prefer the word "theory" and have used it often in articles on criminal theory and tort theory.

Yet a doctrinal foundation of international criminal law may be indispensable. And we should not be afraid of entering into the intersections of law and religion, or at least of the philosophical dimensions of religion. The essential nature of the German *Dogmatik* is the recognition of distinction as well as commonality. The fundamental distinction of all legal systems is that between lawful and unlawful. The alternative is a spectrum of discretion—more or less lawful. It is something like an on/off principle underlying computers; they run on a succession of 0's and 1's, with no fractions to express the intermediate zone. Of course, legal disputes often end in compromise, but these compromises are negotiated against a backdrop of rules and principles that define what lawful and unlawful are.

The common denominator with the work of German theorists is that there cannot be an effective international criminal on the basis of treaties or legislation or case decisions alone. There must a foundational body of thought that provides the cement for the entire structure. The *Dogmatik* is the grammar that enables us to elaborate the finer points of the arguments that constitute positions in legal debate.

I regret to note that these views are shared in the textbooks on international criminal law. Antonio Cassese uses the term "customary international law" to do much of the work borne by the concept of *Dogmatik*.[5] But this translation is obviously misleading. The *Dogmatik* is not law in any conventional sense; it is not customary. More significantly, an important German scholar, Gustav Werle, uses neither the term *Dogmatik* nor the term "customary international law."[6] This testifies to the regrettable fact that the field

[5] *See* ANTONIO CASSESE, INTERNATIONAL LAW 12.4.1 (2d ed. 2005).
[6] *See* G. WERLE, VÖLKERSTRAFTRECHT (2d ed. 2007).

of international criminal law stands in relative isolation from the field of domestic law. This problem will return for a later discussion on necessity and self-defense.

But the concept of *Dogmatik* is too significant to be distracted by the relative isolation of the literature on international criminal law. Let us dig more deeply by focusing on the word itself. The root for *Dogmatik* as well as doctrine is the Latin word *docere* that means "to teach." The idea that the scholars are teaching the rest of us sounds a bit too authoritarian.

Here is a little anecdote from my studies in Germany in the 1960s that might illuminate the problem. I was taking a seminar in advanced private law from a distinguished teacher named Ernst von Caemmerer. The issue was something like the burden of persuasion in contract cases. The professorial treatises held one way on the other matter, and I discovered from a careful reading of the cases that they went the other way. Proud of my discovery, I presented my conclusions in class. Thinking like a common lawyer, I assume that the cases were the primary source of authority and the professorial merely derivative. The brilliant von Caemmerer responded, "The professors decided what the cases mean." There is much truth to this view, even in common law systems, where the professors are not held in such high esteem.

In the common law world, based on the case law system of education, the judges look for validation by being quoted in the case books, and the professors find their confirmation by being cited by other courts. In the last 20 years, however, things have shifted in the American legal academy. Now professors care more about being cited by other professors, particularly in prestigious law journals. This might be a small step toward recognition of von Caemmerer's principle that the scholars decide what the cases (and the statutes) mean.

Yet the way in which this movement toward scholars' law is expressed is not in the concept of doctrine but preferably in the word "theory." Note the dominance of expressions such as "feminist theory" or "queer theory." I have used the terms "tort theory" and "criminal theory" in numerous articles. Some people prefer "tort law theory," etc. If the concept of the *Dogmatik* rings of religious influence, the notions of theory carries connotations of the physical and social science. This is obviously a sign of our times, where since World War II—the same period in which the United Nations and international criminal law started to become important—the physical sciences have become the model of rigorous theoretical work.

Apart from the ins and outs of the concept of theory, there is something to be learned about why the term *Dogmatik* is so difficult to translate into English. The question is closely related to a long dispute about sources of law, namely whether the legal system has a single, a dual, or a triadic source of law. You could believe that all law emanates from one source—either the legislature or the courts. I have never known of anyone to believe this (except perhaps naively), even in the early days of enthusiasm about the French and German civil codes. Or a third source of law could be the executive branches, but this requires a monarchial conception of the presidency.

The task of finding a synthesis among the conflicting sources of law is left to the scholars and their writing and teaching. The students must find a synthesis in their examinations. But here it is worth noting two more important distinctions. In the civil law traditions, students are trained to be judges and becoming a judge is an elective career choice. In the common law tradition, students are trained to be lawyers, to argue both sides of the case, with the synthesis less important. This may be reflective of the relative difficulty and political nature of getting appointed to the bench. A related common law feature is dissenting opinions, which carry on the plurality of ideas in the legal culture.

The model of judging carries with it the idea of formal authority. The judge's like the legislator's positions are respected because of the office they hold. We can call this formal authority. The model of lawyering depends more on the quality of the argument and sometimes on the reputation of the advocate. This is where the element of charismatic authority enters in. An argument by Thurgood Marshall or Clarence Thomas carries more weight than the opinion of a novice. To some extent, we see the impact of charismatic authority in United States Supreme Court, but in recent years both formal and charismatic authority have yielded to political identification, which represents a loss of both kinds of authority.

The role of scholars in the *Dogmatik* and in developing legal theory is based not on formal but charismatic authority and, alas, to some extent on the formal authority of their institutional identification and the status of the law reviews in which they publish. If scholars are not read and not cited, they might as well as not exist. The constant challenge presented in the context of charismatic authority is essentially the following: innovate, win adherents, or die. Put less dramatically, the task for scholars is to find a synthesis among the conflicting formal sources of law, perhaps to modify this consensus and thus to make a consistent, teachable claim about what the law is.

The Restatements of the American Law Institute and the Model Penal Code, primarily the work of scholars, enjoy some formal authority. Yet they also enjoy some charismatic authority based on the prestige of the institutions that have generated them. These unofficial codifications of the law, with built-in efforts to change substance and terminology, have an impact on the legal culture very much like the German *Dogmatik*. Some provisions of the Restatements have vast influence in private law, and the Model Penal Code nearly dominates the field of criminal law in the United States. We will see later, however, there are impressive holdouts from the MPC, namely California.

This long discussion of the *Dogmatik* and its analogues explains the structure of this book. The 12 distinctions advanced as the organizing structure of the book represent a modest step toward a *Dogmatik* of international criminal law. In the best of all possible worlds, some people will find these distinctions useful ways of continuing the conversation that constitutes the foundation of all practical work in the field.

3. The Linguistic Side of International Law

Now we turn to the question why international law is called law and not policy or politics. There is more difficulty here than meets the eye, largely because of a concealed ambiguity in the word law.

All European languages—except Polish and English—have two words for law. There is a sense of law as the right thing, as in the analogues in other languages: recht, droit, derecho, prava, jog, mishpat. In that higher sense of law, the judge can assess what the law is without relying on the formal authority of the legislature, the executive, or other courts. This is the way Lord Coke used the word "right" in *Dr Bonham's Case*[7] when he ruled that a statute of Parliament is null and void if it violates "common right or reason."[8]

Thomas Hobbes picked up on this theme in his imaginary debate between a lawyer, modeled after Coke; and a philosopher, himself.[9] Coke stood for the amoral autonomy of the common law. Hobbes held the view we now call positivist: the law was no more and no less than what the king said it

[7] 77 Eng. Rep. 638 (C.P. 1610).
[8] *Id.*
[9] For an earlier publication of this observation, George P. Fletcher, *New Court, Old Dogmatik*, J. Int'l Crim. Just. (2011).

was. The analogue in international law would be the claim that all law stems from treaties. In fact, there is a school of this stripe, represented by some elite scholars in the United States. In his courageous book, *The Assault on International Law*, Jens Ohlin demolished their position.[10] This should be a familiar theme after the preceding discussion. In effect, this debate between Ohlin and his positivist opponents is about the relevance of scholarly opinion (the *Dogmatik*) in international law.

The argument stylized by Hobbes has gone on now, in one form or another, for nearly five centuries. One side reduces the law to power and will; the other side elevates the law to reason. The former theory is called positivism; the latter has no clear name. It is not natural law—a concept that has no clear meaning. It is best just to say the concept of law has a normative dimension. To be law, it must be good or sound law—Right, droit, derecho, Recht.

The leading scholars of positivism were Hans Kelsen in Germany and H.L.A. Hart in Great Britain. The incentive for the positivist view of law in the 1950s was overcoming the residual influence of National Socialism and increasing the respectability of the Soviet Union. The modern version of Hobbes's parable is the debate between Hart and Lon Fuller that appeared in the *Harvard Law Review* in 1958.[11] The debate is worth some attention because it carries an important message for international criminal law today.

The influence of National Socialism consisted in the perversion of the word *Recht* (Right) in two expressions used by the Nazis. The first was this: *Recht ist der Führers Wille*; and the second was, *Recht ist was dem Volke nutzt*. The unfortunate fact is that a version of both of these maxims is defensible. Take the first, in which the law is the command of the sovereign. This positivist theory of law goes back the nineteenth-century English scholar John Austin. Many respectable thinkers have accepted this view—assuming, of course, that the sovereign was not a homicidal tyrant.

The second maxim is a version of utilitarianism: the right thing to do is the greatest good for greatest number. The problem is limiting the "greatest number" to the racially defined German *Volk*. There are many complications of these views even if cleansed of National Socialist biases. Yet Hart defended the positivist view in 1958 as a way of increasing tolerance in the international legal order. He further developed his theory in *The Concept of Law*.[12]

[10] Jens David Ohlin, The Assault on International Law (2015).

[11] *See* H.L.A. Hart, *Positivism and the Separation of Law and Morals*, 71 Harv. L. Rev. 593 (1958); Lon L. Fuller, *Positivism and Fidelity to Law—A Reply to Professor Hart*, 71 Harv. L. Rev. 630 (1958).

[12] H.L.A. Hart, The Concept Of Law (2d ed. 1994).

Hart made some significant changes relative to Hans Kelsen's *Pure Theory of Law*.[13] Yet Kelsen's work was adopted by many scholars of law as a way of fending off Communist influences. On a trip to Cuba in the 1980s, I met a local professor of jurisprudence and asked him why Kelsen was so popular in Cuba and indeed all of Latin America. He replied, "It was either Kelsen or Communism." He had a point. The positivist theory is nonjudgmental and for that reason, it should be appealing to international lawyers seeking a wide consensus among different kinds of legal regimes. This may account for some of the resistance to the *Dogmatik* and theoretical work, which carry a risk of political association and parochial identification.

In the 1958 debate, Lon Fuller committed himself to a value-based conception of law. He wanted to say that certain Nazi laws were not laws at all, for example, the law requiring children to inform on parents listening to foreign radio broadcasts. Essentially, he wanted the word "law" to stand for the concept of Right (Recht) as originally understood. Fuller developed a revised theory based on what he called "the inner morality of law,"[14] which prescribed certain conditions generally accepted for legislation, such as public notice, clear language, and consistency. The general view is that Hart and Fuller were debating the relationship between law and morality. But in fact, they were disputing the proper meaning of the word Law—a problem caused by there being one word that serves the dual function of distinct concepts in most European systems.

The central creed of Hart's and Kelsen's positivism is that all law is enacted law. It stems from formally constituted authority. Kelsen called the premise for this authority the *Grundnorm* or Basic Norm;[15] Hart called this authority "the rule of recognition"—a term that has more of a sociological than a logical orientation.[16] The Hartian system is explicitly tolerant of any legal system—however dictatorial or abhorrent—that is de facto accepted by other states. In theory of positivism, there is no room for the *Dogmatik*, for precedents in the sense of case law, for customary law, or charismatic authority, indeed for anything that lies outside the constituted authority of a legislature or other enacting body. Treaties would constitute positive law in international law. The alternative is not natural or divine law but simply to

13 *See* Hans Kelsen, Pure Theory of Law (Max Knight trans., 2d ed. 2006) (1967).
14 *See* Fuller, *supra* note 11, at 650.
15 Kelsen, *supra* note 13, at 31.
16 *See* Hart, *supra* note 12, at 100.

avoid confusion: transpositive law. Transpositive law constitutes that which is binding or compelling by virtue of charismatic authority.

In my view, this was essentially a debate generated by our two words for law. There is little doubt that the Nazi laws were formally speaking enacted Gesetze, leyes, or statutes. The Nazis were shockingly meticulous about their murderous activities. They wanted the orders written down and their victims numbered. There is little doubt that their evil laws were not laws in the higher sense of principled laws. The question was whether this formally enacted measure had the merit of being called Recht or Droit.

The right term for international law is not international statutory law or Internationales Gesetz, but Internationales Recht or Droit International and the analogues in all other European languages. And whatever the corruption of the latter word in Nazi jurisprudence, we can rescue the concept from authoritarian and utilitarian influence. This is not to say the word Gesetz or Loi is not useful in expressing principles of legality. We use the term for statutory law invoked in the Rome Statute to refer to positive, enacted law.

The correct way to understand the conflict between positivism and its opponents is to bring to bear the work of Ronald Dworkin, Hart's leading critic, beginning in the 1980s. Dworkin was a master of linguistic argument. He paid close attention to the use of words of relevance to domestic law, but for our purposes also to international law. The major issues were "discretion," "rights," and "principles." His overall strategy was to direct attention away from the positivist attempt to transcend morality in order to accommodate rogue regimes and brought to bear his focus on American law and its structure. The notion of rights is clearly normative and the existence of principles—not enacted but nonetheless less applicable by their moral force—provides the *coup de grace* to a positivist thesis that all law is enacted law.

One of Dworkin's leading books is called *Taking Rights Seriously*.[17] Since we do not use the word Right anymore to refer to objective concept of sound law, the only alternative for Dworkin was to invoke the notion of subjective or personal rights to accomplish the same end. This was a way of disputing the dominance of the positivist conception of law-based law and eliciting the inherent normative structure of the law.

Dworkin's project has many fronts. For our purposes, his most important argument was his stressing the inherent role of principles in order to fend off

[17] Ronald Dworkin, Taking Rights Seriously (1977).

the positive arguments that all law is enacted law. Principles are not enacted. They are binding not because of their "pedigree" but because of their inherent weight and persuasiveness. His favorite example is akin to "No man should benefit from his own wrong."[18] If an heir kills the testator, he should not be able to inherit. Thus, we can see why some readers would take Dworkin's aim to inject the element of morality into the concept of law.

With his emphasis on principles, Dworkin effectively refuted the positivist theory that all law is enacted law. And that is the point of connection for international criminal law. Principles are an acknowledged source of law in the Rome Statute. They have weight, and this weight derives not from their pedigree but from their inherent weight.

Without having the term in his lexicon, Dworkin brought back the *Dogmatik* to the legal thought. He is the ally I would like to have today in international criminal law.

4. The Concepts of Criminal Law

The most significant contribution of the *Dogmatik* for criminal law was the invention of the tripartite system, namely the three levels of analysis that determine the structure of every criminal offense. The first stage, called the Tatbestand, represents the paradigm of criminal conduct. It is sufficient, prima facie, to think a crime is occurring. A good example in the law of war would be bombing a civilian target. If it is found out later that the schoolhouse was, in fact, housing a chemical weapons factory, that would change our understanding of the situation. In 1978, in writing *Rethinking Criminal Law*, I faced serious doubts about how to translate the German term. In the end, I chose the term "definition" instead of "paradigm." The definition simply tells us what the elements of the offense are; it does not include the principle that the definition is a paradigm of criminal conduct, namely that elements include a sufficient number of factors to be incriminating on its face.

The advantage of the "definition" is that it works well for offenses that are malum prohibitum as well as those that are malum in se. In international criminal law, the assumption appears to be that the offenses are malum in se. This was certainly true in the Nuremberg and Tokyo trials, but we cannot

[18] *See id.* at 23–39.

conclude this about the offenses treated in the Rome Statute without further investigation.

If an offense is malum in se, the issues of fair warning and *nulla poena sine lege* are less acute. There are also implications for the relevance of superior orders and mistake of law. Everyone one should know that killing innocents is wrong. But this is not true about offenses created by legislation.

The prohibition of offenses malum in se represents the inverse side of the principle *nulla poena sine lege*. It implies that legislative definition is not only necessary but sufficient for criminalization. An example of a malum in se offense in the Rome Statute would be Article 8(2)(b)(xii): "Declaring that no quarter will be given."[19] Now actually harming prisoners would presumably be a crime malum in se. But is hard to understand how the mere speech act of making a declaration could constitute a crime in and of itself—without a statutory prohibition.

Another feature of criminality, common to virtually all legal systems, is the distinction between two levels of criminality, called misdemeanors and felonies in English. This distinction is an important guide to sentencing and to the post-conviction status of the offender. This is particularly true in American law where felon disenfranchisement has posed a particularly strong threat to democratic voting rights. In many states—still undergoing reform—felons who have served their sentence are still branded with that status and denied the right to vote. In fact, it is argued that George W. Bush, a Republican, won the 2000 election because a half-million felons in Florida could not vote, and the presumption is that they would have voted Democratic.[20] Of course, the election was complicated by many other factors, but it would be a mistake to think that these matters of defining crimes and their levels have no impact on the international legal order.

In fact, the disenfranchisement of felons is justified by a literal reading of the U.S Constitution, enacted in the course of the Civil War, provides: "Neither slavery nor involuntary servitude, except as a punishment for crime whereof the party shall have been duly convicted, shall exist within the United States, or any place subject to their jurisdiction."[21] The interpretation and application of this provision indicates some the perils of the taking statutory language too seriously. First, it says nothing about felons, but apart from that,

[19] Rome Statute, *supra* note 1, art. 8(2)(b)(xii).

[20] *See* Julian Borger & Gregory Palast, *Inquiry into New Claims of Poll Abuses in Florida*, GUARDIAN (Feb. 16, 2001), https://www.theguardian.com/world/2001/feb/17/usa.julianborger.

[21] U.S. CONST. amend. XIII., § 1.

the provision was adopted to abolish slavery. Unlike other all other applicable provisions, it is not directed to the state and its actions but a flat prohibition of the status of slavery. It is possible to read "involuntary servitude" to refer to prison, and the wording seems to suggest the "workhouse"—a precursor to the current practice of simply locking up offenders.

In any event, the reference to "punishment for crime" led to a decision by the Supreme Court, upholding felon disenfranchisement.[22] How felonies as opposed to misdemeanors are defined is a matter of state law. The important point is that the felon has a status that accompanies the offender for life. It violated a critical element of retributive punishment, namely that offender can repay his debt to society.

As we are beginning to see, developing a consistent theory of crime—for the domestic or international setting—is far from an easy task.

Let us return to the example of "declaring that no quarter will be given." Here we encounter not only an example of malum prohibitum but of the paradoxically collective nature of crimes under international law. We can understand that the Geneva and Hague Conventions directed to the actions of states and nations—were collective in nature, but the Rome Statute is supposed to be out individual criminality, "natural persons" as the Statute tells us.[23] How is it possible for a criminal standing alone—outside the chain of command—screaming "no prisoners taken alive" could be committing a war crime?

Similar problems run through all the offenses. I don't see how a singular private individual could be guilty of genocide. The crime is committed against groups, and there the paradigm implied is the war of one nation against another. Interestingly, the crime of aggression refers to the actions of a person in power to implement the policy.[24] This sensible innovation should run through the interpretation of all four offenses held to constitute the "jurisdiction" of the ICC.

The amendment to the crime of aggression would, if extended across the board, deprive me of many standard criticisms of the law of war. My favorite example of an obviously collective crime is the war crime defined in Article 8(2)(a)(vi) of the Rome Statute: "willfully depriving a prisoner of war or other

22 Richardson v. Ramirez, 418 U.S. 24 (1974).

23 Rome Statute, *supra* note 1, art. 25(1).

24 Resolution Adopting Aggression Amendments to Rome Statute, Rev. Conf. of the Rome Statute, Kampala, Uganda, May 31–June 11, 2010, Annex I, 8*bis*, 13th plen. mtg., I.C.C. Doc. RC/Res.6 (June 11, 2010).

protected persons of the right of fair and regular trial."[25] Collective action literally screams off the page: the notions of "war," "prisoner," and "fair and regular trial" entail the participation of many people. If the "person in power" principles were applied, we could make sense of these crimes. Paragraph 8*bis* may have inadvertently salvaged the entire structure of the Rome Statute.

Another problem is posed in the Preamble of the Rome Statute, which defines the jurisdiction of the Court as limited to the "most serious crimes of [international] concern."[26] Since the statute itself defines its jurisdiction to be genocide, crimes against humanity, war crimes, and aggression, plus later defined offenses against the administration of justice, what sense does it make to refer to the "most serious crimes of concern"? Either the reference is redundant or it adds a component of "seriousness" to the crimes already defined. Neither of these alternatives is satisfactory. Redundancy is a dangerous flaw in legislation, and an additional undefined component of gravity raises new problems of judicial activism in violation of the principle *nulla poena sine lege*.[27]

The American approach to criminal law is suffused with constitutional values, namely the right to a jury trial; the distinction between the verdict by the jury and sentencing; and other constitutional protections spelled out in the Fifth, Sixth, and Eighth Amendments to the Constitution. To illustrate the problem, consider two issues of serious concern to the international order. One is denationalization—revoking acquired citizenship. And the second is deportation. Both of these create instability because the international order is based on the assumption that every person is entitled to a home in the international regimes of states and nations. This might be the only home the person every knew (the problem of the "Dreamers" in the United States—the undocumented immigrants who believe their native soil is the United States). The enemy here is homelessness. In the 1970s and 1980s, the major issue of concern to the international order was emigration—particularly from the former Soviet Union. Today the major issue is the flood of refugees from Syria and other trouble in the Middle East. Because these refugees are mostly Muslim and the executive branch of the United States has engaged in unfavorable policies,[28] the refugee

[25] Rome Statute, *supra* note 1, art. 8(2)(a)(vi).

[26] *Id.*, pmbl.

[27] *Id.*, art. 23 ("A person convicted by the Court may be punished only in accordance with this Statute.").

[28] *See* Trump v. Hawaii, 585 U.S. __ (2018).

problem has become intertwined with constitutional issues in the United States. The international legal order must incorporate concern for issues of religious and ethnic discrimination that fall short of the Genocide Statute. Some of these issues come up in our analysis of punishment and its alternatives in chapter 2. Yet in this modest effort, I am not able to address all of these issues. In brief, the concepts of crime and criminal law are more complex than meets the eye. So long as we do not take the claims of the Rome Statute too seriously, we can cope with them. We draw on as many sources as we can to develop a robust theory of international criminal law.

5. The Relevance of the Law of War (or International Humanitarian Law)

The title of Grotius's foundational book, *The Law of War*,[29] is an essential part of the international legal order. This is evident as well in the detailed treatment of war crimes in Article 8 of the Rome Statute.[30] Yet I have written extensively about these issues in *Defending Humanity* with Jens Ohlin[31] and *Romantics at War*.[32] As with other issues treated in this book, I would prefer not to repeat myself more than necessary. If the reader would like a quick summary of *Defending Humanity* and the analysis of Article 51 of the UN Charter, please refer to the recorded six lectures at Washburn University in 2008.[33]

In the spirit of the poles that mark out the domain or law and its opposite, this entire book is organized on a set of 12 distinctions. Some of these are inspired by the German tradition; others are opposed to it. This might be considered the new *Dogmatik* of international criminal law.

[29] Hugo Grotius on the Law of War and Peace (Stephen C. Neff ed., Cambridge University Press 2012) (1625).

[30] Rome Statute, *supra* note 1, art. 8.

[31] George P. Fletcher & Jens David Ohlin, Defending Humanity: When Force is Justified and Why? (2008).

[32] George P. Fletcher, Romantics at War: Glory and Guilt in the Age of Terrorism (2002).

[33] Washburn Law, *Defending Humanity*, YouTube (Dec. 28, 2008), https://www.youtube.com/watch?v=1skzKa1KEMA.

1
Substance and Procedure

Being guilty of an international crime is one thing; being prosecuted and convicted is quite another. Within the realm of international criminal law, both are more highly controverted questions than within domestic criminal law. Being guilty in principle requires the following: first, an identification of a norm under which the suspect would be guilty if the norm applied to him; second, the application of the norm to the offender to conclude that the particular person is guilty.

Initially, this two-stage procedure might take place in the minds of observers, and then, in the minds of people capable of bringing to bear the procedures of the International Criminal Court (ICC) or other international-national tribunals in order to effectuate a conviction. We could expect that those with hands-on experience in seeking convictions would be more likely to have a courtroom-tested, more circumscribed conception of guilt than those who approach the matter without knowledge of local practices and inclinations.

In either case, the notion of liability or guilt requires reasoning in a syllogism. The major premise is the substantive law, and the minor premise consists of the facts that appear to be provable at trial. As to the latter, those with experience in the particular legal system are likely to be more sophisticated about who will be held accountable.

Let us focus on the major premise, for that is the element of substantive law with which this chapter is concerned. The substantive law is typically identified by recourse to a statute or some other source of law. In a common law system, the prosecutor might invoke some rather vague traditional concept such as conspiracy as it is invoked in the American law of war.[1] In the International Criminal Tribunal for the former Yugoslavia (ICTY), there was a similar tendency of appealing to vague definitions in the case law,

[1] *See, e.g.*, Singer v. United States, 323 U.S. 338, 340 (quoting Nash v. United States, 229 U.S. 373, 378 (1913)); Hamdan v. Rumsfeld, 548 U.S. 557, 698–703 (2006) (Thomas, J., dissenting).

particularly of Joint Criminal Enterprise III—a crime deleted in the Rome Statute.[2]

In common law jurisdictions with jury trials, the substantive rule is also stated in the jury instructions. The task of reasoning through the syllogism is then left to the jury who must find the facts, apply the instructions to the facts, and reach a verdict.

In civil law countries, the syllogism is reasoned through the written opinion of the judge. Of course, this depends on the quality of the opinion and, in any event, the reasoning is likely to be as clearly bifurcated between the major and minor premise as it is when the major premise is articulated in instructing the jury. Though, as we shall see, the ICC is an amalgam of common law and civil law structural principles; there is no jury trial, and therefore the syllogism must occur in the reasoning and writings of the judges. A useful experiment for us would be to imagine what those instructions would be like if the judges of the ICC had to articulate them to a jury.

The interpretation and application of the Rome Statute[3] should be easier than the analogous process with any national criminal code. The Rome Statue is limited to four crimes "within the jurisdiction of the Court." Yes, the Rome Statute is embedded in a history of international criminal law including the Nuremberg and Tokyo tribunals,[4] and the special tribunals for Yugoslavia, Rwanda, and Lebanon[5]—not to mention the law of war as it dates back to Grotius[6] and Puffendorf.[7] Therefore, we cannot read the Rome Statute in isolation of its history. Nor we can ignore the multiplicity of languages that bear upon the interpretation of the leading texts of the international legal order.[8]

[2] Prosecutor v. Milutinovic, Sainovic, Ojdanic, Case No. IT-99-37-AR72, Decision on Dragoljub Ojdanic's Motion Challenging Jurisdiction—Joint Criminal Enterprise, ¶ 15 (Int'l Crim. Trib. for the Former Yugoslavia, May 21, 2003).

[3] Rome Statute for the International Criminal Court, July 17, 1998, 2187 U.N.T.S. 3; U.N. Diplomatic Conference of Plenipotentiaries on the Establishment of an International Court, U.N. Doc. A/Conf.183/9 [hereinafter Rome Statute].

[4] *See generally Tokyo Trial* (Netflix miniseries 2016); Henry L. Stimson, *The Nuremberg Trial: Landmark in Law*, 25 Foreign Aff. 179 (1947); Telford Taylor, *The Nuremberg Trials*, 55 Colum. L. Rev. 488 (1955); Jonathan A. Bush, *The Supreme Crime and Its Origins: The Lost Legislative History of the Crime of Aggressive War*, 102 Colum. L. Rev. 2324 (2002).

[5] *See generally* Karin N. Calvo-Goller, The Trial Proceedings of the International Criminal Court: ICTY and ICTR (2006); 2 The Establishment of the Hariri Tribunal (S. Fennell & C. Tofan eds., 2d ed. 2011).

[6] Hugo Grotius On the Law of War and Peace (Stephen C. Neff ed., Cambridge University Press 2012) (1625).

[7] Samuel Pufendorf, Two Books on the Elements of Universal Jurisprudence (Thomas Behme & Knud Haakonssen eds., Liberty Fund, Inc. 2009) (1660).

[8] The six official languages of the United Nations are Arabic, Chinese, English, French, Russian, and Spanish. The leading language of the commentaries is English. In fact, there are many leading

This makes the reading and application of the Rome Statute more difficult than the corresponding process of adjudicating a national criminal case with a single tradition and single governing language.

An additional problem is posed by the phrase "jurisdiction of the Court" present throughout the Rome Statute. The word "jurisdiction" here is not used in the same sense as it is used in the national legal system, and in particular, not as it is used in the common law jurisdictions. The French and Spanish versions of the treaty, both official, rely on variations of the word "competence" (compétènce, competencia), which has the clear connotation of the "defined power of the court." "Jurisdiction," as the word is used in English, presupposes competence of the court. The term is ordinarily used in American law with modifiers, such as "in personam jurisdiction" or "in rem jurisdiction," and is typically used in English in a specific law suit, for example, a civil torts action. We will see in chapter 2 that this kind of jurisdiction in ordinary English becomes important in the Alien Tort Claims Act. Criminal jurisdiction in the United States is based on the territorial principle.

Limitations on competence are necessary to avoid overlapping jurisdiction, particularly in an international setting that does not recognize double jeopardy to prevent prosecution, first in one country and then in another, and another until a conviction is finally reached. These forms of overlapping competence would result in a race to the bottom where the state that could be most easily convicted would acquire an excessive share of the burden to police and suspects.

Consider the case of Adolph Eichmann, a German citizen complicit in the Holocaust, later domiciled in Argentina, kidnapped by Israelis, and indicted and tried in Jerusalem.[9] Here, we see an intersection of the concepts of competence and jurisdiction under international law. Any common law court that had custody of Eichmann could have had the competence to try him. The necessary and sufficient condition for common law criminal jurisdiction is presence of the body in court, however the body might have been secured (Eichmann was kidnapped in Argentina by the Israelis).[10] In civil law

commentaries in German, which is not an official language. *See generally* George P. Fletcher & Jens David Ohlin, Defending Humanity: When Force Is Justified and Why (2008).

[9] Attorney General v. Adolf Eichmann, Case No. 40/61 (District Court of Jerusalem, 1961). The leading commentary is Hannah Arendt, Eichmann in Jerusalem: A Report on the Banality of Evil (1963).

[10] *See* Harriet Sherwood, *Adolf Eichmann's Capture, as Told by the Mossad, in Israel Exhibition*, Guardian (Feb. 15, 2012), https://www.theguardian.com/world/2012/feb/15/adolf-eichmann-exhibition-tel-aviv.

countries, criminal law jurisdiction might extend to persons merely served by process, for example, in the French fraud prosecution of the Scientology leader, L. Ron Hubbard, who was prosecuted in Paris in absentia. In this case, public notification of the pending proceeding was sufficient notice of process.[11]

Still, under conventional principles of international law, Israel had to defend its claim of jurisdiction under one of four principles: universality, active nationality (i.e., of the suspect), passive nationality (i.e., of the victim), or territoriality, namely applicable if the crime was committed on its territory. Israel, as the self-proclaimed state of the Jewish people, asserted the passive nationality principle. The argument is a bit stretched: Israel did not exist at the time of the crime and its recognition in international law is as a secular state, not identified with any particular religion or preexisting nationality.

These points notwithstanding, the post-Holocaust mood in the 1960s created considerable latitude for Israel to extend the borders of international legitimacy. It is doubtful that the same mood prevails today, but this is nothing novel to the evolution of international criminal law. The tolerance of ex post facto trials in Nuremberg and Tokyo was a consequence of the same mood that prevailed immediately after World War II. After all, what the victors should do with their former enemies poses a serious problem. Trials at the borderline of legitimacy are preferable to assassinations, which are ad hoc, often based on mistaken identification, and obviously surrender to the mood of the mob.

All things considered, the imprecision of the use of the term "jurisdiction" tells us something about the Rome Statute as well as about the material it purports to govern. The criminal jurisdiction of U.S. courts is also subject to a form of criticism that might illuminate the situation. The state courts have jurisdiction, based on the territorial principle, over-all common-law offenses. These common law offenses evolved over time based on the needs of the moment. Thus, the principle of jurisdiction might be well-defined, but the offenses themselves are open-ended. The principle of *nulla poena sine lege* has never been accepted as constitutionally binding. Some offenses such as conspiracy are subject to considerable prosecutorial manipulation. For example, all conspirators are liable for the offenses of co-conspirators. The possibilities of overcharging for the sake of plea bargaining are obvious.[12]

[11] For my own participation as an adviser in the case, see George P. Fletcher, My Life in Seven Languages 156–57 (2011).

[12] *Developments in the Law: Criminal Conspiracy*, 72 Harv. L. Rev. 920 (1959).

Federal criminal law is more limited, but not by much. At the inception of the Constitution, 1789, there was no federal criminal law, which is a factor of vital importance to the rise of the Alien Torts Claim Act—as discussed in chapter 2. Since the federal government is also limited by the Constitution, federal criminal jurisdictions should not have a residual common law foundation. But this is not true in practice. A good example, again, is conspiracy, which, according to the federal statute, prohibits a conspiracy to defraud the United States. The contours of "defrauding" the United States have no common law foundation, certainly not in the common law of fraud.[13]

We might sum up this discussion with a recognition of a hydraulic principle in international criminal law. If we seek to apply a principle of *nulla poena sine lege*, we have to be flexible about jurisdiction and competence. By contrast, if we desire instead to be strict on the definition of an offense, we are going to be vague about jurisdiction and competence. This isn't necessarily true wall-to-wall, but it might helpful in understanding the Rome Statute as well as the common law.

Another factor to consider is that the Rome Statute takes the place of a constitution, a federal statute defining offenses, and a common law of crime within the matrix of international law. It is a though it were the Big Bang of the international legal order. The search for legitimacy must end somewhere. Of course, as we navigate past this point, we will come across other issues that serve the interests of defendants in the international dock.

A problem that we leave aside is the general theory of interpretation, a critical issue in light of the multiple binding languages and the disputed relevance of national legal traditions, though recognized in Article 21(1)C).[14] It should be noted, however, that the Rome Statute indirectly includes a principle of interpretation by referring to the "general principles of law derived by the Court from national law of the legal systems of the world. . . ." The word "derived" obviously signals a process of interpretation. The general principle of interpretation in criminal proceedings is strict construction—the meaning that best serves the accused.[15]

[13] *See* 18 U.S.C. § 371 (2018); Haas v. Henkel, 216 U.S. 462, 479–80 (1910) (relying on statutory interpretation alone to dispense of case).

[14] Rome Statute, *supra* note 3, art. 21(1)(c) ("Failing that, general principles of law derived by the Court from national laws of legal systems of the world including, as appropriate, the national laws of States that would normally exercise jurisdiction over the crime, provided that those principles are not inconsistent with this Statute and with international law and internationally recognized norms and standards.").

[15] *See* United States v. Halseth, 342 U.S. 277 (1952).

With all of these preliminary issues considered, we should turn to the major problem that we face in analyzing the four crimes subject to the jurisdiction of the Court: the problem of collective versus individual action. Bear in mind that the historical foundation of the Rome Statute is the adaptation to the individual responsibility of The Hague and Geneva Conventions, which applied to the collective action of states.

1. Collective Action

The paradigmatic crime of collective action is aggression. The idea of collective intrusion in the realm of another nation or state is foundational to the law of war. Article 51 of the United Nations Charter governs the defensive exception to collective intrusion.

One way to begin understanding the contours of "aggression" is to look at the law of trespass, which is a writ large that applies to the actions of collective entities. Thus, the following collective acts define the particular provisions of the original Article 8(2): (a) invasion, (b) bombardment, (c) blockade, (d) attack by armed forces, (e) nonconsensual use of armed forces within the territory of other states, (f) use of territory to perpetuate aggression, and (g) sending of armed bands. Though it is possible to imagine some of these actions committed by individuals acting alone, for example, bombardment (perhaps), on the whole, collective action is inherent in these actions.

The initial reading of Article 8(2), therefore, should be that aggression is a violation of the law of war. Now, getting from the law of war to individual responsibility under the Rome Statute is no easy trick. One of the basic principles of jus in bello[16] is that individuals are not responsible for the otherwise unlawful acts committed in the course of armed conflict. If the four requirements of combatancy are satisfied (uniforms, arms carried openly, chain of command, customary laws of war),[17] no soldier is liable for killing, maiming, assaulting, or engaging in any of the other actions that would otherwise be prosecuted in national criminal courts. Thus, the question is why these actions should be unlawful if they are committed by groups.

[16] *International Humanitarian Law*, Wex Legal Information Institute, https://www.law.cornell.edu/wex/international_humanitarian_law (last visited Aug. 26, 2018) ("[T]he legality of wartime conduction (*jus in bello*, or how states must behave themselves during war)").

[17] International Committee of the Red Cross, IHL Database, Rule 4: Definition of Armed Forces (2018) (citing Hague Regulations, art. 1).

There seems to be the following illogical steps: (1) the law of jus in bello tells us that killing other soldiers is permissible; (2) if the actions are done by collective units, they fall under the principle of aggression, but we cannot or do not know how to apply the principle of collective action to individuals charged in the ICC; thus (3) the 2010 amendment in Kampala becomes necessary.[18]

Now we encounter a problem of interpretation. Criminal statutes should be strictly construed, and this presents a "bramblebush" of issues.[19] The basic tension is between (1) the obviously collective nature of these offenses, understandable in light of the influence of The Hague and Geneva Conventions; and (2) the principle of individual responsibility.

This is just the facade of the thicket. The critical provision in Article 8*bis* (1) provides a qualification: "which, by its character, gravity, and scale, constitutes a *manifest* violation of the Charter of United Nations."[20] In other words, some aggression is acceptable but not too much. This is somewhat disturbing if we are to take the principle *nulla poena sine lege* seriously. Setting aside Article 51 of the United Nations Charter, which we consider later in the chapter on self-defense, the only relevant provision in the United Nations charter is Article 2(4), which provides:

> All Members shall refrain in their international relations from the threat or use of force against the territorial integrity or political independence of any state, or in any other manner inconsistent with the Purposes of the United Nations.[21]

The key concepts here are the threat, use of force, and territorial and political independence. By and large, the explicit prohibitions against aggression can fit into these categories.

The solution to the problem of collective action lies in Article 8*bis* adopted at the 2010 Kampala Conference.[22] If there were a jury instruction based on Article 8*bis*, the judge could simply read the entire provision:

[18] Resolution Adopting Aggression Amendments to Rome Statute, Rev. Conf. of the Rome Statute, Kampal, Uganda, May 31–June 11, 2010, Annex I, 8*bis*, 13th plen. mtg., I.C.C. Doc. RC/Res.6 (June 11, 2010) [hereinafter Resolution].

[19] *See generally* Karl N. Llewellyn, The Bramble Bush: The Classic Lectures on the Law and Law School (2008).

[20] Resolution, *supra* note 18, art. 8*bis*(1) (emphasis added).

[21] U.N. Charter art. 2, ¶ 4.

[22] Resolution, *supra* note 18.

The "crime of aggression" means the planning, preparation, initiation or execution, by a person in a position effectively to exercise control over or to direct the political or military action of a State, of an act of aggression which, by its character, gravity and scale, constitutes a manifest violation of the Charter of the United Nations.[23]

However, it would make far more sense to break the instruction down into the following segments:

(A) *Did the defendant engage in one of the four means of committing the crime: planning, preparing, initiating, and executing?* Within the possibilities arising from such a presentation, the defense would have two subtle moves to make in its litigation strategy that would impact the exact form of the instruction. The first move would be to insist that the judge identify which of the four means he had in mind; and second, to stress that these are presumptively collective actions and that if the defendant did, say, plan, or prepare the crime, we should want to know with whom. The judge could respond that, as in the crime of conspiracy, the defendant might have acted with an unknown person X in planning or preparing the offense.[24] Of course, it is logically possible but highly unlikely that the defendant acted alone. Just debating this question would tie up the court for some time.

(B) *Was the defendant a "person in a position effectively to exercise control"?*[25] The issue of control needs illumination; if the word were clear on its face, the draftsmen would not have added the word "effectively." Is this simply redundant legal drafting? No. The phrases reveal a serious problem in identifying the persons in power who engage in this so-called leadership crime.[26]

(C) *Was this an incident of political or military action?*[27] The problem here is obviously the word "political." Suppose that the agency carrying out the aggression is a private company, an institution that became more common during the American war in Iraq.[28] Does that

[23] *Id.*

[24] Developments, *supra* note 12, at 925 (citing State v. Carbone, 10 N.J. 329, 336–37 (1952)).

[25] Resolution, *supra* note 18, art. 8*bis*(1).

[26] Johan D. van der Vyver, *Prosecuting the Crime of Aggression in the International Criminal Court*, 1 U. Miami Nat'l Sec. & Armed Conf. L. Rev. 1, 8 (2011).

[27] Resolution, *supra* note 18, art. 8*bis*(1).

[28] *See generally* Jeremy Scahill, Blackwater: The Rise of the World's Most Powerful Mercenary Army (2007).

provide insulation against the action's being considered "political?" These are not clear terms, and there is much room for argument.

(D) *Was there a "manifest violation of the Charter?"*[29] First, there will be a need to determine which provision of the Charter is alleged to have been violated. Perhaps it is Article 2(4), which, as indicated, provides that a member shall "refrain . . . from the threat or use of force against the territorial integrity or political independence of any state."[30] This provision raises another set of complex issues, all just as contestable as the ones considered herein. If the drafters of the Rome Statute were confident as to the original meaning of the charter they had in mind, they would not have added the adjective "manifest."[31] Adding modifying words such as "effectively and 'manifest' reveal the drafters" uncertainty.[32] Here are some possibilities: "manifest" could mean simply "large," which is far too vague a term. Or, it could mean "apparent to the naked eye" or to a reasonable person, as in the expression "manifestly unlawful" used in Article 33.[33]

The significance of "manifest" as it is written in Article 8*bis* differs from its use in Article 33 on the defense of superior orders. In the former case, the import of the term is inculpatory. The defendant is guilty in the case of a manifest violation of the Charter.[34] In the latter case, the term is exculpatory of an act in obedience to an order that the defendant did not know was unlawful. In effect, a manifestly unlawful order is one that the defendant should know—just as a reasonable person would—is unlawful. The word "manifestly" thus betokens a form of negligence. This example will be helpful to us later when we scrutinize the issues surrounding the subject of mens rea more deeply.

The point of this exercise has been to demonstrate that if trials before the ICC were able to emulate the proceedings on requesting instructions in a common law jury trial, the lawyers together with the tribunal could reach much clarity in understanding the applicable law.

29 Resolution, *supra* note 18, art. 8*bis*(1).
30 U.N. Charter art. 2, ¶ 4.
31 *See* Resolution, *supra* note 18, art. 8*bis*(1).
32 *Id.*
33 Rome Statute, *supra* note 3, art. 33(1)(c).
34 *See* Resolution, *supra* note 18, art. 8*bis*(1).

However, the discussion here is limited to Article 8*bis* and its recognition of individual action. If the tribunal had to consider the problem of collective action under Articles 5 through 8, there would be an additional level of complexity that could not be easily handled in imaginary jury instructions. I will turn to some of those problems later on in the chapter.

2. Article 6: Genocide

This provision incorporates the Genocide Statute of 1948. The concept of genus-cide—the killing of a type or category of people—was invented by Rafael Lemkin, a Polish Jew.[35] The historical context, the Holocaust, is obvious. The question in interpreting the provision is whether the historical context should be controlling in interpreting the provision in different times and places.

It is clear, historically, that the statute refers to collective action. The Holocaust was the product of systematic work done by the German government. The crime was so new in the history of humanity that no one had a name for it until a German television program adopted the word "Holocaust" in the 1980s. (The term is a biblical reference to a burnt offering.)[36] The French called the mass killing the "Shoah"—or disaster.[37] This is the term used in modern Hebrew.

Article 6 does not explicitly refer to collective action, but it seems clearly implied by the context in which the crime is committed by groups of people against groups of people with the intent to "destroy" them in whole or in part. Since the victims are collective entities and the historical context is obvious, it seems to be a fair inference that the crime must be committed by an organization, a political entity, or even a state (since official capacity is no defense under Article 27).[38] This is true, though only individuals can stand trial for the collective action. Of course, the extension of Article 8*bis* would solve this conundrum as in other contexts. It is important to remember that we cannot assume that Article 8*bis* applies a fundamental principle of the entire Rome Statute's applicable law.

[35] J. Cooper, Raphael Lemkin and the Struggle for the Genocide Convention 4 (2008); Samantha Power, A Problem from Hell: America and the Age of Genocide 47–60 (2002).

[36] 7 *Holocaust*, The Catholic Encyclopedia (Charles G. Herbermann et al. eds., 1910).

[37] Shoah (Claude Lanzmann, 1985).

[38] Rome Statute, *supra* note 3, art. 27.

On the latter questions, here are various factors pointing both directions: (1) Article 22(2) prescribes that the definition of a crime "shall not be extended by analogy."[39] It is not clear whether this provision should apply if the analogy works to the benefit of the accused. But, then again, it is not too clear that avoiding confusion and conceptual morass works to the benefit of one side or the other in the trial. (2) The principles laid out in the Preamble advocate the end of impunity.[40] The arguments could be made that extending Article 8*bis* and limiting liability for collective action could be increasing impunidad contrary to the Court's basic purpose. There is an obvious tension between traditional principles of criminal law (protecting the accused) and the purposes of the ICC (making sure that the "most serious crimes . . ." not go unpunished).[41]

With these issues to one side, let us return to the details of genocide, and, in particular, the NERR requirement—the limitation of protected groups to National, Ethnic, Religious, and Racial groups.[42] There are difficult questions about how to classify the following groups that have been or might be targeted in mass killings: Jews, Gypsies, handicapped, Kulaks, mentally ill, gays, dying people, fetuses, drug addicts. The Statute does not say NERR *or other similar groups*; it merely refers to the four categories. The problem is whether we take Article 22 seriously based on the strict construction of the Statute.[43]

I once posed the question of the mass killings of gays to William Shabas, a leading expert in the area, and he responded that if such an event were to happen, we would amend the Statute to cover the case. He presumably meant that the Statute would apply retroactively. This, of course, is the way international criminal law has worked—at least since the trials in Nuremberg. But, the emergence of a highly detailed Rome Statute, with its commitment to *nullum crimen sine lege*, means that the old Nuremberg style of legal development is no longer possible.

However, it is possible to reconcile Article 22 with Schabas's opinion. The principles of *nulla poena* and *nullum crimen* have two possible purposes. One is to warn possible offenders of their potential liability, and the other is to channel the power of courts into defined paths of possible conviction. In the field of international criminal law, where the evil of the actions should

39 *Id.*, art. 22(2).
40 *Id.*, pmbl.
41 *Id.*
42 *See* Rome Statute, *supra* note 3, art. 6; Steven T. Katz, The Holocaust in Historical Context: The Holocaust and Mass Death Before the Modern Age 131 (1994).
43 Rome Statute, *supra* note 3, art. 22.

be evident to all, the second function of disciplining the court should be obvious. Indeed, precisely because the evils are so obvious, any defendant who appears in court is likely to be unsympathetic and in need of the law's protection.

Yet the disciplining of the courts is in conflict with their mission and the purpose of the Rome Statute, which is to end the impunity of the perpetrators that affected the "peace, security, and well-being of the world."[44] Nonetheless, we could interpret the *nullum crimen* principle in line with the overall purposes of the ICC and endorse a careful extension of the NERR principle to include other groups. Currently, one of the critical issues is the persecution of drug addicts in the Philippines.[45] A complaint against President Rodrigo Duterte has reportedly been filed in the ICC to test the very question of extending the NERR framework.

The situation in the Philippines illustrates a problem that was apparent in other cases of the mass killings of identifiable groups. How exactly, does the mass killing of the NERR and analogous groups threaten the "peace, security and well-being of the world?" The drug addicts in the Philippines are too weak or will be rendered too weak to retaliate.

In many cases, the persecution of NERR groups increases the chances that the repressive regime will collapse, as did the Third Reich after diverting its manpower to the murder of the Jews and the Ottoman Empire after the persecution of the Armenians. There are few cases in history in which genocide increased the prosperity of a nation. One example might be the systematic killing of American Indians in order to conquer the West. Whether self-defeating or not, genocide is still a moral evil and, in that sense, should fit under one of the general purposes of the Rome Statute. If prohibiting genocide does not directly further the general aim of promoting peace and security, then there should be sufficient justification for including the crime under Article 5 as one the "most serious crimes of concern to the international community as a whole."[46]

[44] *Id.*, pmbl.

[45] *Philippines: Duterte's "Drug War" Claims 12,000+ Lives*, Human Rights Watch (Jan. 18, 2018), https://www.hrw.org/news/2018/01/18/philippines-dutertes-drug-war-claims-12000-lives (last accessed 8/2/2019).

[46] Rome Statute, *supra* note 3, art. 5.

3. The Protected Groups, the Details of NERR

Every one of these four categories is highly contested.

A. Nationality

The place to begin is to ponder the difference between nationality and citizenship. For internal democratic purposes, such as voting rights and welfare benefits, the critical concept is citizenship. The inspiring French *Déclaration des droits de l'homme et du citoyen* (1789)[47] emphasized the role of citizens as the bearers of human rights, yet the historical evolution since then and the contextual difference may have changed our perspectives on the relative importance of citizenship and nationhood.

The infamous Dred Scott decision had determined that blacks, even those living in free territory, could never become citizens for purposes of "diversity of citizenship"—a ground for civil jurisdiction in the U.S. federal courts.[48] The context of citizenship here is not unifying as in the 1789 French Declaration, but appositional. Because they are opposed to each other, with different views of the world, the citizens of different states required a federal tribunal to litigate their disputes. Of course, the Dred Scott decision itself has little to do with this rationale of federal jurisdiction; it was a racist decision, pure and simple—probably the most infamous in U.S. history.

Elected to the presidency the year before, Lincoln was outraged, but he was stuck with a Supreme Court appointed by his predecessors. The Civil War was partly a response to the intense divisions about the equality of the races in the United States, but at least initially, Lincoln claimed that the war was about keeping the Union together, with or without emancipation of the slaves.

During the course of the Civil War, Lincoln subtlety shifted the American focus from citizenship to nationhood. His methodology represents one

[47] Declaration of the Rights of Man and of the Citizen (trans.). The document formed the basis of the United Nations Declaration of 1948 and was added to the United Nations Memory of the World Register in 2003 to commemorate its lasting and universal influence. *Original Declaration of the Rights of Man and of the Citizen (1789–1791)*, United Nations Educational, Scientific and Cultural Org., http://www.unesco.org/new/en/communication-and-information/memory-of-the-world/register/full-list-of-registered-heritage/registered-heritage-page-6/original-declaration-of-the-rights-of-man-and-of-the-citizen-1789-1791/ (last visited Feb. 24, 2018).

[48] Scott v. Sandford, 60 U.S. 393 (1857). This case is generally regarded as the worst U.S. decision in history. It contributed directly to the Civil War.

of the most remarkable feats of reinterpretation in the history of lawyers working with documents. The 1776 Declaration of Independence articulates the reasons that United States elected to separate from England. There was no pretense either then, or 13 years later in the Constitution, that Americans would prohibit slavery.

Yet, in the middle of the Civil War, Lincoln found the rhetoric to reinterpret 87 years of history in a way that grounded emancipation, equality, and eventually all Negroes in the country. The Gettysburg Address was only two minutes long, but it became one of the most famous speeches of American history. Here is the opening line:

> Four score and seven years ago, our fathers brought forth upon this Continent a new nation conceived in liberty and dedicated to the proposition that all men are created equal.[49]

It is worth pausing a minute on the dramatic reinterpretation of the Declaration of Independence that these words represent. "Four score and seven" or 87, as subtracted from the year of delivery, yields not the Constitution of 1789 but the Declaration of Independence of 1776. "Our fathers brought forth on this Continent" is a deliberate biblical metaphor. The patriarchs of Judaism brought together the 12 tribes into a single nation of Israel. "Conceived in liberty" repeats the metaphor of birth: in fact, the image of the rebirth of the United States as a country that would respect the equality of blacks and whites alike.

In the Fourteenth Amendment, adopted after the war in 1868, it was made clear that "[a]ll persons born or naturalized in the United States, and subject to the jurisdiction thereof, are citizens of the United States. . . ."[50] Thus, by reverting to the notion of nationhood, Lincoln began the process of establishing a principle of equal citizenship applying to everyone born in the United States, thus overcoming the great scar of slavery that had marred American history since the first slave traders imported Africans in chains.

This snippet of American history explains why nationality is more basic than citizenship and more likely to be a potential source of genocidal behavior. Citizenship is useful and indeed indispensable in a world of international travel, but people rarely hate each other on the basis of their passports. And

[49] Abraham Lincoln, Address Delivered at the Dedication of the Cemetery at Gettysburg (Nov. 19, 1863), *in* ABRAHAM LINCOLN: GREAT SPEECHES 103–04 (John Grafton ed., 1991).

[50] U.S. CONST. amend XIV, § 1.

because citizenship, based on membership in an often-arbitrary set of state boundaries, tells little about the citizen, it is unlikely that anyone would abhor and call for the extermination of everyone with a particular passport. However irrational hatred for certain nationalities may be, there is at least some form of bias for nationalities that can be reconstructed and thus explained—in the way we explain other illnesses of the mind.

The Latin root of "nation" carries with it the idea of being born into a particular condition. There is a progression from family to tribe to the collection of tribes that calls itself a nation. In the beginning of the book of Exodus we see the transition from family to nation: "Now there arose up a new king over Egypt, who knew not Joseph."[51] The Jews went down to Egypt as families and tribes and in their captivity became a nation known to Pharaoh only as slaves. The history of their emancipation had an enormous effect on Lincoln, who was caught in a related struggle for the liberation of black slaves in the United States.

The concept of nationhood took on a new meaning under President Woodrow Wilson and his entry into World War I. The idealized purpose was to liberate individual nations and allow them to become self-governing states, each with its own citizenship. On the basis of this historical account, we can safely conclude that leading up to World War II, nationality was the foundational idea, and citizenship a useful derivative for ordering international affairs.

Of course, why people hate and are given to genocidal behavior remains a bit of a mystery. In the modern world, at least, genocide is not profitable behavior and, in the midst of wartime, the hostility toward an internal segment of the population, such as Hitler's genocide of the Jews, can lead to a waste of resources, loss of the war, and a lasting stigma in international affairs. The assumptions of dictators such as Hitler must be one of the following: (1) they can get away with it, (2) they can rewrite history to vindicate themselves, (3) they believe that they have some divine or historical mission to commit the act, and (4), they can appeal to a mythical base of the population that supports discriminatory (if not homicidal) behavior. Whatever the motive, the perpetrators of genocide are not easily deterred. The best justification for punishing these crimes is retribution and, in some cases, establishing a historical record of the crimes.

[51] Exodus 1:8 (KJV).

B. Ethnicity

This may be the vaguest of the four categories. The Tutsi in Rwanda are sometimes mentioned as a paradigmatic ethnic group.[52] It is not entirely clear why, except perhaps that the arbitrarily imposed distinction between Hutus and Tutsi and the resulting mass killings seemed intuitively to be a case of genocide, and some rationale was necessary to make the conflict fit the Statute.

The term "ethnic cleansing" came into fashion in the Yugoslav wars, another conflict with similar confusion surrounding whether the groups in question fell into historical categories of recognizable distinction. I suppose the differences among Serb, Croats, Bosnians, and other groups were not considered national differences, perhaps because of confusion between state and national members.

It is difficult to pinpoint the minimal content of ethnicity. It has something to do with the "other," but whether it applies to Arabs in the Middle East or dope addicts in the Philippines is open to debate. There is something circular about the concept of the "other" as a legally relevant factor. We are not inclined to use the word unless we sense a significant difference, but between the subjective identification of the other and the objective legal category, there is a yawning methodological gap.

This may be the residual category in the NERR foursome—more subject to manipulation than the other three.

C. Race

The category of race is perhaps the least attractive and most controverted of the four and is often defined in the eye of the beholder.

One example of the complexities surrounding race, especially the difficulties in determining the contours of its meaning, is the caste system in India. Whether this system is a matter of racial classification is complicated because of the ambiguity of race as a classification. Caste may be hereditary, according to Indian culture and region (though now prohibited under law),[53]

[52] *See generally Tutsi People*, Encyclopedia Britannica (2016); *Rwanda: How the Genocide Happened*, BBC News (May 17, 2011), http://www.bbc.com/news/world-africa-13431486.

[53] *Background on Untouchability and Segregation*, Human Rights Watch, http://pantheon.hrw.org reports/2001/globalcaste/caste0801-03.htm#P133_16342 (last accessed 8/2/2019).

but that does not make the hereditary element necessarily a racial marker, similar to blue eyes.

The most prominent racist regimes in modern history have been the United States and South Africa. Of course, Nazi Germany was guilty of this sin as well, as were all of the others listed under the Genocide Statute. But the obsession with race—as opposed to the other three NERR factors—particularly as it relates to blacks in the United States and South Africa, has been an acute and long-standing conflict. The simplified assumption behind the racial biases present in these cases is that light skin is better than darker skin.[54]

In both the United States and South Africa, the system of racial classification privileged those with light skin. In the United States, at least, there was a difference between the Northern free states and the Southern confederacy. Yet, in both parts, we encountered the curse of cases such as *Dred Scott v. Sandford*[55] and, until 1967, the prohibition of marriages between blacks and whites.[56] Perversely, marriages between races were called "miscegenation"—a term that applies to the breeding of animals. These particular burdens imposed on blacks in the United States become more significant when we consider, in the next sections, the kinds of measures besides killing that can constitute genocide under the Convention and the Rome Statute.

The interesting feature of race in the United States is that it was based on blood, not on popular perceptions. In order to prohibit intermarriage, the law required a definition of "Negro" status—interestingly, not of Caucasian status. By the early twentieth century, there emerged in the case law the so-called one-drop rule.[57] The issue was never maintaining racial purity on all sides—but not becoming identified with Negroes in the United States.

In the long struggle to achieve racial equality in the United States, the disadvantaged race has been called by many different names, each being politically correct for the time and incorrect later. The present acceptable range includes "black," "person of color," and "African American," the preferable term depending on context. The issue is so sensitive that an accidental

[54] *See, e.g.*, Henrik Pryser Libell & Catherine Porter, *From Norway to Haiti, Trump's Comments Stir Fresh Outrage*, N.Y. Times (Jan. 11, 2018), https://www.nytimes.com/2018/01/11/world/trump-countries-haiti-africa.html (last accessed 8/2/2019).

[55] 60 U.S. 393 (1857).

[56] Loving v. Virginia, 388 U.S. 1 (1967).

[57] F. James Davis, *Who Is Black? One Nation's Definition*, Frontline, https://www.pbs.org/wgbh/pages/frontline/shows/jefferson/mixed/onedrop.html (last visited Aug. 26, 2018).

reference to "spooks" (which also means ghosts) in Philip Roth's *The Human Stain* generated a college-wide, collective soul-searching about racism.[58]

Offensive words are not the only issues of race present in the United States today. In the last few years, a new movement called "Black Lives Matter" has taken the side of black victims in a series of highly publicized conflicts between black citizens and police.

The Black Lives Matter movement claims that the internal treatment of black citizens in the United States is rife with what they refer to as "structural racism," an issue that stands to have vast repercussions on the political process. Blacks suffer a much higher rate of imprisonment than do Caucasians, Hispanics, or Asian Americans.[59] And, this is true in a country that has the highest per capita rate of imprisonment in the world.[60] As a result of their criminal convictions, African Americans are subject to a form of voter disqualification called "felon disenfranchisement" that applies not only while in prison, but after release.[61] In the presidential election of 2000, millions of black felons were unable to vote, which may have played a role in George W. Bush's presidential victory.[62]

In South Africa, the one-time policy toward race, infamously called apartheid, is based on the policy of different life channels for different races, including whites, blacks, those of mixed race, and Indians. They also faced a problem never faced in the United States: how to classify everyone else—Japanese, Chinese, etc. Jews were always considered whites (which means they never encountered Ethiopian Jews, who would have been classified as blacks). The issues in South Africa represent an attempt at designing a country in Africa, with a large black majority, so that ideally each race could lead a life independent of the others. Things did not work out that way because blacks ultimately became the servant class—even though after the end of apartheid, blacks quickly formed a powerful political party.[63] Interestingly,

[58] Philip Roth, Opinion, *An Open Letter to Wikipedia*, N. YORKER (Sept. 6, 2012), https://www.newyorker.com/books/page-turner/an-open-letter-to-wikipedia.

[59] Inmate Race, FEDERAL BUREAU OF PRISON STATISTICS (last updated Feb. 24, 2018), https://www.bop.gov/about/statistics/statistics_inmate_race.jsp. *See also* George Gao, *Chart of the Week: The Black-White Gap in Incarceration Rates*, PEW RESEARCH (July 18, 2014), http://www.pewresearch.org/fact-tank/2014/07/18/chart-of-the-week-the-black-white-gap-in-incarceration-rates/.

[60] The U.S. prison population rate is 698 per 100,000. Roy Walmsley, *World Prison Population List*, INSTITUTE FOR CRIMINAL POLICY RESEARCH (11th ed.) (2016), http://prisonstudies.org/sites/default/files/resources/downloads/world_prison_population_list_11th_edition_0.pdf.

[61] George P. Fletcher, *Disenfranchisement as Punishment: Reflections on the Racial Uses of Infamia*, 46 UCLA L. REV. 1895 (1999).

[62] *See* THE LONGEST NIGHT, POLEMICS AND PERSPECTIVES ON ELECTION 2000 (Arthur Jacobson & Michel Rosenfeld eds., 2002).

[63] *See generally African National Congress*, ENCYCLOPEDIA BRITANNICA (Feb. 15, 2018).

the South African attitude toward race, as I understand it, was that if you passed as white, you were white.[64] There was no search for a drop of black blood, or a check on parentage, as there was for Jews in Nazi Germany.

The Rome Statute reserves a special note of condemnation for apartheid by listing "the crime of apartheid" as a crime against humanity.[65] In no other case is "the crime of" used to qualify the specifics of a crime. Why is apartheid different in this regard from murder[66] or torture?[67] There is a possible point to the definition "the crime of apartheid" on the ground that some politicians in South Africa advocated apartheid without thinking of it as a crime. There was an analogous movement in the United States under the "separate but equal" movement. Of course, racists attitudes prevail over pretensions of equality.[68]

D. Religion

It would seem that this would be the least controversial of the NERR foursome. By and large, people can choose their religion whereas they cannot choose their nationality (except perhaps by migration), their ethnicity, or their race. There are converts in every religion. Why should people hate each other on the basis of religion, and if they do, are the despised partially responsible in a way in which the victims in the other categories are not?

Freedom of religion is a basic constitutional right in the United States under the First Amendment. Yet arguably, it conflicts with other rights recognized under the U.S. Constitution, namely, the right to marry the person of your choice and the principle of equality that has prevailed since Lincoln's reinterpretation of the phrase "all men are created equal" in the Gettysburg Address. The foundation is the recent decision of the Supreme Court, which has recognized the right of gay persons to marry.[69]

[64] Population Registration Act 30 of 1950, § 1 (xv) (S. Afr.) ("'[W]hite person' means a person who in appearance obviously is, or who is generally accepted as a white person, but does not include a person who although in appearance obviously (sic) a white person, is generally accepted as a coloured person.").

[65] Rome Statute, *supra* note 3, art. 7(1)(j).

[66] *Id.*, art. 7(1)(a).

[67] *Id.*, art. 7(1)(f).

[68] Brown v. Board of Education, 347 U.S. 483, 74 S. Ct. 686 (1954) (overturning the notion of "separate but equal" touted in Plessy v. Ferguson, 163 U.S. 537 (1896)).

[69] *See* Obergefell v. Hodges, 135 S. Ct. 2584 (2015).

A dispute brewing in the United States for a few years and recently decided by the U.S. Supreme Court arose between a gay couple and a baker whom they asked to bake a wedding cake for their nuptials. He refused on the ground that it interfered with his freedom of religion, as he is opposed to gay marriage.[70] The issue arises at the borderline of religious freedom, as it comes into conflict with the basic right to be treated equally.

The other highly disputed issue recently before the U.S. Supreme Court, perhaps with more significance for international law, is the travel ban proposed by President Trump, which restricts immigration access from Muslim-majority nations. Only the third iteration of the travel ban was successful at the Supreme Court while previous iterations were met with consternation in the courts.[71]

In any event, these and other aspects of the NERR classificatory scheme apply only if the action constitutes an attempt with specific intent to inflict one of the specific kinds of damage on a protected group.

4. The Prohibited Actions, Five in All

The first two of this lists are fairly obvious: killing or causing physical or mental harm to members of the group. Yet there is a hidden issue in the phrase "members of the group." In a case in which I appeared as an expert witness in the Eastern District Federal Court in New York, the grandchildren of the Vietnamese directly affected by the use of Agent Orange in the war sued Dow Chemical and others for birth defects that did not show up until their generation.[72] Assuming that Agent Orange was used to inflict harm on the civilians then present in Vietnam and that these civilians were a member of the protected group, were their grandchildren also protected? I think the answer would have to be yes.

[70] *See* Masterpiece Cakeshop, Ltd. v. Colo. Civ. Rights Comm'n, 137 S. Ct. 2290 (2017). The interesting problem is deciding the correct position for the ACLU (American Civil Liberties Union) to take. Both sides raise an issue of civil liberty: freedom of religion versus the foundational principles of private enterprise, and the freedom to do business as one sees fit.

[71] *See* Shadi Hamid, *The Travel Ban, the Law, and What's "Right,"* ATLANTIC (Jun. 28, 2018), https://www.theatlantic.com/international/archive/2018/06/trump-travel-ban-supreme-court/564044/; Doe v. Trump, No. C17-0178JLR, 2017 U.S. Dist. LEXIS 211377 (W.D. Wash. Dec. 23, 2017); Ali v. Trump, No. 2:17-cv-00135-JLR, 2018 U.S. Dist. LEXIS 11789 (W.D. Wash. Jan. 23, 2018) (granting a stipulated motion for extension of stay in light of Trump v. Hawaii, 138 S. Ct. 542 2017 WL 5987406 (2017)).

[72] Isaacson v. Dow Chem. Co., 304 F. Supp. 2d 404 (E.D.N.Y. 2004), *aff'd*, 517 F. 3d. 129 (2d Cir. 2008), *cert. denied*, 555 U.S. 1218 (2009).

Of course, Dow Chemical could defend on the ground that the use of Agent Orange was neither genocide nor a war crime, but, that obvious issue aside, there is an interesting question about who constitutes a member of a protected group and whether harm suffered by subsequent generations is included with the original crime. This issue has also emerged recently in Japan, where the residual effects of the bombs dropped during World War II are being seen in new generations.[73]

The third prohibited action is to impose conditions "calculated" to bring about physical harm. It cannot be the case that the harm is simply an unintended consequence of the Long March of the Navajos to their reservation in New Mexico.[74] The requirement of "calculation" goes beyond knowing or expecting that the physical conditions will cause irreparable harm. The requirement seems inconsistent with a respectable purpose for the "physical conditions."[75] Arguably, detention at Guantánamo Bay for suspects of terrorist activities against the United States (all of whom happen to be Muslims) might cause physical or mental harm, but they are not designed or "calculated" to do so. The mens rea term here requires more than a specific intent to commitment the harm. In the language of homicide, it requires specific intent plus premeditation. It is difficult to find or invent a plausible example of this occurring.

These first three examples of required action indicate a serious problem that affects a wide swath of crimes related to the occurrence of war, and that is, the philosophical problem of double effect.[76] The origin of this doctrine is most often used in explaining the Catholic approach to abortion. Killing the child is lawful if it is the side effect of a meritorious medical procedure.[77] Similarly, killing civilians in wartime is legitimate if it is a side effect of an acceptable military procedure. The arguments for the latter can sometimes be a bit strained, as for example, the claim that the harm to civilians in the

[73] *See* Gabriella Blum, *The Laws of War and the "Lesser Evil,"* 35 Yale J. Int'l L. 1, 1 (2010).

[74] Also referred to as the Long Walk to Bosque Redondo, the Long March was the deportation of the Navajo people from their homeland of Arizona to Fort Sumner in New Mexico, following a "scorched earth" campaign waged by Colonel Kit Carson from 1863 to 1864. After surrendering, approximately 8,500 Navajos were "death marched" in four bands over four hundred miles. Raymond D. Austin, Navajo Courts and Navajo Common Law, A Tradition of Tribal Self-Governance 2–3 (2009).

[75] Updated Statute of the International Criminal Tribunal for the former Yugoslavia, art. 4, *available at* http://www.un.org/icty/legaldoc-e/b.asic/statut/statute-feb08-e.pdf.

[76] *See* Michael Walzer, Just and Unjust Wars: A Moral Argument with Historical Illustrations 153 (1977).

[77] *Abortion*, Diocese of Phoenix, https://dphx.org/respect-life/know-the-issues/abortion/ (last visited Aug. 27, 2018).

nuclear bombing of Hiroshima was lawful because the United States sought to eliminate a train station in Hiroshima. Nonetheless, the doctrine of double effect is indispensable in analyzing liability for inflicting harm on innocent persons.

The fourth ground of trying to "prevent births within the group"[78] is a little mysterious. We can imagine some bizarre ways to accomplish this, such as killing all the men within the group, but that is presumably not what the provision has in mind. Nor does it include the menace of rape in wartime by the target. Rape may generate children of mixed nationality, but it certainly does not have the effect of preventing births. Some examples given in various commentaries are forced sterilization and forced abortions. Again, these measures may have the consequence of lowering the birth rate, but it is hard to see these individualized measures as having the intent to destroy the relevant group in whole or in part. Be that as it may, this may be the correct interpretation of the language.

The last ground of "forcibly transferring children to another group" has some historical precedents in the actions of Christian missionaries in the United States, presumably toward Indian children, and the approach of Australia toward the re-education of Aborigine children (the latter understood as a racial group). The problem here is that these movements were meant to help the children by enabling them to function well in the larger society. Of course, they might as a result lose some of their loyalty toward their parental home or their tribe, but to call education as being any sort of a form of genocide seems to undermine the negative valence of the concept.

5. The Requirement of Intention

This factor links the prohibited action with one of the NERR. The intention must be "to destroy, in whole or in part," the targeted group.[79] The first problem is whether the concept of intention should be interpreted according to Article 30—one of the more poorly drafted provisions of the Rome Statute.[80] The latter distinguishes between the mental element as to conduct and as to consequences. As to the latter, it is sufficient if the defendant

[78] Rome Statute, *supra* note 3, art. 6(d).
[79] Rome Statute, *supra* note 3, art. 6.
[80] Rome Statute, *supra* note 3, art. 30(b)(2).

is aware that the consequence "will occur in the ordinary course of events."[81] The latter phrase is unique in the annals of criminal law theory and practice. I know of no case or statute that invokes the phrase. It comes closer to defining negligence than intentional conduct.

If the "ordinary course of events" test is used, it might be possible to commit genocide by merely allowing the water supply of a protected group to become contaminated or to impose a blockage in wartime that leads the city to suffer starvation.

The factor "in whole or in part" is similarly elusive. The notion of destroying "in part" qualifies the concept of killing an entire genus of people. An example might be the attack in Waco, Texas, in 1994 by federal law enforcement to shut down the compound of an offshoot cult from Seventh Day Adventists.[82] Their purpose was not to kill the Branch Davidians in the cult, but a fire ensued and 76 people died. This example seems to fit the formal requirements of Article 6 but only by bringing to bear the odd principle of intention as an awareness that the harmful effect might "occur in the ordinary course of events."

Unfortunately, the elusive qualifier "in part" adds some support to labeling the killing in Waco as genocide. This kind of distortion could be possible without a coherent theory on why the intention to destroy might apply to only part of the NERR group. There is nothing to suggest that Hitler and the Nazis intended to kill only Jews living in Europe. There was nothing about the Jews' location that added to Goebbels's propaganda and the systematic dehumanization that led to Auschwitz and the other death camps.

One explanation for this confusion might be that genocide is inherently a crime of attempt. No one has ever succeeded in wiping out an entire group under the NERR categorization. They have tried but never quite succeeded. Genocide has been a completed crime only "in part." If that intuitive understanding of history is read back into the required definition of genocide, we have a plausible account of the language we use.

[81] *Id.*

[82] In 1993, federal law enforcement agents with the help of military air support and armored vehicles breached the Branch Dividian compound in Waco, Texas, under the guise of a search warrant for "unlawful possession of a destructive device." The affidavit presented for the search warrant also included discussions of alleged child abuse. A massacre ensued, and numerous men, women, and children were killed in the course of the raid. *See* OFFICE OF SPECIAL COUNSEL, FINAL REPORT TO THE DEPUTY ATTORNEY GENERAL CONCERNING THE 1993 CONFRONTATION AT THE MT CARMEL COMPLEX WACO, TX 131–34 (2000).

In interpreting any provision of law, we need to reconcile the results we obtain from rigorously applied criteria laid out in a statute with our intuitive judgments about the scope of the crime. The killing of the Branch Davidians does not meet our intuitive sense of genocide. The answer might be to rely upon our common sense understanding of language in interpreting the concept of intention originally found in the Genocide Convention than the one now twisted with some other goal in mind in Article 30 of the Rome Statute.

With the topic of genocide finally covered in detail, we can move on to Article 7.

6. Crimes Against Humanity

As we turn the page to a new type of crime, crimes against humanity, we encounter a totally different form of drafting and requisite interpretation. Genocide is a closed book, a numerus clausus, a finite set of categories and methods for committing the offense. In our extensive analysis of genocide, we have had to take seriously the principle of *nullum crimen sine lege*, which literally forbids interpretation by analogy. Yet, in the realm of Crimes against Humanity (hereafter CaH), we are told in a residual clause that the prohibition includes "other inhumane acts of a similar character intentionally causing great suffering or serious injury to body or to mental or physical health."[83] If "similar character" does not invite interpretation by analogy, nothing does.

In the Nuremberg trials, the primary function of CaH was to provide a charge against the Germans for crimes against their own people. Killing Jews in Poland was an armed attack against Poland, but by killing their own citizens, the Germans apparently did not encroach upon international law. The CaH established a principle of the international order directs to the nationals and citizens of one's own country.

Since then, the contours of CaH have swollen and now overlap many aspects of genocide as well as war crimes. This may be due simply to there being no inherent conceptual limit to the crime. In the common law tradition, however, there is a prosecutorial advantage to multiple charges on the same set of facts. They provide a well-known technique to encourage plea

[83] Rome Statute, *supra* note 3, art. 7.

bargaining and the illusion that the defendant is gaining something in the exchange.

The general actus reus of a CaH requires first that it be an act that is part of "a widespread or systematic attack on any civilian population."[84] There follows a list of 10 specific acts, most of which are generally recognized as crimes in domestic law. The general mens rea requirement is "knowledge" of the attack. We do better in developing a coherent understanding of Article 7, CaH, if we ignore Article 30 on mental states and concentrate on the use of the phrase "knowledge of the attack."[85]

As for the problem of collective action, a difficulty arises around the phrase "widespread or systematic attack," but logically one could imagine a single dictator orchestrating these attacks.[86] As we shall see, there might be collective consequences implied in the 10 specific acts.

The thing that these 10 acts have in common is that they are directed against people. That makes sense in light of their being crimes against humanity—human beings. This is true about genocide as well, but not about all cases of aggression and war crimes. Each of the 10 is accompanied by an explanatory sentence in part 2 of the Article. Here are some thoughts on each of them:

1. *Murder.* The first one, oddly, is not defined. The correct term might have been "homicide" to include killings that are partially excused by mental illness under Article 31(1).[87] Even a widespread or systemic attack might stem from the mind of a deranged dictator even if it, as required in Article 7(2)(a), is "in furtherance of a State or organizational policy to commit such an attack."[88]
2. *Extermination.* This is an unfortunate term for a crime. The term in English is usually reserved for the extermination of pests, such as bedbugs. So, far as I know, there is no domestic crime anywhere called "extermination." The explanatory note in Article 7(2)(b) gives an example of what the drafters had in mind: the "deprivation of food or medicine" calculated to bring about the destruction of part of the population.[89] One might think that the word "extermination" would carry

[84] *Id.*
[85] *Id.*
[86] *Id.*
[87] *Id.*, art. 31(1)(a).
[88] *Id.*, art. 7(2)(a).
[89] *Id.*, art. 7(2)(b).

implications of direct and immediate consequences, not of indirect killing via some form of deprivation. And further, one might take the word to imply total destruction. But as we have seen with genocide, the tendency in the Statute is to define crimes by setting a threshold of completion in the field of preparing and attempting the ultimate harm.

In the case of extermination, the background is the history of the siege as an acceptable method of warfare. The Lieber Code (1863) held that it was permissible to deprive a city under attack of supplies as a way of hastening the end of the war.[90] The siege is one move in a tactic of negotiation. Perhaps the critical factor here, as elsewhere, is the import of the word "calculated," as connected with "leading to destruction." This term could be read to mean something more than "expected," perhaps the implication being one of malicious intent, beyond the realm of a negotiation tactic.

3. *Enslavement*. This is apparently designed to prevent human trafficking, particularly of "women and children," which implies that the purpose is not exploiting people for sake of labor (as in the United States before the Civil War) but in preventing females from becoming victims of prostitution. Frankly, it would have been better to explicitly target the crime of selling sex directly. Yet, as with many other crimes, the negative valence of the term "enslavement" far exceeds the wrongfulness of the crime. The bark of the Statute is worse than its bite.
4. *Deportation or forcible transfer of population*. These are not known to be crimes. Deportation in the United States applies only to noncitizens and is not regarded as a criminal proceeding requiring the constitutional protections of the Sixth Amendment. Provided that the deportee has a home country, it is not clear why this should be considered a problem of concern to the international community. The example the drafters might have had in mind is the threat many years later to the deportation of Arabs living on the West Bank.

   There have been some egregious cases of forcible transfer in the aftermath of wars, but the victorious state is often caught between two options, both considered illegal. Think about Israel and its policy toward the West Bank 50 years after the Six Day War. Israel could integrate the West Bank into its territory and give the Arabs the right

[90] *See* Francis Lieber, *Instructions for the Government of Armies of the United States in the Field*, art. 15 (1863) ("Military necessity admits of all direct destruction. . . .").

to vote or remove Arabs from the territory. Both would be severely condemned by the international community. It is no surprise the policy of occupation continues in the hope of a negotiated peace.

5. *Imprisonment or other severe deprivation of physical liberty or violation of fundamental rules of international law.* The intriguing implication here is that there are jus cogens, unwritten principles of international law that are "fundamental." Interesting, because the idea of jus cogens invites the application of principles of custom outside the perimeter of *nulla poena sine lege*.
6. *Torture.* This is a wonderful example for illustrating the position of Justice Potter Stewart toward pornography:[91] he knows it when he sees it. The attempt to define torture may be an unfortunate distraction, and, in fact, give the torturers a defense when they should not have one. Take the psychological torture at Abu Ghraib—humiliation of Muslim prisoners put into dog chains, then exposed to naked women.[92] Of course, the term "mental suffering" is sufficiently elastic to include what we want it to.

   It might have made sense to include some modification of the form: "of the type never proven to yield reliable results." It has never been clear to me why those tortured don't simply lie. Perhaps, there is some fear of retaliation and more severe torture if the lies are proven, but still there is little reason to trust the word of someone who faces the choice of speaking and suffering.
7. *Sexual violence, primarily rape, and forced pregnancy.* There are two distinct wrongs here: one is the obvious harm to women, and the other is the covert aggression that replicates other crimes aimed at holding our international boundaries firm. It is paradoxical that rampaging soldiers, fighting an aggressive war for territory, compromise their overall military goals by generating a population tied in part to the women under conquest. Yet, this provision is hedged by the limiting requirements: (1) the women must be under confinement, and (2) there must be an intent to affect the ethnic composition of (3) any population. Or it must be some other grave violation of international law. The only part that is relatively clear is the prohibition of rape.

[91] Jacobellis v. Ohio, 378 U.S. 184, 197 (1964) (Stewart, J., concurring).
[92] *See* Seymour M. Hersh, *Torture at Abu Ghraib*, N. Yorker (May 10, 2004), https://www.newyorker.com/magazine/2004/05/10/torture-at-abu-ghraib.

8. *Persecution against any identifiable group, etc.* This is a new concept and one to which we bring an intuitive understanding. It essentially means biased prosecution. The grounds of bias are enumerated but our intuition prevails, particularly if there are only a few instances of prosecution of the particular group. The rest of the definition is left entirely vague. A new problem arises because the Statute tries to define gender as exclusively "male or female." Anyone living in the age of LGBTQ (lesbian, gay, bisexual, transgender, queer/questioning) political activism would know that some believe this to be a form of bias in itself.
9. *Enforced disappearance of persons.* This crime needs no explanation, though it receives one out of place as Article 7(2)(I). Everyone should know that it refers to the desaparecidos in Argentina in the 1980s and the inability of the government to respond until the Madres and Abuelas went into the streets.[93] This lead to the notion of impunidad and a basic rationale of the ICC. Thus, we understand the principle of jurisdiction that the national state be "unwilling or unable to prosecute."[94] It is important, however, to note that the victims' groups be substantial. The disappearance of two or three people would not qualify. Although, in fact, the Argentine case has racial, ethnic, and political components in the identification of the victims; this is not required. With a limitation to the historical paradigm, the definition of the crime—in this case as in many others—is overly broad.
10. *The crime of apartheid.* This clause also has a clear historical paradigm. The difference between this and the Argentine case, however, is that prosecution in the ICC would not have a substantive impact on the "crime." Perhaps that is why, as compared to all the other charges, it is labeled a crime.

In review, it is clear that some of these crimes appear to be defined out of whole cloth while others have historical paradigms. When a historical paradigm exists, it should be followed—even though doing so seems to violate other principles of the Rome Statute, namely the principle *nullum crimen sine lege* and the prohibition of punishment by analogy. It is also critical to

[93] *See* RITA ARDITTI, SEARCHING FOR LIFE: THE GRANDMOTHERS OF THE PLAZA DE MAYO AND THE DISAPPEARED CHILDREN OF ARGENTINA 1 (1999); Ronald Dworkin, *Introduction* to COMISION NACIONAL SOBRE LA DESPARICION DE PERSONAS, *in* NUNCA MAS: THE REPORT OF THE ARGENTINE NATIONAL COMMISSION ON THE DISAPPEARED at xi (1986).

[94] Rome Statute, *supra* note 3, art. 17(1)(a).

avoid the confusion on mental state in Article 30(2)(b). These crimes do not simply occur in the ordinary course of affairs. If they do—as for example, the disappearance of persons in a fire or a flood—they are not necessarily criminal. The frequent and contextualized use of the words "intentional" and "calculated" are used repeatedly and take precedence. The more important principle is to make sense of the Rome Statute as a whole in the context of "general principles of law derived by the Court from national laws of legal systems of the world."

Note that nearly all of these offenses are crimes of collective action. It goes without saying that the innovation of Article 8*bis* must apply here as elsewhere or else we would be incapable of reasoning from group to individual responsibility.

7. War Crimes

This is the fourth of the crimes, described in excruciating detail in Article 8, "within the jurisdiction of the ICC" according to Article 5. As we glance over the list, we encounter many of the fundamental issues we have mentioned, and therefore this is a good occasion for review of some jurisprudential issues. Recall that "aggression" is not defined at all in the Rome Statute of 1998 and did not receive its sophisticated individualizing definition until the Kampala Conference of 2010.

War crimes are the quintessential collective crime. Indeed, it is hard to see actions committed in the course of war (or "armed conflict" as international lawyers are inclined to say these days) as anything else. Military action requires organization, a chain of command, and uniforms or other signs of membership that serve both as a license to kill and permission to the enemy to kill. Above all, the law requires the principle of distinction, namely between soldiers and civilians and others hors de combat (sick, wounded, detained).

The entire institution is based on the distinction between just ad bellum and jus in bello. Jus ad bellum addressed the beginning of conflict and is governed by Article 51 of the UN Charter.[95] We are concerned here with in jus in bello, the law that governs combat itself. The distinction is critical

[95] U.N. Charter art. 51 ("Nothing in the present Charter shall impair the inherent right of individual or collective self-defence if an armed attack occurs against a Member of the United Nations, until the Security Council has taken measure necessary to maintain international peace and security. Measures taken by Members in the exercise of this right of self-defence shall be immediately reported to the Security Council and shall not in any way affect the authority and responsibility of the Security

because an unlawful war (e.g., Hitler's attack on Poland) does not entail liability for the soldiers who are lawful combatants in the German army. This principle—apart from being foundational to the law of war—is a matter of decency toward enlisted soldiers. There is no way that an ordinary soldier can be expected to know whether the war, commanded in a far-off place by superiors he has never met, satisfies the requirements of Article 51 or not.

If we ask the general question of why is killing in warfare ever justified, we encounter a puzzle under the categories of traditional criminal law. There are three options: (1) the enemy soldier does not have an interest worthy of protection; (2) the killing is justified as a matter of necessity or self-defense; or (3) the killing is excused on grounds analogous to duress, for example, the soldier is forced to do it. None of these is a plausible account. First, if the enemy was not worthy of respect as a human being, we would not have all these specific laws in Article 8 concerning the treatment of captives. Second, the ordinary criteria of necessity or self-defense do not apply. In Michael Walzer's famous examples of encountering an enemy soldier taking a break and smoking a cigarette, there is no need to kill instead of taking him prisoner.[96] Nonetheless, if the requirements of combatancy are satisfied, either soldier could shoot and kill the other. Third, neither a physical factor nor the higher command is forcing the soldier to act. She can disobey and if under an order to shoot, the order might be "manifestly unlawful."[97] In the final analysis, there does not seem to be any of three lines of arguments, based in criminal law, to justify the killing of combatants.

The interesting implication of Article 32 on superior orders is that war crimes are differentiated from genocide and crimes against humanity on the ground that the other two are always manifestly unlawful (there is no implication about aggression under Article 8*bis*). There is a clue to a point readily understood by glancing at Article 8: there are more war crimes than any soldier could reasonably be expected to know by heart.

The organizing distinction is between international and non-international conflicts (the meaning of the latter category will concern us later). There are 30 distinct crimes in the international category. The numbering depends on whether the use of the word "or" indicates a genuinely alternative charge or

Council under the present Charter to take at any time such action as it deems necessary in order to maintain or restore international peace and security.").

[96] *See* Michael Walzer, Just and Unjust Wars: A Moral Argument with Historical Illustrations 142 (1977).

[97] Rome Statute, *supra* note 3, art. 33(1)(c).

simply an explanatory alternative, for example, "Unlawful deportation or transfer or unlawful confinement."[98] This looks like three distinct charges. In other cases, the "or" just introduces a clarification, for example, "Torture or Inhuman treatment, including biological experiments."[99] This is complicated because "inhuman treatment" is too vague to stand alone as a charge. On the other hand, "biological experiments" is sufficient in itself to constitute a charge.

In the second major heading of Article 8, "not of an international character," we encounter about 20 possible charges. The first conceptual issue in this category is what we mean by the general classification of non-international. If the drafter meant to say "internal," they should and could have said that. Thus, they leave open the terrain to clever legal arguments, particularly about the American wars of the twentieth century. What about the recent war against al-Qaeda in Iraq in 2001? This operation led, as we know, to mass incarceration in Guantánamo Bay and the invention of categories outside the ordinary discourse of warfare, for example, the term "unlawful combatant."

The challenge to Bush was that the Geneva Conventions applied, including the part now incorporated in the Rome Statute as Article 8(2)(a)(ii).[100] The war against al-Qaeda, which came to be known as the War on Terror, was international in one sense and not in another. It clearly crossed conventional boundaries between states and therefore was international, but it was not a war between distinct "nations."

It would make sense to read the entirety of the Geneva Conventions and Article 8 as comprehensive, therefore including all armed conflicts, except those explicitly excluded in Article 8(2)(d): "riots, isolated, sporadic acts of violence, and similar acts."[101] It is difficult to interpret this exclusion without knowing how deeply the category of "non-international disputes" is meant to reach in internal affairs. It is not meant to cover every gunfight in Chicago. The exclusion is deliberately vague.

For the forty-first president, the war in Iraq was justified by the interpretation of "non-international" as "not between states." Thus, a war against al-Qaeda and similar nonstate groups would not be covered. Perhaps by

[98] Rome Statute, *supra* note 3, art. 8(2)(a)(vii).
[99] *Id.*, art. 8(2)(a)(ii).
[100] *Id.*
[101] *Id.*, art. 8(2)(d).

analogy to the tribute that vice pays to virtue, this kind of interpretative move is the tribute of a White House to the principle of legality.

To summarize the key points so far: (1) we are concerned here with jus in bello, not just ad bellum;[102] (2) there is no justification for killing in warfare under the categories of the traditional criminal law; (3) we are dealing with a classical collective crime, presumptively not covered by Article 8*bis*; and (4) the principle of distinction is indispensable to understanding the concept of war crimes.

The final mystery about war crimes is how they are possible, with or without the other four points previously summarized. The inevitability of collective action in warfare (or armed conflict) not only raises the problem of who is liable within the collective but how liability of the individual is possible at all. The notion of warfare suppresses the individual within the collective of the fighting unit. The unexpected beauty of war crimes is that somehow the individual breaks loose from the collective and must stand trial alone, as a unique person, for one of the 25 to 30 charges that we will cover selectively in Section 8 of this chapter.

8. War Crimes: Substantive Highlights

As we read through Article 8, some points stand out and warrant commentary:

1. "Willful killing."[103] One would expect some consistency with other references to homicide, such as to "murder" in the Genocide Statute, Article 7(1). The use of the term "willful" departs from the definition of mental states in Article 30, but the term "unless otherwise provided" in the latter provision permits this deviation. The term occurs many times in the course of defining war crimes. The question is: Why? In light of many inconsistencies in drafting, I don't think one should be taken too seriously. It is presumably just an inheritance from the Geneva Conventions.

[102] *International Humanitarian Law, supra* note 16 ("International humanitarian law governs both the legality of justifications for war (*jus ad bellum*, or when states can resort to war) and the legality of wartime conduct (*jus in bello*, or how states must behave themselves during war)".).

[103] Rome Statute, *supra* note 3, art. 8(2)(a)(i).

2. "Fair and Regular Trial."[104] This is a very intriguing provision, not easy to express in other languages. Both terms "fair" and "regular" warrant extension in the sub-chapter on procedure.
3. "Intentionally directing attacks against the civilian population."[105] Here, the central problem is terrorism—a phenomenon ignored by the Rome Statute. Let us assume, for the purpose of discussion, that terrorists ensconce themselves in civilian targets—hospitals, schools—otherwise treated as civilian institutions. They fight part of the day and then return to live in their "civilian" villages. With the development of drone warfare, the terrorists can be singled out and targeted with minimal impact on surrounding institutions. The problem is whether this is an "intentional attack against the civilian population" when the population is not targeted "as such"—a useful term in the Genocide Statute.

   What makes an installation military as opposed to civilian? Under wartime conditions, just about everything has a military purpose. Suppose it is a steel plant or even a bread factory or—to take a disturbing example—a factory manufacturing Zyklon B, the gas used for genocide in Auschwitz.[106] In small quantities, the gas has a useful purpose, as does just about everything—in appropriate quantities. The problem here is the quantity and the purpose in manufacturing large quantities. Here there might be a conflict between the definitions of "genocide" in Article 8 on war crimes. Genocide is an attack on a civilian population, but it is hard to call it a military attack. Indeed, it is fairly obvious that Hitler, by diverting so much of his resources to the murder of innocent Jews, substantially impaired his own military efforts in Russia, and it may have cost him the battle of Stalingrad and the war.
4. "Clearly excessive in relation to the [military advantage]."[107] This is the way international documents express the issue of proportionality, which is one of those vague expressions that hound the law of war. The fact is that the word "proportionality" is usually used in connection with the requirement of necessity, which means that there is no

[104] *Id.*, art. 8(2)(a)(vi).
[105] *Id.*, art. 8(2)(b)(i).
[106] *See* Jay Akbar, *"The Brain and Heart Are Attacked First . . It Begins with a Stinging Chest and Epileptic Seizures": Trial of "Auschwitz Bookkeeper" Told How Gas Chamber Pesticide Was So Weak It Could Take Holocaust Victims "Longer than Half-an-Hour to Die,"* Daily Mail (May 27, 2015), www.dailymail.co.uk./news/article-3099309/The-brain-heart-attacked-begins-stinging-chest-epileptic-seizures-Trial-Auschwitz-bookkeeper-told-gas-chamber-pesticide-weak-holocaust-victims-longer-half-hour-die.html.
[107] Rome Statute, *supra* note 3, art. 8(2)(b)(iv).

cheaper, reasonable means available for the end in sight. "Necessary and proportional" are typically used together. But, more often than not, the issue is necessity—is there a cheaper means available—rather than the more debatable variable of proportionality or excessiveness. The problem with the latter term is that it is entirely subjective. What is "too much" for one person may not be excessive for another.

5. "Making improper use of a flag of truce, etc."[108] The provision is testimony to the entrenched customs and universal language of jus in bello. There is nothing inherent about the color "white" or a "flag" to indicate surrender. The custom goes back to wars fought by Romans and, independently, by the ancient Chinese. At one time, apparently, a black flag communicated surrender, but a piece of cloth with no color at all is easier to pass off as white to indicate either surrender or a desire for a truce.
6. "Transfer, directly or indirectly, . . . of its own civilian population."[109] This is generally read to target Israel's settling the West Bank beginning in 1977. This provision is reminiscent of the chain of logic that leads to individual responsibility under the Rome Statute. It may be that individuals decided to become "settlers," but they would not be held liable under the Geneva Conventions unless their actions were attributable to the Israeli State. In the beginning, I didn't think this was so easy to do, but then it became apparent that the settlers relied upon Israeli military protection against the Arab population. Thus, we get the problem of collective action and must reason back to individual accountability of a particular settler. This becomes increasingly difficult to do as we move into the third generation of Israelis in the territories, most of whom were born there and know no other home.
7. "Intentionally directing attacks against buildings dedicated to religion, etc."[110] This, again, is a classic issue in the wars fought by Israel against various Arab militias in Gaza and on the West Bank. The problem occurs as a result of the victims using the civilian buildings as places for storing weapons, launching attacks, and hiding militants. The paragraph is qualified by the phrase "provided they are not military objectives." It would seem that if the protected are used for these military purposes, they become military targets. Here the intriguing

[108] *Id.*, art. 8(2)(b)(vii).
[109] *Id.*, art. 8(2)(b)(viii).
[110] *Id.*, art. 8(2)(b)(ix).

problem is whether the issue of military target is more difficult to prove, as compared with Article 8(2)(b)(I), by virtue of the presumptively protected status of the building.

8. "Killing or wounding treacherously."[111] The use of this language, reminiscent of the prohibition against using the white flag falsely, testifies to the element of chivalry in jus in bello. The troops on both sides must fight fairly. It is difficult to know, however, what constitutes a violation. Perhaps the classic example from ancient Greek warfare is the use of the Trojan Horse. Surprise is an essential aspect of military tactics. Yet there are many borderline cases, such as use of the ambush, a concealed weapon, or even a new form of weaponry, such as air power in World War I. The larger question raised by this provision, as applied to many, is balancing the history of warfare with the necessity of innovation. There might be a larger message here as well. Normatively charged terms such as "treacherously" are easy to use in drafting but hard to apply in practice.
9. Seizing the enemies' property, or, of course, destroying it.[112] One of the most vital tasks in fighting a war on foreign soil is managing the supply line. It is one thing to protect the lives of foreign armies, another thing to expect the advancing army to leave the crops intact. A "scorched earth" policy effectively bars the possibility of retreat, which is another reason for Hitler's defeat on the Eastern front. On the other hand, General Grant effectively used this tactic in burning down Atlanta and his march from Atlanta to the sea. The terms "destroying" or "seizing" suggest more profit-oriented purposes. So far as this provision means that there is no apparent tactical advantage to the destruction of property, it makes sense as an aspect of the principle of distinction, for example, protecting civilians in warfare.
10. Employing poison.[113] One of the issues in the dispute is about Americans using Agent Orange as a defoliant in the Vietnam War. The impact was to inflict the kind of damage poison would inflict, even to the point of genetic transmission. This may be an aspect of fighting "treacherously" or it could have been more serious implications for the general ban on relatively easy methods of attacks, such as poisoning the

[111] *Id.*, art. 8(2)(b)(xi).
[112] *Id.*, art. 8(2)(b)(xiii).
[113] *Id.*, art. 8(20(b)(xvii).

food or water supply, which could be done openly without secrecy or surprise. This issue takes us back to the problem of the siege in the analysis of CaH. We can see how difficult it is to form a general theory of jus in bello. The elements of tradition and chivalry constantly conflict with the air of ending the war as quickly as possible.

11. "Committing outrages upon personal dignity."[114] This excessively vague provision is more like a constitutional provision than a rule of jus in bello. The German Grundgesetz begins with the same commitment to human dignity. It is about as useful to troops on the ground as a commitment to equality or fair fighting. Perhaps the word "outrage" restricts the scope of the provision, but again this illustrates the downside of using highly charged words and expecting the principle of *nullum crimen sine lege* to have applicable force. Even if the *nullum crimen* provision is designed only to regulate the discipline of judges, it is difficult to see this end being accomplished by these vague and ill-conceived provisions.

We could think of another purpose of the Geneva Conventions and their purported individualization in the Rome Statute. These are benchmarks in the hope and for progress of humanity toward a more civilized legal order.

These are only about half of the provisions applicable to international warfare. I have selected only the norms that permit original commentary. The reader is encouraged, of course, to read the full list.

Variations on the same theme appear in Article 8(2)(C) on non-international conflicts. The ambiguity of the latter term has already been noted.

The value of this exercise, if there is one, is to raise jurisprudential issues about this intricate and repetitive body of statutory material.

David Sheffer, one of the most prominent scholars and practitioners in this field, campaigned for the addition to the Rome Statute but expressed unspecified reservations in an op-ed article in the *New York Times*, July 1, 2010.[115] In a more recent article, he sets forth the following specific objections:

1) the provision does not cover non-state actors.
2) the modes of aggression do not include cyber warfare.

[114] *Id.*, art. 8(2)(b)(xxi).
[115] David Sheffer, Opinion, *Aggression Is Now a Crime*, N.Y. Times (July 1, 2010), http://www.nytimes.com/2010/07/02/opinion/02iht-edscheffer.html.

3) it is not clear how to accommodate states nominally violating the provision by acting to protect another (R2P).[116]

All of these minor problems, he concedes, are subject to ready amendment.

What I find interesting about this entire debate is that the real achievement of Article 8*bis* is solving the problem of collective action, at least for aggression, and possibly for all the crimes within the competence of ICC.

9. Procedure

In BCCL, the primary example of the intersection of substance and procedure was the burden of persuasion. The progressive lengthening of the period of prescription was a recurrent issue in the German prosecution of Nazis for the crime of murder, originally under a 20-year statute of limitations. The German legislature extended the statute 10 years and finally abolished it. To appear impartial, they also had to do the same for all murderers of the period, including not those connected to the Holocaust.

The theory behind this move is that defendants have a right to rely on the substantive definition of offenses. That is part of the message of the principle *nullum crimen sine lege*. As to procedure, the rules of evidence, and the like, the defendant has no right to rely on these rules in deciding whether to remain in concealment or even to confess his crime and seek privately to make amends with the victim. The procedural rules guide the state and the community in seeking to ensure the proper expenditure of resources on each reported crime.

The German decision might have been a good precedent for Article 29 in the Rome Statute, which has only one simple point: there shall be no statute of limitations for any offense. But there is a revealing ambiguity raised by Article 33, which addresses the defense of superior orders, but then adds a mysterious reference in the title of the article: Superior Orders and Prescription of Law.[117] "Prescription" is the civil law term to refer to a statute of limitations. It has no apparent meaning in English. Article 32 itself says nothing about the time limit for prosecuting offenses, but the structure of the articles provides a

[116] David Sheffer, *The Missing Pieces in Article 8 bis (Aggression) of the Rome Statute*, HARV. INT'L L.J. Online (Apr. 11, 2017), www.harvardilj.org/2017/04/the-missing-pieces-in-article-8-bis-aggression-of-the-rome-statute/.
[117] Rome Statute, *supra* note 3, art. 33.

rationale for recognizing a statute of limitations in the problematic categories of war crimes, where it seems that—as compared with genocide and crimes against humanity—no reasonable person could be expected to master the full list of offenses and know that they all are illegal.

A. Malum in Se, Malum Prohibitum

The useful distinction here is crimes malum in se and malum prohibitum. Crimes malum in se—those that are wrong in and of themselves—invite stricter approaches to mistake of law, the statute of limitations, and superior orders. The theory is that if the defendant commits a crime malum in se, she is fairly expected to have known that she is wrong and subject to censure. Of course, there are many moral misdeeds—lying, refusing to aid another in distress—that are not subject to any legal sanction.

A good example of a crime malum prohibitum is membership in prohibited organization, for example, an organization labeled legislatively as "terrorist." Admittedly, even in the category of war crimes, the language used is often so normatively charged that the crime takes on a morally taboo quality. But, consider for example conscripting children under the age of 15.[118] Whether 15 is too young to fight depends largely on local customs and practices. Also, in many parts of the world, people do not keep accurate birth records, and there is little way of knowing the precise age of young boys.

There is an element of thinking along the lines of malum prohibitum in prohibiting actions on a collective basis and yet insisting on individual responsibility. There is little that specific individuals can know in advance that they are bound by the actions of the collective. The important point is that insofar as the Rome Statute is confused or incoherent on many issues discussed here, it is not fair to the accused to treat all the offenses as malum in se. In particular, because the Rome Statute is committed to the principle *nullum crimen sine lege*, the ICC should be sympathetic to situations posed by mistake of law, superior orders, and the statute of limitations.

This position of skepticism has a textual basis in the presumption of innocence, which prescribes that the prosecution must prove guilt and the Court must be convinced of the accused's guilt beyond a reasonable doubt.[119] Guilt

[118] *Id.*, art. 8(2)(b)(xxvi).
[119] *Id.*, art. 66(2)–(3).

in this sense could simply mean formal guilt, as the word is used in a plea of guilty in common law systems. Formal guilt is closer to the use of the word "liability" in tort law, but punishment requires moral guilt or guilt in a normative sense. This theme is explored further in chapter 2.

B. Procedural Offenses and the Problem of Jurisdiction

Article 70 adds a significant set of offenses to the four primary offenses of "the most serious crimes of concern to the international community as a whole."[120] These are offenses that occur in the proceedings. In the common law they would be labeled "contempt of court."[121] They mostly concern the process of examining witnesses and hearing evidence in court. Perjury and related offenses are subject to direct punishment by the court. They are a good example of procedural offenses that cross the line between procedure and substance.

These procedural violations fall, it is said, within the jurisdiction of the court. Since this is the most significant term in organizational structure of the ICC, we should ponder what the term means. Generally, the use of this term presupposes that the court already exists and that it has inherent authority, for example, to declare parties in contempt. The field of federal jurisdiction in the United States is a major academic and professional field. It is based either on questions arising under federal law or on cases arising in interstate commerce. The latter category exhibits some of the features of complementarity found in the Rome Statute. In the interstate cases, the federal courts apply state law in deference to the residual authority of the latter.

The important point is that the U.S. federal courts are of limited jurisdiction. The Supreme Court is created by the Constitution, the federal courts by statute—but not by the very statute that they are expected to apply. The term "jurisdiction" as used in Article 5 of the Statute bears no resemblance to the jurisdiction of a court, such as the Supreme Court, which has come into existence by virtue of a constitution or a federal statute.

The Rome Statute resembles a constitution. There was a convention in Rome (think Philadelphia) that drafted it, then it was submitted to the member states for ratification, and finally it went through a necessary

120 *Id.*, art. 5.
121 Gompers v. Bucks Stove & Range Co., 221 U.S. 418, 441 (1911).

amendment in the Kampala Conference. The Statute also created a court, just as the U.S. Constitution did. In this respect, it is appropriate to think of the Statute's defining the crimes within the jurisdiction of the ICC.

Yet the Rome Statute reads as well like two other documents: a statute regulating existing courts; and, shall we say, a training manual for all the participants about their roles, what they should do, and the sanctions for their malfeasance. The concept of the judge, as communicated by the Statute, is not comparable to a common law judge who thinks of herself as a sovereign in the courtroom. The ICC judge is more like one of three sequential, roughly equal organs of power. If the defendant gets a "day in court" in the common law, the suspect in the ICC confronts periods of equal difficulty in the office of the prosecutor, the pretrial chamber, and finally the trial court. The appeals chamber will be considered as a potential fourth in the chain.

This is an invitation to explore the general differences between common law and civil procedure and their relative influences on the Rome Statute. But this is an important jurisprudential subject itself and therefore more appropriately explored in chapter 3 on subject and object. To bring this chapter to a close, we shall concentrate on the more abstract question of what it means to guarantee the accused a "fair and regular" trial—implicit in the Statute because not doing so is a violation of the Geneva Convention and therefore a war crime under Article 8(2)(a)(vi). Strictly speaking, the denial of a fair trial only applies to "prisoners of war or other protected parties."[122]

Criminal defendants deserve as much protection as do prisoners of war. Yet, there is something about this wording that remains a little troubling; the use of the word "denial" suggests that the prisoner would have otherwise had the right, and further that there would be something discriminatory about the denial.

The idea that all defendants have a right to a fair trial comes at this from another angle. The common law emphasis on this right is rooted in the notion of a fair fight or fair play in sports. Indeed, the English language overflows with metaphors drawn from sports and games. Consider these: level playing field, do not hit below the belt, do not deal from the bottom of the deck. In a sporting culture, winning fairly is admired. Cheating is contemptible.

By and large, the history of criminal procedure under the Constitution has been to secure rights to the accused that the prosecution already had.

[122] *Id.*, art. 8(2)(a)(vi).

Note some of the details of the Sixth Amendment: (1) speedy and public trial, (2) to be informed of the nature and cause of the accusation, (3) to be confronted with the witnesses against him, (4) to have compulsory process for obtaining witnesses in his favor, and (5) to have the assistance of counsel for his defense.[123] In addition, under the Fifth Amendment, (6) no person shall be compelled to be a witness against himself.[124]

These six rights tend to level the playing field. They can contribute to a fair trial. But there are several paradoxes that arise from the sporting theory of justice. First of all, do we really want to level the playing field? If so, why do we require proof of guilt beyond a reasonable doubt?[125] Why does the same provision specify that the onus of proof is on the prosecutor? Perhaps, to ensure equality between the two sides, as in a torts case, the burden on defenses should shift to the defendant. In fact, what we want is a level field plus an additional level of support for the accused. We do not want to cheat for the sake of the defendant. We want a fair fight, but we place our bets on the accused.

It is also a maxim of the sporting culture that it matters not whether you win or lose but it's how you play the game. On the contrary. We have these maxims stating that it is preferable to let 10 (or 100 or 1,000) guilty men go free than to convict one innocent person. In common law systems, we all allow the defendant to appeal but do not allow the prosecution to do the same.

The purpose of most constitutions is to guarantee the rights of the defendant. That is the purpose of the Fourth, Fifth, Sixth, and Eighth Amendments to the U.S. Constitution. There is no constitutional amendment favoring the rights of victims.

Yet the ICC, founded as it was out of concern for impunidad and the rights of victims, does not seek, as the first order of business, to protect the defendant against an overweening state. For one thing, there is no international state or world government that seeks to protect itself at the expense of the criminally accused. It is understandable, then, that we would encounter these rights deep into the Statute, Articles 65, 66, and 67.[126]

Finally, there is an important linguistic lesson to be learned from the implicit right to a fair trial. The word "fair" is exceptionally difficult to translate into other languages. It usually comes as "just." But there is an extraordinary

123 *See* U.S. CONST. amend VI.
124 *See* U.S. CONST. amend V.
125 *See* Rome Statute, *supra* note 3, art. 66.
126 Rome Statute, *supra* note 3, arts. 65–67.

difference between fairness and justice. A fair trial sometimes produces justice, but not always, often instead focusing on receiving a fair and timely trial. Victims want justice, but the defendants—many of whom are guilty—do not want justice.

Therefore, there is something impressive about the official Spanish translation of Article 8(2)(a)(vi). The approach is not a word-for-word translation but rather a rendering of the entire phrase: *ser jusgado legitima e imparcialmente*. Both of these words are an improvement on the English version and, incidentally, on the French version. If I may translate into English, we can recognize that a "legitimate" trial is what is at stake. The term may be a bit vaguer than "fair trial," but it recognizes the complexities of seeking a level playing field and favoring the accused at the same time. "Impartial" is also an improvement on "regular" trial. There is some sense in which our favoring the accused is arguably compatible with an impartial trial.

The face of justice is blindfolded because she is impartial. She does not favor rich over poor or white over black. Even the blind can recognize that the rich have an advantage in resources, at least in criminal cases. And, there is evidence in the United States that blacks are more readily suspected of crime, more intensively investigated, and as a result make up a vastly disproportional segment of the prison population. There is so much personal prejudice in normal criminal trials that we constantly remind ourselves of the imperative of impartiality.

2
Punishment vs. Tort Liability

According to Blackstone, both crimes and torts are wrongs: one a public wrong and the other a private wrong.[1] Yet in the international arena, the dimension of tort liability has been shunted aside. One reason for this is that in many legal systems, influenced by the dominance of criminal law, a criminal acquittal precludes a subsequent civil trial. In the United States, however, a criminal verdict of not guilty does not bar a subsequent civil trial for damages. In several famous cases,[2] a popular defendant was acquitted by a jury but then found liable for tort damages in another trial, perhaps even another courthouse.

In the international legal order, the tort regime is of particular importance. As we shall see, the Alien Tort Claims Act has a vital role to play either as a backup to a failed attempt at criminal prosecution or the inability to get jurisdiction over a defendant in hiding. Thus, the international regime of tort liability responds to the same concerns of *impunidad* as we find in the Preamble of the Rome Statute.[3]

1. Punishment: In Less Than a Nutshell

There is a long disquisition on punishment in Volume 1 of this trilogy.[4] Without repeating those thoughts, let me add a few remarks appropriate to this chapter. Punishment is the domain of criminal law.

[1] 4 William Blackstone, Commentaries on the Laws of England 5 (1769) (asserting that private wrongs infringe upon civil rights and public wrongs breach public duties owed to the entire community).

[2] Adam Nossiter, *Bronx Jury Order Goetz to Pay Man He Paralyzed $43 Million*, N.Y. Times (Apr. 24, 1996), http://www.nytimes.com/1996/04/24/nyregion/bronx-jury-orders-goetz-to-pay-man-he-paralyzed-43-million.html. B. Drummon Ayres Jr., *Jury Decides Simpson Must Pay $25 Million in Punitive Award*, N.Y. Times (Feb. 11, 1997), http://www.nytimes.com/1997/02/11/us/jury-decides-simpson-must-pay-25-million-in-punitive-award.html.

[3] Rome Statute for the International Criminal Court, July 17, 1998, 2187 U.N.T.S. 3; U.N. Diplomatic Conference of Plenipotentiaries on the Establishment of an International Court, U.N. Doc. A/Conf.183/9 [hereinafter Rome Statute]; *Id.*, pmbl.

[4] *See* George P. Fletcher, Vol. I.

The Grammar of Criminal Law: Volume Two: International Criminal Law. George P. Fletcher.

Liability in tort cases is not officially punishment. In fact, punitive damages imposed by an American jury can have more severe consequences than a brief period in jail. Yet the line between crime and tort is maintained strictly in American jurisprudence, as it should be.

There are two well-known guides to the theory of punishment and its proper measure. The first is the five-part definition by H.L.A. Hart,[5] and the second is Robert Nozick's formula[6] for determining the just level of punishment. I wish to apply these criteria to a controversial recent decision by the Israel Supreme Court.[7] Israel has had a practice of destroying the homes of Arab terrorists, typically after being convicted of their related crimes.[8] This raises problems of collective punishment and unfair treatment, though I have written in the past that it can be justified.[9] The argument relies on two stages: first, the principle of forfeiture to the state for using an airplane or the home as a means for committing an offense, for example, an airplane for transferring drugs or the home as a refuge for terrorists. This is not treated as "punishment" in any legal system, though it is not so easy to circumvent Hart's fivefold test.[10] The second stage is that if the forfeited property belongs to the state, it may dispose of it at will.

The practice of home demolitions has taken a new and controversial twist in the recent decision holding that the Court would not approve the demolition of the homes of Jewish terrorists convicted in 2014.[11] The primary argument of the Court was that the purpose of the demolitions is not punishment but deterrence.[12] There is allegedly a difference in the deterrent value of destroying Jewish homes because there were so many fewer cases of Jewish terrorism. We must assess whether, assuming the facts are true, this a plausible argument and if not, why not. I should add that is not a political issue for me (I am strongly pro-Israel). The problem is the logical coherence of the Israeli Supreme Court's argument.

5 H.L.A. Hart, Punishment and Responsibility: Essays in the Philosophy of Law 4–5 (1968).

6 Robert Nozick, Philosophical Explanations 388 (1981).

7 Jeremy Bob Yonah, *Israeli Court Rejects Request to Demolish Home of Jewish Terrorist*, The Jerusalem Post (July 4, 2017), http://www.jpost.com/Israel-News/High-Court-rejects-request-to-demolish-Jewish-Arab-murderers-house-498731.

8 *Id.*

9 *See generally* George P. Fletcher, *Fairness and Utility in Tort Theory*, 85 Harv. L. Rev. 537 (1972).

10 Hart, *supra* note 5.

11 Yonah, *supra* note 7.

12 *Id.*

We first need to review the concept of punishment and inquire how the policy of deterrence relates to the concept.

According to H.L.A. Hart, punishment must:

1) involve pain, or other consequence normally considered unpleasant
2) be inflicted for an offense against legal rules
3) be of an actual or supposed offender for this offense
4) be intentionally administered by human beings other than offender
5) be imposed and administered by an authority constructed by the legal system against which the offense is committed.[13]

Of these the most vulnerable is point 3, the reasoning being that in the home demolitions, there might be innocent parties affected. They might be considered "supposed offenders" in a collective action. Or they might imply neighbors or members of the family who are guilty by association. The argument by the state in response could be this: OK, all right, this is not punishment according to Hart's criteria but it is still a justified sanction in the name of communal security. The interesting feature of Hart's criteria is that they say nothing about retribution or deterrence as the acceptable rationale for punishment.

The history of punishment supports a policy of retribution, that is, making the punishment fit the crime and thus correcting the imbalance in social benefits and burdens caused by causing harm or even just by seizing the privilege of doing what others may not to do.[14] In that respect, we shall say that retributive justice resembles corrective justice in tort law. In some ways, retributive justice is supported by the goals listed in the Preamble to the Rome Statute.[15] After all, why should we be concerned about "impunity" and insist that "the most serious crimes of concern to the international community as a whole not go unpunished?"[16] The reason is not that impunity is an evil in or itself and should not be tolerated in the world legal order. So interpreted, the Statute resonates with Kant's theory of punishment.[17]

[13] Hart, *supra* note 5.
[14] *See* Nozick, *supra* note 6.
[15] *See* Rome Statute, *supra* note 3, pmbl.
[16] *Id.*
[17] *See* Immanuel Kant, The Metaphysics of Morals (Mary Gregor trans., 1991) (1797) [hereinafter Kant I].

But there are two factors that speak against this interpretation. First, in the same clause that stressed putting an end to "impunity," the Preamble adds: "and thus to contribute to the prevention of such crimes."[18]

The connection between ending impunity and deterrence is explicit. The second factor is that international lawyers are practical people. They are not philosophers in the vein of Immanuel Kant. They want to accomplish something in the future. This is the appeal of deterrence in place of retribution.

The Kantians might parry: Yes, but deterrence is unequal in its application. After you have achieved the requisite amount of deterrence by say X number of convictions, how do you justify X+1 prosecutions, even in terms of dollars and cents? It costs money to prosecute (or to demolish homes); why do this unless the additional action contributes some benefit to society? And how do you prove that the state is getting its money's worth? The United States suffers from both a high crime rate[19] in certain places and a high incarceration rate,[20] perhaps the highest in the world. There is little proof that putting one more person in prison is justified by the consequential savings to society in an allegedly lower crime rate. The truth is that prison itself has a crimogenic effect, and the social benefit of locking up one more person has a dubious marginal benefit.[21] In economic terms the marginal cost may exceed the marginal benefit, and therefore the practice is clearly unjustified in utilitarian terms.

The Kantian falls back on the principle of equality. The Benthamite,[22] advocating deterrence, will respond that equality costs money and what does it accomplish? The proper interpretation of the Rome Statute seems to be that it has specific instrumental utilitarian purposes—to fill in gaps left by the national states "unwilling" or "unable" to prosecute.[23] If the issue is interpreting the Rome Statute, the nod must go to the Benthamites, the utilitarians. The purpose of the Court is not to punish simply as a matter of personal desert, but to achieve equality among the vast number of different practices

[18] Rome Statute, *supra* note 3, pmbl.

[19] The United States had an average homicide rate of 4.9 per 100,000 population over five years. *Many Faces of Homicide*, *in* Global Study on Homicide, United Nations Office on Drug and Crime 43 n.5 (2013) (citing UNODC Homicide Statistics (2013)), https://www.unodc.org/documents/gsh/pdfs/2014_GLOBAL_HOMICIDE_BOOK_web.pdf.

[20] The U.S. prison population rate is 698 per 100,000. Roy Walmsley, *World Prison Population List*, Institute for Criminal Policy Research (11th ed.) (2016), http://prisonstudies.org/sites/default/files/resources/downloads/world_prison_population_list_11th_edition_0.pdf.

[21] *See* Martin H. Pritkin, *Is Prison Increasing Crime?*, 2008 Wis. L. Rev. 1049 (2008).

[22] *See* Igor Primoratz, Justifying Legal Punishment 13 (1989) (Bentham has "[t]he most comprehensive and thoroughly developed" consequentialist account of punishment).

[23] Rome Statute, *supra* note 3, art. 17(1)(a).

around the world. The principle of complementarity is a recognition of diversity among the member states. Some punish more, others less. We could maintain a goal of equal distribution of punishment across the international legal order.

If we leave the issue of equality to one side, there is still something wrong with the Israeli Supreme Court decision in that there are not enough potential Jewish terrorists to justify imposing the same treatment as received by Arab terrorists. The policy of deterrence raises a broader question of Kantian vs. Benthamite theories of morals and thus of just punishment. The Kantian view is that punishment is just or not, depending on the actions of the accused.[24] The Benthamite or utilitarian view is that punishment is justified by its consequence.[25] If deterrence actually worked and did not cause more harm than good, it would satisfy the Benthamite criteria.

The Kantian arguments against the goal of Benthamite deterrence is that it fails to respect human beings as ends in themselves.[26] They must not be sacrificed on the altar of criminal justice in order to achieve some social goal. Their being used as a means to a social goal degrades their humanity, treating them as objects rather than subjects.[27]

Thus, we are left with several issues. If we accept Hart's five criteria of punishment, we encounter the problems of the single offender as opposed to the collective offender, the equal distribution of benefits and burdens in society and the role of punishment in accomplishing this goal, and finally the Kantian imperative to respect the humanity of offenders—not to treat them as a means to our ends.

A retributive theory may be abstract and philosophical, but it also focuses and facilitates debate. Let's consider Robert Nozick's account of just punishment, which clearly lies in the Kantian tradition. His insightful formula is P = r.W where P stands for just punishment, r for degree of culpability, and W the level of wrongdoing.[28] The former varies between 0 and 1, and the latter depends on the egregious nature of the crime: for example, genocide is worse than denying someone a procedural offense, such as denying someone

[24] *See* KANT I, *supra* note 17, at 140 ("must always be inflicted on [an offender] only because he has committed a crime.").

[25] *See* Primoratz, *supra* note 22, at 26.

[26] *See* IMMANUEL KANT, FOUNDATIONS OF THE METAPHYSICS OF MORALS 46 (Lewis White Beck trans., 2d ed. 1990) (1785) [hereinafter KANT II].

[27] *Infra* ch. III.

[28] NOZICK, *supra* note 6.

a "fair and regular" trial. In chapter 6 we explore the meaning of culpability and wrongdoing in the international legal order.[29]

As for the way deterrence applies in the international order, we are left with an additional quandary. When common citizens might be deterred by sanctions—if they are strictly enforced—every dictator and even some democratically elected leaders think of themselves as exceptions to history.

If we are skeptical about deterrence for practical reasons and about retribution for moral ones, there might be a great future in the tort remedy as an effective instruct of justice in the international legal order. Thus, we turn to a study of the Alien Tort Claims Act; its decline in the courts; and its recent, surprising prospect of revival.

2. Torts Remedies—In the Common Law Experience

A tort action requires a victim who has standing to bring suit about an injury inflicted directly or indirectly by a defendant—person or a corporation—who can be sued within the jurisdiction. At the outset we should think of the 50 states, each with its own jurisdiction. Corporations are subject to jurisdiction if they have "minimal contacts" within the state.[30] Individuals are subject to jurisdiction if they are there or have been there.[31] It should be noted that we are using "jurisdiction" here in the normal sense—not in the sense meaning competence in the Rome Statute.

Jurisdiction is of various types, depending on the nature of the lawsuit, for example, for land, personal status.[32] We are concerned about the latter and therefore turn to the "transitory cause of action" as developed in the common law.[33] The cause of action may arise in one place, and typically the law applied would be the lex loci delicti (the law of the place where the tort occurred), but the transitory nature of the cause means that the plaintiff can sue the defendant in any jurisdiction where he can serve process on him.[34] Serving process means essentially that the plaintiff (or an agent called a process server) must actually find the defendant and hand him the complaint

[29] *Infra* ch. V.
[30] International Shoe Co. v. Washington, 326 U.S. 310 (1940).
[31] *See* Hess v. Pawloski, 274 U.S. 352 (1927).
[32] Pennoyer v. Neff, 95 U.S. 714 (1878) (articulating *in rem* and *in personamm* jurisdiction).
[33] *See generally* Brainerd Currie, *The Constitution and the Transitory Cause of Action*, 73 Harv. L. Rev. 36 (1959).
[34] Black's Law Dictionary 760 (abr. 8th ed. 2005).

stating the cause of action and the notice when and where to appear.[35] It is not enough to leave the papers in the defendant's mailbox. Also, in these cases, diplomatic immunity can be a defense against service—for example, while engaged in official business at the United Nations in New York,[36] diplomats can be served as soon as they return to their room at a neighboring hotel.[37]

It may be like a game of tag, but that is consistent with the influence of sports on the culture of the common law and the adversary system (more about that in chapter 3).

Torts suits in the common law offer three major advantages to the plaintiff in the common law as opposed as the tort plaintiff in civil law countries. First, the plaintiff can recover punitive damages, which can be enormous, perhaps 10 or 20 times more than the actual damages, including pain and suffering.[38] Second, the plaintiff has access to first-class lawyers, at least for a serious law suit. The lawyer takes a contingency fee, perhaps 30 percent of the recovery,[39] if the law suit succeeds; and nothing, if it fails. This also serves the communal interest because if the law suit is trivial, the responsible lawyer will not waste his time. Third, liability and damages are determined by a jury in a single verdict.[40] This is desirable for conflicting reasons. On one side, juries are inclined to be more generous than are civilian judges faced with the routine of similar cases; but on the other hand, the jury can compromise on the damage award in an ambiguous set of facts.

It should be noted that the tort suit offers several advantages for the defendant as well. The defendant might be careful enough to evade service of process. But even if forced to stand trial, she has the benefit of well-paid counsel and a rule not available in criminal cases: the defense of contributory negligence. If the plaintiff has put herself in a situation of danger negligently, the defendant has a complete defense (with certain exceptions). The theory is that if the plaintiff has faultfully put herself in harm's way, she is the primary cause of his misfortune.

The interesting implication is that if the defense is based on causation and causation is also required for most criminal offenses (more about this

[35] *See* Fed. R. Civ. P. 4.

[36] Vienna Convention on Diplomatic Relations, art. 31(1)(a)–(c) (1961).

[37] *See id.*

[38] *See* Stephen P. Croley & Jon D. Hanson, *The Nonpecuniary Cost of Accidents: Pain & Suffering Damages in Tort Law*, 108 Harv. L. Rev. 1785, 1789–90 ns. 15, 19 (1995).

[39] *How do I Settle on a Fee with a Lawyer?*, American Bar Ass'n, https://www.americanbar.org/groups/legal_services/milvets/aba_home_front/information_center/working_with_lawyer/fees_and_expenses/ (last accessed 8/2/2019).

[40] *Infra* ch. V.

in chapter 5), we could derive a similar defense in criminal cases. Yet there is a semi-theological principle that prevents systems of criminal law from treating victims as the cause of their own harm. The typical case is taking a walk in a dangerous area at night. An analogous case in, say, genocide, would be continuing to live in Germany after the deportations began. We may think the victim's behavior foolhardy, but it provides no defense to criminal behavior.

The only explanation for this principle, so far as I have been able to find, derives from the principle of victim-sacrifice in the book of Leviticus, the third book of the Bible.[41] This might not be a respectable source for an international legal argument, but I am not making a legal argument here, just explaining why we fail to treat criminal victims like tort victims. The victim destined for sacrifice, it is said, must be pure. If the victim is assumed to be pure, he or she cannot be saddled with the contributory sins leading to the sacrifice. For a Christian example, just think of Jesus at Calvary: no one suggests the willing act of self-sacrifice compromised the Christian belief in the redemption of humankind.

At this point the analogical connection between tort law and criminal law breaks down. Nonetheless, the analogy is illuminating, even only to demonstrate its limits.

Perhaps this is enough to make the common law tort remedy an attractive alternative to the punishment for crime. Since we are concerned, however, with the international legal order, we move to the more intriguing institution that is the Alien Tort Claims Act (ATCA), now called the Alien Tort Statute (ATS). Before turning to the vicissitudes of the ATCA, we should note that in Article 75, the Rome Statute makes some effort to attend to the needs of victims,[42] but this effort, we will see, is minimal at compared to the ATCA and, of course, suffers the same limitations at the rest of the Statute.

3. Alien Tort Claims Act (ATCA)—the Situation in 1789

In order to approach the meaning and purpose of the ATCA, we need to understand a fundamental problem with the American tort remedy. Based as it

[41] George P. Fletcher, Punishment and Responsibility, *in* A COMPANION TO THE PHILOSOPHY OF LAW AND LEGAL THEORY 514, 516 (Dennis Patterson ed., 1996).

[42] Rome Statute, *supra* note 3, art.75.

is on the use of state courts and given the regional biases of American culture in the revolutionary period (many of which remain today), the First Judiciary Act of 1789 created a system of federal courts[43] (the Supreme Court derives from the Constitution itself). The federal courts would have jurisdiction over two kinds of disputes: those arising under federal law and those, based on the common law, arising among citizens of different states or between citizens and between American citizens and foreign citizens or states, with many variations of the above. The point was to recognize that if local courts are biased—"unwilling or unable to do justice"[44]—a more comprehensive basis of litigation was necessary.

The precise language of the Judiciary Act, 1789, reads as the following:

> The district courts shall have original jurisdiction of any civil action by an alien for a tort only, committed in violation of the law of nations or a treaty of the United States.[45]

The Judiciary Act of 1789 has near-constitutional statute, and thus the creation of the ATCA in the statute has that same elevated status. Of course, it is subject to interpretation and reinterpretation. Let us explore some of these possibilities by examining the key terms:

A) district courts—those created by Congress as the initial court for bringing suit. They are subject to appeal to the Courts of Appeal, and then on a discretionary basis to the Supreme Court.
B) original jurisdiction—as opposed to a case removed from a state court to the federal courts.
C) civil action—this means civil as opposed to criminal or administrative. The federal government now has a criminal regime with an extraordinary number of offenses—over 3000 at last count.[46]

[43] History, Recognition of the Need for Federal Marshals, U.S. Marshals, DEPARTMENT OF JUSTICE (last visited March 25, 2018), Service https://www.usmarshals.gov/history/judiciary/judiary_act_of_1789.htm.

[44] Rome Statute, *supra* note 3.

[45] 28 U.S.C. § 1350 (2018).

[46] Gary Fields & John R. Emshwiller, *Many Failed Efforts to Count Nation's Federal Criminal Laws*, W.S.J. (July 23, 2011), https://www.wsj.com/articles/SB10001424052702304319804576389601079728920 (detailing that the last official count of criminal counts was in 1982, with several failed attempts since).

D) by an alien—someone who is not a citizen of the United States. In the original understanding, aliens were simply noncitizens. They might be legal or illegal immigrants.

E) tort only—the latter word means to exclude contract and property disputes. In the late 18th century, however, the general concept of tort liability was not fully developed. Blackstone mentions the word twice to mean a type of "private as opposed to public wrong."[47] The writ system still dominated our conceptual legal structure; that system divided the law of personal injuries into actions in trespass and trespass on the case.[48] Even the basic writ of trespass was subdivided into distinct writs for injuries against the person (vi et armis), trespasses against land (*quare clausum fregit*), and trespass against personal property (*de bonis asportatis*).[49] There were other writs that address some aspects of what we now call torts. The writ system was challenged throughout the 19th century until the Judicature Act in 1873, which codified its end.[50] The concepts of tort law took on a more intrinsic meaning of the word.

F) in violation of the law of nations and G) or a treaty of the United States.

There these last two phrases, F) and G), carry a book's worth of material on international law and the American constitutional system. First of law, the law of nations (same as international law) must be understood to include customary international law as well. Whether it also includes the other sources of law discussed earlier in Article 38 of the Statute of the ICJ[51] or Article 21 of the Rome Statute is open to argument.[52]

The first point is that a federal statute cannot refer to the "law of nations" without a constitutional basis for legislative authority.[53] Congress has the authority under Article I, Section 8, to "define and punish . . . offenses against the law of nations."[54] Interestingly, the word used is "to punish." It says nothing about granting compensation. The problem therefore is more how

[47] Blackstone, *supra* note 1.
[48] 4 Albert H. Putney, Popular Law Library 23 (1908).
[49] *Id.* at 37.
[50] *See* Thomas C. Grey, *Accidental Torts*, 54 Vand. L. Rev. 1225, 1231 n.8 (2001).
[51] Statute of the International Court of Justice art. 38 (1945).
[52] Rome Statute, *supra* note 3, art. 21.
[53] *See* U.S. Const. art. I, § 8.
[54] *Id.*

the common law practice of compensating victims of tort damage under the writ system—not abolished until 1873—enters into the constitutional text and the ATCA—both enacted the same year of 1789.

Another approach, based on the theory of the federal judicial power, relies on the constitutional phrase "arising under . . . the laws of the United States."[55] The argument proceeds in four stages:

1. International law is part of the common law.
2. The common law constitutes part of federal law.
3. Therefore, international should be considered as included within the phrases "laws of the United States."[56]
4. Therefore, a claim based on international law constitutes a claim arising under the "laws of the United States."

There may be some internal logical problems in this argument. The first is the distinction between the common law (singular) and the reference to "laws." The plural in this context refers to statutory laws. The common law is inherently singular.

Assuming the Constitution embraces the common law, is the common law forever frozen at its stage of development in 1789? This raises larger issues about the originalist school of constitutional interpretation and those who adhere to a theory of a living constitution. This debate, as we shall see, enters into the case law.

The alternative to a customary law of nations is an international law based exclusively on treaties, as advocated in recent years by some conservative-leaning international lawyers.[57] One could read F and G together as referring to a "customary international law" or treaty-based international law. Or with some effort, it would be interpreted to mean only "law of nations" as constitutionally recognized—in the view of some, limited to a treaty-based system.

[55] *Id.* at art. III, § 2.

[56] *Id.*

[57] *See* Jordan J. Paust, *In Their Own Words: Affirmations of the Founders, Framers, and Early Judiciary Concerning the Binding Nature of the Customary Law of Nations*, 14 U.C. Davis J. Int'l L. & Policy 205 n.1 (2008).

4. The Dormancy, Initiation, Defeat, and Revival

The history of the ATCA reads like a detective novel. There are heroes and villains, with many revealing signs of American foreign policy and internal corruption. We will illustrate these turning points with critical cases.

A. *Filartiga*

The dormancy period extended from the enactment in 1789 until the first major victory in *Filartiga v. Pena Irala* in the Second Circuit[58] almost two hundred years later in 1980. The case beautifully illustrates the transitory cause of action as the foundation of the tort system and basic issues in the interpretation of the ATCA. The dispute began with torture and murder of the victim in Paraguay.[59] The plaintiffs claiming standing were the victim's relatives living in Washington, DC. The defendant was in the United States when the victim's family managed to serve process on him, after he overstayed his visa and was being held for deportation.

The defendant made a number of classic moves. First, that the case had a remedy under Paraguayan law, the court did not have subject matter jurisdiction, and he objected to the forum per forum non conveniens. But one of the primary issues was whether the case would be governed by Paraguayan law. From the point of Private International Law (Conflicts of law in American parlance), the classic principle is indeed lex loci delicti. But this principle has come under attack in recent Restatements of the law in favor of a more flexible approach based on other factors, such as the residence of the parties.[60]

Because the issue was torture—one of the basic three customary international offenses—along with piracy and slavery—the substantive issues outweighed the argument of deference to local authority.[61] Because the case arose before the Rome Statute, the court paid primary attention to Article 38 of the ICJ Statute with its explicit recognition of scholarly authority.[62] The three-judge panel quote numerous American experts on the evils and futility of torture. Presumably, this interpretation should enter into the "general

[58] Filartiga v. Pena-Irala, 630 F.2d 876 (2d Cir. 1980).
[59] *Id.* at 878.
[60] *See* Restatement (Second) of Conflict of Laws § 145 (Am. Law Inst. 1977).
[61] *See Filartiga*, 630 F.2d at 885.
[62] *Id.* at 881 n.8.

principles" derived from national laws recognized in Article 21(3) of the Statute.[63]

Another pathbreaking aspect of the case was rejecting the claim of forum non conveniens. If all the parties had been resident abroad, this might have been a compelling argument. But the plaintiffs lived in the United States, and therefore was no serious issue about the convenience of the forum.

When the case reached trial, the best defense might have been to tackle the question of torture directly. The allegations of torture and murder were sufficiently strong to move the court beyond the procedural issue, but the concept of torture is undeniably vague. The allegations were that there were marks on the body of the deceased indicated torture, but there might be innocent explanations for these marks.[64] Even if the cause of death was in doubt, the concept of torture invites uncertainty at the fringes of the concept. The Bush administration tried to refer to their treatment of suspects as "enhanced interrogation techniques."[65] No one knows for sure whether sleep deprivation, prolonged solitary confinement, or being bound for lengthy periods by hands or feet constitutes torture.

The classic case of disputed torture was the Abu Ghraib prison in Iraq circa 2003.[66] The Americans exposed Muslim prisoners to a whole series of humiliating situations involving fierce dogs, naked women, and enhanced interrogation. Vice President Cheney admitted that the techniques were abusive but claimed that the techniques were employed by "bad apples." All this is simply to illustrate that good lawyers can easily defend against all but the most extreme cases.

The great achievement of Judge Irving Kaufman and his two colleagues on the panel of the Second Circuit in *Filartiga* was getting past the procedural objection to allow a trial and possible settlement on the substantive issues. In writing the opinion and making the ATCA a viable tool for litigating human rights abuse, they were engaged in a mission beyond the conventional lines of the international legal order.

[63] Rome Statute, *supra* note 3, art. 21(3).

[64] *Filartiga*, 630 F.2d at 878.

[65] Jan Crawford et al., *Sources: Top Bush Advisors Approved "Enhanced Interrogation,"* ABC News (April 9, 2008), http://abcnews.go.com/TheLaw/LawPolitics/story?id=4583256&page=1.

[66] Ifeoma Ajunwa, *"Bad Barrels": An Organizational-Based Analysis of the Human Rights Abuses at Abu Ghraib Prison*, 17 U. Pa. J.L. & Soc. Change 75, 75–77 (2014).

B. Fears of Flooding the Courts

In the years following *Filartiga*, three great fears motivated opponents to the liberal use of the ATCA and its potential impact on the case load of the courts. The concerns were expressed regarding three primary issues: (1) an expansive interpretation of tort law to include modern developments such as recovery for minimal intrusions, strict liability, negligence, and extended causal connections; (2) an expansive interpretation of the law of nations to include contemporary issues such as climate change, free trade, and the law of war; and (3) corporate liability, recognized under general tort principles.

As to the problems of minimal interference, there was no reason to expect the future cases to be about torture. One of the functions of the writ of trespass was to establish boundaries; therefore even the slightest crossing of the line between one person and the property of another or between one person and another would constitute one of the forms of trespass. After all, the tort of battery (trespass vi et armis) is committed by a simple touching without consent.[67] Recognizing the development of the law, however, also includes the countervailing expansion of the defensive issues such as implied consent and various arguments for breaking the causal chain. The last two hundred years of theoretical work in tort law is very rich, and it is not clear that the courts wanted to import all of this development into the ATCA.

Holding the line to the 1789 understanding is debated in the first decision of the Supreme Court on the ATCA, *Sosa v. Alvarez-Machain*.[68] The essential facts are that while the DEA (Drug Enforcement Agency of the U.S. federal government) was conducting drug investigations in Mexico, one of their operatives kidnapped an implicated Mexican doctor named Alvarez-Machain, with the purpose of forcing him to stand trial in Los Angeles—incidentally on charges for torture and murder.[69] After he was acquitted in the LA trial, he sued the Mexican operatives, one of whom was named Sosa, under the ATCA (which the Court started calling the ATS) as well as the DEA under a federal tort claims statute, an exception to the immunity the government would otherwise enjoy.[70]

It's important to highlight the techniques used by the majority to scale back the potential application of the ATCA. There are a few not entirely consistent

[67] *See* Restatement (Second) of Torts §§ 13, 18 (Am. Law Inst. 1975).
[68] 542 U.S. 692 (2004).
[69] *Id.* at 697.
[70] *Id.* at 698.

techniques. One is to insist that the statute is purely jurisdictional: it does not create a new cause of action. The other is to focus on the three claims that Blackstone recognized as violations of international law, which limits the law of nations to the famous trilogy of violations of grants of safe conduct, offenses against ambassadors, and piracy.[71] The important feature of these three is that they interfere with international commerce and in that sense that they should be regarded a violations of the international legal order. The only problem is why aren't they considered torts as the ATCA requires.

The general way to restrict expansive application of the law is to insist on the original understanding of the Constitution and statutes. This position is famously associated with Justice Scalia.[72] The alternative would be called a "living Constitution" associated largely with Justice Black.[73]

There are a few puzzles posed by the originalist position—at least for conservatives like Justice Scalia. One issue is why one should think that the original view of the Constitution or the ATCA would be less appealing to our values—even conservative values—than our present understanding. On the death penalty, for example, Justice Scalia's originalism is out of sync with contemporary European notions of international law. Justice Scalia reveals at the end of his opinion by noting that he does not want "foreigners" to impose their views on Americans.[74] This kind of nationalist sentiment has reasserted itself during the Trump administration, but it will eventually induce a reaction in favor of supporting the international legal order.

In the end, however, Justice Scalia's concurrence (remember that Alvarez lost) harps on the originalist view to reject the ATCA. Justices Breyer and Ginsburg wrote separate opinions about the FTCA and the issue of state immunity.[75] Of the justices joining Scalia in his anti-internationalist concurrence, the only one remaining is Justice Thomas.

The most important implication of *Alvarez* is that the ATCA passed several hurdles. As a statute passed in 1789, it has not suffered obsolescence. The claim was not based on torture but on a relatively minor offense: arbitrary arrest. It did not fall victim to the scorn of Justice Holmes, who ridiculed the common law "as a brooding omnipresence in the sky."[76] Nor did the

[71] Blackstone, *supra* note 1, at 68.

[72] Antonin Scalia, *Originalism: The Lesser Evil*, 57 U. Cin. L. Rev. 849, 862 (1989).

[73] Charles A. Reich, *The Living Constitution and the Court's Role*, *in* Hugo Black and the Supreme Court 133 (S. Strickland ed., 1967).

[74] *See* 542 U.S. at 750 (Scalia, J., concurring).

[75] *Id.* at 751 (Ginsburg, J. and Breyer, J., concurring in part and concurring in the judgment).

[76] S. Pacific Co. v. Jensen, 244 U.S. 205, 222 (1917) (Holmes, J., dissenting).

Blackstonian trilogy gain dominance in our understanding of international law. On the contrary, a new idea emerged in a quotation from the opinion hold of *Marcos* litigation in the Ninth Circuit 1994, a view, which was implicitly endorsed by everyone: the applicable norms of international law must be specific, universal, and obligatory.

Each of these terms requires commentary. The term "specific" should support our previous analysis of Article 8*bis* on the crime of aggression and the issue of extending the principle of individual or specific liability in ascertainable individuals.[77] It also seems clear that these are universal norms. They are even binding on states that have not ratified the Statute. The word "bligatory" seems redundant. Norms are obligatory or they are not norms.

Given these constraints, the ATCA could easily expanded to cover all four crimes outlined in the Rome Statute. Perhaps this possibility of expansion was to become the hidden trap of Sosa.

5. Apparent Defeat: *Kiobel v. Royal Dutch Petroleum Corp.*

It is commonly said that if there is rifle hanging on the wall in the beginning of a Chekov play, you can expect it to be used before the play is over. In the case of the ATCA, two rifles were hanging on the wall.

One was the problem of corporate liability, to be assumed in tort litigation but not so obvious in international law. And the other almost invisible rifle was the issue of exterritorial application.

The basic rule of civil litigation is to follow the money. If you can find a corporate defendant, you have a good chance, at least, of collecting a judgment. Thus, one would think that the financial barons who influence much of American life would resist corporate liability under the ATCA. And they tried in *Kiobel*[78] and are still trying in *Jesner v. Arab Bank*.[79] So far as the theory of tort liability is at stake, there is no doubt that corporations are liable for their torts. And many cases applying the ATCA have held corporate defendants liable, notably *Khulumani v. Barclay National Bank Ltd.*[80] The

[77] *See supra* ch. I.
[78] Kiobel v. Royal Dutch Petro. Co., 569 U.S. 108 (2013).
[79] 138 S. Ct. 1386 (2018).
[80] 504 F.3d 254, 282 (2007).

latter case focused on recovery for supporting apartheid—an evil as obvious as torture.

The two Chekovian rifles are low-visibility options, but they are still there and would be used in corporate efforts to defeat the revival of the ATCA in *Filartiga* and though often in defeat, in all the cases leading to *Kiobel* and *Jesner*.

The facts in the *Kiobel* case are much like those in *Filartiga*, the contemporary foundation for understanding the ATCA. The corporate defendants supported acts of torture against the plaintiffs in Nigeria. The parties expected the Supreme Court argument to be about the corporate issue, but the Court at the final stage asked the parties to brief the question of extraterritorial application of the ATCA,[81] a question never considered in those terms by the Court. They phrased the question of extraterritoriality in a way that revealed which way the majority was leaning: "occurring within the territory of a sovereign other than the United States."[82] This difference in stating the issue turned out to be important. Extraterritorial means something that might be good or bad; interfering in the affairs of another sovereign nation sounds like aggression. (We should recall that this litigation would not have been possible, but for the transitory cause of action and service of process in the United States.)

There was strong precedent against this negative way of formulating the issue (incident with a sovereign other than the United States), namely *Filartiga*. Not surprisingly, the Roberts opinion ignores *Filartiga* in favor of a historical approach rooted in preconstitutional incidents like the Marbois affair.[83] Yet a new issue emerged that would become the focal point between the Roberts majority and the four liberal-leaning justices in concurrence (Bryer, Ginsburg, Kagan, and Sotomajor).

It was essentially a context between two trilogies; one stresses three dimensions of international law that are positivistic in nature (grants of safe conduct, treatment of ambassadors, and piracy).[84] They are positivistic in the sense that they express no enduring values. They are largely matters of international convenience.

[81] *Kiobel*, 569 U.S. at 108.

[82] *Id.* at 122.

[83] *See generally* Gwynne L. Skinner, *Roadblocks to Remedies: Recently Developed Barriers to Relief for Aliens Injured by U.S. Officials, Contrary to the Founders' Intent*, 47 U. Rich. L. Rev. 555, 567 (2013).

[84] Blackstone, *supra* note 1, at 38.

Focusing on the Blackstonian three, the Roberts opinion ignored another trilogy of jus cogens norms of international law, those that are binding by their sheer moral power. They are binding on all international actors and focus on criminal actors that are *hostis humanis generis*—enemies of all mankind.

These peremptory norms cover two crimes, slavery and torture, which have either elapsed or found adequate treatment elsewhere. Slavery is no longer an issue, and torture has since the days of *Filartiga* found statutory treatment in the Torture Victims Protection Act.[85] Thus, the focus was on the third in the trilogy: piracy.

Everyone agreed that the ATCA applied to acts of piracy, but the majority and the concurrence disagreed on the nature of crime and the interpretation is critical for the Roberts position on interfering with the jurisdiction of another sovereign. The traditional view, compatible with the views of the Roberts opinion for the majority, is that piracies occur on the high seas and therefore are subject either to no jurisdiction or universal jurisdiction.[86] Obviously, as a practical matter, the option of universal jurisdiction is preferable. As a result, it is plausible to apply the ATCA to the acts of pirates. The example of piracy, therefore, does not compromise the principle that the U.S. courts should not litigate a dispute occurring "within a territory of a sovereign other than the United States."[87]

The four-vote plurality, authored by Justice Breyer, reasoned that piracy might occur on the high seas but typically occurs on a ship bearing a certain national flag.[88] Therefore as with crimes committed on airplanes, the acts of piracy occur within a jurisdiction other than the United States. The Breyer opinion goes further and argues that today's piracies include acts of war (sinking of the *Lusitania*) and indeed genocide. With a little imagination, the Breyer arguments could absorb the four crimes defining the competence of the ICC as acts of piracy, making the perpetrators "enemies of all mankind."

It is important, however, that the four votes concurrence insists on an American interest in ATCA litigation, but that interest can be satisfied only by "preventing the United States from becoming a safe harbor (free of civil as well as criminal liability) for a torturer or other common enemy of mankind."

[85] 28 U.S.C. § 1350 (2018).
[86] Eugene Kontorovich, *The Piracy Analogy: Modern Universal Jurisdiction's Hollow Foundation*, 45 Harv. Int'l L.J. 183, 184 n.8 (2004).
[87] *Kiobel*, 569 U.S. at 127 (Breyer, J., concurring).
[88] *Id.* at 130 (Breyer, J., concurring).

The safe harbor metaphor—with its figurative invocation of the high seas—is a winning principle for maintaining an American commitment to international legal order.

Although Kiobel is technically a unanimous opinion, the divergence between the Roberts and Breyer opinions indicates a deep riff in the thinking of the Court. As was typical in this decade bridging the Bush and Obama administrations, the vote by Justice Kennedy was critical. In his brief opinion concurring in the result, he simply says that the presumption against extraterritoriality will require elaboration in the future.

That time will eventually come, but for the time being the crucial issue, raised in *Kiobel*, and shunted aside, namely corporate liability, is now before the Court in the case of *Jesner v. Arab Bank*. The second, potentially deadly Chekovian rifle has been taken off the wall.

Simply put, the Bank, with an office in New York, allegedly provides funding for Hamas to engage in acts of war against Israel. A technical problem remains with the way the Roberts opinion in Kiobel shifted the focus away from the Second Circuit's decision banning corporate liability under the ATCA. Arguably that opinion is still binding unless reversed by the Supreme Court. In April of 2017, the Court granted certiorari in a bundle of cases raising the question of corporate liability. That the Court is willing to hear the case is a positive sign, for doing nothing would arguably preclude corporate liability.

However, this is not clear because the primary reason for the Court's taking the case is the split among the circuit courts about corporate liability. And many circuit courts have written convincing opinions affirming corporate liability as implied by the nature of tort liability and also requiring them to address human rights abuses.

3

Subject vs. Object

The distinction between subject and object pervades the substantive law of war and, in general, the distinction between common law and civil law modes of criminal procedure and their relative influences on the procedures of the ICC.

1. Actions and Omissions in the Law of War

In one of the thoughtful law review articles of all time, Robert Cover developed the distinction between jurisgenerative and jurispathetic instruments in the evolution of biblical law and the law in general.[1] Some norms appear and flourish, creating new worlds of meaning. Other norms appear and disappear quickly. In the law of war, the most surprising jurisgenerative norm was the definition of belligerency in Article I of the Annex to the Hague Convention of 1907.

2. Article 1

The laws, rights, and duties of war apply not only to armies, but also to militia and volunteer corps fulfilling the following conditions:

1) To be commanded by a person responsible for his subordinates;
2) To have a fixed distinctive emblem recognizable at a distance;
3) To carry arms openly; and
4) To conduct their operations in accordance with the laws and customs of war.[2]

[1] Robert M. Cover, *The Supreme Court 1982 Term, Foreword: Nomos and Narrative*, 97 HARV. L. REV. 4, 15 (1983).

[2] Hague Convention IV, Annex to the Convention, Regulations Respecting the Laws and Customs of War on Land, sec. 1, ch. 1, art. I (Oct. 18, 1907).

The Grammar of Criminal Law: Volume Two: International Criminal Law. George P. Fletcher.

The implication of noncompliance is that the members of the army or other fighting groups cannot qualify as prisoners of war, with the attendant legal protections. It should be seen as akin to a licensing provision. Those who do not satisfy the conditions do not have a license to fight in wars and qualify as prisoners of war if they are captured. There is nothing that implies criminal or civil liability for the failure to satisfy one of more of these conditions.

There is admittedly some ambiguity in the first provision and in the reference to "a person responsible for his subordinates."[3] The concept of "responsibility" can suggest legal responsibility. Thus, we might have a basis for generating the principle of liability called command responsibility. Since the evolution of international criminal responsibility seizes on whatever threads it can find and weaves them into something new, the first provision of Article I has been surprisingly jurisgenerative.

One of the striking applications of this principle was the American military tribunal trial of General Tomoyuki Yamashita, the Japanese commander of the Philippines, for having been in charge when mass atrocities were committed by Japanese troops against the civilian population.[4] There are many striking and troubling aspects about the trial, including the role of the military commission, the imposition of a death sentence, and the clear abuse of the laws of evidence, in particular, the hearsay rule,[5] but first we should explain how it connects to the topic of liability for omissions in the law of war.

In domestic criminal law, there is considerable doubt about imposing liability for failures to rescue.[6] The classic example is the passer by who sees a child drowning and does nothing about it. The general assumption is that the law needs to impose a special duty of intervention in order to impose liability.[7] One reason for this result—to anticipate the subject of the next chapter—is that the passerby is not considered the cause of the harm. He is not acting, just omitting to act. Therefore, he is arguably not the author of the deed, not the subject. Rather, he is an object upon whom the sentence might be imposed in order to influence others in the future. He could be described

[3] *Id.*

[4] United Nations War Crimes Commission, 4 Law Reports of Trials of War Criminals 1 (1948).

[5] *See* Craig Green, *Wiley Rutledge, Executive Detention, and Judicial Conscience at War*, 84 Wash. U. L. Rev. 99, 151–52 (2006). *See also In re Yamashita*, 327 U.S. 1 (1946).

[6] *See* Liam Murphy, *Benefice, Law, and Liberty: The Case of Required Rescue*, 89 Geo. L.J. 605, 605–06 (2001).

[7] *Id.*

as "responsible" for the drowning, but without a duty to intervene, he would not be liable.

This is precisely the anxiety raised by the Yamashita case. All of the foregoing factors apply: He was in charge, the atrocities occurred under his command, and he failed to act. This was an omission. The problem was how, if possibly, he could be held accountable. This is where the definition of part 1 of the definition in the Hague Convention comes into play.[8]

After extensive proceedings with the result of Yamashita being sentenced to hang, he appealed on a writ of habeas corpus to the Supreme Court.[9] In the majority opinion by Justice Stone, the emphasis is on the phrase "commanded by a person responsible for his subordinates."[10] The issue was not whether the troops committing the atrocities could qualify as belligerents. Rather, the question was the jurisgenerative potential of using a critical phrase to create a new form of liability, which we can call *command responsibility*. Here we focus on the segments one by one:

1. *commanded*—It is not clear whether this refers to someone who already is or might be commanded, say, by the war department in Tokyo.
2. *by a person*—This is surprisingly neutral as between civilians and military personnel.
3. *responsible for*—This phrase could mean "answerable for" and could imply something like the principle of agency, *respondeat superior*.[11] That is, the person commanding the belligerent could be held liable—if this were a matter of private law—for the behavior of his agents. But because this matter arises not in the limited world of private litigants but under the international law of war, the argument might have to be different.
4. *subordinates*—Here again we have an emphasis on the chain of command. In all trials for wartime atrocities, however, we have a basic choice about holding accountable those who actually committed the atrocities or those who actually had command responsibility. Since the Nuremberg trials, we have shown a clear preference for holding the commanders responsible.[12]

[8] Hague Convention, *supra* note 2.
[9] *In re Yamashita*, 327 U.S. at 1.
[10] *Id.* at 15.
[11] Warren Abner Seavey, *Speculations as to "Respondeat Superior," in* HARVARD LEGAL ESSAYS 433 (1934).
[12] *See* Agreement for the Prosecution and Punishment of the Major War Criminals of the European Axis, Aug. 8, 1945, art. 7, 59 Stat. 1544, 1548, 82 U.N.T.S. 279, 288 ("The official position of

Before turning to the impact of Yamashita on the Rome Statute,[13] we should note the dissenting opinions by Justices Murphy and Rutledge.[14] These are mostly concerned with issues of evidence, but underlying them is a significant legal claim ignored by Justice Stone, namely that the due process clause of the Fifth Amendment applies to guarantee the defendant a fair trial.[15] The clause literally holds: no person shall be deprived of life, liberty, or property without due process of law.[16] Since World War II, disputes about "due process" have been a feature of American lawyers resisting policies of the punishment and detainment of enemy combatants.

The legal cases became frequent and conflicted after September 11, 2001, and the attack on the World Trade Center and the establishment of the prison camp in Guantánamo Bay, an area of Cuba leased by the United States from the Cuban government.[17] There were essentially two positions in the debates. One was that the due process clause applied anytime the government asserted its power, and thus is in line with the Murphy, Rutledge dissent.[18] Second was that it applied only geographically to disputes within the territorial jurisdiction of the United States.[19] Although the death penalty was not used, the disputes about detention without a fair trial were much like the controversy in Yamashita.[20]

Now we should explain the jurisgenerative implications of the trial in the Philippines. The most significant is the subsequent adoption of Article 28 in the Rome Statute, which provides in part I: Article 28-Responsibility of commanders and other superiors:

> In addition to other grounds of criminal responsibility under this Statute for crimes within the jurisdiction of the Court:
>
> (a) A military commander or person effectively acting as a military commander shall be criminally responsible for crimes within the

defendants, whether as Heads of State or responsible officials in Government departments, shall not be considered as freeing them from responsibility or mitigating punishment.").

---

[13] Rome Statute for the International Criminal Court, July 17, 1998, 2187 U.N.T.S. 3; U.N. Diplomatic Conference of Plenipotentiaries on the Establishment of an International Court, U.N. Doc. A/Conf.183/9 [hereinafter Rome Statute].

[14] *In re Yamashita*, 327 U.S. at 26.

[15] *Id.*

[16] *See* U.S. Const. amend V.

[17] *See* Hamdi v. Rumsfeld, 542 U.S. 507 (2004). *Cf.* Boumediene v. Bush, 553 U.S. 723 (2008).

[18] *See Hamdi*, 542 U.S. at 529.

[19] *See id.* at 526.

[20] *See id.* at 587–88.

> jurisdiction of the Court committed by forces under his or her effective command and control, or effective authority and control as the case may be, as a result of his or her failure to exercise control properly over such forces, where:
> (i) That military commander or person either knew or, owing to the circumstances at the time, should have known that the forces were committing or about to commit such crimes; and
> (ii) That military commander or person failed to take all necessary and reasonable measures within his or her power to prevent or repress their commission or to submit the matter to the competent authorities for investigation and prosecution.[21]

Several points spring to mind. First, it is important to underscore that we are speaking here of an omission, namely a "failure" to take reasonable measures to prevent the atrocities. Yet the language is slightly different from the Annex to the Hague Convention. We now get a clearer emphasis on "effective command and control."[22] The notion of belligerency invoked in Yamashita, with its emphasis on responsibility, has morphed into a full-fledged crime of command responsibility.[23] Also, the mens rea requirement is more sophisticated than the awkward language in Article 30(2)(b) about the "ordinary course of events."[24] The question becomes whether the commander "should have known" that his subordinates were committing or about to commit such crimes. Yet the drafters created a new problem of command responsibility for subordinates "about to commit" the atrocities.

This is a clear reference to the crime of attempt but differs significantly from the definition of attempts in Article 25,[25] which adopts the Model Penal Code's principle of "substantial step" attempt liability.[26] We will pursue this them in depth in chapter 10.[27] It might have been better for the drafters of Article 28 to stick more closely to the facts of Yamashita than leave the fraught issue of attempt liability, particularly the combination of negligence

[21] Rome Statute, *supra* note 13, art. 28(a).
[22] *Id.*
[23] For an earlier discussion, see George P. Fletcher, *Hamdan Confronts the Military Commissions Act of 2006*, 45 COLUM. J. TRANSNAT'L L. 427, 463 (2007).
[24] Rome Statute, *supra* note 13, art. 30(2)(b).
[25] Rome Statute, *supra* note 13, art. 25(3)(f).
[26] Model Penal Code and Commentaries § 5.01 cmts. 1, 6, at 299, 329 (Official Draft and Revised Comments 1985).
[27] *Infra* ch. X.

and attempts. It is hard to imagine what it means to say that the commander "should have known" that the offense was about to occur.

Despite these drawbacks, we should appreciate the jurisgenerative impact of the Yamashita decision and the subsequent to the drafting of Article 28.

A. Responsibility to Protect (R2P)

A new cycle began with the United Nations Summit conference in 2005, forging a link between the concept of sovereignty and the recognition that each state has a responsibility for its own citizens.[28] The critical concept emerging from the UN conference as well as a 2001 private conference of scholars is the responsibility of each state to prevents its own citizens from suffering a domestic version of the four crimes highlighted in the Rome Statute.[29] No government may sit idly by as its citizens suffer Genocide, War Crimes, Crimes against Humanity, and an internal version of Aggression. The latter crime of ethnic cleansing is defined essentially as one internal ethic group trying to commit genocide against another internal group.

The cited historical precedents of Rwanda in 1994 and Srebrenica in 1995 highlight the importance of ethnic cleansing as a primary motiving factor in the adoption of the R2P.[30] Another example that deserves headline attention is the treatment of the Kurds in Turkey.[31]

The UN Security Council remains involved with succeeding reports and resolutions specifying various trouble spots in the world, primarily in Africa (it should be mentioned that the African states were instrumental in moving the UN Security Council to action).[32]

The philosophical significance of the recognition of R2P is the willingness to modify and contract the concept of state sovereignty that has been the foundation of the international legal order since the beginning of scholarship in the area. Note the contradiction between this contraction of state sovereignty and the aversion toward extraterritorial application the ATCA expressed in the Kiobel case.[33] What else could the latter principle

[28] 2005 World Summit Outcome, G.A. Res. 60/1, ¶ 138, U.N. Doc. A/RES/60/1 (Sept. 16, 2005).

[29] *Id.*

[30] *Supra* ch. I.

[31] Asli U. Bali, *The Perils of Judicial Independence: Constitutional Transition and the Turkish Example*, 52 VA. J. INT'L L. 235, 290–91 n.191 (2012).

[32] *Reports of the Security Council Missions*, U.N.S.C., https://www.un.org/en/sc/documents/missions/ (last visited Apr. 13, 2018).

[33] Kiobel v. Royal Dutch Petro. Co., 569 U.S. 108 (2013).

of legislative interpretation be based on but a respect for the sovereignty of other countries?

The new cycle of the Responsibility to Protect (R2P) awaits the following critical events.

1) The full recognition and application in a concrete case of international responsibility to enforce the R2P. This could happen on a regional, even a bilateral basis if neighboring states feared the spillover effects of, say, ethnic cleansing.
2) A recognition and resolution of the tension between Article 51 of the Charter,[34] which elevates self-defense to the highest principle regulating the use of force and the R2P, which could indeed provoke hostilities triggering the application of Article 51.
3) Most interesting for our purposes is the framing of civil or criminal litigation about these issues in concrete cases. There would no shortage of plaintiffs or victims who have suffered from omissions of other states. The challenging part would be to isolate individuals or groups that are specifically responsible for the particular harm. This might take the imaginative application of Article 8*bis* of the Rome Statute,[35] which individualized responsibility for the crime of aggression.

In any event, we should welcome the emergence of R2P and find the proper means for integrating this new development into the international legal order. To sum up the two inquiries in this part of the chapter on Subject and Object, we have to proceed on the linkage between the concept of subject and the issue of action versus omission.

3. Subject and Object in International Criminal Procedure

Criminal trials presuppose human subjects, agency, and judgment. We can imagine the mechanization of warfare. Indeed, robots might command

[34] U.N. Charter art. 51.

[35] Resolution Adopting Aggression Amendments to Rome Statute, Rev. Conf. of the Rome Statute, Kampala, Uganda, May 31–June 11, 2010, Annex I, art. 8*bis*, 13th plen. mtg., I.C.C. Doc. RC/Res.6 (June 11, 2010).

future armies—even with their programmers long dead. A human trial could not function, however, without the contextual judgment as well as the imperfections that human beings bring to the bar. The primary actors in every trial are the judges, the prosecutors and defense counsel, the witnesses, forensic experts, and those entrusted with keeping order in the court. Secondary actors include the public, both in court and following the trial in the media; the police as investigators; and in the case of jury trials—the lay participants, a crew of consultants about jury behavior, and the scholars who write books that inform the lawyers and judges about the possibilities at trial and appeal.

The players take on different functions in common law and civil law trials. The notion of the accused's guilt or innocence as an object of investigation takes on a stronger significance in civilian trials. Thus, our first task is to explore the ideal types of common law and civil law criminal procedure: one stressing the subjects as the determinative element and the other emphasizing the object of investigation. In the real world, there is more gray in all systems than this black and white contrast. It will be useful, however, to explore the ideal types with their historical associations and then see how these two polar opposites apply in the mixed case of the ICC.

4. Common Law and Civil Law

There are many legal systems within the international legal order, including religious systems, which have limited international application. Among the primary secular systems, the dominant influences are the families of the common and civil law. Families are the appropriate way to describe these two groups for there is great diversity within each one. The common law families are found primarily in the English-speaking world. No English-speaking country has adopted a strictly civil law orientation, though there are some mixed cases like in Quebec and traces still in Louisiana.

The civil law families begin in the French and German codifications, early nineteenth century for France[36] and late nineteenth–early twentieth centuries for the German civil and criminal codes.[37] In the intervening century

[36] Irene Bessette, *French Civil Law System Since 1804*, 73 LAW LIB. J. 336 (1980) (explaining that the French Code "marked the beginning of the modern legal system in France").

[37] Reinhard Zimmermann, *Characteristic Aspects of German Legal Culture*, *in* INTRODUCTION TO GERMAN LAW (M. Reimann & J. Zekoll eds., 2d ed. 2005).

in Germany, the scholars developed a highly sophisticated system of interrelated concepts called the Pandekrecht, which formed the basis for the civil code. In the field of criminal law, the scholars developed their famous *Dogmatik*, mentioned in the Introduction.

In the influence of these legal materials around the world, we see the French codes exported almost all over the world,[38] except for in the English-speaking and the Northern Protestant countries in Europe. The French codes translate easily because, as Napoleon commanded, they are written in clear layman's French. The German codes, by contrast, are written in complicated legal German and therefore do not find ready counterparts in other languages.[39] The German gift to international jurisprudence is the highly sophisticated sets of concepts developed in the nineteenth century, the structural components of the civil code, and the *Dogmatik* in criminal law. These sets are translated in discursive style all over the world, with their greatest influence in Spanish, Italian, Japanese, and to some extent in Chinese and Russian and its neighboring Eastern European countries.[40]

As a general matter, the civil law mentality correlates well with the Catholic religion, and the common law tradition, more than with the Protestant tradition. The explanation for this might be that the both the Catholic Church and the civil law way of thinking require a system of hierarchal authority. The Protestant and common law ways of thinking are more decentralized. Examples of this decentralized way of thinking are the adversarial system, the jury system, and the recognition of parallel authority in the state and federal courts in the United States. Also, it is significant that the United States Supreme Court publishes dissenting opinions, which leads scholars to identify entirely with jurisdictional schools with certain justices.[41]

These American schools of thought, however, have little influence abroad—not even in the other English-speaking countries of the world.

[38] *See* EDGARDO BUSCAGLIA, JR., MARIA DAKOLIAS & WILLIAM RATLIFF, JUDICIAL REFORM IN LATIN AMERICA: A FRAMEWORK FOR NATIONAL DEVELOPMENT 17–18 (1995) ("Most of the civil law countries in Latin America achieved their independence in the nineteenth century and one after the other they adopted civil codes that in many cases were little more than translations of the French code."); P.J. VATIKIOTIS, THE HISTORY OF MODERN EGYPT FROM MUHAMMAD ALI TO MUBARAK 40-41 (1991) (discussing the French influence on Egyptian development).

[39] For an earlier discussion, see George P. Fletcher, *New Methods and Approaches: Jurisprudence, Interdisciplinary Study, and Systems Analysis, Comparative Law as a Subversive Discipline*, 46 AM. J. COMP. L. 683, 697 (1998).

[40] *See id.*

[41] *E.g.*, Justice Breyer is well known for having an interest in comparative law.

American legal concepts, as we shall see, do not readily translate into other languages, even the closely related Germanic and Romance languages.

As for the German influence in international criminal law, the practice of translating the leading treatise of German criminal law contributes to German influence abroad. It is also significant that the Max Planck Institute for Foreign and International Criminal Law in Freiburg, Germany, provides fellowships and recruits fellows from all over the world.[42] Recently they abandoned the requirement that the fellows speak German—in line with the general shift toward English as the language of the international legal order.[43]

Nonetheless, for the study of German law, and I believe for international criminal law, a reading knowledge of German is indispensable. The majority of the relevant texts are still in German, though many have been successfully translated into Spanish. Thus, for a variety of reasons, German criminal law has acquired considerable international influence—even if the dominant language of international discourse has become English. Without a study of European languages and comparative law, American and English scholars are doomed to a restricted domain of discourse.

It is not surprising, then, that the ICC prefers to cite German scholars and those, writing in English, who show a dedication to comparative law, including the German system. The leading example is the citation in Katanga, Lubanga, and Chui—considered in a later chapter on complicity—of three German sources and my own *Rethinking Criminal Law*—a book devoted to the comparative analysis of the then-prevailing views of German, French, Soviet, and American scholars.[44]

It is not easy to explain the influence of German scholarship in international criminal law. One good guess is that the German academic community is highly oriented toward the authority of scholars rather than judges. This is a matter of customary practice that dates back to the beginning of the nineteenth century. It seems to have little to do with the tragedies of World War I and World War II. But why should this custom have taken hold? In the area of private law, the best account is the German rejection of the French model of codification, which led to the nineteenth-century academic explosion, primarily in private law.[45]

[42] Max Planck Institute for Foreign and International Criminal Law, https://www.mpicc.de/en/home.cfm (last visited Apr. 17, 2018).

[43] *See id.*

[44] *See* George P. Fletcher, Rethinking Criminal Law (1978).

[45] *See* Richard A. Posner, *Law, Knowledge, and the Academy: Legal Scholarship Today*, 115 Harv. L. Rev. 1314 (2002) (citing Friedrich Carl von Savigny, Right of Possession (Erskine Perry

There are revealing differences of languages between the two cultures, most notably the use of the world "reasonable" in common law cultures. Other languages have words based on the root "reason" but do not rely on the derivative words as legally important markers. The common law reliance on reasonable care, reasonable force, reasonable time, and similar expression is pervasive. Another peculiarity of English jurisprudence is the concept of fairness, which reveals the connection of the common law to the culture of sports, where fair play is the dominant idea. Neither of these basic American legal concepts is readily expressed in German scholarship.

This is an important point in explaining the purposes of criminal procedure. Common lawyers think of the process as an end in itself. So long is the game is played fairly, the result is presumptively acceptable. As we shall see, the civil law system of procedure emphasizes, as some would say, the finding of truth. The notion of pursuing justice as a "game" is offensive to the civil law mind. With respect to language in the Rome Statute, both the notions of reasonable and fairness are commonly used, revealing a debt to the common law tradition.[46]

5. The Structure of Pre-trial and the Trial in the Two Families

The common law system of procedure, originating in England in the Middle Ages, has come to embody Montesquieu's principle of separation of powers.[47] The lawyers run the trial, the judge manages the trial, and the jury (or a judge sitting in place of the jury) decides the facts. The lawyers are adversaries—that is, they stand for the position of their client—the accused or the state.

But limits to the partisanship of prosecutors have evolved over time. As representatives of the state, they must act in the name of justice, not only in pursuit of winning. They must disclose evidence favorable to the accused prior to trial, and they must follow the rules of evidence, including the

trans., 6th ed., London: S. Sweet 1848)) ("[von Sagigny] argued that Roman Law, essentially a body of common law principles, should be made the basis for German law because it would provide a better framework for German unity and modernization than a code on the French model.").

---

[46] *See* Rome Statute, *supra* note 13, arts. 28, 53, 58.

[47] *Cf.* Laurence Claus, *Montesquieu's Mistakes and the True Meaning of Separation*, 25 Oxford J. of Legal Studies 419 (2005).

avoidance of hearsay statements and witness statements overly provocative and prejudicial to the interests of the accused.[48]

The law of evidence is one of the distinctive features of common law and adversarial trials. It constitutes a major subject in legal education, and it's on the bar examination. No lawyer is qualified to practice without knowing the hearsay rule (inadmissibility of an out-of-court statement to prove the matter asserted) and its manifold exceptions.[49] Another feature of the law of evidence is the exclusion of prior convictions as relevant evidence.[50] All of these rules and exceptions provide fertile ground for advocacy and enhance the status of lawyers at trial.

It should be understood that the ideal application of the adversarial system lies in tort and contract cases, where both sides have an equal claim to justice. Thus, it is acceptable in these private law cases to think about offenses and defenses. The plaintiff proves the former; the defendant the latter. This private law frame of mind also influences issues like the burden of proof and the burden of going forward (sufficient evidence to send the issue to the jury).[51] It also introduces the private law pleading of "confession and avoidance," which means that the defendant concedes the claims of the prosecution and asserts new material, such as a claim of justification or excuse.[52]

No system of criminal law can gain coherence unless it rigorously divorces itself from the private law style. Thus, it may appear desirable that the prosecution not be regarded as the strict adversary of the accused. There are dangers, as we shall see, in thinking of the prosecutor as a neutral public servant.

The saving grace of criminal law is the notion of guilt. We do not speak of guilt in private law trials; the preferred word is liability. Guilt is a highly loaded moral notion. Some of these connotations inevitably seep into the more formalized notion of guilt used in criminal law. The richness of the moral notion is expressed in one of the basic maxims of the common law: *Actus non facit reus nisi mens sit rea*.[53] We should concede, however,

[48] Fed. R. Evid. 403, 801.

[49] "Evidence," 2018 MBE Subject Matter Outline, National Conference of Bar Examiners, http://www.ncbex.org/pdfviewer/?file=%2Fdmsdocument%2F201. (last visited May 9, 2018).

[50] Fed. R. Evid. 609.

[51] *Burden of Proof*, Wex Legal Information Institute, https://www.law.cornell.edu/wex/burden_of_proof. (last visited May 9, 2018).

[52] S.F.C. Milsom, Historical Foundations Of The Common Law 296 (2d ed. 1981).

[53] There is no guilty act without an accompanying guilty state of mind.

that this proposition is not entirely coherent. There are no guilty acts: only combinations of actions and states of mind that render the actor legally responsible. Some of the earlier test cases arose in the law of larceny, where the actor lawfully acquired possession at one moment of time and then decided to keep the goods unlawfully at a later moment.[54] The real point of the maxim is that the element of action and the element of culpability must coincide. It was tempting to convict in these cases. And therefore, the temporal interpretation of the maxim served as a useful restraint.

The opposite of guilt is either not guilty (the legal plea) or innocence. In terms of reputation and employment prospects after the trial, it is not enough for the accused to win on a plea of not guilty.[55]The public will have lingering doubts. The only corrective for an unfounded prosecution is a declaration of innocence. Unfortunately, the legal system is not interested in providing a *way* for the accused to preserve their reputation.

Some support for a declaration of no-guilt-at-all would be found in the now widely accepted presumption of innocence, endorsed by several prestigious codifications.[56] For example, the International Covenant for Civil and Political Rights holds in Article 14(2):

> Everyone charged with a criminal offence shall have the right to be presumed innocent until proved guilty according to law.[57]

This sounds like an important guarantee but it lacks teeth. Everything turns on what it means to found "guilty according to law." The local legal system could impose a low bar for proving guilt or even shift the burden of persuasion on selected issues.

[54] *See* Thomas W. Merrill & Henry E. Smith, *Law and Morality: Property Law: The Morality of Property*, 48 WM. & MARY L. REV. 1849, 1887 (2007) (citing *An Act To Make Better Provision for the Punishment of Frauds Committed by Trustees, Bankers, and Other Persons Intrusted with Property*, 20 & 21 Vict., c. 54 (1857)).

[55] Megan Rose, Opinion, *Innocent but Still Guilty*, N.Y. TIMES (Jan. 17, 2018), https://www.nytimes.com/2018/01/17/opinion/innocent-alford-pleas-guilty.html.

[56] *See* Andrew D. Leipold, *The Problem of Innocence, Acquitted Defendant*, 94 NW. U.L. REV. 1297, 1318 (2000).

[57] International Covenant on Civil and Political Rights, 1966, art. 14, 999 U.N.T.S. 14668 (United Nations General Assembly 1966, in force since 1976).

The Canadian Charter of Rights and Freedoms (1982), Art 11(d) specifies as a basic legal right that:

> Any person charged with an offense has the right . . . to be presumed innocent until proven guilty according to law in a fair and public hearing by an independent and impartial tribunal;[58]

The emphasis on a "fair and public hearing" does indirectly implicate one of the latent concepts in the rhetoric of a presumption of innocence. It is at this point that we encounter the problem posed by the prosecutor as a neutral public servant.

6. Role of the Prosecutor: Neutral or Partisan?

The issue became most acute in the former Soviet Union, where the *procuror* or public prosecutor was considered the paradigm of the neutral public servant. It is rather hard for us to believe today, but in fact there was an extraordinary debate within the Soviet legal system between the late 1940s and the mid-1980s about the status of the presumption of innocence in Soviet law.[59] This debate took place in the literature, in the Supreme Soviet, in the Supreme Court—indeed just about everywhere in the legal culture.[60] And though there are few people now who take this history seriously, let me say on the basis of much research in the field: the Soviet scholars were first rate, though obviously subject to some ideological restraints.[61] The unappreciated fact is that in a dangerous political environment, legal scholarship might be a relative safe shelter.

An abstract legal form like the presumption of innocence was an ideal cover for deeper political debates about the relative power of the "neutral prosecutor" and the judiciary. The procuracy claimed to be the guardian of legality in the Soviet system, presumably because they were under tighter control by the Kremlin, even though they purported to be neutral as between the state and the defense. So, why then would there be an intense debate about the presumption of innocence?

58 Can. Const. (Constitution Act, 1982) pt. I (Canadian Charter of Rights and Freedoms).

59 *See* Christopher Osakwe, *Modern Soviet Criminal Procedure: A Critical Analysis*, 57 TUL. L. REV. 439, 453 (1983). For an earlier discussion, see George P. Fletcher, *The Presumption of Innocence Under Soviet Law*, 15 U.C.L.A. L. REV. 1203 (1968) [hereinafter *The Presumption*].

60 The Presumption, *supra* note 59, at 1222.

61 *See generally id.*

Here is the argument for the procuracy:

> As neutral investigators we have considered both sides fairly. We know the accused has a "right to a defense" (prava na zashchu). We have guaranteed that right by considering the pro and cons and applying the European principle in dubio pro reo (equivalent to proof beyond a reasonable doubt).[62] We would not send the case to trial without having concluded that the accused is guilty. Why then should the trial court presume that he is innocent?
>
> This is the crux of the argument: the conflict between a purportedly neutral prosecutor and the trial court. And there is no doubt that according to our experience, prosecutors are not going to waste their time by bringing dubious cases to trial.

The emphasis should be on the presumption of innocence at trial. The pretrial proceedings may be part of the overall process, but they do not constitute a trial. And the claim that the neutral prosecutor realizes the accused's right to a defense cannot be taken seriously.

Perhaps the real issue beyond the concept of the neutral prosecutor is whether neutrality is even possible in criminal justice. As we shall see, this fundamental issue goes to the heart of the difference between the common law and civil law frames of mind. From the common law perspective, the point of the adversarial system is to engage in competition between supposed equals. The prosecutor's purpose is to prove guilt beyond a reasonable doubt; the defense to seek an acquittal by lawful means.

There are two other points that are worth mentioning about the myth (or ideal) of the neutral prosecution. One of these was implicit in the Soviet debate, namely the desire to divert cases from the ordinary system of criminal justice into alternative methods of reintegrating suspects into ordinary society.[63] The Soviets had developed a system of local informal community courts called "Comrades Courts."[64] The *procuror* would try to divert cases from the ordinary channels of justice into the informal mechanisms of social control—and somehow these community courts appealed to Soviet ideologues as a "withering away of the state."[65] Yet it did not make much sense to assume authority to divert these cases

[62] *Id.* at 1204; Craig M. Bradley, *The Exclusionary Rule in Germany*, 96 Harv. L. Rev. 1032, 1051 (1983) ("[A]ll doubts resolved in favor of the defendant.").

[63] *See generally* The Presumption, *supra* note 59.

[64] Okaswe, *supra* note 59, at 566.

[65] *See generally* Yoram Gorlizki, *Delegalization in Russia: Soviet Comrades' Courts in Retrospect*, 46 Am. J. Comp. L. 403 (1998).

unless the "neutral prosecution" could properly conclude that the defendant was guilty. Many of the same techniques of diversion (traffic school, community service) are achieved in common law systems after a plea of guilty.

7. Legality of Plea Bargaining

Many of these diversionary goals are achieved in the common law by relying on plea bargaining. This is also a dubious way of resolving cases at lower expense to the state and may reveal another dangerous side of the supposedly neutral prosecutor. In a plea bargaining arrangement, the prosecutor makes a number of charges based often on overlapping offenses, for example, one charge for possessing a weapon, another for using it. The jury might thus be encouraged to reach a compromise verdict splitting the difference between the two sides.

Plea bargaining raises a basic point of principle that characterizes the difference between the common law and civil law ways of thinking. The Germans refer to the distinction between *Legälitätsprizip* and *Opportunitätsprinzip*. The former (Legality Principle) means that the prosecutor prosecutes all cases with comparable evidentiary support in exactly the same way.[66] There is no option to grant a lower set of charges to a defendant who pleads guilty. The latter principle of discretionary prosecution (seizing the "opportunity") enables plea bargaining.

Plea bargaining is an accepted part of common law practice, but it is subject to a principled challenge. In a famous 1998 case decided in the Federal Tenth Circuit of Appeal, the question was posed for the first time whether it was legal for a common law prosecutor to offer a lower charge to a witness (or a defendant) in return for her incriminating testimony against a codefendant.[67] The story is worth telling in some detail.

In 1997, Sonya Singleton was convicted of cocaine trafficking and money laundering after a codefendant, Napoleon Douglas, testified against her at trial.[68] In exchange for his testimony, government attorneys promised that they would not prosecute him for other possible offenses and that they would

[66] *See* STRAFPROZESSORDNUNG [STPO] [CODE OF CRIMINAL PROCEDURE], Apr. 7, 1987, Bundesgesetzblatt [BGBL] § 152(2) (Ger.), available at http://www.legislationline.org/documents/action/popup/id/9016/preview ("Except as otherwise provided by law, the public prosecution office shall be obliged to take action in the case of all criminal offenses which may be prosecuted, provided there are sufficient factual indications.").

[67] U.S. v. Singleton, 165 F.3d 1297 (1999).

[68] *Id.* at 1298.

bring his cooperation to the attention of the sentencing judge and the parole board.[69] Singleton was sentenced to 46 months in federal prison. [70] Douglas's sentence was reduced from 15 to 5 years, to be served concurrently with time he had to serve in Mississippi.[71] On appeal, Singleton argued that the district court erred in allowing Douglas's testimony into evidence because it violated the federal bribery statute, which prohibits giving "anything of value to any person, for or because of the testimony" to be given by that person.[72] This was the first attempt in the statute's 50-year history to apply it to prosecutors.

The term "bribery" had long been applied to defense lawyers' effort to make a deal with witnesses on the scope of their testimony.[73] Of course, defense lawyers do not have much to offer in comparison with prosecutors' command over the charging process and influence with judges on sentencing. But if a defense offered to pay a prosecution witness to change his testimony, it would clearly be bribery. Yet, the defense is allowed—at least in the American system—to prepare their own witnesses for trial and perhaps even to provide benefits to them that would be considered "things of value" under the conventional definition of bribery.

Singleton's lawyer had the innovative idea of applying the same principle to prosecutors. After all, it is an "adversarial" system and therefore two opposing sides should be treated equally.

There are practical limits on the ideals of the adversary system. Most of these limits derive from the enormous expansion of drug prosecutions in the 1990s. The Singleton decision has to be understood in the context of the war on drugs and the consequent expansion of the U.S. prison population—arguably the highest per capita incarceration rate in the world.[74] It is not to be assumed, however, that the judges were aware of these interconnecting factors, and they probably would not have considered them relevant to the narrow question before them.

Whether a partisan or an allegedly neutral prosecutor is preferable is still open to debate. We have tried to underscore the dangers of supposed neutrality, but nevertheless the prosecutor as public servant must strive not only

[69] *Id.*
[70] *Id.*
[71] *Id.*
[72] *Id.* at 1299 (quoting 18 U.S.C. § 201(c)(2) (1994)).
[73] *Id.* at 1310.
[74] The U.S.'s prison population rate is 698 per 100,000. Roy Walmsley, *World Prison Population List*, INSTITUTE FOR CRIMINAL POLICY RESEARCH (11th ed. 2016), http://prisonstudies.org/sites/default/files/resources/downloads/world_prison_population_list_11th_edition_0.pdf.

to win but to do justice. When the considerations of clearing the docket and securing convictions by means other than proof in open court, the principles of justice yield to those inefficiencies and prevail over the principles of justice, and the adversarial system seems to lose its appeal.

To state the issue in the governing distinction of this chapter gives us a slightly different perspective. If we treat the defendant as a subject of the process, then plea bargaining enhances the power of the accused to control his own fate. The danger, however, is that the legislature and the prosecution can easily counter this supposed autonomy by increasing the number of overlapping offenses and by overcharging the accused, thus creating the image that he actually gains something in a plea bargain.

A good example is the trial of Bernhard Goetz, in which on the basis of shooting four youths on a New York subway in arguable self-defense, the accused was charged not only with attempted murder, but with various counts of illegal possession of a weapon without a license and the crime of reckless endangerment. [75] In a case like this, the jury can readily compromise, as they in did, convicting Goetz on one of the possession charges.[76]

On the other hand, treating him as an object to be protected—perhaps contrary to his own wishes—may entail some humanitarian benefits. It shields him from a legal system concerned about efficiency as in the Singleton case. Yet it also provides a defense against zealous prosecutors representing victims and politicians who seek vengeance or at least some personal satisfaction or political advantage.

8. Implications in the Rome Statute

These vignettes in legal history and comparative law find expression in the Rome Statute but not in a dramatic way. Article 66 is labeled "the presumption of innocence,"[77] but there might be some indirect recognition of the Soviet debate in the requirement that the accused is "presumed innocence until proven guilty before the Court. . . ."[78] With this clear provision the ICC prosecutor could not plausibly argue that the OTP realized the protections necessary to safeguard the accused against a false conviction.

[75] People v. Goetz, 502 N.Y.S.2d 577, 578 (N.Y. Sup. Ct. 1986).
[76] *Id.*
[77] Rome Statute, *supra* note 13, art. 66.
[78] *Id.*

The rest of the provision is about the burden of persuasion, which has been a more nettlesome problem in American jurisprudence than elsewhere. Most contemporary legal systems insist on the prosecution's proving guilty beyond a reasonable doubt (or in European parlance, recognizing the principle in dubio pro reo), yet some structural features of the Rome Statute suggest an argument for shifting the burden of persuasion on defensive issues. The important provision is Art. 31, which acknowledges the distinction between offenses and defenses and provides guidance on insanity, intoxication, self-defense, and duress.[79] The most suggestive provision, however, is Article 31(3), which allows the trial to recognize new grounds of defense.[80] In other words, the principle *nullum crimen sine lege* does not apply to the grounds "excluding criminal responsibility."[81] We consider two possible additional defenses—(1) necessity and (2) consent in rape cases in an upcoming chapter.

If there are newly recognized defenses at trial, would it be permissible to shift the burden of persuasion to the defendant on the ground that he has received a benefit not recognized in the Rome Statute? There is much to support the permissibility of compromising the benefit of the newly bestowed defense. The defendant should have little ground to complain about receiving "half a loaf" rather than the full benefit of Article 66 on the burden of persuasion. Indeed, from the perspective of persuading the Court, arguing for the compromised position provides an easier task of advocacy.

The issue of diversion to other tribunals, which was a major issue in the Soviet debate, is of lesser concern to the ICC. Indeed under the principle of complementarity, recognized in the Preamble, the opposite is true.[82] The ICC is the court of last resort. It does not receive cases that can be handled by national court systems—the metaphoric parallel to the comrades courts for the procuracy.

9. The Role of the Jury

In some common law criminal trials, the petit jury, consisting exclusively of laypersons, typically 12, has the ultimate, non-reviewable power to acquit, but its findings of guilt are subject to review on procedural grounds.[83]

[79] Rome Statute, *supra* note 13, art. 31.
[80] *See id.*
[81] *See* Rome Statute, *supra* note 13, art. 22.
[82] *See* Rome Statute, *supra* note 13, pmbl.
[83] *See* Green v. United States, 355 U.S. 184, 188 (1957).

Recalling that truth is not the object but obviously of high relevance in the common law trial, the basis for appeal is the allegation of judicial mistakes on the evidence admissible to the jury and mistakes in the instructions to the jury. In a rare case, the defense can secure a reversal on appeal on the grounds that the verdict of guilty is not supported by the evidence.

The jury votes in secret, guided only by the judge's instructions. During their service and deliberations, they are cut off from the media and are barred from discussing the trial if they go home go in the evening. If the trial is subject to a great publicity (the O.J. Simpson trial, for example), the judge can sequester the jury, which means that the jury is locked up in a hotel during the evenings and has no contact with the outside world.[84] Some of these measures may seem extreme to the civil law mind, and in my personal experience I have generally found that the merits and demerits of the jury systems appeal to people largely on their cultural heritage. Lawyers in the civil law tradition rarely see the advantages of the jury, though several have experimented with it for brief periods in an effort to return legal power to the people.

The jury is often thought to be linked to democracy. But there are many democracies in civil law cultures that have no interest in the jury system. The historical and structural linkage to democracy in the common law world is also dubious. The jury is much older than democracy, and it does embody the masses but only a select few of specially qualified of the mass. The jury pool, from which the 12 are ultimately chosen, consists of residents of an area (typically taken from the voting rolls) who are not registered felons.[85] The process of selection is based on a process called voir dire in which lawyers from the two sides question the jurors about their potential biases.[86] This process is a well-developed art form because lawyers want to find out how the jurors lean but are not allowed to ask them directly about private matters. The lawyers must develop hunches bases on tangential considerations such as reading habits, employment, activities, and the like. A whole profession of jury consultants has developed to assist lawyers in making background checks on potential jurors.[87]

If a lawyer is not satisfied with a potential juror, he can challenge him "for cause," in which case the judge decides whether the juror is biased and should

[84] *See* Mary Strauss, *Sequestration*, 24 Am. J. Crim. L. 63, 65 (1996).

[85] *See* Brian C. Kalt, *The Exclusion of Felons from Jury Service*, 53 Am. U.L. Rev. 65 (2003).

[86] *See* Fed. R. Crim. P. 24(a).

[87] Franklin Strier & Donna Shestowsky, *Profiling the Profilers: A Study of the Trial Consulting Profession, Its Impact on Trial Justice and What, If Anything, to do about It*, 199 Wis. L. Rev. 441 (1999).

be dismissed. If this works, the lawyer has at his disposal a certain number of peremptory challenges, for which the lawyers need give no explanation. These peremptory challenges are highly controversial and have been subject to extensive litigation in cases whether they appear to have been used in a racially discriminatory way.[88]

This process of jury selection demands sensitivity to human nature. I recall witnessing a case of jury selection in which the defense had pondered some difficult borderline cases, most notably a nun who presented herself in the pool. The question was whether she would carry too much authority in deliberations and was that good or bad.

Here it is important to recall that a verdict typically has to be unanimous, and therefore the defense always wants to find one or two people who might be holdouts against the majority. If the holdout is stubborn and won't yield to pressure, the judge has no choice but to declare a hung jury, which means that either the prosecution either gives up or has to start all over again.

Another significant feature of trial by jury is the entire law of evidence. Laypeople cannot be trusted with ultimate power and therefore the information the lawyers may present is limited. So far as witnesses provide evidence, the witness must testify under oath—administered before they begin to speak—and are subject to charges of perjury for all intentional falsehoods. The implication of the oath requirement is the elimination, at least in principle of hearsay evidence. A typical example would be witness X claiming that he heard Y say in a bar that the accused X shot Y.

The reason for the rule is a feature of the adversary system—the principle of cross-examination by the lawyers. The statement that X shot Y is not subject to cross-examination and therefore should not be admissible. Alas, the rule is shot through with exceptions where the statement out of court is apparently so reliable that it need not be subject to cross-examination. Some examples are excited utterances and dying declarations.[89] The study of the hearsay rule and all its exceptions is the subject matter of the common law course on Evidence, which is typically missing in the curricula of civil law countries.

Neither the Rome Statute nor the Rules of Procedure and Evidence mention the concept of hearsay.[90] This might be a consequence of the false

[88] *See* 22 Cal. 3d 258 (1978); Batson v. Kentucky, 476 U.S. 79, 89 (1986).

[89] *See* Fed. R. Evid. 804(b); Webb v. Lsssane, 922 F.2d 390, 394–96 (7th Cir. 1991).

[90] *See generally* Rome Statute, *supra* note 13; ICC, The Rules of Procedure and Evidence, Doc. ICC-ASP/1/3 (Sept. 2002).

association of the hearsay rule with the jury system. But the rule is not about the competence of the judge or jury, it is about assessing the relevance of the evidence on the fairness of admitting evidence not subject to cross-examination. A good example of an unfair use of hearsay evidence is the set of depositions of victims collected in the Yamashita case and admitted in the trial against him.[91]

The Civil Law tradition of criminal procedure begins with the inquisitorial system, where the power to investigate, accuse, and judge are located in a single person. This system perfectly exemplifies the perception of defendant and the alleged crime as the object of the investigation. The issue is not fair trial but the truth of the matter. In the course of time, this system was modified first by separating the accusatorial function from the investigative function. This leads to the rule of the prosecutor as a distinct office and eventually to the role of lawyers for the defense, though certainly not to the adversarial principle that the lawyers run the trial. The modern civil law systems are generally thought to exemplify the accusatorial system.[92]

In this century, there have been experiments in many countries of mixing laypeople with professional judges in hearing the case and making determinations of fact and prescribing sentences.[93] This has given laypeople some influence in the processes of justice, but according to all informal reports, the professional judges are still in charge.

There are several consequences of the civilian mode of trial. In principle, there is no law of evidence (after all these are professionals!). The verdict does not require a supermajority, and the verdict and the sentence are made in a single judgment. The latter procedure invites compromise—as you find in American torts cases, where the jury decides liability and damages in a single verdict. In a compromise verdict, a civilian judge unsure about the facts can readily decide to convict on a lesser crime. Of course, the latter form of compromise occurs in common law systems as a result of overcharging.

So far as the law of evidence is concerned, the civilian tradition is affected by the rejection, after the French Revolution, of the legal system of proofs,

[91] *See In re Yamashita*, 327 U.S. at 20.

[92] *See* Michele Panzavolta, *Reforms and Counter-Reforms in the Italian Struggle for an Accusatorial Criminal Law System*, 30 N.C.J. INT'L L. & COM. REG. 577 (2005).

[93] *See* Matthew J. Wilson, *Japan's New Criminal Jury Trial System: In Need of More Transparency, More Access, and More Time*, 33 FORDHAM INT'L L.J. 487, 488 (201).

which prescribed various weights to witnesses of different feudal rank. The demise of legal proofs ushered in the era of "free evaluation of the evidence" and the judicial findings of fact on the basis of "in-time conviction."[94] It is difficult to translate the latter term, but it purports to be the personal subjective conviction of the judge. It is easy to see how these trends also led to a principled rejection of the law of evidence, the rules of which were associated with feudal regimes.[95]

One of the curious things about the evolution of legal ideas in the common law is that institutions associated with feudalism are alive and well. This is true in the law of real property, and it is obvious in the common law rules of evidence. The rules we associate with the jury system and our understandable fear of lay authority find a justification as well in the survival of feudal institutions in common law countries. Thus, we can explain why most common law countries (Cyprus, Israel, India) have rejected the jury system but retained the law of evidence, including some version of the hearsay rule.

The common law world had no chance of bequeathing the jury system to the international legal order. Yet it is critical in the American approach to criminal and civil justice. Indeed, in tort cases, the jury provides an enormous benefit by way of punitive damages. This is true, whether the tort plaintiff sues under the ATCA or simply gets local jurisdiction by serving process on the defendant.

The only bequest of the common law world to the ICC is the adversarial system. The inquisitorial system as it was known in the early history of the civil law systems is largely a matter of history. After the French Revolution, the inquisitorial system became the accusatorial mode of trial. This meant that the process of charging would be distinct from the process of judging. This correlates well with the presumption of innocence.

There may be another possible gift of the common law system to the international legal order, and that is the principle of double jeopardy. Civil laws system generally allow a retrial based on new evidence. Suppose O.J. Simpson confesses after his acquittal. Can he be retried? The answer is no. This principle is not likely to influence the ICC because the entirely foundation of the

[94] *See* Stephen C. Tharman, *Symposium on Comparative Jury Systems: Should Criminal Juries Give Reasons for Their Verdicts?: The Spanish Experience and the Implications of the European Court of Human Rights Decision in Taxquet v. Belgium*, 86 CHI.-KENT L. REV. 613, 615–20 (2011).

[95] *See id.*

Court is avoidance of impunidad and the protection of victims. It is not likely that the ICC would integrate the tort alternative into its thinking. Yet the recovery for damages, particularly for punitive damages, represents a sound alternative to the costly and not particularly useful threat and imposition of criminal punishment.

4
Causation vs. Background Events

An intelligent approach to drafting a criminal code deliberately avoids certain problematic philosophical issues. Among these are the nature of human action, the purposes of punishment, and most importantly for this chapter—the problem of causation. The reason to avoid legislative definitions of these issues is that they are not subject to definitive resolution; they are essentially contested issues. Asking a legislature or even a court to resolve them by majority vote is like asking them to decide whether there was time before the Big Bang. Philosophical issues provide a rich field for legal argument as well as academic commentary. There is no way an advocate can simply cite a single source of law as authoritative on the issue. Ongoing argument about the philosophical problem is indispensable.

The problem of causation runs through the crimes defined by the Rome Statute.[1] The issue is implicit, even if the drafter wisely declined to define the concept. It is obvious that a concern for *impunidad* and the fate of victims presuppose the harm that has occurred to a defined victim, which implies that the harm must have been caused by the crimes defined by the Rome Statute.

Many horrendous harms occur under conditions of war and social upheaval. In these conditions, we do not know whether the harm would have happened anyway or whether it was caused by a specific actor who should be held accountable. Some of these harms are endemic to war—hunger, dislocation, destruction. Some people die naturally. They have car accidents and injure themselves. The deaths need not be caused by agents of interest to us. In that sense, they are the background conditions.

[1] Rome Statute for the International Criminal Court, July 17, 1998, 2187 U.N.T.S. 3; U.N. Diplomatic Conference of Plenipotentiaries on the Establishment of an International Court, U.N. Doc. A/Conf.183/9 [hereinafter Rome Statute].

The Grammar of Criminal Law: Volume Two: International Criminal Law. George P. Fletcher.

To illustrate this point, suppose an armed group passes through a village. When they leave, several corpses are found, but with no signs of bullet wounds or other external signs of violence. We do not know that any soldier in the passing army or the army acting in concert caused the death. The victim might have died from fright but also might have had a heart condition that put him on the edge of death. Death and harms of this sort constitute the background conditions. They have been caused by something in the environment, but not by the armed group, and it is their field of causal impact that concerns us as matter of criminal law. Simplistic fallacies have governed our thinking about causation. The first is the superstitious maxim, post hoc, propter hoc.[2] To exemplify this maxim, when I am writing, the birds sing in the garden at sunrise. Does their singing cause the sun to rise? To think so would is obviously fallacious. There must be something more to causation then the observance of regularly occurring events.

Ironically, the otherwise desirable reform of the Rome Statute in 2010, introducing the principle of individual responsibility under Article 8*bis*,[3] makes it more difficult to prove causation. A faithful application of the Rome Statute requires no less. Yet the statute itself offers no guidance at all on the nature and limits of causation. This is a matter where advocates and scholars must turn to the academic and legal traditions of the common law and civil law cultures. I hope the following discussion of the issue might serve as a stimulus for others to join the debate.

The first thing to do is to address the philosophical issues in general and to illustrate the implicit and sometimes explicit recognition of causal issues in the four principal crimes within the jurisdiction or competence of the court.

The fallacy of holding the armed group or a single individual liable for the death they discover is called post hoc, propter hoc. Even if we observe a constant concatenation of events, we do not have a causal connection. It does not follow that if Beta regularly follows Alpha, Alpha causes Beta. If I go to sleep at dark and rise with the sun, as humans have always done, it does not follow that sleeping causes the sun to rise. Nor does the night, which always precedes the day, cause the earth to turn in a way that makes the sun appear to rise.

[2] *Post Hoc*, Wex Legal Information Institute, https://www.law.cornell.edu/wex/post_hoc (last visited Aug. 28, 2018) ("From the Latin phrase post hoc ergo propter hoc, which means "after this, therefore because of this.").

[3] Resolution Adopting Aggression Amendments to Rome Statute, Rev. Conf. of the Rome Statute, Kampala, Uganda, May 31–June 11, 2010, Annex I, art. 8bis, 13th plen. mtg., I.C.C. Doc. RC/Res.6 (June 11, 2010).

This very issue became the cornerstone of the lengthy debate between the Scottish philosopher David Hume and the famous thinker who never left the city of Königsberg, Immanuel Kant. Hume adopted a conception of causation based on observing the regularity of one thing's following another.[4] The empirical view of causation is simply that it is a regular concatenation of events. If Beta follows Alpha on a regular basis, that means that Alpha causes Beta.

When Kant first encountered Hume's work in translation in the 1760s, he wrote that the issue of causation awakened him from his "dogmatic slumber" and led him eventually to form his pathbreaking idea of a priori concepts—concepts like causation.[5] By 1785, in one of his first major books, *Critique of Pure Reason*, Kant wrote "that the effect does not merely follow upon the cause but is posited through it and follows from it."[6] Allow me to restate this in more down-to-earth terms. The point that was missing in Hume's strictly empirical approach is an idea that I shall call, in layman's terms, "causal energy"—the intrinsic factor that enables Alpha to bring about Beta. Admittedly, the notion of causal energy sounds a bit like mythology, but we are simply trying to give voice to the a priori idea that something more underlies causation than observable facts.

It is understandable that the example discussed during that period was the sun warming a rock. We associate the sun with a source of energy. When we see the impact of the sun's heat, we might well come to Kant's proposition "that the effect does not merely follow upon the cause but is posited through it and follows from it."[7]

There is an analogous relationship between custom and customary law. It is not that custom causes or generates customary law, but there is something like a de facto universalization or near universalization of the behavior among states, the factor of opinio juris renders the custom binding on states. The opinio juris[8] is analogous to causal energy. The individual state support

[4] *See* David Hume, *An Enquiry Concerning Human Understanding, in* Enquiries Concerning Human Understanding and Concerning the Principles of Morals VII, pt. I, at 63–64 (L.A. Selby-Bigge ed., 3d ed. 1975) (1777) ("The scenes of the universe are continually shifting, and one object follows another in an uninterrupted succession; but the power or force, which actuates the whole machine is entirely concealed from us, and never discovers itself in any of the sensible qualities of body.").

[5] Immanuel Kant, Prolegomena to Any Future Metaphysics intr. (Paul Carus ed., Gutenberg Project 1912) (1783) (ebook) [hereinafter Kant, Prolegomena].

[6] Immanuel Kant, Critique of Pure Reason 91 (Paul Guyer & Allen W. Wood, eds. & trans., Cambridge University Press, 1997) (1781) [hereinafter Kant, Critique].

[7] *Id.*

[8] *Opinio Juris (International Law)*, Wex Legal Information Institute (last visited Aug. 28, 2018) ("In customary international law, opinio juris is the second element (along with state practice)

might be presumed in the absence of persistent objection, and certain universal practices—notably maritime law—are so useful that a strong presumption of opinio juris provides the factor that makes the practice binding as customary law.

The basis of the analogy with "causal energy" is that "opinio juris" is always mythical, but it is necessary to identify some source of power that renders customary practices—the regular concatenation of events—as something more that commands our respect.

The way H.L.A. Hart explains the emergence of customary law is slightly different. He begins with certain customary practices[9] (like baring your head in Christian churches or covering your head in Jewish synagogues). And then on the basis of reciprocal expectations, the practice becomes obligatory. A good deal of religious law arises in this way. The critical point is that an internal sense of obligations must accompany the practice in order to render it legally binding. This, then, is the way Kant addressed the surface understanding of causation in Humean empiricism and resolved the fallacy of "post hoc, propter hoc."[10] The legal analogues come to mind as a way of assuring the reader that this is all relevant to our general inquiry into the foundations of the international legal order.

A supposed corrective to the over-inclusiveness of the "propter hoc" fallacy is the almost sound *sine qua non* or "but for" test of causation, used pervasively in legal argument. In order to understand the causal import of the birds singing in my garden, we have to imagine the events leading to the sunrise and ask whether it would have happened anyway. If the sun would have risen anyway, the singing at dawn is not a cause.

We should pause to recognize the degree of imagination required to appreciate the counterfactual condition proposition that the sun doesn't rise, and the birds sing anyway. Typically, we make causal claims without any experience with the counterfactual condition situation. For example: Did the Treaty of Versailles ending World War I cause the rise of Nazism and World War II? Did the prohibition of alcohol in the United States[11] lead to the rise of the Sicilian Mafia several decades later? History is full of these puzzles. The simple reason is that we cannot extricate a single historical event from the

necessary to establish a legally binding custom. Opinio juris denotes a subjective obligation, a sense on behalf of a state that is bound to the law in question.").

[9] H.L.A. Hart, The Concept of Law 100–117 (3d ed. 2012).
[10] Kant, Critique, *supra* note 6.
[11] U.S. Const. amend. XVIII (repealed 1933).

infinite number of events occurring every day and ask whether it would have happened anyway.

In the world of legal disputes, the relevant events stand out from all the background conditions. The relevant factors are the actions of the suspect, the occurrence of harm, and the level of culpability. In Robert Nozick's famous formula, the appropriate level of retributive punishment is defined as P = r.W, where P = punishment; r = the level of culpability (intent or negligence); and W = Wrongdoing.[12] The two factors constitute wrongdoing, action, and harm and are the topics of the next chapter. For now, we are concerned about the relationship between them and whether the action causes the harm. In fact, this is a subtle problem because of the conventional way we describe crimes.

The problem is the relevance of harm to wrongdoing, which is not an easy proposition to solve. Assuming that harm is relevant, we have to inquire whether the suspect's actions caused the harm. To provide additional examples, firing the gun might not have killed the diseased; he might have died anyway. Striking a match might not have caused the fire; there might have been other sources. Yet there are some offenses where the conventional description of the offense presupposes a causal connection. Good examples are rape and larceny. The definition of rape is the sexual violation of the victim.[13] The "violation" might occur by mistake but not by accident.

This distinction requires some reflection. Suppose a child is scalded in the bath. This might happen by mistake if his parent mistook the hot for the cold faucet. It would occur by accident if the parent was reaching for cold but tripped and hit the hot.

It is useful to distinguish between these two types of crime depending on whether "causation" is a distinct element requiring proof. Some crimes have the harmful consequences built-in or implicit in the description of the required action. Larceny requires the dispossession of a chattel.[14] If items are lost, they are not "dispossessed." This crime can occur by mistake but not by accident. The reason is the description of the required action has the consequence built-in. Larceny occurs only when a thief engages in the dispossession. Rape also falls into the same category. This means that causation is not

[12] Robert Nozick, Philosophical Explanations 388 (1981).

[13] Rape, Unif. Crime Reporting Program (Federal Bureau of Invesigations 2013) ("Penetration, no matter how slight, of the vagina or anus with any body part or object, or oral penetration by a sex organ of another person, without the consent of the victim.").

[14] Wayne R. LaFave & Austin W. Scott Jr., Criminal Law § 8.1, at 702 (2d ed. 1986).

a separate element requiring proof. We can refer to these crimes as crimes of unlawful action. Other crimes, conveniently called crimes of harmful consequences, require a distinct inquiry into causation. Most crimes of concern to the international community are crimes of harmful consequences, such as the crime of Genocide in Article 6 of the Rome Statute.[15] The language is replete with causal imagery. Part (a) covers killing, clearly a crime of harmful consequences.[16] Part (b) refers explicitly to causing harm.[17] Part (c) is directed to "inflicting" harsh conditions.[18] Part (d) covers "imposing" measures inhibiting birth.[19] When you impose conditions on someone, you obviously cause them to apply. Part (e) addresses "transferring children," which happens when some agent causes the transfer. [20] One way to test this claim intuitively is to ask the question of whether the five types of harm mentioned in parts (a) through (e)—death, bodily harm, group destruction, birth prevention, genocide—can occur accidentally. The answer is yes. Where causation is an issue—the crime is one of harmful consequences—accidental harm is conceptually possible. We should remember that as discussed in chapter 2, this book includes an analysis of the Alien Tort Claims Act as part of the international legal order. This is useful because the approach to causation in tort law has much to teach criminal lawyers, even if differences between the two fields must also be taken into consideration. Also, certain issues come into focus as a result of comparing the two fields. For example, why is contributory negligence relevant in tort but not criminal cases? Does this have anything to do with the theory of causation? These are nagging questions that demand an answer.

There is a long and engaging a story about the role of causation in the history of the common law of torts and in the deep conflict in the academic debate about the relevance of economic analysis to the just distribution of the losses that victims suffer. We review that history briefly. In the common law of torts, the basis of recovery was defined by the writs of trespass and trespass on the case.[21] The writs were essentially permission from the King's Exchequer to file suit if the facts were sufficient to state a cause of action.

[15] Rome Statute, *supra* note 1, arts. 6(a)–(e).
[16] *Id.*
[17] *Id.*
[18] *Id.*
[19] *Id.*
[20] *Id.*
[21] *See* 3 WILLIAM BLACKSTONE, COMMENTARIES ON THE LAWS OF ENGLAND 115 (William S. Hein & Co 1992) (1768).

Trespass vi et armis[22] lay for directly caused harms against persons. This was essentially an aggression. A good test case was *Scott v. Shepherd* in 1773.[23]

Shepherd threw an explosive squib into a marketplace. A bystander W picked it up and threw it up. R did the same. The squib exploded and injured Scott. The question was whether—in principle—this was sufficient to state a cause of action in trespass, that is, for directly causing harm to another person.[24] At the time a jury could render a special verdict but reserve the question of liability for the judges on the King's Bench. The major dispute among the six judges was whether the appropriate writ was trespass or trespass on the case. As I will show, the argument boils down to a version of the theory of "causal energy." At the time, the distinction between trespass and trespass on the case (the only two relevant writs) was absolute, but no one was quite sure what it was. We should keep in mind that all of this was being debated just a few years before the enactment of the Alien Tort Claim Act in 1789.

It is not to be assumed that judges have always written full opinions and disagreed with each other publicly in writing, but that feature of the legal culture was well recognized by the time of *Scott v. Shepherd*.[25] One of the judges was the famous William Blackstone, who had just published his four volume *Commentaries on the Laws of England*. His argument was that writ of trespass would apply in principle if the injury was direct and immediate, and trespass on the case, if it was indirect and consequential. Blackstone opined that the triple play feature of the case made the injury indirect and as such, trespass would not apply.[26] In other words, the causal energy initially invested by Shepherd was dissipated by W's freely throwing it again, and R's doing it once more. They imported new causal energy, which superseded the initial throw by Shepherd.

The other judges disagreed and reasoned that Shepherd might be liable only under the writ of trespass on the case.[27] Their argument was more about the public danger of throwing the squib than the theory of causation.[28] The judges disagreed with each other, but they might not have been paying much attention to their colleagues' arguments. Of course, judges always decide

22 By force and arms.
23 3 Wils. 403, 95 Eng. Rep. 1124, 2 Black. W. 892, 96 Eng. Rep. 528 (K.B. 1773).
24 *Id.*
25 3 Wils. 403, 95 Eng. Rep. 1124, 2 Black. W. 892, 96 Eng. Rep. 528 (K.B. 1773).
26 *Id.*
27 *Id.*
28 *See id.*

before they write their opinions. And most opinions disappear in the dustbin of history. Yet Blackstone's examples on the issue of causation have lasting importance on clarifying the distinction between the two writs, trespass and trespass on the case, and illuminating the theoretical problem of causation.

Blackstone's most intriguing example is the case of throwing a football into the street.[29] It is kicked around by a hundred other people and then goes through a shopkeeper's window. The intervening causes break the causal chain, but not entirely. There remains a form of indirect causation sufficient for trespass on the case. An example often given to illustrate the difference is the different ways a person's throwing a log into the street can injure a pedestrian. If the log hits the walker on the head, it is a matter of direct causation, and trespass will lie. If the pedestrian trips over the log, the causation is indirect, and the appropriate writ is trespass on the case.

Of course, in an extreme case, the log might have lain there for a long time with most pedestrians learning to walk around it. But, if one of them nonetheless trips over the log, he might be contributorily negligent. In our previously defined terms, the causal energy would have shifted from the log thrower to the pedestrian.

In the history of the common law of torts, there has been a dance around the proverbial log thrower and pedestrian in an effort to impose ultimate responsibility, which was once regarded as a matter of all or nothing. In the case of contributory negligence, the defendant was not liable at all, and thus arose the doctrine of last clear chance.[30] If the log thrower could see that the danger that the log posed to pedestrians, he could enter the street and remove it. Therefore, he would have the last clear chance and be liable according to the writ of trespass on the case. This last move raises the philosophical problem of whether omissions can be causes. If we take the theory of causal energy too seriously, we might see this as a problem. Omissions appear to impart no energy at all. And if the causing actions must be singled out from background events in order to assess their causal import, think of the infinite number of omissions that might be regarded as causes. In cases like *Scott v. Shepherd*, there might be hundreds of people standing by and witnessing the explosive squib in their midst.

There are two distinct ways of penalizing omissions, and one of them has direct relevance to the possible extension of liability under the Rome Statute.

[29] *Id.*
[30] *See id.*

The first is a pure case of liability for failing, say, to plow the snow on the sidewalk in front of your building. The second is committing a standard offense by not intervening when there is reasonable opportunity to do so. Under this second standard of liability, just about any war crime under Article 8(2)(a) could be committed by omission. A soldier could prevent a killing but willfully fails to do so. He could prevent torture but turns the other way. The list goes on and on.

It is true that the duty to rescue is more widely recognized in continental jurisprudence than in the common law.[31] In a famous case, victim Kitty Genovese was stabbed in front of her apartment in Brooklyn; dozens of neighbors knew about her plight and did nothing to rescue her.[32] No one doubts their moral responsibility for failing to act. The problem is difficult to address under the rubric of a duty to intervene.

In all cases of causing harm, there is an implicit duty not to harm, but the duty to rescue takes on special salience in cases of omissions. There is a liability for the omission only if it is violation of duty to the victim. Recognizing a duty of this sort and extending liability to omissions poses a problem under the Rome Statute's commitment to the principle *nullum crimen sine lege*.[33]

Another approach is signaled by the famous book by H.L.A. Hart and Tony Honoré, *Causation in the Law*.[34] They have no difficulty in recognizing omissions as causes. It all depends, in their view, on the expected environment.[35] Say you go on vacations for a few weeks and your doorman agrees to water your plants, as he has faithfully done in the past. This time he forgets, and the plants die. There are several causes of the plants' dying. One of them is the failure of the doorman to water them. Of course, if you had no expectation of his fulling his promise, it would be hard to consider his omission a cause.

We have a conflict based on a physical theory of causation and one based on based on human expectations. The right approach, it seems, would be to combine the "but for" test with a theory of expectations designed to pick out the salient actions and omissions.

[31] *See* Alberto Cadoppi, *Failure to Rescue and the Continental Criminal Law*, *in* THE DUTY TO RESCUE: THE JURISPRUDENCE OF AID 93 (Michael A. Menlowe & Alexander McCall Smith eds., 1993); F.J.M. Feldbrugge, *Good and Bad Samaritans: A Comparative Survey of Criminal Law Provisions Concerning Failure to Rescue*, 14 AM. J. COMP. L. 630, 632–34 (1966).

[32] Martin Gansberg, *37 Who Saw Murder Didn't Call the Police*, N.Y. TIMES (Mar. 27, 1964), https://www.nytimes.com/1964/03/27/37-who-saw-murder-didnt-call-the-police.html.

[33] Rome Statute of the International Criminal Court, art. 22, 2187 U.N.T.S 90 (July 17, 1998).

[34] *See generally* H.L.A. HART & TONY HONORE, CAUSATION IN THE LAW (2d. 1985).

[35] *See id.* at 38.

To return to the theory of causation in tort law, we should examine various responses to the all-or-nothing system represented by the trilogy of negligence, contributory negligence, and last clear chance. The German alternative, enacted in the Civil Code (BGB), is suggestive:

> (1) Where fault on the part of the injured person contributes to the occurrence of the damage, liability in damages as well as the extent of compensation to be paid depend on the circumstances, in particular to the extent the damage is caused mainly by one or the other party.
> (2) This also applies if the fault of the injured person is limited to failing to draw the attention of the obligor to the danger of unusually extensive damage, where the obligor neither was nor ought to have been aware of the danger, or to failing [sic] to avert or reduce the damage.[36]

The critical point is the recognition in the phrase at the end of part (1), "to the extent the damage is caused mainly by one of the other party."[37] This implies that the causation might be relative to the input of either the plaintiff or the defendant. That implies that causation is not an all-or-nothing proposition as maintained in the common law tradition. Causation comes in degrees. The only way to account for this idea is to appeal to the folksy principle of causal energy. The but/for test simply will not account for the BGB's radical innovation.

Innovation is the keyword. There was nothing like this in the French Civil Code.[38] The notion of relative causation is an achievement of the German tradition. Nonetheless, there were interesting signs of this movement in the California Civil Code. Article 1714(a) provides, in its relevant part:

> Everyone is responsible, not only for the result of his or her willful acts, but also for an injury occasioned to another by his or her want of ordinary care or skill in the management of his or her property or person, except so far as the latter has, willfully or by want of ordinary care, brought the injury upon himself or herself.[39]

The language that is suggestively parallel to the BGB's is the phrase "except so far as the latter . . . brought the injury. . . ."[40] This also sounds like relative

[36] Burgerliches Gesetzbuch [BGB] art. 254 (W. Ger.).
[37] *Id.*
[38] *See generally* C. Civ.
[39] Cal. Civ. Code § 1714(a) (2018).
[40] *Id.*

causation based on causal energy. The critical case interpreting this provision is *Li v. Yellow Cab* decided in 1975.[41] Before turning to that case, there are a few things to note about the California Civil Code. First, codes in the American tradition are not succinct, well-drafted provisions that provide the foundation of legal thought and research.[42] They are generally verbose and rambling summaries of the common law. They purport to abolish the prior case law, but instead they are ensconced in it. Nevertheless, the California Civil Code had a certain *je ne sai quoi* to it. Namely there was widespread belief that it derived from the French legal tradition and therefore incorporated civil law principles that might be different from the common law's winner-take-all frame of mind.[43]

The Li case arose from a routine travel accident in downtown Los Angeles.[44] Ms. Li was presumed to be contributorily negligent.[45] Therefore, plaintiff's lawyers had considerable incentive to argue for an interpretation of Article 1714 that would support something like comparative negligence. In fact, there was a considerable literature at the time arguing in favor of comparative negligence as a matter of principle, and many states had already adopted it by legislation.[46] One of the issues was whether the proper method of change of the rule was through legislative action or whether judicial interpretation of the language would suffice.[47] There is another point to keep in mind about American legislation. In the positivist tradition—where law is the command of the sovereign—the tendency is to prioritize legislative intent.

The opinion line of Justice Sullivan's opinion tells it all: "In this case we address the grave and recurrent question of whether we should judicially declare no longer applicable in California courts—the doctrine of contributory negligence, which bars all recovery when the plaintiff's negligent conduct has contributed as a legal cause in any degree to the harm suffered by him, and hold that it must give way to a system of comparative negligence, which assesses liability in direct proportion to fault."[48]

41 13 Cal. 3d 804 (1975).

42 *See* Aniceto Masferrer, *Defense of the Common Law Against Postbellum American Codification: Reasonable and Fallacious Argumentation*, 50 Am. J. Legal Hist. 355 n.2 (2010).

43 *See generally* Caroline Bermeo Newcombe, *The Origin and Civil Law Foundation of the Community Property System, Why California Adopted It, and Why Community Property Principles Benefit Women*, 11 RRGC 1 (2011).

44 *Li*, 13 Cal. 3d at 804.

45 *Id.*

46 *See id.* at 813.

47 *Id.*

48 *Id.* at 808.

Here, the points are readily apparent: (1) this does not appear to be about a provision in the Civil Code but about a doctrine called "contributory negligence"; (2) the emphasis on the word "judicial" suggests that if the common law approach is defective, the legislature should change it; (3) the phrase "legal cause" is unusual but understandable; (4) comparative negligence imposes liability in proportion to fault.

The last line becomes the basis for the court's holding, which is most unfortunate. Comparative negligence, as the California court and presumably the advocates for reform understood it, was not about comparative causal contribution—as found in BGB Art. 254—but about comparative fault in the abstract.[49] But that principle strikes me as slightly incoherent. You find enormous indications of fault that have no causal relevance. Suppose Ms. Li had no brakes, no windshield wipers, and no functioning headlights. But Yellow Cab rammed her on the side where none of these factors were relevant to the accident. Her non-causal negligence should be irrelevant, as indeed non-causal contributory negligence was irrelevant. Perhaps, this does not matter in practice but subsequent courts would be not be well-informed to read the word "fault" to include non-causal factors.

With respect to the supposed influence of French law over the decision, the court cites a comment made in the annotation to a Louisiana code provision and the French Civil Code sec. 1813,[50] which led it to the provision in Louisiana, the single state in the Union that more or less adopted civil law thinking. But the code references are irrelevant. *Faute commune*—the French analogue to comparative negligence—was not added to the French code until 1879, after enactment of the California Civil Code.[51]

The remarkably honest quality of the California court's opinion is that it rejected many of the arguments that would have made its task much easier. The point was that adopting comparative negligence in California was not implied by the Code; nor was it the intent of the framers, and not really predicated on civil law influences.[52] It was not based on a theory of relative causation but on the less satisfactory theory of comparative fault. The guide to their decision was the widespread literature rejecting the common law approach and favoring a change to comparative fault. But why not wait, and let the legislature do it?

[49] *See id.*
[50] *Id.* at 818–19.
[51] *Id.*
[52] *See id.*

At this point the Court introduces a technique called prospective overruling, generally reserved for constitutional changes.[53] The majority recognized that many litigants relied on the common law system in preparing their cases for trial, and therefore held that their opinion applied "to all cases in which trial has not begun before the date this decision becomes final in this court," but not to those already begun.[54] As in many other respects, the California Supreme Court was at the cutting edge of activist judicial thinking.

Our survey of the developments of theory in American tort law, all of which are highly relevant to application of the Alien Tort Claims Act, comes toward a close with our consideration of the crown jewel of the parade on the theory of causation, *Palsgraf v. Long Island Railroad Company*[55] This is another exploding package case reminiscent of the squib that prompted Blackstone's analysis of direct causation at the beginning of our survey. The difference is that now we encounter a path of reasoning in Justice Cardozo's opinion for the majority that declares, in finale, "the law of causation, remote or proximate, is thus foreign to the case before us."[56] That facts of the case were simple. The guards of the Long Island Railroad helped a man carrying a package board the train. The package carrying fireworks fell and exploded, causing a scale on the other side of the station to fall on the wholly unsuspecting Mrs. Palsgraf, who sued for her injuries.[57]

Justice Cardozo's opinion for the four-vote majority is eloquently written, perhaps too eloquently, to recognize the simple fact that the railroad's negligence could be readily established for having pushed the passenger in boarding, perhaps even for not providing greater security checks on those entering the station. The court concedes that, that might have been negligence against the passenger.[58] If so, why should Ms. Palsgraf not recover?

Cardozo's reflections on this point generate a theory of tort law that precede an analysis of causation. The key point is that negligence is a relational idea. It is negligence toward a specific person. It is simply what a reasonable person would do to someone to whom he owes a duty not to harm. The duty is based on specific expectations of harm, or more eloquently in Justice Cardozo's words: "[T]he orbit of the danger as disclosed to the eye of

[53] *See id.* at 813; Walter V. Schaefer, *The Control of "Sunbursts": Techniques of Prospective Overruling*, 42 N.Y.U. L. REV. 631 (1967).
[54] *See Li*, 13 Cal. at 829.
[55] 248 N.Y. 339 (1928).
[56] *Id.* at 346.
[57] *Id.*
[58] *Id.* at 355–56.

reasonable vigilance would be the orbit of the duty."[59] Cardozo also stressed the probable negligence of the guard toward property.[60] For Mrs. Palsgraf, the alleged negligence was to her person.

The essential reasoning is that negligence in the abstract is not a tort. It must result in the commission of a wrong, and the wrong must be to a specific person for a specific harm. The reasoning is a bit circular because tort means wrong in French. Therefore, Cardozo's reasoning boils down to one claim, namely that the tort of negligence must be established by the violation of the duty of reasonable care toward a specific person. The Court cites *Scott v. Shepherd*, but the reasoning shows how far we have come since the days of trespass and direct vs. indirect causation.[61] Justice Andrews begins his influential dissent by falling back on the more traditional definition of negligence as an "act which unreasonably threatens the safety of others" and thus takes the real question to be proximate cause, a term of art.[62] This theme is repeated in various ways and is well supported by case citations. In the end, the diverging opinions come down to whether negligence is a purely private tort, as defined by Justice Cardozo, or a wrong to the public, as considered by Justice Andrews.

The import of Justice Andrew's conception of tort law is that we must cope in all but the simplest cases with the concept of causation, and indeed with a theory of causal energy as I have outlined the concept in this chapter. To explain the concept of causal energy and how it dissipates into the surrounding environment, Andrews invokes the metaphor of a stream: "The spring . . . is joined by tributary after tributary. The river, reaching the ocean, comes from a hundred sources. No man may say whence any drop of water is derived. They are [eventually] so commingled that all distinction is lost."[63]

This is a distinctive style of legal reasoning, one that is more suited to the artificial legal task of trying to fathom when causal energy becomes "so commingled" with other sources of energy "that all distinction is lost." My sympathies in this watershed dispute are with Justice Andrews, but that is of less importance than the fundamental questions of (1) whether we must address the issue of causation as part of the question of assessing liability and (2) what that conception of causation means in legal terms.

[59] *Id.* at 343.
[60] *Id.*
[61] *Palsgraf,* 248 N.Y. at 346.
[62] *Id.* at 347 (Andrews, J., dissenting).
[63] *Id.* at 352.

I confess that I fell under the influence of Justice Cardozo's eloquence and his preference for a relational theory of torts in the single article of influence I ever wrote about tort law.[64] The thrust of the article was to critique the economic analysis of law that threatened, at that time, to take over the academic field of tort law. The challenge for many academics in the last 50 years has been to rescue tort law as a repository of our best intuitions of corrective justice as opposed to the influential views, stemming mainly from Guido Calabresi and Richard Posner, which have attempted to reduce all of tort law to a calculus of efficiency.[65]

The argument of my 1972 article is that we can restate the corrective justice function of tort law under a paradigm of reciprocity.[66] The claim is that someone, causing a non-reciprocal risk to others, say, by flying airplanes over residential property, is liable for the consequence of a crash. If the plaintiff is also flying a plane, the risks would be reciprocal and therefore there would no liability. This explains why airplane owners are strictly liable for ground damage but not liable, in the absence of faulty, for mid-air collisions or for harm to passengers.

The most significant case explained by the paradigm is one of the great chestnuts of tort law, *Vincent v. Lake Erie Trans. Co.*[67] A shipowner moored his vessel to a wharf in Lake Erie as a storm was imminent. As the intensity of the storm compounded, the shipowner retied the ship to stabilize it in the storm. As a result, the banging of the ship damaged the dock and the owner sued to recover. The question is why.

Under the circumstances, the shipowner was acting reasonably to protect his property. One interesting argument for recovery, developed in German jurisprudence, is that because the dock owner would not be entitled to release the ship into the pending storm, which would inevitably result in its destruction, he should receive compensation for the loss of his right of self-defense.

Thus, an applicable provision under the BGB would be found in the book on property rather than the law of obligations. Looking at the problem as a matter of corrective justice, my argument was that the shipowner imposed a non-reciprocal risk on the dock owner and therefore should pay for the consequence. The basic principle under this theory is a theory about personal

64 George P. Fletcher, *Fairness and Utility in Tort Theory*, 85 HARV. L. REV. 537 (1972) [hereinafter *Fairness*].

65 *Id.* at 531 n.1.

66 *Id.* at 542.

67 109 Minn. 456 (1910).

security that traded on John Rawls's then just published *A Theory of Justice* and the equal entitlement of all persons to the same basic liberty.[68] My argument was that we are all entitled to the same basic security compatible with a like security to all.[69] A non-reciprocal risk violated our right to basic security.

This is the point at which I now recognize the influence of Cardozo's opinion in *Palsgraf*.[70] Our entitlement to universal security is violated merely by the expectation of harm. It is not a problem of causation as Cardozo claims. It is about the relationship between the shipowner and dock owner. One imposes a non-reciprocal risk on the other, and a result becomes liable in principle.

In a devastating critique in the 2003 *Notre Dame Law Review*, Professor Heidi Hurd claims that without the element of causation, there can be no coherent theory of tort liability.[71] She argues that the notions of risk and reciprocity are infinitely manipulable. And there is no doubt that she is right about much of that. The critique is worth reading because it is so funny and personal. Alas, I never properly responded to Professor Hurd's critique. In my 2008 book, *Tort Liability for Human Rights Abuses*, my focus is on the influence of the ATCA with perhaps undue attention to some other issues of tort theory.[72] As we return to the field of criminal liability and in particular liability under the Rome Statute, we should summarize some of the elementary points about causation. It turns out that the principle of causation is essential for a sound theory either in tort law or criminal law. The elements of causation can be summarized under the principle that B will occur if and only if A occurs. A refers to a necessary condition and B to a sufficient condition. The element of necessary condition has led to many puzzles, such as whether only actions can cause harm, whether omissions can be causes. We conclude in line with H.L.A. Hart and Tony Honoré's classic test, unexpected omission can indeed by causes.

The problem of sufficient conditions derives from the "but for" test. The problems posed by this test are legion, and we found that to solve of them we needed to use the unscientific concept of causal energy.

68 *See generally* John Rawls, A Theory of Justice (1971).

69 Fairness, *supra* note 64, at 544.

70 *See generally Palsgraf*, 109 Minn. 456 (1910).

71 Heidi M. Hurd, *Nonreciprocal Risk Imposition, Unjust Enrichment, and the Foundations of Tort Law: A Critical Celebration of George Fletcher's Theory of Tort Law*, 78 Notre Dame L. Rev. 711, 718 (2003).

72 George Fletcher, Tort Liability for Human Rights Abuses (2008).

As a transition example to investigation causal issues in the law of war under the Rome Statute, consider the problem of alternative sufficient conditions, illustrated in this famous hypothetical case. Two independent actors plan to kill a victim about to set forth on a hike through the desert. The first fills the hiker's canteen with poison. The second drills a hole in the canteen. The hiker dies, but who causes it? The victim would have died as a result of the poison, or he would have died because of the hole in the canteen. It was also a sufficient cause of his death that there was no alternative source of water in the desert. All the alternatives satisfy the "but for" test.

The law of war is replete with alternative sufficient causes. Two or three distinct battalions converge on the village at the same time. Any one of them is sufficient for the pillaging and the mass harm that occurs.

The "but for" test is rarely up to the task but the notion of causal energy does not always work either. There seems to be the indispensable element of shifting reliance on one concept or another, as the occasion arises. This is not very scientific and should leave us with a sense of modesty about our task. We should be grateful that the Rome Statute does not attempt to define causation. The notion is best left to the attempts of scholars to make sense out of this morass of philosophical problems. The least we can say is that a good advocate will be aware of the conflicting theories and use the one that bests the needs of the case.

Although these reflections on causation in negligence cases are important, they might be of greater value in analyzing liability under the ATCA than under the Rome Statute, where the primary mode of liability is intentional. The question is how the problem of causation differs in cases of intentional crime.

Is the metaphor of causal energy still apt? I argued in this direction with regard to intentional torts in my 1972 *Harvard Law Review* article, but I think I was squeezing the concept in my overarching notion of non-reciprocal risk taking.[73] Even if that distortion in the case of intentional torts might have been excusable, the same arguments do not work for intentional crimes. First, the concept of causation in intentional crime is the primary case, not an afterthought to the analysis of negligence. The vast majority of crimes are committed intentionally, and only a few are subject to liability for negligence.

A clear indication of the different structure of intentional criminality is the role of *attempt*, defined in the Rome Statute in Article 25(3)(f)[74] and the

[73] *See* Fairness, *supra* note 64.
[74] Rome Statute, *supra* note 1, art. 25(3)(f).

subject of extended analysis in chapter 10. For now, the principal points are that (1) there is no crime of attempt in the case of negligent conduct, and (2) the attempt is under the control of the agent but the subsequent causal implications are not. That is, the suspect can aim and fire the gun, but he has no control over the path of the bullet. The control of the agent is critical for the theory of deterrence as the justification of punishment. The threat of sanctions can deter whether the agent unleashes a deadly force, but they cannot influence the course of nature. Looking back on our analysis of negligence in cases ranging from *Yamashita* and Article 28 of the Rome Statute[75] to the extensive analysis of tort law in this chapter, we assumed that the negligent conduct encompassed the occurrence of the harm. That is, the actor was negligent with regard to the harm itself. Intentional conduct has a different structure, one to be explored in chapter 7.[76]

Thus, we are left with the issue of causation in the case of intentional crimes, however different this problem may be from the foregoing analysis of causation in tort law. The most important point is one that should resonate with the structure and purpose of the Rome Statute, namely the nearly sacred status of victims, as expressed in the Preamble.[77] The problem of victims' rights concerns us in the next chapter.[78] Now the critical point is the impact of victim status on the analysis of causation. In referring to the status of victims as nearly sacred, I am addressing the fact that we do not consider the causal input of the victim in analyzing the causal contribution of the defendant. The victim can go jogging at midnight in Central Park and then be the victim of rape, as actually happened in the late 1980s.[79] The victim is assumed to be innocent, a causal blank slate. The victim could be a Jew in Germany in 1938, refusing to leave his home, and suffering deportation to Auschwitz. Blaming the victim in these cases is considered an outrage.

Why does the victim receive this special treatment in the field of intentional crime? The best answer I have found that trades on the semi-sacred status of the victim is the concept of the temple sacrifice or *korban* as explicated in the first five chapters of Leviticus.[80] The sacrificial animal must be pure, and thus so far as we think by analogy with the biblical *korban*, we

[75] *Supra* ch. III.
[76] *Infra* ch. VII.
[77] Rome Statute, *supra* note 1, pmbl.
[78] *Infra* ch. V.
[79] *But cf.* Joshua Kleinfeld, *A Theory of Criminal Victimization*, 65 Stan. L. Rev. 1087, 1098 n.42 (2013).
[80] Leviticus 1–5.

assume that the victim is also pure, innocent, non-responsible for becoming the sacrificial object of the criminal act.

In a sophisticated article, Jan van Dyke, a Dutch criminologist, picks up the argument I first made on this point in a lecture and develops it into a sophisticated account of Jesus as a sacrificial lamb.[81] From his point of view, the stunning feature of Jesus as korban is that it explains how Jesus could be both a victim of crime while the crucifixion is revered as an act of Christian redemption.

For all its special characteristics, the problem of causation in intentional crime still faces many of the problems that arose in our analysis of negligence, for example, the problem of intervening causes breaking the causal chain. The case of Bernhard Goetz illustrates the problem. Goetz shot four young blacks in the New York subway in the late 1980s. One of the them ended up paralyzed for life arguably as a result of negligent treatment he received in the hospital.[82] The argument of breaking "the causal chain" rarely works when in criminal cases.

Even if an intentional killing in the hospital might not break the causal chain, say, if a mob boss is subject to an attempted assassination and while recuperation in the hospital, he faces renewed attacks that kills him. Something comparable to the arguments of Justices Cardozo and Andrews comes into play here, but with an expansive view of foreseeability. This might be due to the heightened causal energy of the initial attempt. The important thing about the structure of intentional crimes is that although the attempt might be the foundation of the crime, the victim's death is indispensable for a charge of homicide. The problem is that the death might occur sometime later. The common law attempted to cope with this problem by imposing a time limit on the gap between the action and the death. The common law rule was that the victim had to die within a year and day of the initial assault.[83] In the late twentieth century, many states abolished the rule by legislation.[84] In a famous case that went all the way to the U.S. Supreme Court, *Rogers v. Tennessee*, the defendant claimed that abolition of the rule violated the due process clause, specifically as an ex post facto law.[85] In fact, in his

[81] Jan Van Dijk, *In the Shadow of Christ? On the Use of the Word "Victim" for Those Affected by Crimes*, 27 CRIM. JUST. ETHICS 13, 15 (2008).

[82] *See* People v. Goetz, 68 N.Y.2d 96 (N.Y. Sup. Ct. 1986).

[83] Jeffrey F. Ghent, *Homicide as Affected by Lapse of Time Between Injury and Death*, 60 A.L.R.3d 1323.

[84] *Id.*

[85] *See* Rogers v. Tennessee, 532 U.S. 451 (2001).

case, there was no legislative change but rather a wise decision by the legislature to abstain from trying to define the relevant rule of causation. The court affirmed the Tennessee conviction, but in one of his classic dissents, Justice Scalia relied on the ex post facto clause of the Constitution.[86]

The winning argument in the case seems to be that the rule was not a rule of causation at all but merely a rule of evidence about causation. With the advance of the forensic sciences, rules of thumb about this kind of evidence should give way to more sophisticated understandings of the cause of death.

A shift in the rules of evidence is merely procedural and does not affect the substantive principle that the offender must cause the death of the victim. In terms of the Rome Statute, a change in the law of evidence does not compromise the rule *nullum crimen sine lege*.[87]

There are several messages to derive from this chapter. First, causation pretends to be a scientific concept, but in the end, the analysis boils down to the mythical notion of causal energy. Second, the notion of causal energy explains the rise of comparative negligence in tort law. Third, we are left with some doubts about whether comparative causation should be relevant in international criminal law.

[86] *Id.* at 469; U.S. Const. art. I, § 9, cl. 3.
[87] Rome Statute, *supra* note 1, art. 22.

5
Victims and Offenders

The victim is invisible in the definition of crime but omnipresent in the prosecution and sentencing of offenders. In the International Legal Order, in particular, the victim is front and center, both in the ICC and in lawsuits under the Alien Torts Claim Act. The reasons for this are both obvious and, we hope, resonant with deeper meaning. The ICC's purpose of overcoming impunity of offenders in their home countries puts victims at the forefront in a way in which no national legal system does, and for tort recovery, the injured plaintiff is an elementary plank (building block?) in the cause of action.

Crime is typically defined by the actions of the offender, and the victim is an incidental consequence. There are many victimless crimes, such as those in the sexual and reproductive arena, which in the United States at least are no longer subject to prosecution on constitutional grounds.[1] The argument for decriminalization is the privacy of the offender, but privacy of the victim can, paradoxically, become an argument for criminalization under the right to a private life codified in the European Convention on Human Rights.[2]

The Korban and the Duality of Victimhood. Before turning to the more specific role of victims in criminal cases, we should take note of the quasi-religious significance of the dual sense of victimhood as recognized in most languages of Western societies. The victim appears both in criminal court and in religious contexts such as the victim of sacrifice. The dual sense is seen in the Hebrew word korban, the German opher, the Arabic udhiya, the Russian zhertva, and in the Latin basis for the English word, victima. Indeed, this is true in all languages except a few that seek to avoid the religious connotations by referring to the victim as the "injured person."

The implication of this association is that the victim is assumed to be blameless and pure as was required for the temple sacrifice according to the book of Leviticus.[3] Thus, we can explain why the contributory negligence

[1] *See* Lawrence v. Texas, 539 U.S. 558 (2003); Griswold v. Connecticut, 381 U.S. 479 (1965).

[2] Convention for the Protection of Human Rights and Fundamental Freedoms, art. 8, 213 U.N.T.S. 221 (Nov. 5, 1950).

[3] *See* Leviticus 1–5 (KJV).

The Grammar of Criminal Law: Volume Two: International Criminal Law. George P. Fletcher.

of the victim is not considered by way of mitigation of the defendant's guilt. Classic examples are Goetz's sitting down amidst four seemingly dangerous young thugs[4] and the Central Park Jogger's taking her runs at night against all safety precautions.[5] The concept of victimhood also arises in warfare—although not in a routine case of jus in bello, but there might be victims of surprise attacks, war crimes, nuclear bombings, the use of chemical weapons, and the like.

The most dramatic application of this duality arises in the Christian interpretation of the crucifixion at Calvary. For a brilliant exposition of Jesus as both a sacrifice to redeem humanity and a victim of persecution, see the article by the Dutch criminologist Jan van Dijk.[6]However, we should note some doubts about referring to the plaintiff in tort disputes as the victim. This usage is not entirely consistent with the theory about the Korban and purity. The plaintiff in tort disputes, as we have discussed at some length, need not be free from blame, and indeed the evolution toward comparative negligence encourages a recognition of fault on both sides. In the pivotal California case, *Li v. Yellow Cab*,[7] discussed in chapter 4, establishing comparative negligence in the state, the court reasoned that the aspect of negligence subject to comparative is relative fault. This hardly makes sense, as noted earlier, unless the negligence at stake has a causal impact.[8] If we insist on a purely causal interpretation of the plaintiff's contributory fault, we can reconcile tort litigation with the theory we have advanced about the Korban.

The boundaries of victimhood. In the course of litigation in high-profile criminal cases in the United States, there is often controversy about the proper use of the term "victim." Of course, prosecutors would always like to refer to the witness as the victim, but that is precisely the matter in dispute, and the defense should always object. In the *Goetz* case, Judge Crane ordered the lawyers to refer to the accused as the "young man." Even after a verdict, there can be controversy about the concept of victimhood, depending on the kind of defense interposed. If the defense is a justification defense, then the injured party's use of force is lawful, and therefore it is a bit odd to refer to party suffering the legitimate force as the victim. If the issue is a matter

[4] *See* People v. Goetz, 68 N.Y.2d 96, 100 (N.Y. Sup. Ct. 1986).

[5] *But cf.* Joshua Kleinfeld, *A Theory of Criminal Victimization*, 65 Stan. L. Rev. 1087, 1098 n.42 (2013).

[6] Jan Van Dijk, *In the Shadow of Christ? On the Use of the Word "Victim" for Those Affected by Crimes*, 27 Crim. Just. Ethics 13, 15 (2008).

[7] 13 Cal. 3d 804 (1975).

[8] *Supra* ch. IV.

of excuse, in insanity or duress cases, the injured party can still properly be called a victim. In the midst of the trial, none of this is established. Therefore, even if the defendant has a good claim of self-defense, he still cannot refer to himself, properly, as the victim of an unlawful attack.

The role of the victim at trial and at sentencing is another matter of dispute. In common law proceedings, the tendency is to remove victims as well as other possible witnesses from the courtroom until it is time for them to testify. This makes a certain amount of sense if the objective of the defense might be to elicit contradictions among the witnesses' testimony. In a civil trial based in the French or German tradition, the victims are better represented at trial because first the victim can be a civil party joining his suit with the criminal case, and further, because the system of professional judging relies upon the judge's expertise to sort out possible conflicts among the parties.[9] Thus, the adversarial system seems to be less beneficial for victims at trial.

At sentencing, however, common law victims may have an advantage. They can make personal victim impact statements, which in my view are inconsistent with any rational purpose of sentencing, and might fulfill victims' desire to seek vengeance or even to forgive the accused. If any victims matter in the criminal process, say as the beneficiaries of deterrence, they are future victims taken as a composite of the population. Victims in homicide cases are a special problem for purposes of these statements. First, there is a problem of defining who the victim is and second, why that person should have any bearing on either the finding of guilt or the sentence.

The role of victims has converted the criminal law into a political instrument that must be responsive to particular constituencies. The process probably started with the *desaparecidos*—the forcibly "disappeared"—in Argentina of the 1980s and the anguished marches by the *Madres* and *Abuelas* (Mother and Grandmothers) insisting on justice by prosecuting the offenders.[10] This is one of the factors that generated the concept of *impunidad* (impunity) and the necessity of prosecuting every serious crime, either

[9] *See, e.g.*, John H. Langbein, *The German Advantage in Civil Procedure*, 52 U. Chi. L. Rev. 823 (1985).

[10] *See* Rita Arditti, Searching for Life: The Grandmothers of the Plaza De Mayo and the Disappeared Children of Argentina 1 (1999); Ronald Dworkin, *Introduction* to Comision Nacional Sobre La Desparicion de Personas, Nunca Mas: The Report of the Agentine National Commission on the Disappeared at xi (1986).

domestically or internationally. On the surface of things, the Rome Statute[11] does not appear to be responsive to particular communities of victims, which as we will see, is the history of victims' rights in the United States. Yet the predecessors to the Rome Statute—namely the regional courts such as the ICTY and ICTR, were obviously responsive not just to victims in general but to the political necessity of responding to the victimization of particular groups, such as Croats[12] and Tutsis.[13]

1. The Rome Statute—from a Comparative Perspective

The proceedings envisioned before the ICC are, as in most cases, a mélange of common law and civil law principles. Take, for example, sentencing and the relevance of victim impact statements at the post-trial phase. The idea that the sentence should be prescribed in a separate hearing is a common law innovation, a practice that was employed by the ICTY and was designed to permit judges to consider a range of evidence not admissible at trial.[14] This evidence might include not only hearsay evidence, victim impact statements, but also prior convictions as an indication of dangerousness.[15] Since the philosophy of sentencing in the ICC is obscure (whether retribution, deterrence, incapacitation, or rehabilitation are prioritized), the factors determining the proper number of years appear to depend entirely on the discretion of the

[11] Rome Statute for the International Criminal Court, July 17, 1998, 2187 U.N.T.S. 3; U.N. Diplomatic Conference of Plenipotentiaries on the Establishment of an International Court, U.N. Doc. A/Conf.183/9 [hereinafter Rome Statute].

[12] *See* United Nations Int'l Crim. Tribunal for the Former Yugoslavia, http://www.icty.org/ (last visited Jun. 15, 2018) ("The International Criminal Tribunal for the former Yugoslavia (ICTY) was a United Nations court of law that dealt with war crimes that took place during the conflicts in the Balkans in the 1990s.").

[13] *The Genocide*, United Nations Int'l Residual Mechanism for Crim. Tribunals, http://unictr.unmict.org/en/genocide (last visited Jun. 15, 2018) ("Genocide, crimes against humanity and war crimes were perpetrated on a horrific scale, primarily against Tutsi civilians and moderate Hutus.").

[14] *See* Allison Marston Danner, *Constructing a Hierarchy of Crimes in International Criminal Law Sentencing*, 87 Va. L. Rev. 415, 426 n.37 (2001); Mirjan Damaska, *Evidentiary Barriers to Conviction and Two Models of Criminal Procedure*, 121 U. Pa. L. Rev. 506, 536 n.65 (1973) ("The continental trial is not bifurcated into the guilt determinative and sentencing stage, as is the case in America.").

[15] *See* ICTR Rules of Procedure and Evidence, rule 85(A)(vi), at http://www.ictr.org (basic documents) (last modified Nov. 3, 2000); ICTY Rules of Procedure and Evidence, Rule 85(A)(vi), at http://www.un.org/icty/basic/rpe/IT32rev18.htm (last modified Dec. 13, 2000) (stating that either party may present evidence that "may assist the Trial Chamber in determining an appropriate sentence"); *id.*

Trial Chamber.[16] It is common, by the way, for codified criminal law to remain agnostic about the purposes of punishment. This is true in the Model Penal Code[17] and, so far as I know, of the European codes. Clarity about these matters is reserved for philosophers like Kant and Bentham.[18]

The confusion about the purposes of punishment come through clearly in the Preamble of the Rome Statute, which insists that the most serious crimes not go unpunished.[19] Why should punishment be an important principle? The only reason suggested is that ending impunity would "contribute to the prevention of such crimes."[20] No one has ever offered convincing proof that punishment deters crimes, especially among the kinds of dictators and collaborators who might be tried before the ICC and who are likely to think of themselves as above both local law and international law. After all, the general principle of jurisdiction in the ICC is that the local governments are "unwilling or unable" to try the suspects.[21] If preventing future crimes were the purpose of the Court, then the most important means to accomplish this end would be the following: publicity of the Court's judgments (including possible misrepresentation of those judgments) and a high probability of prosecution. Neither of these seem to be a top priority of the Hague.

It is not fashionable these days to insist on retribution as the proper guide to punishment, namely in the strict Kantian sense that the punishment fit the crime and that no offender be allowed to escape his just deserts. A strict Kantian system might lead to some forms of punishment that are considered cruel and unusual by contemporary standards (e.g., castration for rape, the death penalty for homicide), but at least the philosopher from Königsberg offered a coherent principle of justice governing the sentence.[22] Deterrence is not a principle of justice but rather a utilitarian standard that, in Kantian terms, engages in the evil of treating of the offender as a means to a social end.[23] The principle of Kantian punishment is to treat the offender as an end in himself. This is a sound philosophical principle but difficult to execute in practice, and raises questions such as how does one justify the common

[16] *See id.*

[17] *See* Michele Cotton, *Back with a Vengeance: The Resilience of Retribution as an Articulated Purpose of Criminal Punishment*, 37 Am. Crim. L. Rev. 1313, 1318–24 (2000).

[18] For an earlier discussion of these philosophers, see ch. III.

[19] *See* Rome Statute, *supra* note 11, pmbl.

[20] *Id.*

[21] Rome Statute, *supra* note 11, art. 17.

[22] Immanuel Kant, The Metaphysics of Morals 130 (Mary Gregor ed. & trans., Cambridge University Press 1996) (1797).

[23] *Id.* at 473.

mode of punishment in the modern world of imprisonment? The paradox of punishment in the modern world is that we believe that it is necessary, but we have no coherent theory about what it should be and how to measure the proper degree of punishment.

Yet it might be true that the Kantian system rules us from the grave. The imperative of ending impunity, regardless of the cost and consequences, evokes the spirit of retributive justice but then pairs this imperative with the widely shared pragmatic ambition of deterring future offenses. This mixing and matching of the purposes of punishment is characteristic of modern legislation. Muddling through is all that we can expect in a world where we feel the imperative of ending impunity, but we are confused about what to do with offenders.

The problem might lie in the distinct purposes of the public, particularly the victims and their families, one the one hand, and the practically minded professionals who draft the codes and manage the system of trial and punishment, on the other hand. The public might seek vengeance, which they make seem less primitive by claiming that at stake is a principle of justice. The professionals, on the other hand, are aware of the enormous costs of trials and incarceration and find no personal gratification in seeing justice done for its own sake. The unsubstantiated principle of deterrence lends an air of practical purpose to the system of trial and punishment.

The major issue that we confront in interpreting the Rome Statute is whether the purpose of the ICC should protect individual victims or collective victims defined as they are in Article 6 on Genocide by their nationality, ethnicity, race, religion, or analogous factors (e.g., sexual orientation, drug addiction).[24] If we are leaving aside War Crimes for the moment, it seems fairly clear that the purpose of the Statute is to protect collective victims. There are several clues to this in the definitions of Aggression and Crimes against humanity as well as Genocide.

In Crimes Against Humanity, the introductory clause refers to the requirements of (a) a widespread of systematic attack against (b) any civilian population.[25] It is hard to make sense of these terms as reference to anything but collective victims. This is followed up by the lists of "acts" that constitute a violation of Article 7. The concepts of extermination, enslavement, and enforced disappearance of persons are not coherent unless they are referring

[24] Rome Statute, *supra* note 11, art. 6.
[25] Rome Statute, *supra* note 11, art. 7.

to "groups" as the Genocide provision refers to them. Yet, admittedly, some of the provisions of Article 7 could apply to individual victims, for example, murder, torture, rape, or the catch-all provision, Art. 7(1)(k): "other inhuman acts of a similar character intentionally causing great suffering, or serious injury to body or to mental or physical health."[26] In summary, Article 7 is ambivalent about whether in principle its focus is on collective or individual victims. Yet I argue that the general purpose should be understood to protect collective victims.

In the Crime of Aggression, as defined by Article 8*bis* at the Kampala Conference in 2010, the objective is rather obviously collective victims.[27] We just need note the language used: "invasion" of another state, "bombardment," "blockade," "attack by the armed forces," etc.[28] There is nothing in this provision that would indicate a concern about individual victims. I recommend these changes be made, yet in an earlier discussion of Article 8*bis*, I praised the drafters for recognizing individual as opposed to collective responsibility for the perpetrators. It seems to be clear, as a result, that the focus on collectives or individuals need not be the same when we are considering perpetrators or victims. The combination of individual perpetrators and collective victims would be a novel idea in criminal law and worthy of serious consideration.

Finally, with regard to War Crimes, in Article 8, we have a fairly clear recognition of individual victimhood—at least within the confines of this Article. These are many of the same crimes mentioned above in discussing Crimes Against Humanity, in particular willful killing (odd change in wording from "murder" in Article 7); homicide; torture; and, in general, causing excessive suffering and destruction of property.[29] Yet, there is a mystery in thinking, about how individuals as agents can commit war crimes. The notion of war presupposes an appropriate collective unit engaged in armed conflict against another collective. Individuals acting alone cannot commit war crimes. They might be vandals, guerillas, terrorists, but that does not mean that they are acting on behalf of a military force engaged in armed conflict.

To understand the notion of the relevant collective agent in armed conflict, we have to refer, as does Article 8 itself, to the four Geneva Conventions of

[26] *Id.*

[27] *See* Resolution Adopting Aggression Amendments to Rome Statute, Rev. Conf. of the Rome Statute, Kampala, Uganda, May 31–June 11, 2010, Annex I, art. 8bis, 13th plen. mtg., I.C.C. Doc. RC/Res.6 (June 11, 2010).

[28] *Id.*

[29] Rome Statute, *supra* note 11, art. 8.

1949.[30] The conventions are all treaties among the High Contracting Parties, which means that in principle only states and their governments are bound by the treaties.[31] The Geneva Conventions are themselves influenced by the Lieber Code of 1863 in the United States,[32] which contains the classic definition of war in Article 20:

> Public war is a state of armed hostility between sovereign nations or governments. It is a law and requisite of civilized existence that men live in political, continuous societies, forming organized units, called states or nations, whose constituents bear, enjoy, suffer, advance and retrograde together, in peace and in war.[33]

Again this supports the principle that only states and their governments engage in warfare. This means that the identity of the individual soldier is submerged in the collective and bears no individual responsibility for ordinary killings in the course of the war. This is critically important because many distinguished theorists have argued that if the initial outbreak of the war is illegal under Article 51 of the UN Charter (jus ad bellum), then every killing in the course of the war is illegal.[34] This would be an inhumane policy. No soldier could do his duty without anxiety about whether, say the outbreak of war between Israel and Egypt in 1967, was the fault of one side or the other. The cleavage, then, between *jus ad bellum* and *jus in bello*, is fundamental to a humane law of war.[35]

The intriguing problem is how Lieber can be right about the collective nature of war and yet individuals can be liable for their own actions. That is, they must, so to speak, break out of the collective and stand responsible

[30] *Id.*

[31] *See* Geneva Convention for the Amelioration of the Condition of the Wounded and Sick in Armed Forces in the Field, Aug. 12, 1949, 6 U.S.T. 3114, 75 U.N.T.S. 31; Geneva Convention for the Amelioration of the Condition of Wounded, Sick and Shipwrecked Members of Armed Forces at Sea, Aug. 12, 1949, 6 U.S.T. 3217, 75 U.N.T.S. 85; Geneva Convention Relative to the Treatment of Prisoners of War, Aug. 12, 1949, 6 U.S.T. 3316, 75 U.N.T.S. 135; Geneva Convention Relative to the Protection of Civilian Persons in Time of War, Aug. 12, 1949, 6 U.S.T. 3516, 75 U.N.T.S. 287.

[32] *See* Sean Watts, *Reciprocity and the Law of War*, 50 Harv. Int'l L.J. 365, 391 n.144 (2009).

[33] Francis Lieber, *Instructions for the Government of Armies of the United States in the Field*, art. 20 (1863).

[34] *See, e.g.*, Noah Weisbord, *Prosecuting Aggression*, 49 Harv. Int'l L.J. 161, 171 (2008).

[35] *International Humanitarian Law*, Wex Legal Information Institute, https://www.law.cornell.edu/wex/international_humanitarian_law (last visited Aug. 26, 2018) ("International humanitarian law governs both the legality of justifications for war (*jus ad bellum*, or when states can resort to war) and the legality of wartime conduct (*jus in bello*, or how states must behave themselves during war)".).

for what they do as individuals. This is the one of the intriguing, unsolved puzzles about the law of war—along with the mysterious transition from the illegality of *jus ad bellum* to the legality of *jus in bello*.

There is much to be learned from the conflicts that consumed internal American politics from the late 1970s to the mid-1990s and continue, sometimes in aggravated form, in the year 2018. The conflicts originally swirled around the status of gays, blacks, Jews, and women as victims of crime. Of course, the political cases that made the headlines resulted not from specific cases, but the public reactions—often expressed in demonstrations, marches, and even violence—attached to group identities. New groups have become salient in the last two decades, in particular Muslims, but the situation of African Americans in the time of Blacks Lives Matter has become even more apparent.[36] Given the statements of the Trump administration, Mexicans are now forming as a collective against discrimination.[37] The poor—however defined—have also become a suffering minority in a society of ever-increasing income disparities.[38]

In the international arena, much of the work of the special international criminal tribunals derived from ethnic conflict—in particular, in the former Yugoslavia between Serbs and Croats and in the ICTR after the mass victimization of the Tutsis.[39] One is tempted to say that these are conflicts between majority and minority groups but women are not a minority and often, in situations of conflict of concern to the international community, the victims might even constitute a vast majority in their particular country. The best example of this is the crime of apartheid—the only offense that the Rome Statute lists as among other Crimes Against Humanity but also identifies explicitly as "the crime of apartheid."[40]

Let us focus more specifically in the four groups that drew so much attention in American politics of the 1990s.

Gays. In the late 1970s, San Francisco became a major attraction for gays and lesbians as well as hippies and other unconventional groups. Among those who moved there and got elected to the Board of Supervisors were

[36] Niraj Chokshi, *How #BlackLivesMatter Came to Define a Movement*, N.Y. Times (Aug. 22, 2016), https://www.nytimes.com/2016/08/23/us/how-blacklivesmatter-came-to-define-a-movement.html.

[37] Patrick Gillepsie, *Mexicans March Against Trump: "Bad Hombre for the Whole World,"* CNN (Feb. 13, 2017), https://www.cnn.com/2017/02/12/americas/mexico-trump-protest/index.html.

[38] Inequality.org, https://inequality.org/about/ (last visited Jun. 28, 2018).

[39] *See supra* notes 12 & 13.

[40] Rome Statute, *supra* note 11, art. 7(1)(j).

Harvey Milk, an openly gay advocate for gay rights;[41] Carol Ruth Silver, an unconventional colleague of mine from the University of Chicago, who was particularly interested in the rights of the Chinese minority in San Francisco;[42] George Moscone, the Italian American mayor;[43] and, contrary to the general pattern of breaking with convention, there was Dan White, a former police officer.[44] Interestingly, Diane Feinstein, the current senior senator from California, was also on the City Council.[45]

The state had just voted down Proposition 6, which would have precluded homosexual teachers from becoming teachers.[46] It was a long time before the Supreme Court would decide the issue of gay marriage in *Obergefell v. Hodges*[47] and recognize the rights of gays and lesbians to equal protection of the law under the Fourteenth Amendment.[48] To understand the riots that occurred over the killing of Harvey Milk and the conviction of Dan White for manslaughter,[49] we must obviously grasps the conventions of the time.

There is no evidence that Dan White's killing of Harvey Milk (and almost forgotten, George Moscone) was an expression of homophobia, yet that hardly mattered to the gay community's identification with the victim. The death penalty loomed over Dan White on the double-murder charge, but in May 1979, after an 11-day trial, the jury came back with a verdict of manslaughter.[50] Many people thought that if White had killed just Moscone, a straight man, he would have been convicted of murder.[51] But given the climate of the time, adding Milk as a victim could have made some people think that the killing was somehow a service to society.

[41] *See* Randy Shilts, The Mayor of Castro Street: The Life and Times of Harvey Milk (1985).

[42] *See Carol Ruth Silver*, Jewish Women's Archive, https://jwa.org/people/silver-carol (last visited Jun. 18, 2018).

[43] *See* Shilts, *supra* note 41.

[44] *See* John Geluardi, *Dan White's Motive More About Betrayal Than Homophobia*, SF Weekly (Jan. 30, 2008), https://archives.sfweekly.com/sanfrancisco/dan-whites-motive-more-about-betrayal-than-homophobia/Content?oid=2166110.

[45] *Biography*, United States Senator for California, Diane Feinstein (last visited Jun. 19, 2008), https://www.feinstein.senate.gov/public/index.cfm/biography.

[46] *See* Karen M. Harbeck, Gay and Lesbian Educators: Personal Freedoms, Public Constraints (1997).

[47] 135 S. Ct. 2584 (2015).

[48] *Id.* at 2593.

[49] Teneille Brown & Emily Murphy, *Through a Scanner Darkly: Functional Neuroimaging as Evidence of a Criminal Defendant's Past Mental States*, 62 Stan. L. Rev. 1119, 1205 n.319 (2010).

[50] *See* People v. White, 117 Cal. App. 3d 270, 278 (1981).

[51] *See* Daniel Zuaro, *"The Times of Harvey Milk" and Milk*, Odyssey (Apr. 11, 2017), https://www.theodysseyonline.com/the-times-of-harvey-milk-and-milk.

The marching began during the trial, peacefully, but on the night of the verdict, some five thousand people gathered on the streets and began rioting, overturning police cars and setting them on fire.[52] The gay community obviously felt undervalued by the reduction of the charge to the lowest possible finding of criminal homicide, but the real conflict was not about gay rights at all.

Along with other progressive communities, San Francisco of the late 1970s was particularly receptive to the mantra: not bad but mad.[53] In other words, crimes like the double killing by Dan White derived not from their evil sentiments but from their psychiatric condition. The crux of the problem was the way in which the levels of criminal homicide were then defined. Murder, either in the First or Second Degree, requires malice aforethought. A killing without malice aforethought is just manslaughter.[54] The Model Penal Code had attempted to rid the criminal law of the concept of malice, but California, for good or ill, had retained its Penal Code from the nineteenth century.

Even more to the point, psychiatrists were permitted to testify on the issue of malice, even though it is a legal and not a medical concept.[55] Moreover, psychiatrists are called to testify on insanity as a legal concept, distinct from any medical definition.[56] The field of psychiatry has its own assumptions, some of them incompatible with the principle of free will that underlies criminal responsibility.[57] Perhaps one could be a perfectly good psychiatrist and be committed to the principle of biological determinism, namely that individuals who commit crimes never really make a choice to do so. In fact, there is a deep philosophical debate about compatibilism and incompatibilism, namely whether free will is logically compatible with psychological determinism.

[52] *See* Alistair Cooke, *Harvey Milk Killing*, BBC Radio, http://www.bbc.co.uk/programmes/articles/1ycH79Fb1fpX6gvM5WYmGGN/harvey-milk-killing (last visited Jun. 19, 2018).

[53] *See* Michael Corrado, *Automatism and the Theory of Action*, 39 Emory L.J. 1191, 1206 n.44 (1990).

[54] 6 California Criminal Defense Practice § 142.02 (1)(ϵ) (2018).

[55] *See* Kenneth W. Salter, The Trial of Dan White 234 (1991) (Dr. Delman testified that Dan White lacked "the capacity to have malice.").

[56] *See, e.g.*, State v. Guido, 191 A.2d 45, 5253 (N.J. 1963). *See also* John F.W. Meagher, *Crime and Insanity the Legal as Opposed to the Medical View and the Most Commonly Asserted Pleas*, 14 J. Am. Inst. Crim. L. & Criminology 46, 46 (1923).

[57] David L. Faigman et al., Science in the Law: Social and Behavioral Science Issues 4 (2002) ("The underlying principle associated with insanity, lack of responsibility for 'involuntary' actions is ancient. Excusing, and then treating, the insane for their antisocial acts and violent propensities is, perhaps, the mark of a civilized society.").

At the trial of Dan White, one of the psychiatrists, Dr. Jerry Jones, testified to what he must have regarded as a professional belief in determinism, namely that no one ever freely chooses to do anything.[58] If that was his assumption, he should have had no trouble generating testimony favorable to the defendant. But, in fact, the testimony got snared in self-contradiction. Dr. Jones testified that "a person cannot make choices." But then later on cross-examination, the following exchange occurred:

Q: Was he at that time capable, just prior to the shooting, of make a decision: Shall I shoot him or not?
A: You can't not act. So he was capable of acting, behaving, and he was behaving.
Q: He made a choice, didn't he?
A: O.K. I said you cannot not make a decision. Yes, Yes.[59]

In fact, the prosecutor and the psychiatrists stumbled upon a deep philosophical conflict between compatibilism and incompatibilism. This is not an easy matter to resolve, and surely too complicated for lawyers and medical experts in a criminal trial. Even if philosophers were considered expert witnesses, the criminal trial is no place for a philosophical debate.

But with regard to the trial's impact on victims' rights, the critical testimony came from another psychiatrist, Dr. Martin Blinder, who testified in the following pseudoscientific mode:

> There is a substantial body of evidence that in susceptible individuals large quantities of what we call junk food, high sugar content with lots of preservatives, can precipitate anti-social and even violent behavior.[60]

This testimony, which came to be known as the "Twinkie defense,"[61] is the exact opposite of Dr. Jones's claim that general determinism precludes the possibility of a decision or a choice to kill. Here, we have a specific account of the way a person's diet can lead him to kill. In hindsight, 25 years later, these extremes of psychiatric arrogance seem to belong to a different era. Yet

[58] *See* George P. Fletcher, With Justice for Some: Victims' Rights in Criminal Trials 27 (1995).

[59] *Id.*

[60] *Id.*

[61] *See* Kelly Snider, *The Infamous Twinkie Defense—Fact or Fiction?*, 9 Annals Am. Psychotherapy Ass'n 42, 43 (2006).

in the trial of Dan White for two homicides, these conflicting perspectives on human behavior could have influenced the jury to reduce the conviction from murder to manslaughter.[62] True, the burden of prosecution was on the prosecution to prove malice (a legal concept distinguishing murder from manslaughter) beyond a reasonable doubt.[63] And yet a conviction requires a unanimous vote by the 12 jurors. Bringing in this "junk philosophy" and "junk science" could easily have garnered more dissenting jurors.

There are many messages of the trial of Dan White and the subsequent riot of the gay community in San Francisco. First, specific communities at specific moments of history will identify with particular victims—like Harvey Milk—and feel collectively depreciated by the failure of the legal system to achieve equal justice for all. We should not forget that George Moscone, an Italian American, was also a victim, yet the Italian American community did not respond. Indeed, the killing of Moscone should have alleviated the sense of the gay community that they, specifically, were humiliated by the verdict. Also, the concentration of the gay community in San Francisco gave them a sense of grievance that they might not have had if the events and the trial had occurred in Boise, Idaho.

These historical contingencies suggest that the trial of Dan White was simply a historical anomaly. This is also not true. The events, the testimony by the psychiatrists, the verdict, and the riot were characteristic of the time and place. It may be that gay rights have retreated to the background but the trial was not simply about gays. In fact, it was not explicitly about gays at all. Yet each group of victims has the potential for attracting the identification of others—who decided that the relevant point of contact is sexual orientation rather than nationality, ethnicity, race, or religion (the relevant categories under the Genocide Statute).[64] The abuses and mistakes of the Dan White trial and the response by the gay communities mark the cases as a memorial in the history of victims' rights.

[62] *See White*, 117 Cal. App. 3d at 278.

[63] *See id.* at 277.

[64] Convention on the Prevention and Punishment of the Crime of Genocide, 102 Stat. 3045, 78 U.N.T.S. 277 (Dec. 9, 1948).

2. African Americans

To shift gears from homosexuals to African Americans as victims is to move from a significant issue in its time and place and to rewind and skip forward at the same time. The course of American history includes slavery, emancipation, segregation, lynching, and the battle against racism, the remnants of which persist even today. The tension in American race relations is reflected in the ever-shifting vocabulary: persons of color, blacks, and African Americans. Our sensitivity is heightened by disagreement about who belongs to the category and why. South Africa applied a test of appearances: if you passed as white, you were white.[65]

Unlike other forms of discrimination considered in this book, prejudice against blacks was based and continues to be based, in part, on stereotypes. These stereotypes include blacks as good athletes, sexually potent, and prone to crime. It is not surprising that a disproportionate percentage of our prisoners are black. The cycle begins on the street with poverty and stereotypes of "thug" manners of dress, resulting in confrontations with the police, higher rate of arrests, and ultimately, mass incarceration. The coup de grâce is that released felons have until recently not been able to vote in many southern states.[66] In fact, felon disenfranchisement meant that a half million blacks could not vote in Florida in the 2000 controversial presidential election of George W. Bush.[67]

There has been no shortage of demonstrations and riots by blacks with a grievance primarily against the police. The Watts riots in South Central Los Angeles in 1965 were the first of many that have occurred since World War II.[68] That war, it should be said, was of critical importance in raising the consciousness of African Americans. Within a few years after Harry S. Truman ordered the integration of the army, the Supreme Court mandated the integration of the schools,[69] and there seemed to be a hint of racial equality in

[65] Population Registration Act 30 of 1950, §1 (xv) (S. Afr.) ("'[W]hite person' means a person who in appearance obviously is, or who is generally accepted as a white person, but does not include a person who although in appearance obviously (sic) a white person, is generally accepted as a coloured person.").

[66] Billy Corriher, *Changing the South's Harsh Rules to Restore Voting Rights to Former Felons*, Inst. for Southern Stud. (Apr. 27, 2018), https://www.facingsouth.org/2018/04/changing-souths-harsh-rules-restore-voting-rights-former-felons (citing Christopher Uggen, Ryan Larson & Sarah Shannon, *6 Million Lost Voters: State Level Estimates of Felony Disenfranchisement, 2016*, Sent'g Project (Oct. 6, 2016)).

[67] *See* Julian Borger & Gregory Palast, *Inquiry into New Claims of Poll Abuses in Florida*, Guardian (Feb. 16, 2001), https://www.theguardian.com/world/2001/feb/17/usa.julianborger.

[68] *See generally* Gerald Horne, Fire This Time: The Watts Uprising and the 1960s (1995).

[69] Brown v. Bd. of Educ., 347 U.S. 343 (1954).

American law. But the problem of the enforcement of constitutional rights has always been the necessity of state action. Private discrimination in clubs, schools, housing, service at lunch counters—all of these instances have created a challenge in the struggle to realize the promise of the Gettysburg Address that all men are indeed created equal and must be treated equally.[70]

The struggle of the NAACP and other organizations favoring racial equality is ongoing, day to day—and even more acute in the present day. Yet the milestones are important. One of the major steps was *Loving v. Virginia*, which held that a prohibition on interracial marriage was unconstitutional.[71] That this decision came near a half century before *Obergefell* granting gays the same right of marriage should not be taken as a major turning point. In fact, there is a strikingly low rate of black/white intermarriage—as compared to, say, intermarriage in the American Jewish community, that is, marriages between Jews and non-Jews. Legal possibilities do not often change cultural patterns. And the social contact between blacks and whites in the United States remains surprisingly low.

On the plus side, the policy of affirmative action in university and law school admissions has led to higher representation of minorities in business and the professions.[72] Unfortunately, the primary argument against affirmative action is precisely the clause of the Constitution most favorable to African American interests, namely the equal protection clause of the Fourteenth Amendment. The policy of affirmative action remains under severe attack in the courts and may not survive in the long term. The downside of affirmative action is that black graduates of prestigious law schools are often taken to be less qualified than their white peers.[73]

In criminal trials, the factor of race enters in manifold ways. We have mentioned the likelihood of arrest, the management of jury trials, and our special concern in this chapter: the identification of the black public with black victims. First, we will consider criminal trials and jury selection.

Beginning with a case that arose right after the Civil War and with the enactment of the Fourteenth Amendment, *Strauder v. West Virginia*,[74] we have

[70] Abraham Lincoln, *The Gettysburg Address* (Nov. 19, 1863), *in* Lincoln on Democracy 307 (Mario M. Cuomo & Harold Holzer eds., 1990).

[71] 388 U.S. 1 (1967).

[72] *But cf.* Richard H. Sander, *A Systematic Analysis of Affirmative Action in American Law Schools*, 57 Stan. L. Rev. 367 (2004).

[73] *Cf.* Dan Slater, opinion, *Does Affirmative Action Do What It Should?*, N.Y. Times (Mar. 16, 2013), https://www.nytimes.com/2013/03/17/opinion/sunday/does-affirmative-action-do-what-it-should.html.

[74] 100 U.S. 303 (1879).

confronted the problem of racial bias in several stages of jury selection. First, the voting roles determine the range of names that fall into the pool—the group from which the 12 persons is ultimately selected—and are further shaped by the use of peremptory challenges, namely the options that lawyers have to use to reject jurors based on their intuitions of whether the particular juror will lean their way or not.[75] The lawyers pose questions to the prospective jurors in a process called voir dire and then exercise their challenges.[76]

Voir dire is an elegant ritual in itself. The lawyers ask questions of the prospective about some obvious matters such as whether they know any of the victims, witnesses, or other parties in the case. If they do, the prospective juror can be dismissed "for cause"—implying probable bias. The judge rules on whether there is cause or not. Yet the real purpose of voir dire is not to establish these obvious factors of bias but to probe the cultural loyalties of the jurors—what newspapers do they read, what TV shows do they watch, their religions. A whole profession of jury consultants has developed to advise lawyers about these intangible factors and also to do research into the backgrounds of the possible jurors.[77]

After the challenges for cause are exhausted, the lawyers have an opportunity to use "peremptory challenges," that is, rejecting a prospective juror on the basis of intuition alone. The use of these challenges can testify to the innate trial judgment of the lawyers, but they can also be an invitation to racially-informed trial intuitions. In the landmark case of *Batson v. Kentucky*,[78] a black defendant was tried and convicted of burglary by an all-white jury. The jury was rendered all white by the prosecution's use of peremptory challenges to exclude four prospective blacks from the jury.[79] The Supreme Court reversed the conviction primarily on grounds of the Fourteenth Amendment's principle of equal protection of the laws.[80] The decision has ramifications through the legal system, including discrimination based on sexual orientation.

There are two cases of lasting significance in the field of racial discrimination and community identification: one on the side of victims; and one,

[75] *See* 2A Patrick L. McCloskey & Ronald L. Schoenberg, Criminal Law Advocacy: Jury Section 1.03(4)(b)–(c) (1997) (describing peremptory challenges for cause).

[76] *Id.*

[77] Franklin Strier & Donna Shestowsky, *Profiling the Profilers: A Study of the Trial Consulting Profession, Its Impact on Trial Justice and What, If Anything, to do about It*, 199 Wis. L. Rev. 441 (1999).

[78] 476 U.S. 79 (1986).

[79] *Id.* at 83.

[80] *Id.* at 84.

contrary to my general thesis focusing on victims on the side of the defendant. The leading case in the 1990s was the Rodney King case, which was a routine case of police officers stopping a speeding driver on a Los Angeles freeway.[81] At the scene of the stop, two other black passengers peaceably exited the car and cooperated with the officers. Rodney King resisted, which led to a massive beating by the police—all of which was caught on videotape.[82] Thus the uncontroversial speeding charge was converted into a leading case of alleged police brutality. Since then, with the advent of Black Lives Matter, the conflict between police and black citizens has become a recurrent phenomenon.

Just to focus on the racial aspects of the trial, the most significant move in the state trial was a ruling to change the venue away from downtown Los Angeles because the judge appeared to have engaged in an illegal gesture of sympathy toward the prosecution.[83] Presumably there was no other judge downtown who could handle the case, and therefore the interesting question—related to the problem of a racially diverse jury—was whether to move the case. They could have changed the venue to Oakland, a racially diverse community, but instead they sent the case to the closest country court within driving distance, namely the predominantly white suburb of Simi Valley in the San Fernando Valley.[84] The trial proceeded with a predominantly white jury consisting mostly of retired police offers and security personnel.[85] As such, the trial ended in an acquittal of the four primary police officers—with horrific consequences. Six days of rioting followed in Los Angeles, resulting in more than 50 deaths and massive property damage in the amount of $1 billion.[86] The consequence dwarfed the San Francisco riots, which had occurred 13 years earlier.

This is not to say that the defense did not use several clever ploys to win an acquittal from the sympathetic jury. They broke down the videotape frame by frame to undercut the brutality in the speed, number and duration of the blows to King's body.[87] They formulated a theory about why King, once on the

[81] Koon v. United States, 518 U.S. 81, 85 (1996).
[82] *Id.* at 86.
[83] Powell v. Superior Court, 283 Cal. Rptr. 777, 792 (Cal. Ct. App. 1991).
[84] *L.A. Hearing on Venue of Police Trial*, NAT'L L.J., June 1, 1992, at 35.
[85] The jury was comprised of ten whites, one Latina, and one Asian. *See Measure on Change of Venue Rules*, L.A. TIMES, May 22, 1992, at B4.
[86] Anjuli Sastry & Karen Grigsby Bates, *When LA Erupted in Anger: A Look Back at the Rodney King Riots*, NPR (Apr. 26, 2017), https://www.npr.org/2017/04/26/524744989/when-la-erupted-in-anger-a-look-back-at-the-rodney-king-riots; *New Initiatives for a New Los Angeles: Final Report and Recommendations*, Senate Special Task Force on a New Los Angeles, Dec. 9, 1992, pp. 10–11.
[87] Kimberle Crenshaw & Gary Peller, *Reel Time/Real Justice*, 70 DENV. U. L. REV. 283, 285 (1993).

ground, rolled toward them. This was a "Folsom roll"—something prisoners learned as a way of fighting guards.[88] In addition, the prosecution referenced police policies that could not be documented in court. In the final analysis, however, in the mind of the public, in particular the African American public in Los Angeles, the trial was a betrayal of both King and the community.

The saga of Rodney King reveals another feature of American criminal justice with relevance for the international legal order. When a state court acquits a defendant in a highly charged case, particularly those involving racial justice, the federal government can bring its own prosecution in federal court for a deprivation of civil rights.[89] The government must specify the constitutional right violated by the defendants. There is no right against police brutality, per se. But it is possible to adapt the Fourth Amendment right against unreasonable searches and seizures to cover an unlawful seizure (or beating) of a person.[90] And since not every state court acquittal generates a federal trial, there is an obvious political dimension as well. The political tragedy in Los Angeles was obvious. The state courts satisfied the test, unwilling or unable to do justice.

The federal trial took place in downtown Los Angeles, in which two blacks were empaneled on the jury.[91] The operative rule was not simply the Batson policy (just extended to the defense in McCollum) of avoiding discrimination in jury selection. The judicial imperative was to ensure some racial representation on a jury hearing a case of police brutality against a black citizen. A judge can influence jury selection in several ways—for example, by turning down borderline dismissals for cause and by coaxing the juror to give an appearance of impartiality. The echoes of the riots in the aftermath of the Simi Valley verdict, made this policy imperative.

Yet the jury system cannot function with fixed quotas for specific groups in the society. For one thing, we would never concur on the relevant groups—rich, poor, men, women, religious, secular, Republicans, Democrats. The jury is not a democratic institution. It must vote unanimously, not by majority as in democratic elections, and the jurors themselves are admonished not to be influenced by their personal interests, as voters obviously are. They

[88] Seth Mydans, *The 81 Seconds That Shaped 2 Years Return to Center Stage in Los Angeles*, N.Y. Times (Feb. 22, 1993), https://www.nytimes.com/1993/02/22/us/the-81-seconds-that-shaped-2-years-return-to-center-stage-in-los-angeles.html.

[89] *See* 18 U.S.C. § 242 (2018).

[90] Koon v. United States, 518 U.S. 81, 88 (1996).

[91] Allen v. City of Los Angeles, No. CV 91-2497 JGD (Tx), 1995 U.S. Dist. LEXIS 13929 Case (D. Cen. Cali. Jan. 13, 1995).

must decide on the evidence and according to the judge's intrusions. They vote as nameless minds in a collective entrusted with the American system of justice. And apart from the remedy of the federal civil rights action, the American jury has the ultimate, unreviewable power to acquit.[92] An apt analogy is the power of the Dalai Lama, who has ultimate power to decide in his community in Tibet but is surrounded and fenced in by advisers who control his actions.

Thus, the jury selection in the federal trial of the officers who beat up Rodney King was in a paradoxical bind. There had to be some black representation on the jury, but not because they would be loyal to King; not because this would be the democratic thing to do; and not because a verdict of guilty was preferable to one of not guilty. It is not easy to express what was at stake other than generating an appearance to the black community that the trial would be fair and impartial.

There is an analogous issue in the selection of judges on the ICC according to Article 38 (a).[93] The judges must represent the major legal systems of the world, constitute an equitable geographical representation, and include a fair number of male and female judges. Each one of these requirements is open to serious dispute. Whether the religious systems of the world are included—Islamic law, Talmudic law—is highly questionable, yet there is no doubt that these systems are applicable in certain countries, for example, Iran and Israel. The requirement of geographic representation is desirable, but it is not clear why it is important. And further, the requirement of a "fair" share of men and women is intriguing for several reasons. The concept of fair distribution might be the appropriate standard for black and white jurors in the Rodney King case. "Fairness" in this context is a vague standard. It means not too little, not too much. We could accept that in American jury selection, but the additional point of requiring men and women raises new questions. We will encounter the problem of jury selection in a rape case below, but in this context, I am not sure what is at stake. This gender requirement as well as the requirement of geographical distribution sound more like an employment provision than a standard of impartiality in the composition of the court.

Perhaps even more important than the jury selection in King's federal trial was the decision of the prosecution to call King as a witness.[94] As the victim

92 United States v. Dougherty, 473 F. 2d 1113, 1132 (1972).
93 Rome Statute, *supra* note 11, art. 38.
94 Mydans, *supra* note 88.

in a criminal trial, he is not represented by counsel, and the defense has no interest in contradicting the police officers' statements and the supposedly expert analysis of the videotape. King offered a convincing account of his behavior. The press had been a victim of its own bias and failed to report King's side of the story during the state trial. King appeared neatly dressed. He explained why he was speeding and evading the police stop (he was afraid of going back to prison).[95] Most importantly, he offered an alternative account of why he appeared to charge one of the officers at the outset, the critical part being the officer's saying "Oh we are going to kill you, n****r. Run."[96] That was enough. The use of the N word is a conversation stopper in polite American society. The same thing happened when Officer Mark Fuhrman testified in the O.J. Simpson case a few years later. Tapes revealing his use of the N word, after his initial denial, destroyed his credibility.[97]

In the end, two of the officers were convicted and under the federal sentencing guidelines, Judge Davies delivered sentences at the low end of the spectrum.[98] They appealed on a number of issues, including the rulings on the challenges to the jurors. Not only did they lose the appeal, but the appellate court instructed that the trial court raise the sentences.[99] It is hard not to say that this was a political decision influenced by the riots and the factors that led the federal court to take the case in the first place.

Another postscript to the federal trial is that King went back to state court and sued the officers as well the Los Angeles Police Department for tort damages in the amount of $4 million.[100] Yet, the central question remains, was a victim vindicated in the court system? In the long run, the system proved that it could work—even against the police—if only this was the last case of the struggles between black defendants and the police. Just in the last few years, there has been an explosion of identified by the now-familiar

[95] Rogers Worthington, *Cops Threatened They'd Kill Me, King Testifies*, Chi. Tribune (Mar. 10, 1993), http://articles.chicagotribune.com/1993-03-10/news/9303190691_1_baton-blows-rodney-king-racial-epithets/

[96] *Id.*

[97] Chris Spargo, *Mark Furhman's Racist Tapes: The Full Transcript of Key OJ Simpson Detective saying N-Word 41 TIMES and Detailing Racially-motivated Violence Involving Members of LAPD*, Daily Mail (Mar. 30, 2018), http://www.dailymail.co.uk/news/article-3514002/Mark-Fuhrman-s-racist-tapes-transcript-key-witness-OJ-Simpson-case-saying-N-word-41-TIMES-detailing-incidents-racially-motivated-violence-involving-members-LAPD.html.

[98] *Koon*, 518 U.S. at 90.

[99] *Id.*

[100] *See* John L. Mitchell, *Rodney King's Lawyers Bill City: $4 million*, L.A. Times (Sept. 24, 1994), http://articles.latimes.com/1994-09-24/news/mn-42417_1_rodney-king-case.

names of the victims: Michael Brown,[101] Tamir Rice,[102] Eric Garner,[103] Trayvon Martin.[104]

It is worth remembering the most important line associated with Rodney King: "Can we all get along?"[105]

3. Jews

If there was an incident in the Jewish community comparable to the Harvey Milk and Rodney King-related riots, it was the killing of Yankel Rosenbaum in Crown Heights, Brooklyn, in the same summer that the federal trial began in the Rodney King case.[106] The circumstances of the killing were much like those of the two other cases. Crown Heights is the home of the Lubavitcher Hasidic community. Their synagogue at 770 Riverside Parkway is as holy to them as the Vatican to Catholics.[107] The changing neighborhood, the influx of many poorer residents, would not lead the faithful to follow other Jews to more affluent neighborhoods. The Rebbe was treated like the leader of other Hasidic communities—a cross between a priest and a prophet. His followers would ask his advice about the most detailed aspects of their personal lives.

In the 1980s, as a professor at Columbia Law, I organized a trip to Cuba, which was difficult in those days. One of my students, a follower of the Rebbe, wanted to come along. She requested and received the Rebbe's permission to do so. While the rest of us were interested in tourism and meeting university-related people, her de facto mission was to find the Jews still living in Cuba and do what she could to help them.

[101] Elliot C. McLaughlin, *Fatal Police Shooting in Missouri Sparks Protests*, CNN (Aug. 11, 2014), https://www.cnn.com/2014/08/10/justice/missouri-police-involved-shooting/.

[102] Sean Flynn, *The Tamir Rice Story: How to Make a Police Shooting Disappear*, GQ (Jul. 14, 2016), https://www.gq.com/story/tamir-rice-story.

[103] Video, *'I can't breathe:' Eric Garner Put in Chokehold by NYPD Officer*, GUARDIAN (Dec. 4, 2014), https://www.theguardian.com/us-news/video/2014/dec/04/i-cant-breathe-eric-garner-chokehold-death-video.

[104] Dan Barry et al., *Race, Tragedy and Outrage Collide After a Shot in Florida*, N.Y. TIMES (Apr. 1, 2012), https://www.nytimes.com/2012/04/02/us/trayvon-martin-shooting-prompts-a-review-of-ideals.html.

[105] Video, King: 'Can We All Get Along?,' ABC NEWS, https://abcnews.go.com/US/video/rodney-king-16589937.

[106] John Kifner, *A Boy's Death Ignites Clashes in Crown Heights*, N.Y. TIMES (Aug. 21, 1991), https://www.nytimes.com/1991/08/21/nyregion/a-boy-s-death-ignites-clashes-in-crown-heights.html.

[107] *See* Joseph Berger, *Officer Fatally Shoots Man After Stabbing in Brooklyn Synagogue*, N.Y. TIMES (Dec. 9, 2014), https://www.nytimes.com/2014/12/10/nyregion/brooklyn-synagogue-stabbing.html.

Though the Jews have largely left Cuba, they have remained rooted within walking distance of their synagogue. The same is true of other Jewish sects in Brooklyn, Lakewood, New Jersey, and, of course, in Israel. The critical factor in this geographic concentration is Orthodox rule prohibiting driving on the Sabbath and holidays. Walking to synagogue is the only way of getting there.

A conflict between the Hasidim and the local black population was inevitable. The trigger was an automobile accident on August 19, 1991, in which a motorcade carrying the Rebbe, Menachem Schneerson, struck a car, killing one young African American and severely injuring another.[108] Several ambulances appeared on the scene, but the accident had already initiated anti-Semitic demonstrating, which increased in intensity as evening fell.

The accident and its aftermath were a trigger for deep-seated resentments about the allegedly preferential medical and police services afforded to the Jewish community.[109] There is also a history in New York of private Jewish defense organizations, notably the Jewish Defense League and a private ambulance service.[110]

In the course of the rioting, a 16-year-old Lemrick Nelson Jr. stabbed and killed a visiting Australian scholar, Yankel Rosenbaum. The legal proceedings were much like those in the Rodney King case—acquittal in state court, conviction in federal court for violating the victim's civil rights.[111] The difference was that the legal case only exacerbated the violence, mainly because blacks leaders like the Reverend Al Sharpton invoked anti-Semitic themes.[112] By August 22, over 1,800 police officers had been dispatched to quell the riots.[113] In total, 152 of these officers and many citizens were injured.[114]

There are several lasting images associated with the episode. First, when the blacks started marching across the Brooklyn Bridge, they chanted "no

[108] Ari L. Goldman, *Rabbi Schneerson Led a Small Hasidic Sect to Prominence*, N.Y. Times (Jun. 13, 1994), https://www.nytimes.com/1994/06/13/nyregion/rabbi-schneerson-led-a-small-hasidic-sect-to-world-prominence.html?sq=schneerson&scp=4&st=nyt.

[109] Kifner, *supra* note 106.

[110] *See id.*

[111] David Stout, *The Case That Rocked Crown Heights*, N.Y. Times (Aug. 15, 1996), https://www.nytimes.com/1996/08/15/nyregion/the-case-that-rocked-crown-heights.html.

[112] *See* William Saletan & Avi Zenilman, *The Gaffes of Al Sharpton*, Slate (Oct. 7, 2003), http://www.slate.com/articles/news_and_politics/ballot_box/2003/10/the_gaffes_of_al_sharpton.html.

[113] Edward Shapiro, Crown Heights: Blacks, Jews, and the 1991 Brooklyn Riot (2006).

[114] Edward Shapiro, *Interpretations of the Crown Heights Riot*, 90 Am. Jewish Hist. 97, 97–122 (2002).

justice, no peace."[115] The same slogan was invoked in the more current protests by blacks against police brutality.

On the other side, many Jewish defenders decried the behavior of the blacks as a "pogrom"—the label used for the repeated attack in nineteenth-century czarist Russia against the Jews.[116] The term was used in Jewish circles for a few decades. The Columbia Professor Michael Stanislawski weighed in to point out that pogromist were always supported by the state.[117] Jews also referred to the rioting as the American Kristallnacht, the 1938 night in which the Nazis destroyed Jewish shops and signaled the coming of the Holocaust.[118] These are obvious metaphors that indicate the level of Jewish insecurity; the details are not as important.

As an American Jew born after Kristallnacht, I had long assumed these anti-Semitic buzzwords were long interred with the ashes of Auschwitz. Then came the comments by Donald Trump in August 2017, which blamed both left and right extremists for the violence in the Charlottesville rallies.[119]

My general assumption, however, is that Jews are no longer a victims group as they were 75 or even 25 years ago. The relative security of Israeli society (with a life expectancy rate much higher than the United States)[120] and the rapid assimilation of American Jews has meant that as compared even to Muslims coming to the United States, we are in a land of opportunity. Witness the nearly successful presidential campaign of Bernie Sanders—a man who once lived in the midst of the Brooklyn cauldron that generated the Yankel Rosenbaum case.[121]

[115] John Kifner, *Tension in Brooklyn; Blacks March by Hasidim Through a Corridor of Blue*, N.Y. Times (Aug. 25, 1991), https://www.nytimes.com/1991/08/25/nyregion/tension-in-brooklyn-blacks-march-by-hasidim-through-a-corridor-of-blue.html.

[116] Shapiro, *supra* note 114.

[117] *Id.*

[118] *Id.*

[119] Michael D. Shear & Maggie Haberman, *Trump Defends Initial Remarks on Charlottesville; Again Blames Both Sides*, N.Y. Times (Aug. 15, 2017), https://www.nytimes.com/2017/08/15/us/politics/trump-press-conference-charlottesville.html.

[120] *The World Factbook*, CIA, https://www.cia.gov/library/publications/the-world-factbook/rankorder/2102rank.html (Israel has the 12th highest expectancy.).

[121] Jason Horowitz, *Bernie Sanders's '100% Brooklyn' Roots Are as Unshakeable as His Accent*, N.Y. Times (Jul. 24, 2015), https://www.nytimes.com/2015/07/25/us/politics/bernie-sanderss-100-brooklyn-roots-show-beyond-his-accent.html.

4. Women

There are many differences between the injustices toward gays, blacks, and Jews under the law; injustices that resulted in riots; and the traditional discrimination toward women. Gays and Jews never required a constitutional amendment to gain the right to vote. Black men acquired the vote in the Fifteenth amendment in 1865, as an immediate consequence of the Civil War.[122] Women remained disenfranchised until the Nineteenth Amendment in 1920.[123] It may be that wars expand our sense of inclusion in the body politic. But the status of women under the law involved the body in a different sense.

Sex, motherhood, the assumed caring function in the home—all of these factors generate a different dynamic. Men are not likely to think of this a form of discrimination. Yet we have never had a female president, and it is unlikely that misogyny did not play a part in the 2016 election. The differences with the three other categories prompts one to think that this issue can be understood only at a psychoanalytic level—surely beyond my ken.

One of the obvious arenas of gender differentiation is the religious Abrahamic traditions of Judaism, Christianity, and Islam. Read any translation of the Bible and you will find that God is male; the prophets are 99 percent male; God gives the Torah to men; Jesus is male; and the position of women correlates well, and indeed defines the degree of religious liberalism. This is obvious in Judaism: the minyan (the 10-person prayer group minimum) must be all men in the Orthodox tradition, but the conservative and reform provide a larger leadership role for women. The Catholic tradition is based on the dominance of men. These details are offered not as criticism but as an explanation of how male supremacy has come to be taken for granted in Abrahamic cultures.

With regard to status of women in the law, the critical question is virginity and sexual suppression. This is taken to an extreme in honor killings and female circumcision, which have no biblical warrant. Yet the Doctrine of the Virgin Birth is central to Christian doctrine, and this can only imply a tradition of relating sex to impurity. The specific area of national and international criminal law shaped by these sexual attitudes is the law of rape and, specifically, the doctrine of consent.

122 U.S. Const. amend. XV.
123 U.S. Const. amend. XIX.

There are two references to rape in the Rome Statute; the first is Article 7(1)(g), rape as a crime against humanity.[124] This means that the rape must occur on a widespread and systematic basis and more tellingly, with knowledge of the "attack."[125] The latter point is critical because rape presupposes non-consent of the victim. This issue has been the point of friction between traditionalists and feminists in debating the approach toward rape in common law jurisdictions. The question is whether non-consent is an element of the crime that the prosecution must allege and prove or whether consent is a "ground for excluding criminal responsibility" to be raised at trial according to Article 31(3).[126]

The second reference to rape and the analogous sexual crimes mentioned in Article 7 are as a war crime in Art. 8(e)(vi), the portion of Article 8 that applies only to non-international armed conflicts.[127] It is not clear why there should be a principled difference on this point between international and non-international situations of conflict. Whether non-international means domestic is a point we leave aside for the moment. The advantage of Article 8 over Article 7 is that in the former case, there is no need to prove a "widespread and systematic" attack.

The central problem in both of these cases of rape is consent, and in particular, mistaken consent. This is a rather common problem both between acquaintances who are dating and between strangers under the intimidating impact of an occupying army. The root of the problem is the nature of consent. Is it something like a license given by the victim to the offender? Or it simply a factor bearing on the good faith belief by the defendant that the sex is desired by both parties? The latter position would incorporate the well-known doctrine of private knowledge as apparent consent, which is sufficient to create a contract or to avoid tort liability.

Before concluding this section on victims in national and international criminal law, I should mention the recent decision by the ICC on compensation for victims under Article 75 of the Statute.[128]

To my regret, the Court seems to overlook the evidentiary problem of whether someone is a victim while the case is pending, for example, the assumption that the crime caused the harm.

[124] Rome Statute, *supra* note 11, art. 7(1)(g).
[125] *Id.*
[126] Rome Statute, *supra* note 11, art. 31(3).
[127] Rome Statute, supra note 11, art. 8(e)(vi).
[128] The Prosecutor v. Germain Katanga, No. ICC-01/04-01/07 (Mar. 24, 2017), https://www.icc-cpi.int/CourtRecords/CR2017_05121).

This sums up our treatment of victims in national and international criminal law as contrasted to the status of the offender. In fact, most of the remaining chapters are devoted to an analysis of the issues bearing on the responsibility of the offender. Yet a few comments are in order.

There are two kinds of criminal law as recognized in German theory, namely *Tatstrafrecht* and *Täterstrafrecht*, translated as act-oriented criminal law and actor-oriented criminal law. That is, do we focus on a specific act isolated from the actor's personality and character, or do we focus on the actor as a dangerous type? Both of these approaches entail victims and both are compatible with other assumptions of the Rome Statute.

As between the two approaches to criminal responsibility, it is difficult to maintain act orientation as a matter of principle.

From the perspective of deterrence as the purpose of punishment, the rational focus would be on actor types, even physical characteristics and other factors, such as the XYY chromosome, which led some geneticists in the 1960s to claim, falsely, that the extra chromosome was correlated with a higher rate of criminality.[129] This practice was associated with the criminology of the German and Italian fascists. It is now taboo, but the question that remains is whether the dangerousness of the offender is relevant for any purpose other than sentencing (and even in the latter case, predictions of dangerousness are dubious).

It is true that systems of civil commitment are based on the dangerousness of the person. Thus, even after an acquittal for reasons of intoxication or insanity,[130] the offender should be subject to civil commitment only if he or she poses an ongoing threat to the community. The problem with the latter standard is that it is not guided by objective standards—anything the judge decides is dangerous is ipso facto dangerous.

We see in the principle of act-oriented criminal law, one of unexpected benefits of a disciplined Kantian retributivist approach to criminal responsibility. Paradoxically, the position of practically minded people in international criminal law is to favor deterrence as the proper purpose of sanctions, as noted in the Preamble to the Rome Statute:

[129] *See* Daryl B. O'Connor et al., *Exogenous Testosterone, Aggression, and Mood in Eugonadal and Hypogonadal Men*, 75 Physiology & Behav. 557, 565 (2002) (finding that exposure to additional testosterone does not correlate to aggression).

[130] Rome Statute, *supra* note 11, arts/ 31(a)–(b).

"And thus to contribute to the prevention of such crimes." Admittedly, the purpose of prevention might be a side effect of retributive sanctions. But we should remember that Kant argued that even if the world were to disband, we should execute every last murderer languishing in prison.

Between the victim and the offender, we obviously have the fact of the crime. In American criminal law, some distinctions among types of crimes have become highly influential in light of the exceptional high rate of arrest, conviction, and incarceration, particularly among African Americans and Latinos. One of these is between crimes malum prohibitum and crimes malum in se, those that are wrong because they are prohibited and those that are wrong in and of themselves. Virtually all the crimes defined in the Rome Statute are malum in se, but there are some crimes that are punished simply because the law of war so dictates.[131]

The most serious mistake of American criminal justice, fortunately avoided in the Rome Statute, is the labeling of more serious offenses as felonies rather than misdemeanors. The concept of the felon lies deep in recesses of English and Roman legal history. It is usually defined by a minimal term in prison. The egregious consequence in the modern system is the disenfranchisement of felons, even after they are released from prison.

Another problem we derived from the concept of felony is the so-called felony-murder rule, as opposed to misdemeanor-manslaughter rule. If someone committing a felony accidentally kills another, he is held liable for murder.[132] This rule obviously ignores the principle of individual culpability and has very little to say for it. Rules of this sort resemble the practice of overcharging. They are useful for prosecutors in securing a plea bargain.

There is much to be learned from national legal systems, but also in the spirit of the ICC, properly understood, the international legal order should call upon the "general principles of law" derived from national legal systems but also avoid the mistakes that are entrenched in their historical practices.

[131] An example is that of the crime of declaring that no quarter will be given. Rome Statute, *supra* note 11, arts. 8(2)(b)(xii), 8(2)(3)(x).

[132] *See* George Fletcher, Rethinking Criminal Law § 4.4.7 (1978); W. LaFave & A. Scott, Handbook on Criminal Law § 71 (1972).

6
Offenses and Defenses

The Rome Statute[1] draws a clear line between the four crimes subject to the jurisdiction of the Court and the grounds for excluding criminal responsibility in Article 31.[2] Let us refer to the distinction between these offenses and defenses as the "distinction." The significance of the "distinction" should not be underestimated. For example, the principle of *nullum crimen sine lege*, which applies to the former but not the latter, as evidenced by Article 31(3), permits the recognition of new defenses at trial.

The four classic defenses of insanity, intoxication, self-defense, and duress spelled out in Article 31 are subject to controversy. Among the major legal systems of the world, there is considerable divergence in approaching these issues. We will turn to each of them, but first, we must address the question of why it is important to make the distinction between offenses and defenses. As we noted in chapter 6 with regard to the issue of consent in rape cases, the issue could be stated either way: non-consent as an element of the offense *or* consent as "a ground excluding criminal responsibility." Yet is not an accident that new defenses are compatible with the rule of *nullum crimen* but new offenses are not.

There are basically two reasons for the *nullum crimen* principle. One is to warn defendants of their possible liability. The other is to control the discretion of judges. From the defendants' point of view, new defenses appear to be a benefit and not a burden.

Therefore, defendants have no reason to object to the increased possibility of acquittal. Yet this might be an illusion, as the example of consent in rape cases illustrates. Every defense can be restated, in negative form, as an element of the offense. For example, the principle of self-defense in a case of

[1] Rome Statute for the International Criminal Court, July 17, 1998, 2187 U.N.T.S. 3; U.N. Diplomatic Conference of Plenipotentiaries on the Establishment of an International Court, U.N. Doc. A/Conf.183/9 [hereinafter Rome Statute].

[2] *See* Rome Statute, *supra* note 1, art. 31.

The Grammar of Criminal Law: Volume Two: International Criminal Law. George P. Fletcher.

alleged aggression under Article 8*bis* could be restated as this: Every nation not under attack which acts prohibitively is guilty of aggression.[3]

Blurring the "distinction"—converting defenses into elements of the offense—might be more difficult for two of the "grounds" listed in Article 31, namely insanity and intoxication (duress is more controversial). If the issue is fair warning, this has no application to the insanity and intoxicated defenses. By definition, the insane and intoxicated defenses are incapable of controlling their actions in response to a legal prohibition. Therefore, the only relevant reason for listing these defenses in Article 31 would be to restrain the discretion in the application of the law. We can call this the principle of judicial control.

But if judicial control is the issue, then we should have a closed list of defenses and not permit deviation under Article 31(3). As such, there seems to be more to the distinction between offenses and defenses than verbal gymnastics.[4]

In common law systems, there have been always been procedural issues associated with this offense and defense distinction. For example, the burden of proof was historically on the prosecution to prove offenses, but often the burden shifted to the defense on matters that society disfavored—like the defense of insanity—or new defenses under the Model Penal Code, such as entrapment[5] or mistake of law.[6] Shifting the burden functions as a procedural surrogate for a restrictive definition of the defense.

This phenomenon has not been restricted to the common law. The Prussian Criminal Ordinance of 1805 required the defendant to prove exculpatory issues, such as the age of consent in a statutory rape case.[7] There is no necessary correlation between the inquisitorial method and the risk of non-persuasion. The inquisitor might have had doubts at the end of investigation but then must decide for or against the defendant. This is the reason that the burden of persuasion is best expressed as a de facto risk of non-persuasion at the end of the trial, whether in the inquisitorial or adversary system, and with or without a jury.

[3] Resolution Adopting Aggression Amendments to Rome Statute, Rev. Conf. of the Rome Statute, Kampala, Uganda, May 31–June 11, 2010, Annex I, art. 8bis, 13th plen. mtg., I.C.C. Doc. RC/Res.6 (June 11, 2010).

[4] The distinction is concerned with, inter alia, non-consent vs. defense, fair warning, and judicial restraint.

[5] MODEL PENAL CODE § 2.13 (AM. LAW INST., 1962).

[6] *Id.* at § 2.04.

[7] *See* GEORGE P. FLETCHER, BASIC CONCEPTS OF CRIMINAL LAW 94–95 (1998).

Apart from the burden of persuasion, there is a critically important burden on the prosecution or the defense. In a common law trial, with a jury, the question is whether there is enough evidence to warrant a jury instruction on the issue. Too many instructions would reduce the jury's focus on the decisive issues of the trial. In civil law systems, the analogue to jury instructions is the judge's duty to write an opinion justifying his or her finding on the evidence. Again, to be meaningful, the opinion should focus on the salient issues of the trial.

The Rome Statute uses some conventional techniques for addressing these issues and also for leaving them subject to argument. One is the approach to superior orders in Article 33, a rather significant issue in the law of war.[8] Basically, the provision says that orders by a commander provide no defense to one of the four basic crimes unless, among other things, "the order was not manifestly unlawful."[9] First, we have to ask, what does "manifestly unlawful" mean? It must refer to a kind of decision by the subordinate that should have been obvious under the circumstances. The interesting problem is the implicit shift in the burden of persuasion. How can the prosecution prove the negative, namely that the action was, in fact, manifestly unlawful?

All of these issues become more complicated if we bring to bear Article 66 entitled "The Presumption of Innocence."[10] According to Art. 66(3), the prosecution must prove guilt beyond a reasonable doubt and the Court must be so convinced.[11] It is not clear what these provisions mean in practice. This kind of language is used in common law jury instructions, and lawyers are quite familiar with explaining to the jury that a reasonable doubt does not include any inkling of doubt.[12]

Reasonable is an indispensable word, not normally translated into the legal terminology of other official languages of the Rome Statute. Yet, in fact, the other versions of the Rome Statute follow the English lead and translate the provision verbatim. Article 66, including the reference to the presumption of innocence, follows a template of American jurisprudence.[13]

[8] Rome Statute, *supra* note 1, art. 33.

[9] *Id.*

[10] Rome Statute, *supra* note 1, art. 66.

[11] *Id.*

[12] *See* Robert C. Power, *Reasonable and Other Doubts: The Problem of Jury Instructions*, 67 Tenn. L. Rev. 45 (1999).

[13] *See* Rome Statute, *supra* note 1, art. 66.

Yet in all legal systems, the notion of guilt—the criterion of liability that must be proved beyond a reasonable doubt—is problematic. The term is used in both a formal and factual sense.

When a defendant pleads guilty in a common law trial, the plea does not mean he is, in fact, guilty.[14] He is just making a procedural move, which determines the next steps of the trial. Of course, even if the jury decides that he has been proven guilty beyond a reasonable doubt, this does not mean he is guilty.[15] An estimated hundred thousand factually innocent prisoners are among the more than two million inmates in the United States.[16]

Unfortunately, the way criminal procedure works in the United States and other systems is that innocence as such is not a ground of appeal. Every convicted criminal could claim innocence, and the appellate court cannot retry every case. Article 81 of the Rome Statute, rendering every error of fact a basis for appeal, is not coherent as written.[17] There are many irrelevant facts and insignificant though accurate facts. The structure of the legal system must find a proper balance between protecting the innocence and the necessity of finality—however brutal that might sound.

These issues aside, Article 65 reveals a significant if inadvertent perspective on the use of the expression "proof beyond a reasonable doubt."[18] The criterion of whether the Court should accept the admission of guilt is whether it is "satisfied" by the submissions of the prosecution.[19] This is closer to the civil law tradition of proof, which is expressed in variations of the French expression "in time conviction." The French version of the Rome Statute requires that the court be "convinced" of the defendant's doubt.[20] This is closer to the subjectivist pattern of civilian jurisprudence.

"Civilian" in this context is a reference to the principles introduced by the French Revolution and the Code Civil of 1804.[21] The large significance of words that refer to the personal conviction of the court is that they deliberately reject the quantitative approach to evidence, as signaled by terms like

[14] *See When the Innocent Plead Guilty*, INNOCENCE PROJECT (Jan. 26, 2009), https://www.innocenceproject.org/when-the-innocent-plead-guilty/.

[15] *See* Hugo Adam Bedau & Michael L. Radelet, *Miscarriages of Justice in Potentially Capital Cases*, 40 STAN. L. REV. 21 (1987).

[16] Justin Rohrlich, *Why Are There Up to 120,000 Innocent People in US Prisons?*, VICE NEWS (Nov. 10, 2014), https://news.vice.com/article/why-are-there-up-to-120000-innocent-people-in-us-prisons.

[17] *See* Rome Statute, *supra* note 1, art, 81.

[18] *See* Rome Statute, *supra* note 1, art. 65.

[19] *Id.*, art. 65(2).

[20] *See* Statute de Rome de la Cour pénale international [Rome Statute], *supra* note 1, art. 65 (Fr.).

[21] *See generally* C. CIV. (Fr.).

the "burdens of proof" and "reasonable doubt," which were associated with the system of "legal proofs" that prevailed in the *ancien regime.*[22] As in other areas of the common law, the language and policies in use since the Middle Ages have adapted well to the conditions of modernity.

The notion of guilt in Article 66 leaves open the range of issues on which the Court must be convinced. Obviously, the prosecution's burden of persuasion includes the elements of the four primary offenses and indeed the particular offenses against the administration of justice under Article 70.[23]

The problem becomes acute in the area of defenses, namely Article 31. There is an area of considerable controversy in the history of the common law, which managed to recognize both the presumption of innocence and reversal of the burden of persuasion of the defensive issues covered by Article 31. The way to think about this is to imagine that the defendant remains silent during the trial. What does the prosecution need to prove in order to justify a conviction?

The way Blackstone defined the common law position on homicide is instructive: "Now homicide, or the killing of any human creature, is of three kinds; justifiable, excusable, and felonious."[24] Note that the definition covers the killing of any human creature, which implies that suicide (Selbstmord—or murder of the self) was also prohibited.[25] In light of the religious foundations of the prohibition, this is the only logical position to take.

To provide some light diversion, consider the way Shakespeare mocks the law in *Hamlet* after Ophelia's suicide and presents the question of whether the grave diggers can justify a funeral in one of my favorite passages in *Hamlet.* Shakespeare writes a satiric defense of Ophelia's suicide by drowning in order to vouchsafe her a Christian burial.

Hamlet, Act 5, Scene 1 (in modern English)

OTHER: I'm telling you, yes. So finish that grave right away. The coroner examined her case and says it should be a Christian funeral.

GRAVEDIGGER: But how, unless she drowned in self-defense?

OTHER: That's what they're saying she did.

[22] *See* A. Esmein, Histoire de la Procedure Criminelle en France [History of Criminal Procedure in France] 399 (1882) (Fr.).

[23] *See* Rome Statute, *supra* note 1, art. 70.

[24] 4 William Blackstone, Commentaries on the Laws of England 176 (1769).

[25] *See id.*

GRAVEDIGGER: It must be se offendendo. It cannot be else. For here lies the point: if I drown myself wittingly, it argues an act. And an act hath three branches—it is to act, to do, to perform. Argal, she drowned herself wittingly.

GRAVEDIGGER: Sounds more like "self-offense," ["se offendendo" in the original, a play on "se-defendeno"]if you ask me. What I'm saying is, if she knew she was drowning herself, then that's an act. An act has three sides to it: to do, to act, and to perform. Therefore she must have known she was drowning herself.

OTHER: No, listen here, gravedigger sir—

GRAVEDIGGER: Let me finish. Here's the water, right? And here's a man, okay? If the man goes into the water and drowns himself, he's the one doing it, like it or not. But if the water comes to him and drowns him, then he doesn't drown himself. Therefore, he who is innocent of his own death does not shorten his own life.

OTHER: Is that how the law sees it?[26]

Shakespeare uses not only puns on the common law of se defendendo—the forerunner of self-defense as a justification—but satirizes the act/omission distinction by supposing that Ophelia is drowned involuntarily by something like a tsunami. The wit of the Bard should convince us not to take our conceptual distinctions too seriously—even if that is all we as lawyers have.

Se defendendo was originally an excuse at common law and eventually became a justification, as will be discussed in chapter 8. The distinction between excuse and justification—now recognized by virtually all the legal systems of the world—makes it unfortunate that these categories are not explicitly recognized in Article 31. Yet implicitly they govern the structure of the article and also feature in the language of particular provisions. The first two sections on insanity and intoxication refer de facto to excuses; and the latter two to issues, self-defense, and duress, generally taken to be claims of justification. An excuse acknowledges that the conduct is wrongful and impermissible but not subject to blame. A justification addresses the question of whether the conduct is wrongful. In order to understand the implications of justification and excuse, let us take a closer look at the details of Article 31.

[26] WILLIAM SHAKESPEARE, HAMLET act 5, sc. 1 (SparkNotes 2003) (1600).

1. Grounds for Excluding Criminal Responsibility

(1)(a): The person suffers from a mental disease or defect that destroys that person's capacity to appreciate the unlawfulness or nature of his or her conduct or control his or her conduct to conform to the requirements of law.[27]

2. Insanity

The definition of insanity in part (1)(a) conceals important distinctions but also includes references to historical debates about the concept. I permit myself to use the term even though it is absent from the provision itself. The German term—*Unzurechnungsfähigkeit*—in fact parallels the label being used: incapable of being held responsible.[28]

The first thing to note is that insanity might arise at three or four different points of a criminal trial. The first question is whether the defendant is capable of standing trial. For example, if he makes an admission of guilt, can he later challenge it on the grounds that he was not competent or sufficiently responsible to confess his guilt? The second concept is retrospective—to the time of the deed; and third is after the trial and sentence, whether the convicted person is capable of serving his sentence. There is no logical connection among these three different concepts of mental incompetence.

The problem of competency to stand trial expresses a critical feature of the common law approach to criminal procedure. The defendant manages the trial. If he is not competent, the trial cannot proceed.[29] If the defendant is found incompetent, the alternative is civil commitment, often an extralegal way of avoiding an open confrontation with an enemy of the government.[30] A good example is the confinement of Ezra Pound, the fascist poet confined in St. Elizabeth's hospital in Washington, DC, from the time of his arrest in Italy in 1945 for making alleged treasonous radio broadcasts until his release in 1958.[31] Of course, if he were convicted of treason, he could have

[27] *See* Rome Statute, *supra* note 1, art. 31(1)(a).

[28] *See* Markus D. Dubber, *Citizenship and Penal Law*, 13 NEW CRIM. L. R. 190, 200 (2010).

[29] *See* S. BRAKEL & R. ROCK, THE MENTALLY DISABLED AND THE LAW 444–53 (1971).

[30] *Id.*; Jesse H. Choper, *Consequences of Supreme Court Decisions Upholding Individual Constitutional Rights*, 83 MICH. L. REV. 1, 138 (1984).

[31] *See* Jean Stefancic & Richard Delgado, *Panthers and Pinstripes: The Case of Ezra Pound and Archibald Macleish*, 63 S. CAL. L. REV. 907, 907 n.1 (1990) (citing E. TORREY, THE ROOTS OF TREASON: EZRA POUND AND THE SECRETS OF ST. ELIZABETHS (1984)).

been executed, but the procedures of a criminal trial are significantly more onerous than commitment, considering the burdens of a jury trial, the presumption of innocence, stricter rules of evidence, and so forth.[32]

Insanity after the trial refers to the problem whether the convicted person understands the meaning of his punishment. This has been a major issue in the U.S. death penalty cases, but in principle the problem is the same in all cases. The problem is respecting the convict as a person rather than a caged source of danger. This problem has arisen elsewhere in this book, namely in discussing the purposes of punishment. If the issue is deterrence as the Preamble of the Rome Statute suggests, ending impunity "thus to contribute to the prevention of such crimes,"[33] the issue of respecting the convict as a person as end in themselves also arises. In Kantian terms, treating the defendant as a person means viewing him as an end in himself, not as a means used to promote some social goal.[34]

Intuitively, the definition of insanity in Art. 31(1)(a) refers to insanity at the time of the deed.[35] Yet it is drafted in the present tense, namely not that the person suffered but "suffers."[36] The implicit danger is that acquittal by reason of insanity would entail automatic civil commitment, which is in fact a common phenomenon and one subject to attack by earlier generations of criminal theorists.[37] As we shall see, other aspects of the definition confirm the danger of treating the person acquitted on these grounds as being dangerous to himself or others and therefore properly subject to civil commitment.

All of these references to insanity implicate the testimony of psychiatrists. Indeed, it would be difficult to consider the concept "mental disease or defect" without expert testimony. Yet, as we have discussed, the issue of insanity is not strictly a medical concept.[38] And the problem that has often typically arisen—notably in the Dan White/Harvey Milk case discussed in the previous chapter—is overreaching by the expert witness.[39] This is difficult to avoid, largely because the judge or jury is not capable of drawing the

[32] *See* 18 U.S. Code §§ 4241, 4247 (2018).
[33] Rome Statute, *supra* note 1, pmbl.
[34] *See* Immanuel Kant, The Metaphysics of Morals 130 (Mary Gregor ed. & trans., Cambridge University Press 1996) (1797).
[35] *See* Rome Statute, *supra* note 1, art. 31(1)(a).
[36] *Id.*
[37] *See generally* George E. Dix, *Major Current Issues Concerning Civil Commitment Criteria*, 45 Law & Contemp. Probs. 137 (1982).
[38] *Supra* ch. V.
[39] *Id.*

conclusions required by the definition of the insanity defense. Yet there remains a gap between medical and legal discourse that is difficult to bridge and is subject to lawyerly manipulation.

The next thing to note is that the definition of insanity at the time of the deed reveals the distinction between justification and excuse. The issue is whether the mental illness destroys the capacity of the accused to appreciate "the unlawfulness" of his action. The reference entails the distinction between claims of justification that bear on unlawfulness and those that do not. The claim of part (1)(a) does not include appreciation of any of the terms that bear on insanity itself.[40] It is irrelevant whether the accused grasps that he has a mental disease or defect. The question of insanity is reserved exclusively for the Court.

The difficulty with the phrase "destroys the capacity" is that the claim of insanity is not about the general capacity of the accused. It is about his particular action. Recall the discussion of act-oriented and actor-oriented criminal law in chapter 5. The same distinction applies to versions of the insanity defense. Insanity should properly focus on the particular act, not on the general capacity of the accused. An actor orientation makes the excuse resemble infancy. The Rome Statute Article 26 makes it clear that the status of being under 18 years old at the time of the offense exempts the actor from liability.[41]

It is tempting to think of insanity as akin to infancy because both legal categories function as mechanisms for shunting the case to a different system of court, one to a juvenile court,[42] the other to a civil court deciding on civil commitment. This temptation is revealed in the nineteenth-century California Criminal Penal Code Sec. 26, which provides at the outset:

> All persons are capable of committing crimes except those belonging to the following classes:
>
> (1) Children under the age of 14, in the absence of clear proof that at the time of committing the act charged against them, they knew its wrongfulness.
> (2) Persons who are mentally incapacitated.[43]

[40] *See* Rome Statute, *supra* note 1, art. 31(1)(a).
[41] Rome Statute, *supra* note 1, art. 26.
[42] *See* Barry C. Feld, *Criminalizing Juvenile Justice: Rules of Procedure for the Juvenile Court*, 69 Minn. L. Rev. 141, 275 n.528 (1984).
[43] Cal. Pen. Code § 26(1)–(2) (2018).

The provision clearly views these defenses as actor oriented, except that in the case of infants, an exception is recognized for those sufficiently mature to understand the wrongfulness of their conduct. The notion of wrongfulness in this context is much like the term "unlawfulness" in the Rome Statute, though perhaps—in line with the status orientation of the defense—the wrongfulness might apply to the crime in the abstract, not the particular execution charged at trial.

The latter clause about "capacity to control conduct to conform to the requirements of law" signals a reference to another test for insanity in American jurisprudence called the "irresistible impulse" test, which poses the complex question whether the mental illness caused the crime to occur.[44] The causal question stands in sharp contrast to the "appreciation" clause at the beginning of (1)(a), which is essentially about knowledge in line with the classic M'Naghten rule.[45] The danger of this test is that it seems to make expert testimony even more indispensable; the philosophical complexity of the issues of determinism and free will are beyond the professional competence of both psychiatrists and lawyers. And perhaps for good reason, philosophers do not qualify as expert witnesses.

The tendency toward "status" or actor-oriented thinking in approaching insanity produces its own significant lawyerly response under the label of "temporary insanity."[46] The claim is best suited for cases sometimes called "heat of passion" such as killing a spouse's lover caught in the heat of passion. In the context of warfare, one could easily imagine many situations like this, such as witnessing war crimes, the killing of fellow soldiers, rape, torture, and the like. This might be useful under the Rome Statute. The only thing that stands in way of the assertion of temporary insanity is the reference to "mental disease or defect."

Finally, for comparative purposes we should look at Section 20 of the current German Penal Code:

> *Ohne Schuld handelt* [one acts without guilt], *wer bei Begehung der Tat* [if in the commission of the act] *wegen einer krankhaften seelischen Störung, wegen einer tiefgreifenden Bewußtseinsstörung oder wegen Schwachsinns*

[44] *Irresistible Impulse Test*, Wex Legal Information Institute (last visited July 19, 2018), https://www.law.cornell.edu/wex/irresistible_impulse_test.

[45] *Insanity defense*, Wex Legal Information Institute https://www.law.cornell.edu/wex/Insanity_defense.

[46] 1 M. Hale, The History Of The Pleas Of The Crown 32 (1778).

> *oder einer schweren anderen seelischen Abartigkeit* [because of various mental conditions] unfähig ist [the actor is incapable], *das Unrecht der Tat einzusehen* [of appreciating the unlawful or wrongful nature of his act] *oder nach dieser Einsicht zu handeln.* [or of acting in accordance with this appreciation].[47]

This test has the following advantages: (1) It begins by making it clear that insanity is an excuse negating guilt, not a factor bearing on the unlawfulness of the conduct; (2) it enumerates various mental conditions that might or might not call for expert testimony; (3) the term Unrecht does the work of unlawfulness or wrongfulness but in fact has richer moral overtones. It comes close to the original M'Naghten language of "not knowing the difference between Right and Wrong."[48] But it also has the disadvantage of including the irresistible impulse test.[49]

3. Intoxication

This test in part (1)(b) parallels the definition of insanity in part (1)(a) with intoxication taking the place of "mental disease of defect." It is clear for the same reasons that intoxication functions as an excuse. But there are several complications. A minor one is the kind of intoxication at stake—alcohol, drugs, or some other source. A major issue is the level of intoxication. This is a familiar problem in drunk driving (DUI) cases in light of differential capacities to function under the influence of a mind-altering substance. The provision again uses the phrase "that destroys that person's capacity to appreciate the unlawfulness" of his conduct.[50]

The phrase "destroys that person's capacity" seems too extreme in the context of the four major crimes within the jurisdiction of the court. It is alleged that Hitler's pilots used methamphetamines in order to stay up and fight three days in a row.[51] Their capacity to recognize the nature of their conduct—if they were, say, bombing civilian targets—was not completely

[47] STRAFGESETZBUCH [StGB] § 20 (Ger.).
[48] *See id; Insanity defense, supra* note 44.
[49] *See id.*
[50] Rome Statute, *supra* note 1, art. 31(1)(a).
[51] *See* Megan Garber, *'Pilot's Salt': The Third Reich Kept Its Soldiers Alert With Meth*, ATLANTIC (May 31, 2013), https://www.theatlantic.com/technology/archive/2013/05/pilots-salt-the-third-reich-kept-its-soldiers-alert-with-meth/276429/.

destroyed. Ignoring problems of degree in this context distorts the nature of the excuse. Insanity may be a case of completely destruction of capacity (though this is also dubious), yet intoxication is clearly not.

The overriding difference between insanity and intoxication is that the latter is often voluntarily induced. That means that it is a progressive state of incapacity, a matter of relative incapacity, which is different in different people. Without an on-the-spot test (again, common in drunk driving situations), it is almost impossible to tell whether the particular suspect had too many drinks or not. If a breathalyzer is used at the time of the traffic stop, one might have an accurate assessment of the degree of intoxication, though without knowing whether the suspect could perform the routine tests that police officers use to determine the degree of incapacity.

In the situations governed by the Rome Statute, these considerations seem beside the point. No one is going to conduct a sobriety test in the course of genocide, a crime against humanity, aggression, or a war crime. In the case of insanity, thinking of the claims as an ongoing condition alleviates this problem. In the context of intoxication, that is not possible.

Article 31 is correct in identifying the problem of intoxication as self-induced. Here is the relevant language stipulating an exception for voluntary intoxication:

> Unless the person has become voluntarily intoxicated under such circumstances that the person knew or disregarded the risk that as a result of the intoxication he or she was likely to engage in [criminal] conduct. . . .[52]

It would be preferable to separate these two clauses, as in some national legal systems, and treat intoxication as an excuse, considering voluntary intoxication at the time of the deed, with a separate risk-taking offense drafted by analogy to Article 28, Responsibility of Commanders.[53] The latter is a risk-taking offense, based on negligence as indicated by the requirement the commander knew or "should have known that the forces were committing or about to commit such crimes."[54] In fact, the Rome Statute reveals rich variations on the concept of negligence without ever identifying the concept, which is well recognized in all systems of criminal law as a mental element or form of culpability.

[52] Rome Statute, *supra* note 1, art. 31(1)(b).
[53] *See* Rome Statute, *supra* note 1, art. 28.
[54] *Id.*

The fact is that the risk-taking offense is relatively minor, something like driving without a license or engaging in hostilities without wearing a uniform. Taking these risks generates harm in a small fraction of the cases. Yet these two prongs, collapsed in the treatment of intoxication, are typically confused in international criminal law. A good example is *Ex Parte Quirin* where German troops landed off the coast of Long Island in June 1942, buried their uniforms on the beach, and then proceeded inland before they were captured.[55] They could have been treated as prisoners of war, but President Roosevelt insisted that they be tried before a military tribunal.[56] All eight were convicted of the novel offense of being an "unlawful combatant"—essentially trying to engage in sabotage and other acts of war while not wearing a uniform.[57] This was a risk-taking offense, but their actions were treated as though they had actually caused harm. The Military Commission hearing the case found all eight guilty and sentenced two who cooperated with the prosecution to long prison terms and the other six to death.[58] The latter were executed with a few months.[59] The quality of justice is often strained under wartime conditions.

4. Legitimate Defense

As we move to the second half of Article 31, we encounter an implicit recognition of the distinction between excuse and justification, the latter two as claims of justification. But first we should clarify what the latter term deriving from the Latin *jus facere* actually means. There is some dispute about the matter. Literally, it translates as "to make lawful." It would not be accurate to interpret the term as make "just," though "just" does derive from the word "jus." Etymology is not destiny. The basic idea is that the action is compatible with the normative notion of law or *jus*.

As well recognized in the literature of criminal law, a justification does not make the ostensible commission of the offense disappear, as though it never happened. In terms of common law pleading, a justification is in the nature, not of a demurrer, denying the cause of action, but of a plea in confession and

55 Ex parte Quirin, 317 U.S. 1, 20–23 (1942).
56 *See id.*
57 *See* Joseph E. Persico, Roosevelt's Secret War: FDR and World War II Espionage 204 (2002).
58 *Id.*
59 *Id.*

avoidance. It recognizes that the crime has been committed, but there are good reasons, extrinsic to the harm caused by the crime, for regarding the action as lawful.

There are several reasons why the distinction between excuse and justification is important in the structure of criminal liability. The basic principle is that a justified action, one that is rendered lawful, cannot be countered by another justified action. In so far as the two excuses undermine competence—by analogy to infancy—they would still be applicable against those who use force against justified force. There are also implications with regard to the law of complicity.[60] In principle, those who assist someone acting in self-defense are not liable for contributing to the harm that accrues to the attacker.

Still on the level of language, some explanation is required for the use of the term "legitimate defense." The common law terminology is self-defense, which is a justification for response to attacks against oneself. Defending against attacks against family members and others standing in close personal proximity were, at common law, viewed as excuses. In *Defending Humanity*, Jens Ohlin and I argued in favor of a general theory of justifiable force by analogy to the approach in European legal systems.[61] The term is *Notwehr* in German and *légitime défense* in French. The French concept is expressed in the official French version of Article 51 of the United Nations Charter, which recognizes a *droit naturel de légitime défense.*[62] Admittedly, the English version relies on common law terminology and posits "an inherent right of self-defense."[63] But the danger of the latter term is to entrench common law distinctions among the defense of self, the defense of others, and the defense of property.

The purpose of the UN Charter is to impose conditions for the peaceful resolution of international disputes and limits the use of force by nation–states as a single exception and applicable only until the Security Council takes "measures to maintain international peace and security." The principle of single exception encourages the use of the term "legitimate defense." The term is to be favored as well because all legal systems outside the common law used similar terminology, which unites all the particular claims of the common law into a single general defense, which we call legitimate defense.

[60] *Infra* ch. XI.

[61] George P. Fletcher & Jens David Ohlin, Defending Humanity: When Force is Justified and Why? (2008).

[62] U.N. Charter art. 51 (Fr.).

[63] *See id.* (Engl.).

The theory of legitimate self-defense borders on the separate justification of necessity, not mentioned in the Rome Statute. Necessity is based on the principle of balancing evils and is in fact enthroned by the Model Penal Code in Section 3 as the general principle underlying all claims of justification.[64] As will be explored in detail in chapter 8, the principle of necessity derives from private law. We should consider necessity as a possible extension of Article 31, which permits the recognitions of additional grounds excluding criminal liability.[65]

The definition of legitimate defense in Article 31(1)(c) raises many of the issues discussed so far. The prolix paragraph is best restructured to make the essential theme and its qualification in the case of war crimes. First, the basic ground of justification consists of (a) acting to defend oneself or others (b) reasonably, (c) against an (d) imminent and (e) unlawful use of force (f) proportionate to level of the attack. And (g) implicitly, the defense must be undertaken knowing of the attack. Each of these seven factors requires analysis both of principle and of the actual language used in Article 31(1)(c).

Acting to defend oneself or others. Since we are speaking here of all crime with the exception of one species of war crime, we have to try to imagine how this might work. The crimes of concern are collective enterprises, and they are sufficiently grave to be of concern to the international community. A typical case, therefore, might be the commission of aggression by invasion of another country. The language "oneself" suggests that a single individual is going to invoke legitimate defenses against a national aggressor. The example invokes fantasies of Superman against an evil kingdom.

The inclusion of the defense of others suggests a collective defense that might be more plausible. Yet there is no doubt that these provisions in Article 31 are pitched to individuals as the cases of insanity and intoxication demonstrate clearly. Perhaps the paradigm case of legitimate defense is one I have envisioned in the hypothetical of the Polish farmer, based on an incident that occurred in World War II near Clermont-Ferrand in France:

Nazi soldiers are marching past a Polish farm. A farmer appears to tend his crops but in fact he has a rifle hidden under his hoe. He knows of the Nazi attacks on both the Polish army and the civilian population. As the soldiers

[64] *See* Model Penal Code § 3 (Am. Law Inst., 1962).

[65] "At trial, the Court may consider a ground for excluding criminal responsibility other than those referred to in paragraph 1 where such a ground is derived from applicable law as set forth in article 21. The procedures relating to the consideration of such a ground shall be provided for in the Rules of Procedure and Evidence." Rome Statute, *supra* note 1, art. 31(3).

pass, he pulls out his gun and starts shooting. Is he defending against an attack against himself or others? He appears to be, even though his conduct, as discussed below, is arguably a war crime on his part.

Perhaps the better way to interpret this language is to focus entirely outside the law of war. One might imagine a fight by one civilian (or perhaps an off-duty soldier) against another. Yet it is hard to imagine that this hypothetical case could be of concern to the international community—even in part.

Reasonably. Whether self-defense must be reasonable is a classic problem in the domestic law of self-defense. The entire Goetz case revolves around this issue.[66] According to the facts generally recognized, Goetz was riding on the subway in New York during a period of high crime in the city.[67] Four tough-looking youths approached him and asked him for five dollars.[68] He took this to be a threat and took out a concealed pistol and fired five shots, severely injuring four of the youths.[69] The issue was whether his sincere belief in danger was sufficient or whether his belief had to be measured against a community standard of appropriate behavior. The Court decided for the latter, and his defense of self-defense failed to absolve him of his criminal behavior. He was convicted for illegal possession of the gun he used.[70]

Yet the standard of the "reasonable person" is always adapted to the circumstances in which the person is acting. Those circumstances include his perception of danger, his own prior experience with violence, and his mental condition at the time. In the context of crimes considered under the Rome Statute, these factors would also include the behavior of other persons in the conflict, both allies and enemies.

The hidden issue in this clause is that the attack might be reasonably (and sincerely) believed to be impending without there being any attack at all. In the international arena, it is important that there be an attack—or at least some proof.[71] It is not enough to argue, as did George W. Bush with regard to Iraq, that he believed they possessed weapons of mass destruction.[72] My

[66] People v. Goetz, 68 N.Y.2d 96, 105–106 (N.Y. Sup. Ct. 1986) [hereinafter Goetz I].

[67] *Id.* at 100.

[68] *Id.*

[69] *Id.*

[70] People v. Goetz, 73 N.Y.2d 751 (N.Y. 1988) (affirming Goetz's conviction and sentencing) [hereinafter Goetz II].

[71] *See* Rome Statute, *supra* note 1, art. 61(5); Beth Van Schaack, *Negotiating at the Interface of Power and Law: The Crime of Aggression*, 49 COLUM. J. TRANSNAT'L L. 507 (2011).

[72] *See* President George W. Bush, *Ultimatum Iraq Speech*, Cross Hall, White House (Mar. 17, 2003), https://www.theguardian.com/world/2003/mar/18/usa.iraq.

favorite example of proof is Adlai Stevenson's showing pictures at the UN of Cuba's construction of missile sites.[73]

Against an imminent attack. The concept of imminence has been problematic both in international and domestic criminal law. It is not even mentioned in Article 51 of the UN Charter, but insofar as domestic criminal law is the guide to international standards, imminence is obviously required.[74] The problem is, what does it mean? Well, we all know that it means not too soon, and not too late, but it there anything more intelligent we can say about it? The problem is acute in the battered women cases, where often men threaten their wives with a beating at night and do not carry through until the next day. The tension lies between the use of force that is autonomous and that which is responsive to an attack. The more the action appears to be autonomous, the less likely we are to consider the attack imminent. This is paradoxical because legitimate defense is not supposed to be a case of semi-involuntary conduct, but perhaps there is some confusion in the Rome Statute produced by association with duress in in Art. 31(1)(d), which requires imminence.[75]

Unlawful use of force. The use of this term confirms the implicit recognition of the distinction between justification and excuse. Actions committed by the insane and the intoxicated are merely excused and therefore their attacks are unjustified. A legitimate defense is not unlawful and therefore we arrive at the conclusion, sometimes contested in the literature, that a legitimate defense is not permitted against conduct that is committed in legitimate defense. If "unlawful" is interpreted to mean permissible, then it might be possible to recognize a legitimate defense on both sides of a two-person conflict.

Proportionate to the level of the attack. The first point is that in keeping with the general confusion in the literature on this point, the paragraph does not mention the necessity of the defense. In most controversial cases of disproportionate force, there is a preliminary issue of whether the use of force was even necessary. For example, in the Goetz case, it was often argued that Goetz had many less-costly remedies than firing his gun. He could have just shown the gun as he claimed to have done in the past.[76] He could have fired into the roof of the subway car. This is often the case in international conflicts

[73] Michael Dobbs, *The Day Adlai Stevenson Showed 'Em at the U.N.*, WASH. POST (Feb. 5, 2003), https://www.washingtonpost.com/archive/lifestyle/2003/02/05/the-day-adlai-stevenson-showed-em-at-the-un/24420f12-5f7a-4f2d-b91e-2b84e04ee6ab/.

[74] *See* U.N. Charter art. 51.

[75] *See* Rome Statute, *supra* note 1, art. 31(1)(d).

[76] *Goetz*, 68 N.Y.2d at 106.

as well. But as soon as one examines the actual balancing of interests, the problem becomes too vague for resolution. For example, was it necessary for the United States to use nuclear weapons against Japan in World War II?[77] If the alternative was an invasion by U.S. troops, then the question is how many men should the United States have been willing to sacrifice arguably to save Japanese lives. The analogous question for Goetz is how much of a risk should he have endured by merely showing the gun in order to lower the cost against those who were aggressing against him.

From a comparative perspective, there have been two basic approaches to the problem of proportionality: the common law and the German approach. The common law developed by drawing an analogy between capital punishment and self-defense.[78] This is a false analogy because self-defense is not a form of punishmen.t but nonetheless it has served to limit the use of self-defense against minor attacks. It is generally agreed that for attacks less than homicidal, self-defense is permissible against rape and grievous bodily harm, but not against theft or other assaults on interests in property.

The German approach started by reference to Section 32 of the Penal Code, which recognizes self-defense in all cases that are necessary to preserve the interests of the defender.[79] Thus. the courts faced a repeated challenge of whether they could limit self-defense in theft cases.[80] My favorite case for teaching purposes is the defense against the apple thief, where a property owner had no means to protect his orchard but to shoot the escaping thief.[81] A similar case in the Uno was held to be a violation of the victim's civil rights under 18 USC 242.

The most intriguing German solution was to invoke a doctrine of private law called *abus de droit* or *Rechtsmisbrauch*. That is, the defender has rights to defend his property at all cost but doing so may be a misuse of his rights.[82]

[77] *See* David Kaiser, *Why the United States Dropped Atomic Bombs in 1945*, TIME (May 25, 2016), http://time.com/4346336/atomic-bombs-1945-history/.

[78] *See, e.g.*, Christopher H. Wellman, *The Rights Forfeiture Theory of Punishment*, 122 ETHICS 371, 374 (2012) ("[S]elf-defense is commonly understood in terms of rights forfeiture, and the most sophisticated debates in these areas are more specifically about whether so-called aggressors and threats can forfeit their rights by merely posing a threat to others.").

[79] *See* StGB § 32.

[80] *See, e.g.*, Judgment of Sept. 20, 1920, Reichsgericht, Ger., 55 Reichsgericht in Strafsachen [RGSt] 82.

[81] *See* Reichsgericht [RG] [Supreme Court 1880–1945] Sept 20, 1920, 55 Enstscheidungen des Reichsgerichts in Strafsachen [RGSt] 82 (F.R.G.).

[82] *See* George P. Fletcher, *The Right and the Reasonable*, 98 HARV. L. REV. 949, 952 n.21 (1985) ("Judgment of Jan. 22, 1963, Oberlandesgericht, Bavaria, 16 NEUE JURISTISCHE WOCHENSCHRIFT [NJW] 824. The defendant attempted to frighten a woman out of a parking spot by driving toward her. On the defendant's plea of self-defense, the court found that although the driver had a right to the parking spot, he had used a degree of force that was excessive and therefore an "abuse of right." This

This solution brings into focus the relative pervasiveness of "reasonableness" in common law thinking. By putting the word "reasonable" in the definition of the standard of self-defense, we need not invoke the principle of *abus de droit*. It is argued that this difference in doctrinal approach is one of the clear differences between common law and civil law thinking. The Rome Statute follows the common law on this point.

The defense must be intentional or knowing. This is generally taken for granted, but there is a position in the literature, notably advanced by Paul Robinson, in favor of so-called objective justification.[83] A good example is the hypothetical of the bomb thief. Someone at the beach steals a backpack. He is arrested and the police find the backpack contained a bomb that was about to explode. In fact, the thief saved many lives. Is his conduct justified? Robinson argued yes.[84] My view is that this position confuses the question of harm with the issue of justification. There was no harm in the case of the bomb thief, and harm is generally assumed to be an ingredient of all completed offenses.

5. Duress

Duress traditionally occupies a conflicted position between the categories of justification and excuse. In one version, it is an excuse based on external pressure overwhelming the voluntary capacities of the actor. In this version, it is applicable in cases of homicide as well as minor offenses. In the alternative, it is a justification based on balancing the interests of the person under duress and the victims. This split does not exactly parallel the differences between common law and civil law thinking noted above in the theory of legitimate defense. It turns out that there are several positions in the common law and perhaps alternatives to the complicated German model in the civil law jurisdictions. It is not surprising to find at the end of this survey that the position in Rome Statute Article 31(1(d) is an amalgam of conflicting approaches to duress.

doctrine was invoked more recently in Judgment of Nov. 24, 1976, Oberlandesgericht, Hamm, 30 NJW 590, 592.").

[83] *See generally* H. Robinson, *A Theory of Justification: Societal Harm as a Prerequisite for Criminal Liability*, 23 UCLA L. Rev. 266 (1975).

[84] *See generally* Paul H. Robinson, *The Bomb Thief and the Theory of Justification Defenses*, 8 Crim. L.F. 387 (1997).

The general idea of duress is that someone who commits a crime is not entirely free to choose whether to do it or not. The constraint on freedom is based on an external threat or coercion imposed by another. This means that there is always another perpetrator on the scene, namely the one who forces—so to speak—the primary party to act. Duress is generally regarded as an excuse due to the requirement of "overwhelming the will."[85] Yet it can take on some of the characteristics of a justification based on balancing evils.

For one common law approach, note the rather simple provision laid out in the nineteenth-century California Penal Code, Article 26, which provides:

> All persons are capable of committing crimes except those belonging to the following classes. Persons (unless the crime be punishable with death) who committed the act or made the omission charged under threats or menaces sufficient to show that they had reasonable cause to and did believe their lives would be endangered if they refused.[86]

This provision does not even use the word "duress" and clearly does not distinguish between justification and excuse. It falls into the error of associating defenses with infancy, namely with a condition that renders the actor incapable of committing any crimes. Indeed, this provision is framed in the plural, which fails even to recognize that duress for one person might not be duress for another. Also, even if we want to interpret this as an excuse, it would only be a limited excuse—not applicable in homicide and other capital cases. That limitation suggests a balancing of interests at the extremes. The death penalty is still formally available in California for the following list of crimes: "First-degree murder with special circumstances; military sabotage; death in the course of train wrecking; treason; perjury causing execution of an innocent person; fatal assault by a prisoner serving a life sentence."[87] These are variations of homicide, but no one has been executed since 2006; hundreds are waiting on death row, and the state is embroiled in efforts to reform the system.[88] In view of the state of the death penalty in California, it

[85] *See, e.g.*, Model Penal Code § 213.1 commentary at 314.

[86] Cal. Pen. Code § 26(6) (2018).

[87] *Appendix Table 1, Capital Offense, by state, 2016*, at 9, *Capital Punishment, Bureau of Justice Statistics*, U.S. D.O.J. (Apr. 2018), *available at* https://www.bjs.gov/content/pub/pdf/cp16sb.pdf. *See* Cal. Pen. Code § 190 (2018).

[88] *See* Paige St. John & Maloy Moore, *These Are the 747 Inmates Awaiting Execution on California's Death Row*, L.A. Times (Aug. 24, 2017), http://www.latimes.com/projects/la-me-death-row/.

would be better to interpret Article 26 of the California Code to limit the defense to homicide cases.

The Model Penal Code has a more refined provision in Article 2.09, which provides:

> (1) It is an affirmative defense that the actor engaged in the conduct charged to constitute an offense because he was coerced to do so by the use of, or a threat to use, unlawful force against his person or the person of another, that a person of reasonable firmness in his situation would have been unable to resist.[89]

This has the advantage of not limiting the defense to threats of homicide and importantly places it outside the general provisions on Justification in Article 2 and locates instead in the General Principles of Liability and not Article 3.[90] Yet the provision is identified as an affirmative defense.[91] What this means is that according to Article 2.04(d), there must be enough evidence to take the claim to the jury—not shifting the burden of persuasion to the defense.[92]

Shifting the burden of persuasion (risk of non-persuasion), if even by a preponderance of the evidence, would hardly be compatible with the spirit of the Rome Statute. It runs contrary to the presumption of innocence and the duty of the prosecution to establish guilt by proof beyond a reasonable doubt. Yet it is not surprising that in the common law tradition, which cannot completely extricate itself from what I call the "private law style"—that is, thinking of these defenses on the model of private litigation—there is a tendency in many jurisdictions to shift the burden of persuasion on some if not all defensive issues.

With respect to duress, MPC Art. 2.09 contains some interesting qualifications in parts (2) and (4). Incidentally, part (3) contains a snippet of legal history, noting and abolishing any residual influence of the principle that a woman acting in the presence of her husband is coerced.[93] Part (2) contains an exemption, parallel to the one we note above with regard to intoxication: if the defendant recklessly (or negligently for crimes punished by negligence) placed himself in a situation in which "it was probable that he

[89] MODEL PENAL CODE § 2.09 (AM. LAW INST., 1962).
[90] *See id.*
[91] *Id.*
[92] MODEL PENAL CODE § 2.04(d) (AM. LAW INST., 1962).
[93] MODEL PENAL CODE § 2.09(3) (AM. LAW INST., 1962).

would be subjected to duress," he cannot claim the defense.[94] The same critique of the intoxication applies here. It might be preferable to have a minor risk-taking offense of subjecting oneself to a coercive situation, and then an excuse for acting under coercion.

Part 4 of MPC Article 2.09 recognizes that the excuse overlaps in some cases with the principle of justification under Article 3.02 of the MPC, which recognizes the general defense of necessity or acting to pick the lesser evil where some choice is necessary.[95] We explore those issues in chapter 8.

To return to the Rome Statute on duress, the significant elements are these: (a) the conduct must be "caused by duress resulting from" a threat, (b) of imminent death or of captaining or imminent serious bodily harm (c) against that person or another person, (d) the person acts necessarily and reasonably to the threat, provided that (e) the person does not intend to cause a greater harm than the one sought to be avoided, (f) the threat may be made by other persons or constituted by other circumstances beyond that person's control.[96] (g) The seventh point is that where such a ground is derived from applicable law, additions to the requirements of duress can be made using authority from Article 21. We will comment on each of these seven points in comparison with the California Penal Code and the Model Penal Code.

(a) The conduct must be caused by duress resulting from a threat.

This phrase is unfortunate for two reasons. It repeats the word duress—the one it is trying to define. Worse, it invokes the notion of causation. In chapter 4, we spent some time on how difficult it is to give a good account of causation. To invoke the concept here is unfortunate and without parallel in the provisions under comparison. When we speak of behavior being caused, we enter a difficult philosophical realm about the relevance of free will and determinism. There are many philosophers who quite sensibly think that all of our behavior is caused but we are nonetheless free to choose our next move. This is the compatabilist school, as opposed to the incompatabilists who claim that determinism precludes the possibility of free or autonomous will.[97] This is a deep and mysterious issue in the philosophy of Immanuel Kant.

[94] *Id.* at § 2.09(2).
[95] *Id.* at § 2.09(4).
[96] *See* Rome Statute, *supra* note 1, art. 31(d).
[97] *Supra* ch. V.

(b) of imminent death or of continuing or imminent serious bodily harm
Leaving aside the issue of causation, the coercion must result from at least the threat of imminent bodily injury. It is not clear why the threat of physical confinement should not have the same effect. This seems to be particularly true, for example, in a case of kidnapping, where the threat is to another person.

(c) against that person or another person
That the threat may be to another person undermines the claim that the threat "causes" the response under duress. Yet it is not clear what the right word would be. The focus should be on the comparison of dangers that we can expect of a reasonable person under the circumstances.

(d) the person 'acts necessarily and reasonably to avoid the threat
The reliance on the word "reasonable" in the California Code and the MPC reveals a prominent feature of American legal discourse, absent from the civil law tradition. In this context, it is the key to understanding duress as a defense. There are some situations in which we can indeed expect people to endure some threats and this becomes obvious in point (f) below as well as in the California exception for homicide.

(e) the person acts "necessarily and reasonably to avoid the threat"
The element of acting "necessarily" requires some comment. This implies, as in the general claim of necessity, that there is no cheaper means of avoiding the threat. This is the classic problem in the law of war and in the theory of self-defense of, say, using nuclear weapons when conventional weapons would do. In the Goetz case, it would have been enough to merely show the gun instead of shooting. Yet every time a less-costly means is chosen, the actor takes risks on himself. In the case of legitimate defense, because it is a case of justification, it seems incorrect. In the context of this provision on duress, which as we see as mixed cases of justification and excuse, the choice of less-costly means might be fairly be expected. Yet as this mixture includes an element of "overpowering the will," the choice fairly to be expected might not properly be qualified as "rational."

(f) provided that the person does not intend to cause a greater harm than the one sought to be avoided
In this provision we encounter a clear collision between a theory of justification and excuse. It is characteristic of a claim of justification to balance evils, but apart from that problem, we now have a balancing of intentions. The causal question drops out altogether.

(g) The threat may be made by other persons or constituted by other circumstances beyond that person's control.

There some ambiguity here between "by other persons" and "that person's control." Is the Rome Statute referring to the same people? It seems that the first reference is to people who are imposing the conditions of duress and the latter to some factor—like a time bomb—that is beyond everyone's control. I suppose that could make sense if the issue is simply generating an excuse for the defendant's committing a crime within the jurisdiction of the Court. The problem, however, is that the purpose of his action must be to avoid the threat. "Avoid" must have the connotation of canceling out or overcoming. If the threat emanates from a cause beyond everyone's control, it is not clear how that is possible.

All things considered, Rome Statute 31(1)(d) is the most poorly drafted of the four and therefore the most difficult to analyze. A large part of this difficulty stems from ambiguity as to whether the provision should stand as a theory of excuse or justification. The first two, insanity and intoxication, are clearly excuses. Legitimate defense is a justification, and therefore one would expect that duress would also be defined as a justification, but in fact is a mixed case with elements of both. In defense of the provision, one might say that mixing the two categories might be justified by the complexity of the problem.

7
Intention vs. Negligence

The Rome Statute[1] tells us both too much and too little about what it calls "Mental State" in the three parts of Article 30.[2] It gives us more information than we can sensibly apply with regard to intentional offenses and tells us nothing about other mental states, notably negligence; and indeed it fails to articulate a principle about why "mental states" are even relevant.

Lawyers trained in the common law tradition are familiar with the concept of *mens rea* and the maxim *actus non facit reus nisi mens sit rea.* Literally this means that there is no criminal (or guilty) act without a criminal (or guilty) mind.[3] The problem is that there are both descriptive and normative interpretations of *mens rea* and of the maxim. The descriptive interpretation is typified by cases in the early history of larceny when the actor would receive possession of the good at one moment of time and decide to keep it at a later moment.[4] The descriptive proposition held that the relevant action and the relevant intention had to occur at the same time.[5] Before the emergence of embezzlement as a distinct crime at the end of the eighteenth century, this was a pivotal question of criminal liability.[6] If the actus reus occurred fist (taking, acquiring possession) and the mens rea later (intention to deprive the owner), there was no crime. Needless to say, the detail surrounding these issues became the subject of intense litigation.

[1] Rome Statute for the International Criminal Court, July 17, 1998, 2187 U.N.T.S. 3; U.N. Diplomatic Conference of Plenipotentiaries on the Establishment of an International Court, U.N. Doc. A/Conf.183/9 [hereinafter Rome Statute].

[2] *Id.*, art. 30 ("Unless otherwise provided, a person shall be criminally responsible and liable for punishment for a crime within the jurisdiction of the Court only if the material elements are committed with intent and knowledge.

For the purposes of this article, a person has intent where: (a) In relation to conduct, that person means to engage in the conduct; (b) In relation to a consequence, that person means to cause that consequence or is aware that it will occur in the ordinary course of events. For the purposes of this article, "knowledge" means awareness that a circumstance exists or a consequence will occur in the ordinary course of events. "Know" and "knowingly" shall be construed accordingly.").

[3] *See Black's Law Dict.* (5th ed. 1979).

[4] Wayne R. LaFave & Austin W. Scott, Jr., Criminal Law § 8.1, at 702 (2d ed. 1986).

[5] *See, e.g.*, T. Plucknett, A Concise History Of The Common Law 449–51 (5th ed. 1956).

[6] *See id.*; George P. Fletcher, *The Metamorphosis of Larceny*, 89 Harv. L. Rev. 469 (1976).

The Grammar of Criminal Law: Volume Two: International Criminal Law. George P. Fletcher.

In the context of the Rome Statute, there are many offenses that might pose this problem. Consider the war crime of "taking of hostages."[7] Suppose in the course of hostilities, the invading army acquires some prisoners of war and then finds, at a later point, that they could threaten to harm the POWs as a way of coercing the enemy to retreat.

Would the threat retroactively convert the taking of prisoners with good intention into a taking of hostages with a mental state that generates liability? A strict approach to the principle nullum crimen sine lege might lead the court to follow the pattern that caused problems in the history of larceny. If the larceny problem was resolved by creating the crime of embezzlement, the hostage hypothetical could be resolved by creating a new crime of treating a POW as a hostage.

The normative or moral interpretation of mens rea holds that the term equivalent to a guilty mind, for example, a basis for blaming the actor for his conduct, is something not possible in the face of the defenses considered in the last chapter. For example, the maxim requiring mens rea would put into play a claim like insanity that would preclude a finding of moral guilt. The tension between the descriptive and normative view of mens rea is inherent in any system of criminal law that seeks both to define the law clearly and yet justify punishment of the guilty. Punishment is by its nature condemnatory, that is, it expresses a moral judgment and therefore invites the normative interpretation of the basic principles of the system. A good example of the normative approach is seen in *Davis v. U.S.*, which held that a plea of not guilty explicitly raised the issue of insanity to the extent that it introduced a reasonable doubt.[8] An insane defendant could not satisfy the requirement of mens rea and therefore would not be guilty.

The principle *actus non facit reum nisi mens sit rea* is a characteristic feature of the common law. It was never enacted as a statute or born by a decree of the English king.[9] It emerged from the case law of solving practical conceptual problems posed by the examples given above of larceny and insanity. This is important because it is obvious that many philosophical concepts required for a functioning criminal law are never officially enacted. We might say the same about the difficult concepts of intention, human

[7] Rome Statute, *supra* note 1, art. 8.

[8] *See* Davis v. United States, 160 U.S. 469 (1895).

[9] *See* 2 Frederick Pollock & Frederick Maitland, The History of the English Law 449–511 (2d ed. Cambridge University Press 1968) (1898) (tracing the origin of *actus non facit reum nisi mens sit rea* to St. Augustine).

action, causation, and the purpose of punishment. That does not mean they should be ignored, but as fundamental philosophical and policy issues, they should be debated by scholars until a consensus emerges and thus become a "general principle" of law as mentioned in Rome Statute 21(1)(c).[10] Admittedly, Article 38 of the International Court of Justice is more helpful in identifying the opinions of scholars as a source of law.[11] In continental legal cultures, in particular the German *Dogmatik*, scholarly teachings are a prominent source of law.[12]

The accepted German definition is quite simple: Intention (Vorsatz) is knowing and desiring the realization of the definition of the offense. The element of desire (Wollen) is critical here because it introduces an element of personal identification between the actor and the harm and thus provides a basis for blaming his conduct. It is also significant that the German definition focuses on the definition of the offense and thus leaves out considerations of wrongdoing (justification) and attribution (excuse).

The downside of the German approach is its rigorous commitment to the bipartite division of all forms of culpability into the categories of dolus and culpa—presumably a legacy of Roman legal terminology. Thus, it becomes problematic to deal with borderline cases of risk taking. This are grouped under the heading of *dolus eventualis*, and there have been many disputes in the German literature about the right way to define this middle ground.[13]

From a practical point of view, these definitions do not matter much, but they do try to capture the essential difference between dolus and culpa (intention and negligence).

Of the two or more approaches recognized in the common law tradition—and dominant in tort law—is to rely just on knowledge, leaving aside considerations of desire that identify the actor more closely with the harm. The common definition is that the actor intends the result if he has knowledge to a substantial certainly that the result will follow. The classic case is *Garret v. Dailey* in which a child moved a chair when it appeared that the

[10] Rome Statute, *supra* note 1, art. 21(1)(c).

[11] Statute of the International Court of Justice, Oct. 24, 1945, article 38, 59 Stat. 1055 ("The Court, whose function is to decide in accordance with international law such disputes as are submitted to it, shall apply . . . subject to the provisions of Article 59, [i.e. that only the parties bound by the decision in any particular case], judicial decisions and the teachings of the most highly qualified publicists of the various nations, as subsidiary means for the determination of rules of law.").

[12] For a discussion of the triparte system, see *supra* Introduction.

[13] *See, e.g*, G. Taylor, *The Intention Debate in German Criminal Law*, Ratio Juris 17(3): 346–80 (2004).

plaintiff might sit down on it.[14] The plaintiff fell and was injured. The state court upheld her claim and enshrined this definition based on knowledge. Two points distinguish the situation of tort law from the problem of culpability in criminal law. First, it did not matter that the child was not quite six years old and would, as an infant, not be liable for a criminal act.[15] Second, in tort law, even though there can be punitive damages, the lawsuit and judgment are not a basis for blaming and punishing the defendant.[16]

The American Law Institute made three critical decisions in attempting to reform and codify the common law in the development of the Model Penal Code. The first was to abandon the term "intention" altogether simply on the ground that the case law had become too confusing and complicated.[17] The second was to depart from the cleavage between intention and negligence and instead to recognize four states of culpability in the iconic provision §2.02(2), which is worth stating in full:

(2) Kinds of Culpability Defined
  (a) Purposely. A person acts purposely with respect to a material element of an offense when:
    (i) if the element involves the nature of his conduct or a result thereof, it is his conscious object to engage in conduct of that nature or to cause such a result; and
    (ii) if the element involves the attendant circumstances, he is aware of the existence of such circumstances or he believes or hopes that they exist.
  (b) Knowingly. A person acts knowingly with respect to a material element of an offense when:
    (i) if the element involves the nature of his conduct or the attendant circumstances, he is aware that his conduct is of that nature or that such circumstances exist; and
    (ii) if the element involves a result of his conduct, he is aware that it is practically certain that his conduct will cause such a result.

[14] *See* Garret v. Dailey, 279 P.2d 1091 (Wash. 1955).
[15] *See* A.W.G. Kean, *The History of the Criminal Liability of Children*, 53 LAW Q. REV. 364, 370 (1937).
[16] For an earlier discussion on tort compensation theory, see George P. Fletcher, *Punishment and Compensation*, 14 CREIGHTON L. REV. 691 (1981).
[17] *See* MODEL PENAL CODE §2.02 (1985).

(c) Recklessly.

(i) A person acts recklessly with respect to a material element of an offense when he consciously disregards a substantial and unjustifiable risk that the material element exists or will result from his conduct. The risk must be of such a nature and degree that, considering the nature and purpose of the actor's conduct and the circumstances known to him, its disregard involves a gross deviation from the standard of conduct that a law-abiding person would observe in the actor's situation.

(d) Negligently.

A person acts negligently with respect to a material element of an offense when he should be aware of a substantial and unjustifiable risk that the material element exists or will result from his conduct. The risk must be of such a nature and degree that the actor's failure to perceive it, considering the nature and purpose of his conduct and the circumstances known to him, involves a gross deviation from the standard of care that a reasonable person would observe in the actor's situation.[18]

This provision might be the most successful contribution of the MPC. Many European scholars admire its solution to the problem of *dolus eventualis*—namely, recognizing the middle category of recklessness.[19] A careful reading reveals several additional contributions. First, the MPC introduces element analysis, which became the basis for drafting Article 30 of the Rome Statute. The range of elements for differentiating levels of culpability are (a) nature of the conduct, (b) the result, and (c) attendant circumstances.[20] It is not clear whether Article 30 of the Rome Statute purports to follow this set of distinctions. The Rome Statute includes the nature of the conduct and the result (called the "consequence") but it is not clear whether it includes attendant circumstances. Article 30(3) refers to knowledge that "a circumstance exists or a consequence will occur in the ordinary course of events."[21] It is not clear what circumstances might be relevant in this passage and whether the latter phrase beginning "will occur" applies to the circumstances

[18] *Id.*

[19] *See, e.g.*, Jens David Ohlin, *Targeting and the Concept of Intent*, 35 MICH. J. INT'L L. 79, 89 n.45 (2013).

[20] *See* MODEL PENAL CODE § 2.02.

[21] Rome Statute, *supra* note 1, art. 30(3).

as well as the consequence. That is, it could be read in either of two ways: (a) knowledge that the attendant circumstances exists or (b) knowledge that the consequence will occur in the ordinary course of events.

Of the approximately 50 war crimes in Article 8, the most significant surrounding circumstance is whether the crime is "committed as part of a plan or policy or as part of a large-scale commission of such crimes."[22] This factor is surely not part of the action or the result. Therefore, it must be an attendant circumstance. The appropriate reading would be option (a) above. The alternative (b) might apply in a case such as shooting in the death and the expectation of death.

But recall the requirement of "intent and knowledge."[23] It is difficult to pair the ordinary meaning of "intent" with the expectation that the consequence will occur as an ordinary consequence. The appropriate reading is "intent or knowledge."

Focusing on the consequence or result of the action in defining the mental elements invokes the relevance of harm. In fact, the criminal law typically insists on actual harm to a person or property before even undertaking an inquiry into the actor's mental state. In tort law, there would never be an inquiry into fault without a plaintiff who was harmed. This should also be the focus of the Rome Statute. It is hard to imagine the problem of impunity without harm to actual victims. True, there is a crime of attempt recognized in Article 25(3)(f),[24] and we will undertake a closer look at inchoate crimes without actual harm in chapter 9.

Whether by design or not, the definitions of acting recklessly and purposely in the MPC teach us something about the distinction between wrongdoing and blameworthiness. It will be recalled that this was the focus of the discussion of the defenses enumerated in Article 31 of the Rome Statute. In the MPC, the wrongdoing component is expressed in reference to the "substantial and unjustifiable risk" of bringing about the material element.[25] This is the same for recklessness and negligence. The difference between them

[22] *Id.* art. 8(1).

[23] *Id.* art. 30.

[24] *Id.* article 25(3)(f) ("Attempts to commit such a crime by taking action that commences its execution by means of a substantial step, but the crime does not occur because of circumstances independent of the person's intentions. However, a person who abandons the effort to commit the crime or otherwise prevents the completion of the crime shall not be liable for punishment under this Statute for the attempt to commit that crime if that person completely and voluntarily gave up the criminal purpose.").

[25] Model Penal Code, *supra* note 15, §2.02(2)(d).

appears in the second section of parts c and d. Recklessness requires "a gross deviation from the conduct of a law-abiding person."[26] The assumption is that the gross deviation is conscious. Negligence is based, as in the classic definition from the law of torts, on the conduct of "a reasonable person under the circumstances."[27]

The important point is that negligence is based on the fault of not knowing. The actor should have known but he did not. The classic instance of this kind of fault in the Rome Statute is in Article 28, Command Responsibility, which states explicitly in part (a) that the commander is liable if he "should have known that the forces [under his command] were committing or about to commit such crimes."[28] Note that recklessness refers to a law-abiding person, but in the context of negligence, the relevant standard is the reasonable person in the actor's situation. The problem has always been whether personal factors enter into the definition, for example, experience, intelligence, pressures of warfare, expectations of superiors, and other characteristics.

The tension in the history of tort law has been the objective and subjective standards of negligence. The problem has always been whether the notion of fault implies some personal and subjective commitment to the action. This issue has been intensely debated in criminal law as well, as typified by the trial of Bernhard Goetz for shooting four unarmed young African Americans on the New York subway in the 1980s.[29] The case became a classic, illustrating the problem of defining the reasonable person under the circumstances. Did it matter, for example, whether Goetz had been mugged before on the subway? Did it matter whether the prior assailants were black or white? Did it matter how they were dressed, whether the subway was coming or going to a black neighborhood? Goe, in fact, was carrying a concealed weapon without a license. That is another important factor bearing on the problem of inchoate liability, discussed in the next chapter.

There are some material elements of the offenses, which no legal system would expect to be encompassed with the mental element or mens rea. A good example is causation. Yet the Rome Statute seems to include causation within the mental element when it refers in Article 30(2) to knowledge that the "consequence will occur in the ordinary cause of events."[30]

[26] *Id.* §2.02(2)(c).

[27] *See* RESTATEMENT (SECOND) OF TORTS § 284 (Am. Law Inst. 1965).

[28] Rome Statute, *supra* note 1, art. 28(a)(i).

[29] People v. Goetz, 502 N.Y.S.2d 577, 578 (N.Y. Sup. Ct. 1986).

[30] Rome Statute, *supra* note 1, art. 30(2)(b).

This resembles the tort standard of foreseeability, but as every student of the *Palsgraf* case knows, foreseeability depends on the particularity with which we define the consequence.[31] A burglar may anticipate harm, but he would not foresee that breaking and entering someone's home would set off an automatic weapon that would kill someone standing across the street.

Recalling the earlier discussion of "causal energy," the appropriate question is whether someone committing a crime intentionally brings more causal energy to the events than someone committing it negligently.[32] An analogous question is whether omissions, coupled with "awareness that the consequence will occur in the ordinary course of events" encompasses fewer consequences that an overt act (however acts and omissions might be conceptualized). My intuitions—as well my expectation of judicial intuitions—are that intentional conduct introduces more causal energy to the course of events. This is obviously not a scientific observation.

The notion of material elements suffers from the same ambiguity as the principle of nullum crimen sine lege. We do not know whether it applies to "grounds for excluding criminal responsibility."[33] We dealt with the latter issue under the theory of objective justification. The notion of "mental elements" supposedly refers to subjective considerations, that is, matters that occur in the mind without any necessary external manifestation.[34] This can be a serious problem for inchoate offenses, such as attempts in Rome Statute 25(3).[35] The question of when an attempt leaves the realm of thought and crosses the line of criminality has been long debated and will become the focus of the next chapter.

Essentially, negligence lives in the fault of not knowing. There is a duty to know but the duty is not satisfied. One could well understand skepticism about negligence from the perspective of mens rea as an actual mental state. Some earlier theorists of American law have opposed punishment for negligence in the criminal law and even those who accept it, such as the distinguished British scholar Glanville Williams, consider negligence a less significant basis for criminal liability than conscious states such as intention, knowledge, and recklessness.[36]

[31] Palsgraf v. Long Island R.R. Co., 162 N.E. 99 (N.Y. 1928).
[32] *See supra* ch. IV.
[33] Rome Statute, *supra* note 1, art. 31.
[34] *See id.* art. 30.
[35] *Id.* art. 25(3).
[36] *See generally* G. Williams, Criminal Law: The General Part (2d. 1961).

The problem is why there is duty to know of risks latent in one's conduct. This is a classic problem in rape cases where disputes have long attended the problem of date rape. In a famous 1975 case in the United Kingdom, three soldiers met the defendant Morgan in a bar, and he supposed told them that his wife was "kinky" and enjoyed being forcibly subjected to intercourse.[37] All three of them raped her while the others held her down and smothered her screams.[38] The House of Lords held that honest belief was a defense but nonetheless upheld the conviction on the ground that no reasonable jury would have believed the claim.[39] The case illustrated the blurring of the line between substance and procedure, namely the principle and evidence.

Yet if it is true that the perpetrators really did not know of the wife's opposition, it would be a good example of the fault of not knowing. The danger of the "should have known" standard is that it is subject to easy manipulation but if we keep in mind the blurred line between substance and evidence, we can see that would be true of all mental states.

Still there is a problem in the ordering imposed by the MPC. Negligence is the least culpable of the four states of mind and indeed, unless negligence is explicitly required, the position of the MPC is that one of the three conscious states is required. It is hard to know here whether the interpretation of mens rea as a conscious decision determines this outcome.

The principle of nullum crimen must have some bearing on the presumed necessity of including Article 30 in the Statute. Could it be the case that one of the two arguments (fair warning and judicial guidance) accounts for the existence of this definition of mental states, however unsuccessful it might be? Could the principle of fair warning apply? The better answer is no: if people are told what crimes not to commit, it hardly makes sense to inform them as well not to commit them intentionally. Perhaps the alternative principle of judicial guidance might be relevant so far as it determines how lawyers argue cases and courts write opinions justifying conviction. There might be a third factor that justifies Article 30, and that is the teaching function of the Rome Statute for students and lawyers. In that respect, my critique of the provision is unsound.

[37] D.P.P. v. Morgan, 2 All E.R. 347 (1975); A.C. 182 (1976).
[38] *Id.*
[39] *Id.*

8

Harming vs. Trying

Offenses and Attempts

A quick look at the four crimes within the jurisdiction of the ICC, as described by the Rome Statute,[1] reveals that they are about concrete harming: killing, torture, rape, and invasion.[2] Some of the sub-crimes within these categories address completed actions even though the harm is less tangible, for example, deportation[3] and biological experiments.[4] It is difficult to reduce this variety of crimes to specific harms to persons or property. There may be a hidden logic in Article 30's reference to the more-encompassing term "consequences" instead of the more concrete notion of harm.[5]

Significantly, the four crimes are committed by action rather than omission. The only conceivable crime of omission might derive from R2P, the responsibility to protect, a duty imposed by the Security Council, on its member states.[6] Yet this is a collective responsibility, and there has been no effort by the international community to apply a version of 8*bis* to individual leaders who fail to comply with their national duties to protect their populations against the four crimes within the jurisdiction of the court (with ethnic cleansing taking the place of aggression).[7]

The motivating question of this chapter is whether the codification of criminal attempts in a statutory regime that emphasizes completed crimes with consequences to personal or property interests is appropriate. The beginning of our reasoning on this topic should be the Preamble of the Rome

[1] Rome Statute for the International Criminal Court, July 17, 1998, 2187 U.N.T.S. 3; U.N. Diplomatic Conference of Plenipotentiaries on the Establishment of an International Court, U.N. Doc. A/Conf.183/9 [hereinafter Rome Statute].

[2] *Id.*, art. 5.

[3] *Id.*, art. 7(1)(d).

[4] *Id.*, art. 8(2)(a)(ii).

[5] *Id.*, art. 30(2)(b).

[6] 2005 World Summit Outcome, G.A. Res. 60/1, ¶ 138, U.N. Doc. A/RES/60/1 (Sept. 16, 2005).

[7] *See, e.g.*, Khaled Yacoub Oweis, *Assad Forces Fire on Protestors Across Syria*, Reuters (Aug. 1, 2011), https://www.reuters.com/article/us-syria/assad-forces-fire-on-protesters-across-syria-idUSTRE76T02020110802.

The Grammar of Criminal Law: Volume Two: International Criminal Law. George P. Fletcher.

Statute, which clearly identifies concern for *impunidad*—the interest in justice to victims—as the primary rationale for the Rome Statute.[8] It is difficult to square the language of victimhood with the general punishing conduct that does not reach completion, that is, an attempt.

Attempts are one form of inchoate offense, that is, offenses that fall short of causing the harm or engendering the victimhood that would come with the completed offense. The standard example of an inchoate offense is possession of an object or tool that might be used to cause harm. The danger of possession offenses is that they generate too broad a sweep and, if taken literally, cut into many permissible and desirable activities. Some of these, like the private possession of illegal narcotics and automatic rifles, imply a criminal purpose, though others, like the possession of counterfeit money or credit cards may be accidental. On the whole, possession offenses create a large swath for prosecutorial discretion, and therefore, the Rome Statute probably chose the correct path to omit them.

The advantage of the crime of attempt over possession offenses is the implicit requirement of intention to cause harm or at least to realize the prohibited conduct. The trade-off, however, is that though the mens rea is well defined, the actus reus is inescapably vague. The problem is always how much the actor must do on the spectrum—from thought through the various stages of action to the final result of causing harm or instantiating the required "consequence" of the completed offenses.

1. Punishment of Attempts

The field of attempts generates four challenging jurisprudential problems. First, it matters in both domestic and international criminal law to consider the rationale for punishing attempts or completed conduct. Should the punishment be reduced based on how far the actor has gone toward realizing the harm that the statute seeks to prevent? Presumably, if he has done nothing, just had homicidal thoughts, he would be guilty—under any test of liability—for just thinking evil. Paradoxically, the earliest statutory crime in English came close to punishments for thoughts, namely the Treason Statute of Edward III (1351).[9] The core of the crime was "compassing; the death of

[8] Rome Statute, *supra* note 1, pmbl.

[9] *See* Treason Act, 1351, 25 Edw. III, c. 2, stat. 5 (Eng.) ("[I]magine the death of our Lord King.").

the king."[10] Yet the statute also required an overt act, and there has been some dispute about whether the overt act was a required actus reus or merely an evidentiary requirement to insure that the "compassing" or intending was firm—more than a fantasy.[11]

Assuming that the action has progressed from pure thoughts toward the completion of the criminal goal, the question is how the theory of punishment bears on the issue that we shall call the "red line" between non-punishable preparation and punishable attempt. For purposes of analyzing the "red line" we should leave aside the crime of treason, which has a history distinct from the rest of criminal law.[12] As it has been refined in the U.S. Constitution, Article III, sec. 3, treason is limited to "levying war against the United States or in adhering to their enemies, giving them aid and comfort."[13] "Adhering" is the modern version of compassing the death of the King. It is not surprising that treason is defined in the U.S. Constitution and the evidentiary requirements are also specified.[14] The reason for this special concern about proving treason is that all the founders—the 56 men who signed the Declaration of Independence and pledged their "sacred honor"—were fearful of the possible abuses of treason.[15]

The constitutional definition of treason both affirms and denies treason as a thought crime as it seems it was in 1351.[16] The affirmation is present in the possibility of proving guilt by defendant's confession in open court.[17] It is denied by the alternative requirement of two witnesses to the same overt act in furtherance of the treasonous purpose.[18] The term "overt act" is useful for our purposes, which are to inquire into the overt act required for an attempt to cross the red line. The important point is that we think of the over act as the actus reus of the attempt, not as proof of a treasonous intention.

We have not answered the question how proceeding on the spectrum from thought to the completed crime should affect punishment for it. Treason is, in principle, subject to the death penalty, though not applied since the Haupt

[10] *Id.*
[11] *See id.*
[12] *See generally* James Willard Hurst, The Law of Treason in the United States: Collected Essays (1971).
[13] U.S. Const. art. III, § 3.
[14] *Id.* ("No person shall be convicted of treason unless on the testimony of two witnesses to the same overt act, or on confession in open court.").
[15] *See* Cramer v. United States, 325 U.S. 1, 21–22 (1945).
[16] *See* U.S. Const. art. III, § 3.
[17] *Id.*
[18] *See id.*

case in 1945,[19] which is another reason to consider it an outlier to our general project of resolving the jurisprudential issues raised by definition of criminal attempt. Leaving treason aside, we should ponder when an actus reus crosses the enigmatic red line.

Thus, we bracket out the death penalty for treason (which may largely symbolic anyway) and consider what the just punishment would be for progressing on the spectrum from thought to completion of the crime. If the purpose is deterrence, the only thing that can be deterred are actions subject to the defendant's control. He cannot control his thoughts (another reason to regard the model of treason as irrelevant). He cannot control the consequences of his action, namely whether the bullet hits its target or anything that depends on the contingent chain of physical causation. In this respect, the defendant's action—in stages ranging from pure thought to realization of his plan—should be the core crime. But note that this way of looking at things converts the criminal prosecution from concern about *impunidad* and victims (the avowed purposes of the ICC) to one concerned about the prevention of future crime (a subsidiary purpose of the ICC, according to the Preamble).

We will address the issue of just punishment for attempts crossing the red line, but first we consider the other two jurisprudential issues posed by the field of attempts. The third relevant conundrum is the choice of means that, by their nature, cannot generate the complete offense. These are called impossible or inapt (German: *untaugliche*) attempts.[20] The fourth problem is the renunciation of the attempt if the actor, for some reason, has a change of heart. Since the action is inchoate, not completed, it should seem possible to change one's mind. The problem is distinguishing proper from improper motives for the renunciation. If the actor sees a police officer and thus recants, that is different from a sudden concern for the welfare of the victim.

The four possible purposes for punishment are retribution, general deterrence (of other people), specific deterrence (confinement of the particular actor), and rehabilitation.[21] Oddly, in the context of the Rome Statute, we have to add a fifth purpose: avoiding *impunidad*, or giving the victims the sense that they are not ignored and that justice is be pursued.[22] Each of these poses problems.

[19] *See* Haupt v. United States, 330 U.S. 631, 646 (1947) (Murphy, J., dissenting) (observing that the defendant's sentence was reduced to a life sentence).
[20] *See* Entscheidungen des Reichsgerichts, bd. 1, p. 439.
[21] S. REP. No. 225, 98th Cong., 2d Sess. 38, 50 (1984), reprinted in 1984 U.S.C.C.A.N. 3183, 3233.
[22] Rome Statute, *supra* note 1, pmbl.

Retribution or just deserts, as defined in the lex talionis[23] in the Bible and in the secular tradition by Immanuel Kant,[24] might be adjusted for the field of attempts, but it is hard to see how. The basic principle of retribution is an eye for an eye. How does one punish an attempt to put out an eye? What about a stab at the offender's eye but one that misses? Another theory of retribution is that the offender consents to the punishment.[25] He brings it upon himself. If this were true, we would not need police forces, and indeed there would be no problem of *impunidad*.

We can leave aside rehabilitation because no one has ever figured out how to bring this about.[26] I suppose this method would have to include voluntary psychotherapy rather than electric shock treatments. This is extremely expensive, and it ignores the particular kind of perpetrator that we are likely to encounter in the international legal order, as discussed in the following point.

If the purpose of punishing attempts is social control—essentially deterrence, and even perhaps incapacitation—the motivating principle would be based on the principle of efficiency or cost/benefit analysis. Thus, the guiding philosophy would be that of Jeremy Bentham rather than the retributive orientation of Immanuel Kant.[27] First we should consider the benefits of threatening a criminal sanction. We would have to know the likelihood of criminal conduct over time and the possibility of deterring that conduct by a criminal sanction. The kinds of conduct envisaged by the Rome Statute, and the actors who would tend to commit the crimes within the jurisdiction of the ICC, are not readily subject to deterrence. They are often dictators who think they are above the law, and if they were subject to arrest, they would resist with their own military troops. Even if these actions were subject to deterrence, it would largely be a fantasy to imagine a concrete number to ascribe to the benefit

Now as to the costs. Consider the ten million dollars or more that the United States pays to imprison every suspect in Guantanamo (and there, alas, the government does not even pay for a fair trial)[28] or roughly $32,000 for every inmate in the overcrowded prison system of the United

[23] *Lex Talionis*, MERRIAM-WEBSTER (2018) ("[L]aw of retribution in kind: an eye for an eye").
[24] For an earlier discussion, see *supra* ch. II.
[25] *See, e.g.*, CARLOS S. NINO, THE ETHICS OF HUMAN RIGHTS (1991).
[26] *See* MODEL PENAL CODE: SENTENCING REPORT 28–29 (2003).
[27] *Supra* ch. II.
[28] *See Wasted Opportunities: The Cost of Detention Operations at Guantanamo Bay*, ACLU (Feb. 7, 2017), https://www.aclu.org/issues/national-security/detention/wasted-opportunities-cost-detention-operations-guantanamo-bay.

States.[29] Does anyone even care whether this investment in housing people (not to mention the U.S. death penalty) is efficient in cost/benefit terms? To even begin this calculus, we would have to calculate whether prisons prevent crime by deterrence of incapacitation or generate more crime by facilitating prison gangs and depriving felons of the possibility of leading normal lives after release (e.g., impact on employment records, voting rights, possibility of deportation). Unfortunately, we do not know the answer to the question of whether a single dollar of this huge investment is worthwhile. When it comes to questions of crime and fear of crime, we do not always make rational decisions.

The economic analysis becomes even more complicated when we consider that lots of people make an honest living off crime—lawyers, police, prison guards, those who build prisons, and academics like myself who write and teach about crime. If there were no crime, we would all be about of a job—so too would the ICC. The point is that the economics of crime—and therefore the efficiency of punishments—are far more complicated than they appear.

For most of Article 25(3), we cannot easily separate out the issues of attempting and complicity in the commission of the offense. The core provision on the crime of attempt as such is Article 25(3)(f), which invokes the three challenging jurisprudential issues mentioned at the outset:(a) crossing the threshold into the realm of criminality, (b) impossible attempts, and (c) renunciation or abandonment.[30] We consider the issues in the order that they appear in the provision.

The first sentence of Article 25(3)(f) raises the first problems of the threshold and impossibility. But it does so in ways that raises more problems than it solves. We consider an edited version of the sentence, including the clause introducing Article 25.

2. Threshold Issues

"A person shall be criminally responsible and liable for punishment for a crime within the jurisdiction of the Court if that person:(f) attempts to

[29] *Annual Determination of Average Cost of Incarceration*, Prison Bureau, FED. REG. (Jul. 19, 2016), https://www.federalregister.gov/documents/2016/07/19/2016-17040/annual-determination-of-average-cost-of-incarceration.

[30] *See* Rome Statute, *supra* note 1, art. 25.

commit such a crime by taking action that commences its execution by means of a substantial step. . . ."[31]

The first problem to note is that the actor becomes liable for one of the four crimes detailed in Articles 6 through 8bis and presumably the offenses under Article 70[32] but not explicitly for the attempt. The indictment should identify one of those provisions rather than Article 25(3)(f).

Many phrases have been tossed about in Western legal systems to capture the line between preparation (sometimes called "mere preparation") and attempt.[33] The three most three prominent expressions all have different connotations: (a) last-step attempt,[34] (b) substantial step,[35] and (c) commencement of the execution.[36] The notion of "last-step attempts" came into currency in the mid-nineteenth century as the common law began to develop a case law of attempt liability.[37] The courts derived the crime of attempt from the common law of completed offenses and therefore defined the threshold linguistically as close as possible to the completed offense.

The question is why the English courts decided to do this. The judges must have had the intuition that the mere accident of missing the target (shooting cases provide the most convenient paradigm) should not be a sufficient ground for insulating the actor with a bad motive from liability. It is doubtful that they gave much thought to the purposes of retribution or deterrence. Of course, the law could have developed the other way around, with the firing of the shot (arrow, burning spear, etc.) as the basic offense. But punishment is one of the most primitive actions that human beings engage in. It existed long before there was a jurisprudence of punishment, and in its primitive state it would have imposed on some patent visible harm that the punishment sought to expiate. That meant that the completed offense had to be the point of departure.

From the perspective of the Rome Statute, the advantage of the "last-step" test is that it ties attempt liability to a specific victim and therefore immunity

[31] *Id.*

[32] *Id.*, art. 70 ("Offences Against the Administration of Justice.").

[33] *See, e.g.*, WAYNE R. LAFAVE, CRIMINAL LAW § 11.4(a), at 588 (4th ed. 2003).

[34] MODEL PENAL CODE § 5.01 cmt. 4 (AM. LAW INST. 1985) ("Last Proximate Act") ("There is general agreement that when the actor has done all that he believes necessary to commit the offense in question, he has committed an attempt.").

[35] *Id.*

[36] CENTRE INTERARMEES DE CONCEPTS, DE DOCTRINES ET D'EXPERIMENTATIONS, MINISTERE DE LA DEFENSE, DIA—5.2: L'USAGE DE LA FORCE EN OPERATION MILITAIRE SE DEROULANT A L'EXTERIEUR DU TERRITOIRE NATIONAL 14 (July 25, 2006), http://www.cicde.defense.gouv.fr/IMG/pdf/20060725_np_ema_emp-1_dia-5-2-usage-force-hors-tn.pdf.

[37] *See, e.g.*, R v. Eagleton, (1855) 169 Eng. Rep. 826, 835-36 (Crim. App.).

for the last-step *attemptor* could raise issues of *impunidad*. In the expression used by Oliver Wendell Holmes, Jr, the transition from mere preparation to criminal attempt should be based on "the nearness of the danger, the greatness of the harm, and the degree of apprehension felt."[38]

The "apprehension" might be "felt" not by the potential victim but by others who witness the action or hear about it. Regardless of who was impacted by the danger, there was some kind of harm to an actual victim present in the last-step attempt. Unfortunately, this conceptual connection between the crime of attempt and the occurrence of harm was difficult to maintain. First, for the purposes of law enforcement there is no reason not to push back the point of potential arrest and imprisonment as far as possible. Second, in an important article written in 1930, Thurman Arnold argued that every crime requires a different threshold of liability.[39] Thus, the shooting example did not apply across the board. An attempted homicide by poisoning would occur as soon as the poison was put in the coffee cup. An attempted larceny would occur as soon as the perpetrator picked up an object that he knew belonged to another. A universal concept of attempting based on the last step did not seem plausible.

We should mention that Thurman Arnold's argument is ignored by the drafters of the Rome Statute, who assume that a single concept of attempting applies across the board.[40] But for reasons that are not entirely clear, that single concept would not be the principle of the last step based on the apprehension felt. There was admittedly a flaw in the apprehension text, as indicated by an Alabama case decided in the 1950s, in which a black man was convicted of attempted assault with an intent to rape for following a white women; the jury was permitted to consider the race of the white prosecutrix and black defendant as they pertained to the development of "social conditions and customs" in the determination of the defendant's intent.[41] The danger is that "apprehension" can become a subjective test and therefore responsive to local biases.

The phrase "substantial step" comes from the utility-minded Model Penal Code. It represents the opposite approach from the last-step principle. The idea is to push back the threshold of liability as far as possible. The Soviet

[38] O.W. Holmes, The Common Law 68 (1881).

[39] *See* Thurman W. Arnold, *Criminal Attempts—The Rise and Fall of an Abstraction*, 40 Yale L.J. 53 (1930).

[40] *See generally* Rome Statute, *supra* note 1.

[41] McQuirter v. State, 63 So. 2d 388, 390 (Ala. Ct. App. 1953).

system, it is worth noting, had no compunctions about punishment of "preparation,"[42] but the linguistic divide between preparation and attempt has held firm in Western legal systems.

While we are on the Model Penal Code, we should mention that the relevant provision punishes those "acts or omissions" that constitute a substantial attempt.[43] This raises intriguing theoretical questions about when an omission can constitute a substantial step or how the issues of impossibility and abandonment could apply to an omission. It is not easy to find offenses in the Rome Statute that are committed by omission, but there is always the third-party case of omission, for example, a third party ignores the aggression planned by a neighboring state, or the duty imposed by the Security Council to protect the local population, R2P.[44]The rationale for pushing back the threshold as far as possible is not so much for the purpose of justifying punishment but to provide a rationale for early intervention by the police. The problem in the United States is that principles of law enforcement may be distorted by racist motives. For example, in the *Papachristou* case, the Supreme Court declared unconstitutional a Jacksonville, Florida, ordinance that prohibited "vagrancy" on the ground that it for vagueness, in that it " 'fails to give a person of ordinary intelligence fair notice that his contemplated conduct is forbidden by the statute.' "[45]

The Model Penal Code, drafted in the 1960s, a decade before the *Papachristou* case, exposes itself to the same criticism.[46] The MPC favored the "substantial step" test in order to facilitate early intervention. The vice of this test seems to be the same as in *Papachristou*. It seems that any test for attempt liability or early intervention by other means can lend itself to racist distortion. Perhaps the right approach to attempt liability is simply to bracket off this danger and proceed as well as we can—leaving the problem of racist prosecution in the hands of law enforcement.

The best criminological argument for early intervention was developed by James Q. Wilson with his famous "broken windows" thesis.[47] In fact, in

[42] Criminal Code of the RSFSR, art. 15.

[43] Model Penal Code § 5.01 (Am. Law Inst. 1985) (Requirements of "Substantial Step" and Corroboration of Purpose problem.).

[44] 2005 World Summit Outcome, G.A. Res. 60/1, ¶ 138, U.N. Doc. A/RES/60/1 (Sept. 16, 2005).

[45] Papachristou v. City of Jacksonville, 405 U.S. 156, 162 (1972) (citing United States v. Harriss, 347 U.S. 612, 617 1954).

[46] *See, e.g.*, Commonwealth v. Hamel, 752 N.E.2d 808, 815 (Mass. App. Ct. 2001) ("The Code thus tends to broaden the base of criminal attempt, to make convictions easier to reach.").

[47] James Q. Wilson & George L. Kelling, *Broken Windows: The Police and Neighborhood Safety*, Atlantic, Mar. 1982, at 29.

New York of the 1980s, broken car windows were a common phenomenon and a sign of lawlessness under Wilson's theory.[48] The incentive for thieves might not have been the car but simply the car radio. Graffiti on the subway was another sign of lawlessness.[49] The principle was that early intervention would increase the general respect for law and thus help to prevent major crimes as well. In my experience, there is a lot of truth to this. Under the influence of this theory, the crime rate in New York dropped drastically.[50]

The middle ground between the theory of "last step" and the theory of "substantial step" is captured by the phrase "commencing the execution" in Article 25(3)(f) of the Rome Statute.[51] This phrase derives from the French Penal Code of 1830.[52] It represents a clear desire to separate the attempt from "mere" preparation and thus a step in favor of not necessarily of fair warning but of control over the judiciary and the police tendency to roam freely, targeting seemingly dangerous stereotypes—in the United States, typically African Americans.

The Rome Statute mixes the Model Penal Code substantial step test with the European "commencing the execution" test.[53] Perhaps this is a gesture toward finding a common denominator but the result is confusing, and there is no reason to think the drafters had anything in particular in mind. The soundest guide to interpretation should be, in the spirit of the Preamble, maintaining a link to victimhood.[54] This probably implies a preference for the European test, which is also a compromise between the two extremes represented by the last step and the MPC approach. But there is also an argument in favor of the original Holmesian test of last-step attempts,[55] which links the attempt more closely to an actual victim, and therefore is in line with the guiding principle of the Rome Statute, namely avoiding *impunidad*.

At this point we should be reminded of an issue typically ignored in the theory of criminal law. The principle "actus non facit reus nisi mens sit rea" implies that there actually be an actus reus in the act of attempting. It is not enough to believe that you are commencing the execution. You must actually do so. The danger being avoided is what the Germans called

[48] *Id.*

[49] *Id.*

[50] William J. Bratton, *Broken Windows and Quality-of-Life Policing in New York City*, NYPD (2015), http://www.nyc.gov/html/nypd/downloads/pdf/analysis_and_planning/qol.pdf.

[51] Rome Statute, *supra* note 1, art. 25.

[52] *See Code Pénal*, art. 121-5 (Fr.).

[53] *See generally* Rome Statute, *supra* note 1, art. 25.

[54] *See id.*, pmbl.

[55] Holmes, *supra* note 38.

"Gesinnungsstrafrecht"—a crime based not on actual danger to a victim but merely on the intentions of the actor.[56]

The commentary to the Model Penal Code, which seems to be the low point in our consideration of options, actually refers to "the circumstances as the actor believes them to be."[57] And some commentary to the Model Penal Code informs us that "the actors mind is the best proving ground of his dangerousness."[58] In other words, the purpose of punishing attempt is to find dangerous people, as revealed by their state of mind in taking the initial steps on the spectrum from pure thought to the occurrence of harm to a victim.

There are several problems here. First, we don't exactly know what "dangerousness" means. There is a threshold of dangerousness—more subtle than the red line in the law of attempts—that separates ordinary people from "criminal types." The calculus of dangerousness would be something like the Learned Hand test for negligence—the probability of a crime in some undefined period of time multiplied by the likelihood of the crime.[59] Believing that there really is a mathematical test of dangerousness is naive, but perhaps one of those archetypical beliefs that derives from the criminal law.

The California Penal Code, the primary alternative to the Model Penal Code in the United States, is just as poorly drafted as the MPC, if not more so. According to Sec. 21a, you can be guilty of an attempted crime in California if:

> You specifically intended to commit a certain crime; and
> You performed a direct (but ineffective) act toward committing that crime.[60]

Even worse than this definition is the prescribed penalty: if the charge is attempted murder, the maximum penalty is life imprisonment.

As we turn to the next set of issues, we should appreciate the dangers of shifting from a criminal law based on actions to one based on dangerous criminal types. The greatest abuses of criminal law occur when the punishing authorities shift their focus from the actus reus to the mens rea. A sound

[56] *See* KLAUS MARXEN, DER KAMPF GEGEN DAS LIBERALE STRAFRECHT 188 (1975) ("Criminal law based on attitudes.").

[57] MODEL PENAL CODE §5.01 cmt. (AM. LAW INST. 1985).

[58] H. Wechsler, W.K. Jones & H.L. Korn, *The Treatment of Inchoate Crimes in the Model Penal Code of the American Law Institute: Attempts, Solicitation and Conspiracy*, 61 COLUM. L. REV. 571, 579 (1961).

[59] *See* United States v. Carroll Towing Co., 159 F.2d 169, 173 (2d Cir. 1947).

[60] *See* Cal. Pen. Code § 21a (2018).

criminal law requires both, but the actus reus—the attempt in the real world—should precede the pursuit of a mens rea rendering the actor guilty. This is true, however difficult it may seem to define the red line separating preparation from attempts.

3. Impossibility

Article 25(3)(f) continues: "but the crime does not occur because of circumstances independent of the person's intentions."[61] This is a reference to the classic field of impossible ("ineffective" in the California code)[62] or in the German idiom, "inapt" (*untaugliche*) attempts.[63] The probability of a case of this sort coming before the ICC is minimal. Yet the field poses some intriguing questions of drafting as well as criminal theory. To appreciate these problems, we should imagine some hypothetical cases that could conceivably come to the attention of the ICC. Consider attempted genocide. As in Rwanda, a group like the Hutus make radio broadcast calling for the slaughter of another group like the Tutsis.[64] It turns out, however, that the radio stations are jammed and no one hears them. Or consider another example under Art 6 (d)—imposing measures intended to prevent births within the group.[65] In fact, abortifacients forced on women in the group are simply harmless powders.

The field of war crimes, in particular Art. 8(2)(a), is replete with the possibility of impossible attempts.[66] Someone tries to kill but the gun is jammed. Another tries to impose unlawful confinement (Art. 8(2)(a)(vii),[67] but the lock in the door does not work. These examples are easily multiplied across the crimes of Article 6. The question is whether they should be punished—specifically, in a criminal law that properly values the actus reus as well as the mens rea.

We should notice here that we are far removed from the purposes of the ICC as outlined in the Preamble. As mentioned at the outset of this chapter,

[61] Rome Statute, *supra* note 1, art. 25(3)(f).
[62] *See* Cal. Pen. Code § 21a (2018).
[63] *See* Entscheidungen des Reichsgerichts, bd. 1, p. 439.
[64] RTLM broadcast, Apr. 15, 1994, *reprinted in* Rwanda: Les Medias Du Genocide (Jean-Pierre Chretien et al. eds., 1995), at 194.
[65] Rome Statute, *supra* note 1, art. 6(d).
[66] See Rome Statute, *supra* note 1, art. 8(2)(a).
[67] *Id.*

it is not easy to locate a victim of the attempt, and therefore there is a remote connection to the purpose of avoiding *impunidad* as originally understood. There are therefore two remaining purposes to guide our interpretation of impossible attempts. One would be deterrence (the next time the *attemptor* might be more effective), and the other more plausible rationale is that we have simply entered an area guided by traditional rules of criminal law that provide a historical foundation for the Rome Statute.

The poisoning cases are illustrative of the field and are significant for our purposes because they bear a relationship to the Agent Orange litigation, in which I was an expert witness.[68] The United States used a poisonous defoliant in Vietnam, which generated birth defects in subsequent generations who ate vegetables grown on the land.[69]

For our purposes, the two relevant hypothetical cases are (A) using too little poison to have a deadly effect; or (B) using something that is not poison at all, for example, putting sugar in someone's coffee under the mistaken belief that sugar is arsenic. Now in both of these cases, the attempt is impossible, ineffective, or inapt—depending on the which legal tradition determines our usage.

To articulate a distinction between case A and B requires us to abstract from the particular case to a class of cases. As a general matter, poison, in sufficient amounts, will claim a victim. Lots of sugar, though not healthy, will not result in a proximate death. Therefore, it seems plausible to punish the case of too little poison and not the case of sugar. The problem is how we justify abstracting the case to general pattern of cases like the hypothetical cases A or B.

One answer to this conundrum might be that appellate courts never decide particular cases. They are always seeking, implicitly or explicitly, to provide guidance for the future. Therefore, it makes sense to abstract the specific case to class of cases, resulting in liability for too little poison but not for using sugar. The language used by courts to capture this intuitive distinction is often colorful. My favorite is a 1920 English case that posed the question of whether the would-be attempter was "on the job." In case A yes, case B no. I suppose "on the job" represents a form of abstraction. The "job" represents a class of events.

[68] *See* Vietnam Ass'n for Victims of Agent Orange v. Dow Chem Co., 517 F.3d 104 (2d Cir. 2008).
[69] *Id.*

Getting lost in these metaphors is hardly a rational way to solve cases. We would never incorporate that language into legislation, but it seems to be an integral part of legal discourse. If we are bequeathed the distinction of possible and impossible attempts, it is not clear how if we punish attempts, we could avoid the issue. The only rationale perspective on the pursuit of the right metaphor is to capture the idea that the attempt must appear dangerous to an ideal observer—not necessarily someone who is there but who might be there. The use of metaphors is just as precise as inquiring whether a hypothetical observer would sense in difference in the apparent dangerousness of case A or case B.

Our engaging in this esoteric analysis prompts me to question an assumption made earlier about the purposes of punishment in international criminal law, namely retribution or deterrence. The assumption was that international lawyers are practical people and therefore favor deterrence, however dubious it might be in reality. Yet practical people would not create a system of liability for attempts that requires this degree of philosophical refinement.

Now we should consider impossible attempted crimes by omission. Omission requires a specific duty to act. For an example, lifeguards are liable for failing to rescue drowning swimmers. But suppose that a buoy in the ocean looks like a swimmer, and suppose that someone rigged the buoy to simulate screaming "help" and the lifeguard ignored the screams. It turns out that no harm occurred, but the lifeguard has nonetheless violated his duty to intervene. Analogous cases are easy to imagine in the international arena, some of them famous. Consider attempted genocide by omission. It would be easy to prevent the genocide by providing food, water, or shelter, but in fact it is impossible to reach the targeted country in time. If there is the proper intent, those that refused aid that unbeknownst to them could not have reached the destination in time anyway would be guilty of an attempt by omission (impossible in fact). Many have criticized the United States for not bombing the tracks leading to Auschwitz.[70] Suppose that bombing the tracks would not, in fact, have prevented the Germans from carrying out genocide (e.g., simply shooting the prisoners in the trains). Given an evil intent (not true in fact), this would have been an impossible attempt by omission. At

[70] *See, e.g.*, Tom Brooks-Pollock, *Pope Francis: Why Didn't Allies Bomb Railway Routes Taking Prisoner to Auschwitz?*, INDEPENDENT (Jun. 22, 2015), https://www.independent.co.uk/news/world/europe/pope-francis-why-didnt-allies-bomb-railway-routes-taking-prisoners-to-auschwitz-10336001.html.

this point, the analysis of the crime of attempt seems more like a set of logical puzzles than a clarification of a body of law that might see application.

Another puzzle in this area is a variation on impossibility, where the problem is legal rather than factual. For one thing, shooting two gay people on the streets of New York would not constitute genocide. The gun jams and therefore the attempt is impossible. The killing of the gays would not fall within the National, Ethnic, Race, or Religious definitions,[71] and the attempt is no legally impossible, at least if we assume that the principle of *nulla poena sine lege* holds firm. The only problem with this position is that the term "ethnic" is subject to easy manipulation.

Although some of these examples seem like we stepped through Alice's Looking Glass and we are jousting with the Jabberwocky, we are merely trying to explore the implications of the Rome Statute, as they were inherited from the history of theoretical work in the criminal law. The emphasis should be on "theoretical" because in fact there are very few cases to support any of the arguments concerning impossibility.

4. Abandonment

The Rome Statute devotes an entire verbose sentence to this issue, which essentially is this: if the attempter changes his mind, he is not guilty.

The concept of abandonment confirms the inchoate nature of attempted crime. If the perpetrator has completed the crime of aggression, he cannot nullify the crime by ordering the withdrawal of his army. But the crime has crossed the red line from preparation and attempt but still is not complete, the offender can change his mind—but obviously the change of heart must be purely voluntary.

It is easy to imagine the cases that are not voluntary. Unexpectedly defensive power might prompt a retreat. Perhaps condemnation by the UN might have this effect. Indeed, one might have doubts about whether any change of heart is ever completely voluntary. Therefore, the burden of proof becomes critical. Since the prosecution must attempt beyond a reasonable doubt, an assertion of abandonment by the defense would not change the burden on the ultimate issue of guilt. The prosecution would have to prove that the abandonment was involuntary.

[71] *See* Rome Statute, *supra* note 1, art. 6.

The indirect implication of this provision is that it establishes one of the fundamental requirements of all criminal liability, namely criminal actions must be voluntary. We have seen early references to this issue in considering the defense of insanity and intoxication, which render the conduct involuntary. Interestingly, in establishing its prima facie case, the prosecution need not prove that the criminal action was voluntary. We assume that to be true unless there are special circumstances are present, which are captured in these criminal defenses.

The crime of attempt may not fit within the scheme of avoiding *impunidad* as the primary purpose of the ICC, but its inclusion in the statute provides a basis for understanding some of the foundational principles of criminal liability.

9

The Law of War and Its Many Distinctions

The format of this book has been to focus on a particular distinction, the assumption being that the legal mind functions at it its best while facing sharp alternatives. The supreme distinction, here, is between lawful and unlawful. However, in the law of war, the distinctions multiply beyond control. Whether troops fighting abroad constitutes war is itself a disputed question; there has been a tendency in recent years to use "armed conflict"[1] or "police action."[2] The last U.S.-declared war was on December 8, 1941, the day after the Japanese attack on Pearl Harbor.[3] This has represented a shift of power from Congress to the president and the executive branch. The president is Commander in Chief, the head of the executive power, but he cannot go to full-scale war without a declaration of war by Congress.[4] We can refer to this as the internal American problem of engaging in legal warfare.

However, the internal problem has little bearing on international law. For the purposes of analyzing the Rome Statute[5] and, in particular, Article 8 on war crimes, we have to assume an international perspective. Most countries in the international legal order are not democracies, and the internal allocation of power is not relevant to whether they violate Article 8.

The complexity of Article 8 challenges the mind, with at least 50 distinct offenses.[6] Our purpose here is not to review these details but to elaborate on

[1] *See, e.g., How Is the Term "Armed Conflict" Defined in International Humanitarian Law?*, Opinion Paper, Int'l Committee of the Red Cross (Mar. 2008) (last visited Nov. 14, 2018), https://www.icrc.org/eng/assets/files/other/opinion-paper-armed-conflict.pdf.

[2] *See, e.g.*, Thomas M. Franck & Faiza Patel, *The Gulf Crisis in International and Foreign Relations Law: UN Police Action in Lieu of War: "The Old Order Changeth,"* 85 A.J.I.L. 63, 63 (1991) ("The new alternative to traditional wars of self-defense is collective police actions by the members of the international community.").

[3] *See generally* Marvin Kalb, The Road to War: Presidential Commitments Honored and Betrayed (2013).

[4] See U.S. Const. art. I, § 8 ("The Congress shall have power . . . to declare war. . . .").

[5] Rome Statute for the International Criminal Court, July 17, 1998, 2187 U.N.T.S. 3; U.N. Diplomatic Conference of Plenipotentiaries on the Establishment of an International Court, U.N. Doc. A/Conf.183/9 [hereinafter Rome Statute].

[6] *See* Rome Statute, *supra* note 5, art. 8.

The Grammar of Criminal Law: Volume Two: International Criminal Law. George P. Fletcher.

the perspectives necessary to grasp the general structure of war crimes in the international legal order.

1. Collective Action and Individual Action

This distinction—that between lawful and unlawful—will be of central importance throughout this commentary. We have discussed it at length in the context of aggression and the importance of Article 8bis, adopted at the 2010 Kampala Conference. Importantly, individuals do not engage in warfare, yet the Rome Statute is about individual responsibility for war crimes. To illustrate the problem, consider a famous story about the highly regarded English professor at Columbia, Edward Said. He once crossed the border from Jordan into Israel while throwing rocks and shouting, "I declare war against you, thou Zionist entity." Sorry, Edward, this did not "declare war." You may have been engaging in an act of vandalism, but not of warfare. The implication of this story (whether true in entirety or not) is that collectives, consisting of individuals, go to war (armed conflict, etc.), and yet only individuals are liable in the ICC.[7] The logic generally goes something like this—individuals acting in collectives engage in warfare, the collective is engaged in a grave breach of the Geneva Convention of 1949, and from this we infer individual liability under Article 8.[8] The problem in the example of the anti-Zionist Columbia professor is that he tried to reduce this complicated three-step waltz to a single step. Ordinary observers might be puzzled by the necessity of this left-right-left, but it is inherent in the history of the law of war.

The next problem we face is properly labeling this collective, and learning or demonstrating whether it exists. It might be called the state, the government, the country, the people, or the nation. This is a difficult question, presumably dependent on the language we are using. There are six official languages of the Court (Arabic, French, English, Russian, Spanish, and Chinese)—British and American English being considered as a single language.[9] The language of diplomacy used to be French, but since World War

[7] *See* Rome Statute, *supra* note 5, art. 25(1) ("The Court shall have jurisdiction over natural persons pursuant to this Statute.").

[8] *See International Military Tribunal (Nuremberg), Judgment and Sentences*, 41 AM. J. INT'L L. 172, 220–21 (1947) ("[T]hat international law imposes duties and liabilities upon individuals as well as upon States has long been recognized. . . . Crimes against international law are committed by men, not by abstract entities, and only by punishing individuals who commit such crimes can the provisions of international law be enforced.").

[9] *See* Rome Statute, *supra* note 5, art. 30.

II, English has become dominant.[10] French is, in fact, more useful for some purposes, for example, the law of self-defense.[11] The term "legitime defense" includes the defense of others as well as the defense of oneself.[12]

The disadvantage of linking the Rome Statute to the languages dominant in the Security Council—that is, the victors in World War II—is that a good deal of the sophisticated literature in international criminal law is written in German. In fact, on the basis of my experience, I would say that one cannot understand the general structure of criminal law without reading the German commentaries. The Max Planck Institute for Foreign and International Criminal Law in Freiburg is one of the world's centers for theory of criminal law.[13] Things have obviously changed in the 70+ years since the end of World War II, and this commentary should be mindful of current political realities. Just as Russian took the seat of the Soviet Union and Communist China took the seat formerly held by the Republic of China (Taiwan), the German point of view cannot be ignored. In fact, we often use the expression "five plus one" to refer to the nations of the Security Council, plus Germany.[14]

So much for modern languages. In fact Latin continues to dominate the field of distinctions in the law of war, as it did in the time of Grotius, *De Jure Belle ac Pacis*.[15] The critical distinction today is between Jus ad Bellum and Jus in Bello, namely between the Right to Go to War and the Law governing combat in war, for example, Article 8 of the Rome Statute. Note that the verbal distinction between "right" and "law" does not exist in English, unlike European languages, which distinguish clearly between Recht (pravo, droit, law as principle)[16] and Gesetz (zakon, loi, law as rules)[17]. The notion of law in science, for example, gravity, is always the same as the word for the written law, the law as rules.

[10] *See* Barbara Crossette, *Diplomatically, French Is a Faded Rose in an English Rose Garden*, N.Y. Times (Mar. 25, 2001), https://www.nytimes.com/2001/03/25/world/diplomatically-french-is-a-faded-rose-in-an-english-garden.html.

[11] *See* George P. Fletcher & Jens David Ohlin, Defending Humanity: When Force is Justified and Why (2008).

[12] *See id.* at 66–67.

[13] Max Planck Institute for Foreign and International Criminal Law, https://www.mpicc.de/en/home.cfm (last visited Apr. 17, 2018).

[14] *See, e.g.*, Kirsten Boon et al., 116 Terrorism: Assessing President Obama's National Security Strategy 644 (2011).

[15] Hugo Grotius On the Law of War and Peace (Stephen C. Neff ed., Cambridge University Press 2012) (1625).

[16] Recht translates as "right."

[17] For an earlier discussion of these concepts, see George P. Fletcher, Two Modes of Legal Thought, 90 Yale L.J. 970, 980–84 (1981).

The Rome Statue purports to be committed to the principle *nulla poena sine lege* and even imposes the principle of strict construction, interpretation in favor of the defendant.[18] "Lege" in this context is a declined form of lex, law as rules rather than as principle. In the history of jurisprudence, the idea that the law consists of enacted rules, as in the rules enacted in the Rome Statute, is called the positivist theory of law.[19] In a few words: all law is enacted law. The opposing school of jurisprudential thought goes by various names, but the keyword is the notion of Right, as expressed in Ronald Dworkin's anti-positivist book, *Taking Rights Seriously*.[20] There is no doubt that international criminal law, beginning with the Nuremberg and Tokyo trials, expressed a transpositivist perspective. But this may have been because there was little choice at the time.

The best example of a transpositive perspective revolves around aggression, a debate so controversial that it was not included in the Rome Statute until the Kampala Conference of 2010 (Article 8bis).[21] The Nuremberg Tribunal derived the crime of aggression from the German Russian non-aggression pact of 1939, which both countries violated by invading Poland. This was a diplomatic treaty and certainly not intended as a basis for imposing criminal liability.

In a final analysis, however, the law is never authoritatively laid down. A finite number requires interpretation in case law and in subsequent treatises, such as this one. Then, the cases and the treatises require interpretation. This is rendered more complicated in the international legal order, with the use of multiple official languages and the addition of other languages, which are indispensable to the understanding of criminal law. There is no end to the process, as there is no finite set of words in any modern living language.

The overarching distinction in the law of war is between jus ad bellum and jus in bello. Jus ad bellum is governed by Article 51 of the United Nations Charter, which reads:

> Nothing in the present Charter shall impair the inherent right of individual or collective self-defence if an armed attack occurs against a Member of the

18 Rome Statute, *supra* note 5, art. 22(2).

19 *See, e.g.*, H.L.A. Hart, *Positivism and the Separation of Law and Morals*, 71 Harv. L. Rev. 593 (1958).

20 Ronald Dworkin, Taking Rights Seriously (1977).

21 *See* Resolution Adopting Aggression Amendments to Rome Statute, Rev. Conf. of the Rome Statute, Kampala, Uganda, May 31–June 11, 2010, Annex I, art. 8bis, 13th plen. mtg., I.C.C. Doc. RC/Res.6 (June 11, 2010).

United Nations, until the Security Council has taken measures necessary to maintain international peace and security. Measures taken by Members in the exercise of this right of self-defence shall be immediately reported to the Security Council and shall not in any way affect the authority and responsibility of the Security Council under the present Charter to take at any time such action as it deems necessary in order to maintain or restore international peace and security.[22]

Our analysis of this provision illustrates the problems of interpretation. The first is a global issue about the purpose of the provision. The general assumption is that Article 51 regulates the international law of jus ad bellum. That means that it defines the international version of the law of self-defense as we know that concept in domestic law. Frankly, I prefer the interpretation of a Dutch student at Columbia, Annemieke van Versefeld, which states that it is not about self-defense at all, but rather about issues that come to us in the law of contracts. The doctrine is called "frustration of purpose." The leading example is a case called *Krell v. Henry*.[23] The defendant sold tickets to the coronation of King Edward VII.[24] The coronation was called, and therefore, the courts held, the tickets should be refused. What this means in the context of Article 51 is that "if an armed attack occurs" all bets are off—all treaty obligations are suspended—until the Security Council takes measures to maintain international peace and security.

But law requires us to make the conventional assumption that Article 51 is about self-defense and thus directed to the issue of jus ad bellum. Let's look at some of the problems generated by this view:

What does the Charter mean by the following:

A) Nothing in the present Charter, (B) shall impair, C) the inherent right, of D) the individual or collective, to E) self-defense, F) armed attack, G) occurs H) Member of the United Nations, I) measures, and J) international peace, K) and security.[25]

A) nothing in the present Charter. This is an intriguing beginning because it suggests that the Charter is all that matters to an

[22] U.N. Charter art. 51.
[23] Krell v. Henry, 2 K.B. 740, 752 (1903).
[24] *Krell*, 2 K.B. at 741.
[25] U.N. Charter art. 51.

understanding of Article 51 as a statement of the international law of self-defense. This could not be possible in light of the missing terms required for an adequate definition of self-defense.[26]

B) shall impair. Impairment is a matter of degree. Yet the Charter implies a total elimination, not just a limitation.

C) inherent right: First, the notion of a right. In the famous Hohfeldian scheme of legal relations, a personal right implies that someone else is under a duty of compliance.[27] That means that you cannot have rights on both sides of a conflict. But in the international context, you could theoretically have a UN police action generating a right of self-defense by the invaded country. "Right" in this context does not mean a Hohfeldian right but rather a right against the whole world.

This point is strengthened by the notion of an inherent right. In the French translation, this is a droit naturel, a natural right, which seems to be a little easier to understand. The only problem is that positivists deny the existence of natural rights. The Rome Statute is committed to a positivist view of international criminal law (*nulla poena sine lege*), but it does not follow that the UN Charter is so committed. Neither the Charter nor the Rome Statute could function without interpretation, but this is particularly true in the case of the Charter where there are radically different readings available and, as we proceed with an interpretation based on jus ad bellum and self-defense, we find that many critical terms are missing (e.g., unlawful, imminent plus other factors limiting self-defense, necessity, proportionality, knowing or intentional use of force).

The notion of right or rights has played a critical role in the internal jurisprudential debates in the United States. The positivist tradition, represented by Hans Kelsen, *Die Reine Rechtslehre*,[28] and H.L.A. Hart, *The Concept of Law*,[29] stood for a notion of law based on a value-free judgment. For Kelsen, binding law was derived from a Grundnorm, a logical premise inherent in a system of binding law.[30] Hart converted this argument into a sociological

[26] *Infra* note 15.

[27] Wesley Newcomb Hohfeld, *Fundamental Legal Conceptions as Applied in Judicial Reasoning*, 26 Yale L.J. 710, 718–20 (1917).

[28] Hans Kelsen, Pure Theory of Law (Max Knight trans., University of California Press 1967) (1934).

[29] H.L.A. Hart, The Concept of Law (2d ed. 1994)

[30] Kelsen, *supra* note 29.

principle, rule of recognition, which generated an internal system of binding law.[31] In the context of the Rome Statute, the rule of recognition is the principle that the Rome Convention, plus the Assembly of State Parties, could enact binding rules. Yet there are still open-ended issues in the international legal order, for example, the residual effect of the regional tribunals, the ICTY, plus the impact of general principles of international law.[32] The enduring problem in this, as in every other legal context, is the role of interpretation in generating binding law.

In retrospect, the implicit political motivation of positivism was to avoid moral judgments about some of the actions of the Soviet Union, for example, the denial of Jews who sought to emigrate (the "refueseniks" and their alleged abuses of psychiatric expertise.) The "gulag" (governmental prison camps) became a familiar meme. My own experiences in negotiating with officials of the former Soviet Union are recorded in *My Life in Seven Languages*[33] and in Telford Taylor's *Courts of Terror*.[34]

In response to the positivist school of thought, Ronald Dworkin established his career as a legal philosopher by emphasizing the notion of "rights" as a value-based claim in an American, or indeed any domestic, legal culture.[35] I employed the same idea—Raising Rights Consciousness—in a series of post-Communist summer workshop for lawyers from Communist legal systems.

This basic distinction between jus and lex (Recht, droit, derecho, vs. Gesetz, loi, ley) is found in all Western legal systems, except English and Polish. In the common law, there once was a notion of Right comparable to the European notion. One finds in *Dr. Bonham's Case*, a precursor of judicial review in the United States, as holding a statute of Parliament null and void as if it violated "common Right or Reason."[36] The distinction between the two words for law is played out today in Quebec, where the issue is whether to translate "the common law" as le droit commun or la loi commune. The issue of translation turns on whether we conceived of the common law as

[31] HART, *supra* note 30, at 214.
[32] *See* Rome Statute, *supra* note 5, art. 21(1)(c).
[33] GEORGE P. FLETCHER, MY LIFE IN SEVEN LANGUAGES 58–71 (2011).
[34] *See* TELFORD TAYLOR, COURTS OF TERROR (1976).
[35] *See* Dworkin, *supra* note 21.
[36] The basic principle in that case was whether one could be a judge of one's own case. *See* Dr. Bonham's Case, 77 Eng. Rep. 638 (C.P. 1610).

Right (droit) or as law in the sense of lex and the way that phrase is used in the Rome Statute Article 22.[37]

Individual or collective.

Nations act as individuals. The United States, though composed of many pseudo-sovereign states, is treated as a single individual in terms of international law and warfare, expressed by the actions of its government. There may be a problem as to the unrecognized states, but that issue is precluded by the unfortunate limitation of Article 51 to member states of the UN. There is an element of circularity in this logic. Take, for example, the conflict between the Jewish and Palestinian peoples, recognized in the UN partition plan of November 29, 1947—a famous date in Israeli history.[38] Why would the UN have recommended the partition or separation of the states if it hadn't assumed that these "peoples" were entitled to statehood? Israel has since gained acceptance in the United Nations, but the Palestinians have not.[39] As we shall see, this creates some problems under Article 51. Collective self-defense presumably applies to organizations like NATO and SEATO where the attack against one member is taken to be an attack against all.

Self-defense. The English phrase here is misleading. The French version legitime defense (or German: Notwehr) makes it clear that the notion includes the defense of others. This is critical in cases where one nation intervenes to protect a nation under threat when itself is not under attack. Of course, in U.S. history, we have interpreted the notion of "self" rather broadly. For, during the period of the Communist threat, we thought of the self as the entire democratic world. In the current era of American nationalism, we might see a different interpretation of the "self." Even more interesting than the change of sentiments over time is the focal point of interpretation. If we are looking at this provision from the perspective of the French, German, or Russian versions of the charter and their respective legal systems, we the use the broader term associated with legitime defense.

The biggest problem raised by the European perspective is the problem of proportionality of the defensive response. In the domestic law of the United

[37] Note that Article 22(2) of the Rome Statute contains the conventional rule on interpretation, namely in favor of the accused. *See* Rome Statute, *supra* note 5, art. 22.

[38] G.A. Res. 181, U.N. GAOR, 2d Sess., Supp. No. 11, at 322-43, U.N. Doc. A/RES/181(II) (Nov. 29, 1947).

[39] *See History of the Question of Palestine*, U.N. (last visited Nov. 14, 2018), https://www.un.org/unispal/history/.

States, one cannot resist a nonlethal assault by killing the aggressor.[40] But, can a nation resist an attack with nuclear weapons?

In this context, German law is not a good model. They have struggled for decades to impose a limitation on subjectively necessary self-defense.

The distinction between necessary and proportional self-defense is often confused, particularly in the international context. Necessity mean that lesser means would not have been effective. Assessing whether this is true requires a counterfactional conditional judgment, that is, what would have happened if atomic bombs had not been deployed in Hiroshima and Nagasaki? Short of invasion, the allies did not think any other means would have sufficed. There is, of course, no way of knowing this, much less proving it. Furthermore, the judgment of necessity imposes risks on the decision maker. One can see this clearly in the *Goetz* case, where Bernhard Goetz pulled a hidden revolver and shot four kids surrounding and threatening him on the subway.[41] Many critics of Goetz said he didn't have to shoot. It may have been enough to show the gun. The question is whether he should have been required to take the risk of the gun being ineffective, or perhaps inspiring further spontaneous violence the group that was threatening him. In brief, a strict rule of necessity imposes additional costs on the party defending himself.

"Proportionality" poses a different question, one that presupposes necessity. The question is whether the use of nuclear weapons was simply "too much." In the domestic context of self-defense, a similar problem is posed by questions such as resisting an assault or rape by killing the aggressor. In the international context, where the defense of one's own territory is at stake, there appears to no limit to the amount of force that nations would use when deemed to be necessary. In the *Goetz* case, again, the question of necessity was whether it was enough merely to show the gun, or whether that would have increased his risk. The question of proportionality, then, is whether seriously wounding or risking the death of his assailants was too much of a cost for them to pay.

It's important to keep in mind that self-defense is not punishment. If it were treated as such, the proportionality limitation would be stricter; you cannot use the death penalty for a parking ticket. The biggest problem in the international content is whether the implicit nature of the categories of warfare determine proportionality, for example, cyber, conventional, nuclear,

[40] *See* Model Penal Code § 3.04 (Am. Law Inst., 1962).
[41] *See* People v. Goetz, 497 N.E.2d 41 (N.Y. 1986).

etc. Is it disproportionate enough to escalate the category of warfare? The problem in this context is that the proposed categories (cyber, conventional, nuclear) are a matter of customary practices in the law of war.

It could have been an issue at the end of Worl War II to introduce jet planes or faster tanks.

Note that in the context of jus in bello, proportionality is clearly an issue. As provided in Article 8(b)(iv), it is a war crime to: "Intentionally [launch] an attack in the knowledge that such attack will cause incidental loss of life or injury to civilians or damage to civilian objects. . . . which would be clearly excessive in relation to the concrete and direct overall military advantage anticipated."[42]

Excessive means "disproportionate," so, is it possible that the proportionality is not relevant in jus ad bellum but becomes a critical issue in just in bello, the definition of war crimes. Of course, this is possible—and just one of the mysteries of the logical transition from the collective law of jus ad bellum to individual responsibility for war crimes.

An armed attacks occurs.

If taken literally, this phrase is difficult to understand, except on the van Versefeld interpretation. Therefore, we should look at some problems raised in individual words: A) *armed* seems to preclude the major problem in contemporary warfare, namely cyber warfare; B) *attack* implies aggression, as covered in Article 8*bis* of the Rome Statute;[43] C) *occurs* implies the critical nature in observing that the attack actually takes place. Lying about weapons of mass destruction—as some claim the Bush administration did with regard to Iraq—is not enough.[44] Baseless threats by North Korea do not suffice. This is the difference between the domestic law of self-defense, for example, the *Goetz* case, where the reasonable perception of an attack is sufficient; and the international law of self-defense, where the attack must actually occur.

A) The notion of "armed" has obviously evolved since the time of knights and jousting. I assume the swords are no longer enough, much like guns without ammunition would not suffice, and airplanes without bombs might be borderline ineffectual. However, as we know now

[42] Rome Statute, *supra* note 5, art. 8(b)(iv).
[43] *See* Resolution, *supra* note 21.
[44] *See* President George W. Bush, *Ultimatum Iraq Speech*, Cross Hall, White House (Mar. 17, 2003), https://www.theguardian.com/world/2003/mar/18/usa.iraq.

from numerous terrorist attacks on domestic soil, a simple automobile can suffice.[45]

B) At the time of this writing, the United Kingdom has complained about the alleged Russian use of nerve gas to assassinate a former spy on British soil.[46] The prime minister has treated this as an attack against the United Kingdom. History is wrought with these borderline and difficult-to-prove cases of alleged use of gas and chemical warfare.[47] One provable example was the United States' use of Agent Orange in Vietnam.[48] The impact of this "herbicide" was felt by Vietnamese civilians nearly two generations later. The United States and Dow Chemical defended their action on the ground that their purpose was simply to defoliate the jungle. This suggests that the element of attack requires a specific purpose. In the U.K. case, mentioned earlier, the Russians may not, and likely did not, have the purpose of committing an attack on British soil. It just so happened that the former spy happened to be in the United Kingdom when he was vulnerable.[49] Based on the United Kingdom's response, the principle might be this: if it feels like an attack, it is an attack. But, this certainly could not be true. Hypochondriac nations are not entitled to more protection.

C) *Occurs.*

The use of the present tense is important. If the attack is over, retaliation is not permissible. When is the attack over? This is not clear. Consider the Israeli occupation of the West Bank. Assuming that there was an attack in 1967, the problem is whether a third generation of occupation implies that the attack is ongoing. I am afraid that the analogy between domestic and international self-defense breaks down in this content. In the domestic context, the attack is over when the aggressor is rendered incapable of further physical action. This does not happen in the international context, when a new generation carries on with grievances of the past.

[45] *See, e.g.*, *From Westminister to Nice: Vehicle Rampage Attacks in US and Europe*, TELEGRAPH (Aug. 14, 2018), https://www.telegraph.co.uk/news/0/westminster-nice-vehicle-rampage-attacks-uk-europe/.

[46] *See* Richard Perez-Pena, *Former Russian Spy Poisoned by Nerve Agent, British Police Say*, N.Y. TIMES (Mar. 7, 2018), https://www.nytimes.com/2018/03/07/world/europe/russia-spy-nerve-agent.html.

[47] *Id.*

[48] *See* Vietnam Ass'n for Victims of Agent Orange v. Dow Chem Co., 517 F.3d 104 (2d Cir. 2008).

[49] *See* Perez-Pena, *supra* note 46.

Look also at the iconic example in the law of war as posed by the Cuban Missile Crisis. Suppose it was true that the Soviet Union was installing Intermediate Range weapons in Cuba. Was this an attack? I don't think so; most international lawyers in 1962 thought that the U.S. blockade was illegal.[50] It was limited interference with the freedom of the seas for a limited purpose. What this example shows, more interestingly, is that the notion of attack depends on the act/omission distinction. That is, the U.S. was motionless in maintaining the blockade, once established. It was up to Soviet Premier Nikita Khrushchev to decide whether to turn back. Who was attacking whom in this situation?

Member of the United Nations.

This is a dubious provision, illustrating a serious gap in the Charter. The biggest questions that arise are the rights of Palestinians and whether the occupation since 1967 constitutes an ongoing attack. Palestine has been an observed in statutes drafted by the United Nations, but the way the General Assembly formulated their status in 2012 was that they are a *non-member observer*.[51] (Apparently, the UN has forgotten about the assumptions made in the proposed partition of November 19, 1947). If they are not officially a member, then they are not protected under Article 51. This makes little sense if the charter is about self-defense.

The UN Security council has largely removed itself from mediating between the parties.[52] The recurrent demands are for direct, face-to-face negotiations. Also, the only progress on the occupation of the West Bank came in the Oslo Accords of 1993.[53] It is obviously preferable for the parties themselves to reach a compromise than for the UN Security Council to impose a solution.

Measures.

The use of this word raises the temperature. The implication seems to be the sending of a UN Peacekeeping Force. The possibility of a UN "invasion" raises troubling questions, both practical and theoretical. The practical

[50] *See, e.g.*, Quincy Wright, *The Cuban Quarantine*, 57 AM. J. INT'L L. 546 (1963).

[51] *General Assembly Grants Palestine Non-Member Observer State Status at U.N.*, U.N. NEWS (Nov. 29, 2012), https://news.un.org/en/story/2012/11/427052-general-assembly-grants-palestine-non-member-observer-state-status-un.

[52] Colum Lynch, *U.N. Once Again Center Stage for Israeli-Palestinian Conflict*, WASH. POST. (Sep. 17, 2011), https://www.washingtonpost.com/world/national-security/un-once-again-center-stage-for-israeli-palestinian-conflict/2011/09/08/gIQA6cBuaK_story.html?noredirect=on&utm_term=.f0ecd0482056.

[53] *See Oslo Accords, Twenty Five Years Later*, NPR (Sept. 13, 2018), https://www.npr.org/2018/09/13/647329036/oslo-accords-25-years-later.

question is whether the defending country could invoke 51 in self-defense. The more theoretical question is whether two conflicting nations (or an international organization and a nation–state could both have a right of self-defense.A lot depends on the interpretation of the word "right." In the domestic legal culture, one cannot have a right of self-defense against someone who is rightfully exercising self-defense. But, if the vocabulary is shifted to "permission" to use force instead of a right do so, the theoretical problem might be solved. However, in its current formulation, the problem remains. The issue resembles the relationship between jus ad bellum and jus in bello. The two must be logically distinct or the troops could not function without automatically committing a war crime. The same danger applies to the UN peacekeeping forces. Someone might have to explain why the right of self-defense under Article 51 doesn't apply to them. If the argument is that they are exempt because Article 51 itself refers to measures by the Security Council, the implication might be that they cannot commit war crimes either.

International Peace and Security.

The first word "international" raises problems if the primary issue is the relationship between the Palestinians and the Israelis (again, the problems of the Middle East). "International" means that the conflict occurs between two nations. Nations are different from states; at least, this was the position maintained by Abraham Lincoln in the American Civil War and by Woodrow Wilson in World War II. As opposed to states, which are recognized under international law by other states, nations are simply born. Lincoln's argument in the Gettysburg Address of November 1863 was that Americans are united by birth and therefore blacks and whites, northerners and southerners, constituted a single nation "indivisible."[54] Woodrow Wilson claimed that after World War I, every nation should have its own state.[55] Things have not worked out that way. Gypsies are presumably a nation, constantly persecuted, and they have never received a state.[56]

The concepts of "peace and security" should not be taken literally. "Peace" is often used in the idiom "peace and quiet." But, how long must things be quiet in order to say that peace prevails? We live in an age threatened with nuclear war. Does that mean we are at peace? The term actually becomes

[54] Abraham Lincoln, *The Gettysburg Address* (Nov. 19, 1863), *in* LINCOLN ON DEMOCRACY 307 (Mario M. Cuomo & Harold Holzer eds., 1990).

[55] *See* Woodrow Wilson, *The Fourteen Points Address* (1918), *in* 1 WAR AND PEACE 155 (1970).

[56] *See generally* Walter Otto Weyrauch & Maureen Anne Bell, *Autonomous Lawmaking: "The Case of Gypsies,"* 103 YALE L.J. 323 (1993).

more ambiguous when coupled with "security." The effort to assure security through armaments, particularly nuclear weapons and ICBMs, actually increases insecurity. Since the threats of wars with the former Soviet Union, the West has been familiar with the dangers of "mutual assured destruction." Disarmament would increase peace and security, insofar is it could be equally observed and enforced. But, the Security Council cannot do much in this analysis except by quiet diplomacy.

The points stated above attempt to fit the language of Article 51 into a mold of self-defense. Rather than take the language too seriously, it might be better just to assume six variables in the international law of self-defense. An (i) imminent, (ii) unlawful, (iii) armed attack by a collective met by a defensive response that is (iv) necessary, (v) proportional, (vi) and knowing or intentional.[57]

The next step in the argument is making the transition from jus ad bellum to jus in bello. The Rome Statute's Article 8 is about the latter, and we must examine the latter set of war crimes, or at least the general structure of the complicated set of 50 odd war crimes. The problem is the asymmetry of the two categories. Assuming that the UN could intervene in only one side of an armed conflict, how do we get to the symmetrical situation in which both those aggressing and those defending can commit war crimes? This is an inescapable problem (as is the problem of the peacekeeping forces committing war crimes). It could not be the case after the German attack on Poland that only one side could commit war crimes. We know from the Nuremberg and Tokyo tribunals that the victors will prosecute the losers. But the victors do not do that as a matter of principle, but as an extension of victory. The virtue of the ICC, many believe, is that it does not represent either the victors or losers, no more than any permanent tribunal in a nation–state is or should be biased toward a political party or orthodoxy.[58]

Furthermore, an asymmetrical approach to war crimes would create an intolerable situation for the troops engaged in battle. How is an ordinary soldier—even a commander—supposed to know whether his side violated Article 51 or not? War crimes make sense only insofar as individual soldiers are treated as responsible for their actions, regardless of who started the war.

[57] For my lecture summarizing these six issues, see https://www.youtube.com/watch?v=KvfFa9Xy3NU.

[58] *See* Statement by Susan Dickson, UK Legal Counsellor at the UN at the UN High Level Event on the 20th Anniversary of the Rome Statute, Marking 20 Years Since the Adoption of the ICC Rome Statute, July 18, 2018, at https://www.gov.uk/government/speeches/marking-20-years-since-the-adoption-of-the-icc-rome-statute.

A. Superior Orders: A Detour

At the opposite extreme, another relevant question can be asked: Why are soldiers not liable for all actions that entail criminal liability under local law? Killing, assaulting, the use of poison—all of these are crimes in every legal system. Why should soldiers—that is, combatants—be exempt? The relevant arguments would be (1) there is no harm in killing the enemy, (2) the action is justified, or (3) the action is excused. None of these is satisfactory. Of course, there is harm in killing other human beings, regardless of nationality and uniform. There might be an argument that because combatants are subject to being killed as well, there is an element of reciprocity that does not exist in domestic law. In that limited sense, one could say there is no relevant harm. An argument of justification would have to be based on an order given by a superior in the order of command. The problem of superior orders is addressed in Article 33 of the Rome Statute, but this provision is difficult to follow. Here's why.

The background assumption is that superior orders normally alleviate a subordinate combatant of criminal responsibility. The entire system of military discipline is based on following orders.[59] Being subject to a chain of command is a condition for being a combatant. Indeed, Japanese General Yamashita was held liable in a postwar military commission for failing to supervise his troops in the Philippines.[60] The assumption was that his subordinates would follow orders and therefore he was liable on a theory of command responsibility.[61] This is the case that generated Article 28 of the Rome Statute.

The general trend since World War II, however, has been the decline of "following orders" as a sound defense.[62] This is presumably a reaction to perceived atrocities committed by German and Japanese soldiers in the widespread killing of civilians by Einsatzgruppen and in death camps such as Auschwitz. The assumption is that if ordinary soldiers had taken more personal responsibility, they would not have committed these war crimes. I have

[59] "The military is built on 'total and unqualified obedience [to orders] without any hesitation or doubt.'" *See* YORAM DINSTEIN, THE DEFENSE OF "OBEDIENCE TO SUPERIOR ORDERS," *in* INTERNATIONAL LAW 69–70 (1965) (quoting the Kafr Kassem case (Military Court, Central District 3/57, Military Prosecutor v. Melinki), 17 Pesakim (D.) 90, 213 (Israel 1957)).

[60] UNITED NATIONS WAR CRIMES COMMISSION, 4 LAW REPORTS OF TRIALS OF WAR CRIMINALS 1 (1948).

[61] *Id.*

[62] *See* Aubrey M. Daniel, III, *The Defense of Superior Orders*, 7 U. RICH. L. REV. 477, 483 (1973) (discussing conviction of First Lieutenant William L. Calley for participation in My Lai Massacre).

my doubts, and there is certainly no way of knowing. Many issues must be left to speculation, including: (1) how many Allied troops also committed these crimes; (2) the extent to which the foot soldiers were animated by personal racial hatred, or whether they were merely following orders; (3) the simple confusion that results from being under enemy fire. My personal view is that we should be more sympathetic to soldiers on the front lines who are certainly following orders.

Contrary to the general principles of military discipline, Article 33 of the Statute begins on the assumption that following an order is not a sound defense.[63] But if three conditions are satisfied, submission to authority could be a defense—thus adding another ground for excluding criminal responsibility according to Article 31. These conditions are first, the subordinate being under a legal obligation to obey the superior in question.[64] The only problem here is raised by the word "legal." Presumably, a serious risk of court martial or mandated penalty in the case of disobedience would be sufficient.

The second condition is that the subordinate not have known that the order was unlawful.[65] In light of the third condition, namely, that the order not be "manifestly unlawful," this is probably redundant.[66] "Manifest" implies that the subordinate should be able to tell that, under the circumstances, the order is unlawful. It is ultimately a standard of negligence. A reasonable subordinate under the circumstances should have known that the order is unlawful. None of this is particularly sympathetic to the soldier in the field, and thus the entire Article 33 runs contrary to the general purpose of jus in bello, which is to protect the ordinary soldier from liability simply because his superior officers or government have ostensibly violated the principles of Article 51 of the UN Charter.

The saving grace for lower-ranking soldiers is that there are simply too many violations of jus in bello to try all of them. What we know from the Nuremberg and Tokyo trials, as well as from the ICTY and other ad hoc tribunals, is that the courts will generally try the leaders, not the foot soldiers. This is simply a matter of efficiency, not of principle, and it seems rather obvious when we consider the sheer number of war crimes created under Article 8.[67]

[63] *See* Rome Statute, *supra* note 5, art. 33(1)(a).
[64] *See id.*
[65] *Id.*
[66] *See id.*
[67] See *id.*, art. 8.

The only way to analyze the 50 war crimes defined in Article 8 is to group them, as the Article itself does. There are five relevant groups, each posing special problems. The first consists of eight crimes derived from the Geneva Conventions of August 12, 1949.[68] Article 8(2)(a) provides that they must be "grave breaches" and that they must be against persons or property protected under the Conventions.[69] Thus, we see a rather clear reference to the principle of distinction. The persons protected are those "hors de combat"—the sick, the wounded, POWs, chaplains, and, obviously, civilians. This has given rise to a euphemism for the law of war: International Humanitarian Law (IHL).[70] Thus a "humanitarian" purpose seems to be protecting those "hors de combat." But, there is nothing humanitarian about prosecuting war crimes. It is as though we called domestic criminal law "domestic humanitarian law." Pun aside, there are serious implications to whether we look at the purpose of a statute as protecting those "hors de combat" or prosecuting war criminals.

The orientation of the treaty, convention, or statute affects the burden of persuasion and the general principle of interpretation, namely Article 23(2) of the Rome Statute. Do we interpret strictly to protect the accused or those protected by the humanitarian purposes of IHL? I suppose it depends on the context. In the prosecution of war crimes, regardless of their historical origins, the burden of persuasion and principles of interpretation must protect the accused.

B. War Crimes and Their Complexity

The structure of war crimes is based on collective action. First, they must be committed, according to Article 8 of the Rome Statute, "as part of a plan or policy or as part of a large-scale commission of such crimes." Perhaps an individual could pull off this "plan or policy" but it is unlikely. Further, many specific crimes presuppose a collective group of actors. Here is a sample list from the many war crimes defined in Article 8:

68 *See id.*
69 *Id.*
70 *See generally* THE HANDBOOK OF INTERNATIONAL HUMANITARIAN LAW (Dieter Fleck ed., 2d ed. 2008).

1. "Compelling a prisoner of war or other protected person to serve in the forces of a hostile Power."
2. "Wilfully depriving a prisoner of war or other protected person of the rights of fair and regular trial."
3. " Taking of hostages."
4. "The transfer, directly or indirectly, by the Occupying Power of parts of its own civilian population into the territory it occupies, or the deportation or transfer of all or parts of the population of the occupied territory within or outside this territory."[71]

This sample list makes the point. There are many war crimes that require the coordinated conduct of large numbers of people. No one, acting alone, can compel a person to serve in a hostile army, deprive someone of a fair trial, take hostages, or transfer their civilian population into an occupied territory. It is conceivable that a commander might be able to mobilize his subordinates to engage in these collective crimes, but the subordinates—or at least some of them—must cooperate. The commander's criminal purpose is validated and reinforced by subordinates willing to carry out his orders.

It is important to see how this structure differs from ordinary domestic crimes, in which the paradigm is the individual acting alone. If there are others involved, they are co-perpetrators or accessories. But the commander is not treated as an accessory to the crime committed by his subordinates; he is simply fully liable as a perpetrator. The traditional criteria of complicity do not readily adapt to these situations of collective criminality.

All these points noted, let us look more closely at the first group of war crimes under Article 8(2)(a). The first is "wilful killing."[72] The notion of "willfulness" as a form of mens rea is not recognized under the Model Penal Code or any European Code that has come to my attention. The implication might be that the mens rea reveals an even greater personal commitment to the action than captured in Article 30 on "intent" and "knowledge." But it is not clear what the addition might be. For the defense, I would argue that the "willful" element in this context include knowledge that the intended victim is alive, a combatant, and "hors de combat." For the prosecution, the best claim might be that Article 30 on the mental element controls the reading of Article 8.

[71] Rome Statute, *supra* note 5, art. 8.
[72] *Id.*

Next, under Article 8(2)(a)(ii), we encounter torture and related offenses.[73] Torture itself has a disputed history. The first of these historic debates is over whether various techniques of "enhanced interrogation" (a term used during the George W. Bush administration) constitute torture.[74] The famous incident at Abu Ghraib—essentially the psychological intimidation of Muslim prisoners—posed the question of whether torture must be a physical, "hands-on" abuse. As though the provision anticipated this problem, it includes other "inhuman treatment."[75] Whether sleep deprivation, being frightened by dogs, being handcuffed for more than 24 hours, being denied a proper place to defecate—all of these are arguably inhumane. The problem is that conventional American prison practices—being held for years on death row, solitary confinement, risk of violence and sexual assault from fellow inmates—also seem inhumane under this standard. The same provision includes "biological experiments" as an example of inhumane treatment (arguably, this is also an example of torture—it is not clear from the text of the Statute). Now what is a biological experiment? The notion of an experiment suggests a trial run in which the outcome is relevant. One can imagine biological warfare but not "experiments." This idea does not seem compatible either with IHL or the law of war.

The remarkable feature of torture is that many believe that it works. On one hand, why would anyone provide accurate information when lying about something hard to verify? On the other, is a prisoner going to lie when a lie would produce an even greater respite and possibly more torture when and if the falsehood *is* identified? Some say that there is a Santa-Clause-like quality to this act of desperation and some even refer to it as cowardice. Others, however, including some politicians, believe in it. It may simply be that some people—like John Yoo during the Bush administration—become identified with the issue and then continue to propagate its effectiveness. Furthermore, it would be difficult to say the negative—that it *never* works, and even demonstrating that it frequently doesn't work may be impossible. Additionally, there is always ticking bomb—a time-sensitive issue that may prompt less-than-efficient decisions—that would tempt the reasonable to resort to extreme actions. Suppose the information is that an atomic bomb is hidden under New York City and one person supposedly has the information

[73] *Id.*

[74] Jan Crawford et al., *Sources: Top Bush Advisors Approved "Enhanced Interrogation,"* ABC News (April 9, 2008), http://abcnews.go.com/TheLaw/LawPolitics/story?id=4583256&page=1.

[75] Rome Statute, *supra* note 5, art. 8(2)(a)(ii).

but will not talk. Otherwise reasonable people would be tempted to resort to some borderline techniques of interrogation. In a hypothetical situation of this sort, even Alan Dershowitz, one of the best legal minds of his generation, said he would resort to "torture" warrants, thus getting the judiciary involved. Of course, one way is to avoid the controversial nature of the word and employ a euphemism—like "enhanced interrogation techniques." The unfortunate truth is that no one really knows where ordinary interrogation ends and true torture begins.

Part (iii) of Article 8(2)(a) poses problems other than ambiguity of "wilfully," namely the notion of "Suffering."[76] Any military engagement causes suffering to the civilian population. Just entering a bomb shelter and anxiously waiting for the signal to leave is a great cause of suffering. Even threatening war is a cause of anxiety and suffering, especially for children. Most Americans born around World War II recall the anxiety produced by the Soviet and American policies of Mutual Assured Destruction. Interestingly, a puzzling comma appears in the language of the Article after the word "suffering."[77] This would be a delight to grammar enthusiasts. What does this imply and why is there no comma later in part (iii) referring to "body or health"? Is it a war crime to cause serious injury to health? The provision can be read that way. Yet all deprivation induced by warfare is injurious to the health both of those under attack and those engaged in aggression.

Part (iv) raises many new problems. First, it is directed toward property. One thinks here of the Nazi looting of paintings and the later disputes, represented beautifully in the film *Woman in Gold*.[78] But, destruction and appropriation, both covered in the provisions, are obviously different. Yet the provision reads: "destruction and appropriation."[79] Is this disjunctive or conjunctive? Will either do, or does the war crime require both? It is more logical to read the provision as disjunctive, but it is not clear if destruction alone should be a crime. Simply destroying property might be a tort, but it is not treated as crime in any domestic code that I am aware of.

The alternative to just destruction of property is appropriate, which justified a claim to get it back. Again, this is a tort remedy, not a criminal prosecution. Destruction of some property, such as animals dangerous to others, would be a social service. Also, some destruction, even willful destruction,

[76] *Id.*
[77] *Id.*
[78] WOMAN IN GOLD (Origin Pictures 2015).
[79] Rome Statute, *supra* note 5, art. 8.

is inevitable in the fog of war. Given the sheer number of war crimes and the unlikelihood of strict enforcement, the drafters should have avoided these "dead letter" provisions.

From a theoretical point of view, however, Article 8(2)(a)(iv) becomes even more complicated with the addition of the phrase "not justified by military necessity" and then "carried out unlawfully and wantonly."[80] The concept of necessity deserves a chapter in itself. But, essentially, necessity depends on a balancing of competing interests and a finding that the expected benefits exceed the expected cost. Utilitarian codes, such as the Model Penal Code, treat necessity as the foundation of all defenses. This might be appropriate for neutral observers who are adept at estimating the risk of doing harm and the likelihood of military benefit, but this approach cannot be fairly expected of partisans in armed conflict.

One interesting sidelight is the way in which the drafting of Article 8 generates problems of reconciliation with the rest of the Statute. Necessity is not even listed among the "grounds for excluding criminal liability" and yet is linked in this provision in the phrase "justified by military necessity."[81] My 2008 book provides an extensive analysis of the differences among aggressive necessity, defensive necessity, and self-defensive.[82] Each of these has a different standard for excessive force.

Note that the phrase is "justified" not "excused" by necessity. The distinction between justification and excuse is fundamental to the theory of defense but not recognized clearly in the Statute—although Article 31 implicitly does so by ordering the "grounds" as excuses (insanity and intoxication first) and then justifications (self-defense and duress).[83]

Article 8(2)(a)(iv) gets more complicated by adding the requirement that the appropriation or destruction be carried out "lawfully and wantonly."[84] As with unlawfulness, we run into a problem of circularity. The Rome Statute purports to be a statement of the relevant legal rules. After all, the basic idea is *nullum crimen* and *nulla poena sine lege* (Articles 22 and 23). So, what does the provision mean by "unlawfully" if not proscribed by the Statute itself? And then the requirement of "wantonly." This was a phrase once used in

[80] *Id.*
[81] *Id.*
[82] Fletcher & Ohlin, *supra* note 11.
[83] Rome Statute, *supra* note 5, art. 31.
[84] *Id.*, art. 8.

common law systems to define murder—"wanton disregard of human life."[85] But, no one quite knows what it means. Yet, it is definitely a mental state and thus runs contrary to spirit of *nulla poena sine lege* and definitions of mental elements under Article 30. In all fairness, however, we recall the proviso in Article 30—"unless otherwise provided."[86] There are many forms of mens rea in the Statute that are "otherwise provided."[87]

Moving on now to Article 8(2)(a)(v), we encounter a different set of complications. The crime is forcing a protected person to serve in a hostile military unit. It is hard to image the historical paradigm for this provision. Let's begin with the notion of "a hostile power."[88] Presumably that refers to a power hostile to the military force that is committing the war crime. One wonders whether today this covers powers, such as Al Qaeda and ISIS, which are hostile to the United States and its allies.

We live in an era of undeclared wars coupled with tensions between the United States and various nations, such as Syria and North Korea. There are charges against the latter of sending workers abroad, say to China, and keeping the wages that the workers should receive. There might be a subtle form of coercion in this case, but China is hardly a hostile power and the workers are not required to serve in the Chinese military. Thus, without a historical paradigm, we are at a loss to figure out the implications of this provision.

However, part (vi) of the Article is a little easier to comprehend, though it raises serious problems of comparative law. Let's us begin with the mens rea of "wilfully."[89] The ambiguities of this term have already been discussed. To consider a different angle on this problem, let us look at the French version: First, "willfully" is rendered as intentionally.[90] This is unfortunate because the same word is used in the French version of Article 30 is the equivalent of the English word "intentionally." Perhaps French is less rich in its specific terminology.

Even more interesting is the French version of a fair trial. The French equivalent of "fairly" is "réguiliérement." This is an unusual translation. Typically,

[85] *See, e.g.*, Uniform Code of Military Justice, 1950, Text, References and Commentary based on the Report of the Committee on a Uniform Code of Military Justice to The Secretary of Defense ("Morgan Draft"), at 144.

[86] Rome Statute, *supra* note 5, art. 30.

[87] *See id.*

[88] *Id.*, art. 8(2)(a)(v).

[89] *Id.*, art. 8(2)(a)(iii).

[90] *See* Statute de Rome de la Cour pénale international [Rome Statute], *supra* note 5, art. 8 ("Le fait de causer intentionnellement de grandes souffrances . . .") (Fr.).

the French equivalent of a "fair trial" is "un process juste"—a just trial. The notion of fairness cannot be captured in any of the official languages of the Rome Statute that are connected to the Continental inquisitorial tradition. A fair trial is much more than either a "regular" trial or a "just" outcome. First, a regular trial could be good or bad, with a jury, without a jury, based on presumption of innocence or not. Our assumption has to be that this provision represents a common denominator of civilized legal systems.

The problem is that we have two civilized legal traditions—the common law adversarial model and the inquisitorial model. The former is based on the principle of equal adversaries battling it out in court, as though the tougher advocate would be more likely to generate a fair result. The alternative inquisitorial model is justified in modern times by the claim that it represents a way of seeking the truth—by analogy to a scientific exploration. Neither of these is fully satisfactory. The common law tradition treats the trial as something like a boxing match: may the better, or more just and legally correct, man win. The inquisitorial tradition ignores the corrupting influence of centralized power. Further, it is difficult to prove that a criminal trial establishes the truth. We do try to avoid the conviction of the innocent, but the presumption of innocence justifies the acquittal of many guilty defendants.

We have to muddle through in this area as in many others.

On the whole, in the Rome Statute, the adversarial model is dominant, as is the trend in the world as a whole following the legal system built in the traditional United States. The interesting part of the Statute, as compared, say, with the American Bill of Rights, is the commitment both to the interests of victims and of defendants. But this raises a different angle on the adversarial model. Typically, we think of the prosecution as opposed to the defendant as the competing perspectives. When we add the victim, we generate a triangular model of advocacy. The prosecution must be committed not to the victim, but to the pursuit of justice in the abstract and within the bounds of precedent. Victims are sometimes motivated by vengeance or political advantage, particularly in cases of large-scale ethnic conflict. In the ICTY, the Croats and Serbs took careful note of how many were prosecuted from each camp. The triangular model of the adversarial system is a new and challenging phenomenon. It is safe to say, however, that this is not what we expect under the concept of a fair trial under Article 8(2)(a)(vi).

Part (vii) raises issues of ambiguity. The war crime consists in three alternative parts, A) unlawful deportation, B) transfer, C) unlawful confinement. Since the word "unlawful" is used in parts A and C, but not in B, we can assume that prohibition against "transfer" need not be unlawful. Transfer presumably refers to relocation of population without cause and therefore so egregious to be considered unlawful per se—either domestically or internationally.

In contrast, deportation is a war crime (of course, when committed as part of a "plan" or "policy"), on the condition that it is "unlawful." Again, we have the circularity of the Statute, which supposedly defines what is unlawful on an international level. Perhaps the Statute is referring to "unlawful" under domestic law, but then we must be talking about the domestic law of the deporting power. A good example perhaps is the proposal by a right-wing party in Israel to deport all Muslims on the West Bank to Jordan. Of course, this only applied to those Muslims who were not citizens of Israel. A less-inflammatory word for this process would be "resettlement." Now what make this "unlawful" under Israeli law? If the government is doing this, how can it be unlawful under domestic law? Maybe the idea is that the government is acting ultra vires—beyond its internal constitutional authority. But if that is the case, why is it the business of the ICC to enforce the constitutional law of a sovereign nation?

One option, which is appealing as a matter of comparative law, is to interpret "unlawful" in the European sense of being contrary to the law understood as Recht, droit, derecho, prava—law as principle rather than lex or statutory law. I find this the most plausible and the most consistent with the history of international law, but it does run counter to the attempt of the Rome Statute to codify international criminal law.[91]

"Unlawful confinement" raises many of the same issues. Maybe the detention of suspects in Guantánamo Bay could be a violation under this provision, but we need to make a lot of assumptions in order to reach this conclusion. The best way to support this claim would be to merge several of the war crimes under the Rome Statute. Some believe that the military commissions resulting in this confinement do not provide a fair trial and that the detentions are a violation of the U.S. Constitution's Sixth Amendment guaranteeing a jury trial, confrontation of witnesses, and other rights not recognized in the military commissions.

Another way to apply this provision might be to the holding of suspects before trial without bail, as guaranteed under the Eighth Amendment of the U.S. Bill of Rights. But, this move suggests two maneuvers for anyone

[91] *See* Rome Statute, *supra* note 5, art. 23.

seeking to uphold repressive measures against the challenges of the Rome Statute. The first is to switch back and forth between the common law and Continental inquisitorial traditions. Under Continental legal systems, pretrial administrative detention is acceptable. The second maneuver is to shift from theory to practice. In reality, American jails are full of people being held without trial, largely because they cannot afford the bond required to be released. Typically, the bail bond requires a down payment that is kept by the private bail bond company, even if the defendant shows up for trial.[92]

The last of this first set of provisions seems straightforward, but it masks some serious problems. "Hostages" are held, presumably, for ransom. The problem might be the intention required. Prisoners are routinely exchanged in armed conflict, but they might be captured and held, as bargaining chips, until the hostile forces have prisoners to exchange. In the Israeli-Arab conflict, Israel was willing to trade Palestinian prisoners in return of the remains of deceased Israeli soldiers.

As soon as we turn the page on hostages, however, we discover a long and intriguing history of kidnapping and highjacking largely designed to take hostages as bargaining chips. In the days of the USSR and Iron Curtain, highjacking was motivated largely by the desire to escape to the West. I was an expert witness in the case of Detlev Tiede, who highjacked an airplane flying out of Gdansk, Poland, and landed it in Tempelhof Airport in West Berlin.[93] He was tried and defended himself largely on the ground of the necessity of fleeing the Communist system. Trials of this nature are largely political, and it was not surprising that he was convicted of a minor offense and free to leave immediately after the trail.

It is worth noting that necessity is one of those grounds that should have been included in Article 31. Necessity is, in fact, the mother of all claims of justification. The only problem in the Tiede case is the risk was not imminent. There was nothing special about that time in East Germany—no heightened risk that required an extreme action that endangered the lives of others. Highjacking has been largely eliminated as a risk in airplane travel, perhaps at the cost of privacy to passengers who must subject themselves to searches before boarding.

[92] *See Bail Bond*, INVESTOPEDIA (last visited Nov. 17, 2018), https://www.investopedia.com/terms/b/bail-bond.asp.

[93] United States v. Tiede, 86 F.R.D. 227, 228 (U.S. Ct. Berlin 1979).

This concludes our analysis of the first eight provisions under Article 8(2)(a).

The next set of 26 offenses are labeled "serious" violations of the laws and customs applicable in international armed conflict.[94] The definitional approach here displays some special characteristics. Some of them appeared to be based on collective actions, others on individual actions. We must consider them in subgroups.

The first four begin with the word "intentionally."[95] While it is possible for two or three people to intentionally take a walk together, or even a larger group to act together if they are subject to military discipline, we should recall the discussion above about superior orders. Following orders is minimally available as a defense. Thus, it runs counter to the grain of the Statute to assume that large collectives act together intentionally.

Assuming that we are talking about collectives acting together intentionally, what does the word mean as a form of mens rea? The history of controversy about this word centers on the distinction between direct and indirect intentions. This distinction is of great relevance in the law of self-defense. The immediate object of defensive action may not be to harm the aggressor but rather to thwart the attack. This distinction gained currency in the Catholic Church's disputes about abortion. An operation that indirectly kills the fetus is acceptable, but not one directly aimed at taking the life of the fetus.

If we approach this issue on the assumption of command responsibility, we can understand the point of Article 8(2)(b)(I). It reads like the Genocide Statute. Under the first prong of the provision, the attack may not be launched against the civilian population "as such."[96] I think this implies a narrower reading of "intention." A good test case is the American bombing of Hiroshima. Of course, the United States could say that had some military target, for example, a train station, but that is all cover for a rather obvious attempt to intimidate the Japanese population and the military into surrendering. The problem is that if we take the U.S. claim at face value, the oblique killing of thousands falls under the definition of "intentionally directing an attack against the civilian population."[97] A good case can be made for both sides.

[94] Rome Statute, *supra* note 5, art. 8(2)(b).
[95] *Id.*
[96] *Id.*, art. 6.
[97] *Id.*, art. 8(2)(b)(ii).

Another violation of Article 8(2)(b)(I) is intentionally directing at attacks "against individual civilians not taking direct part in hostilities."[98] This is unfortunately becoming a recurrent problem in modern warfare, largely due to the development of drone strikes. The principle of gentlemanly warfare, face-to-face combat, has been out of date since the development of air power. But, at least airplanes are subject to anti-aircraft fire in a modern "gentlemanly" exchange of technological power. Drone operators, however, may be underground in a bunker. Even more frightening is the possibility of computer programs designed to operate autonomously. In that case, who would be acting intentionally? Could be it the programmer? Would actions taken by the computer be under less scrutiny by enforcers of international law just because it had no intent?

The other problem raised in part (I) is the concept of "civilians" not taking direct part in hostilities. This has become rather common in contemporary terrorist activity. We have a new phenomenon of fighters who are farmers by day and armed terrorists by night. Are they civilians, and, if so, are they taking direct part in the hostilities? We should remember that this provision is governed by the introductory clause referring to the "laws and customs applicable in international armed conflict." Each of these words is problematic.

Leaving aside our discussion of the words "law" and "laws," the intriguing problem here is the customs of international armed conflict. Customs are constantly evolving, and there is a major difference between customs and customary law. Everyone has his own view of what customs are. Do we take off our head covering in places of religious worship? In churches, yes; in mosques and synagogues, no. For the custom to become customary law, it must be recognized as binding. It is rare for customary practices to become legally binding. The only example I can think of is the law of the sea.

"Direct part in hostilities." This suggests the possibility of taking an indirect part in the military conflict. It looks as though the programmer could be liable under this interpretation. Also, there are many people in the military who do nothing more than deliver the mail or translate from one language to another. Suppose they are civilians themselves hired for these special tasks. Are they an indirect part in the hostilities? It is anyone's guess.

The biggest problem of warfare in the age of terrorism is that each side follows its own rules. In large part, as between Muslims and others in the Middle East, these particularistic rules—for example, the role of women—is

[98] *Id.*, art. 8(2)(b)(i).

what these wars are often about. We are running up against up the edges of jus in bello, which is designed to create a common set of rules to protect soldiers from liability for the aggressive and illegal behavior of their commanders and political leaders.

Another problem is the definition of "hostilities."[99] It seems that this refers to actual fighting. But it is hard to know when the hostilities begin and end. Were there hostilities on December 8, 1941, the days after the Japanese attack on Pearl Harbor? Or on September 12, 2001, immediately after the attack on the World Trade Center? There is always the possibility of a single strike without an intention to continue the aggressive actions.

Part (ii) of Article 8(2)(b) penalizes an intentional attack on "civilian objects, which are not military objects."[100] The problem here is the distinction between direct and oblique or indirect intentions. This is a familiar problem in the law of self-defense. Of course, no one can ever determine whether the U.S. nuclear attack on Hiroshima was designed to take out a military target or simply to intimidate the Japanese military. The notion of a "military object" is also puzzling. Why should the Statute be concerned about protecting property? Everything in the enemy's economy serves a military purpose. Without bread and clean water, no army can function. So, it appears, a distinction is drawn between direct military instruments and societal instruments vital to the military's existence; otherwise the Article fails to draw any restriction.

Trespasses on property need not be extensively addressed here. This is because, generally, in domestic criminal law, trespasses against real or personal property are treated as torts nor crimes. The analysis of these 50 offenses takes us back to the problem of chapter 2, the role of tort liability in the international legal order. There is no apparent reason why the ICC should take on these issues and add to the uncertainty of prosecutorial discretion.

Part (iii) may be more plausible than part (ii). The essential point is that it is a crime to direct an attack against a non-fighting unit that seeks to eliminate the suffering on the battlefield. Here we can see a good reason to call this body of law "international humanitarian law." Criminalizing the action is way of serving this purpose. At the end of this part, however, the language reverts to "international law of armed conflict." These additional words may confuse more than they clarify. First, what body of international law are they

[99] *Id.*
[100] *Id.*

referring to? And is it about humanitarian assistance or jus in bello? These questions have concerned us before.

Part (iv) raises some issues that appeal to economists. The issues are posed by an application of cost/benefit analysis. We will not repeat the mens rea issues posed by "intentionally" and "in the knowledge." The economic issues are the anticipated costs and benefits of launching an attack. These concepts recapitulate the famous Learned Hand test for negligence. But there are special problems posed by applying the domestic law of negligence in the context of international hostilities.

The relevant damage to be anticipated is the loss of life or injury. There are many injuries caused by hostilities, including the common PTSD.[101] More complicated is the damage done to succeeding generations. The use of Agent Orange as a defoliant in Vietnam is an example. I was an expert witness in the case of the Vietnamese survivors against Dow Chemical for manufacturing and distributing the herbicide.[102] The damage did not show up until the third generation. This raises serious problems of causation, which we have considered at length in chapter 4.

As to the benefits, the military advantage is obvious: the possibility of moving through the underbrush without encountering hidden enemy snipers. The more interesting question is why American forces in Vietnam should take a neutral view on the costs and benefits of using Agent Orange. Warfare is, by its nature, a partisan activity. It might be true that the costs to an enemy enter into the equation at some point, but imposing a strict cost/benefit analysis is confusing the rule of a judge with the role of engaged military personnel.

The problem with the subjective military point of view is the relevant discount factor for enemy troops. Consider the bombing of Hiroshima and Nagasaki contrasted to an American invasion of Japan. The assumption is that this would have cost many American lives, but how do we compare our lives with theirs? There is a similar problem in the theory of self-defense. The lives of aggressor are worth less than those of the defenders but still worth something. If not, we wouldn't have the entire system of "international humanitarian law."

[101] *See* Karen McVeigh, *Syrian Children Suffer Staggering Levels of Trauma and Distress—Report*, GUARDIAN (Mar. 6, 2017), https://www.theguardian.com/global-development/2017/mar/06/syria-children-suffering-staggering-levels-of-trauma-save-the-children-report-warns.

[102] *See* 517 F.3d at 104.

The inclusion of the adjective "incidental" to modify the anticipated cost of the military action raises an issue of double effect.[103] As a principle assumed in the law of self-defense, the harm to the aggressor may not be directly intended but incidental. This is called the principle of double effect, and it is a rather subtle modification of the mens rea required in self-defense. The principle has an important application in the law of abortion. It is not permissible to intend the death of fetus (considered a human life) but acceptable if the death of the fetus is incidental to a required medical operation. The problem, of course, is the totally subjective nature of this principle. There is no way to prove the contrary.

Part (v) is relatively straightforward except for the notion of "military objective."[104] Everything is more or less a military objective. More intriguing is the symbolism of their being undefended. The war crime requires an attack on a defended community. This principle expresses the traditional principle of reciprocal warfare. There is something unfair about attacking an undefended person or community, and this is expressed in the language of the Article 8(2)(b).

The same principle of unfair combat continues in part (vi).[105] The puzzling part is the addition of the phrase "at discretion" after the requirement of surrender.[106] What other kind of surrender could there be? And whose discretion is implied? There are two problems. One is whose discretion is at stake; the surrendering soldier or the capturing soldier? And what does the term mean? In the history of philosophy, the latter question has generated a great deal of discussion. The term originally had the meaning of "wise" or "mature" as in the phrase "age of discretion." Then it was adopted in American administrative law to mean a range of acceptable outcomes. Then the term was applied to judicial decisions to imply that judges decided not on the basis of the law or justice but in the interest of some social purpose like protecting the environment. The latter connotation of "discretion" would obviously be inconsistent with the guiding principle of the Rome Statute, *nulla poena sine lege*, and with precedent-based principles of enduring American domestic law.

Part (vii) begins with a rather clear inchoate offense, namely an attempt to deceive the enemy by using a false flag. The use of a deceptive flag then

[103] *See* Rome Statute, *supra* note 5, art. 8(2)(b)(iv).

[104] *Id.*, art. 8(2)(b)(v).

[105] *See id.*, art. 8(2)(b)(vi) ("Killing or wounding a combatant who, having laid down his arms or having no longer means of defence, has surrendered at discretion.").

[106] *Id.*

becomes a completed offense when the deception results in death or serious bodily injury. There are some difficult issues. The flag must be one of the "enemy," but we are discussing undeclared wars without an official enemy.[107] Presumably this would apply to the flag of ISIS. More problematic is the causal factor of leading to death or serious bodily injury. In the fog of the battlefield, this is difficult to ascertain. All harmful consequences are overdetermined. In the end, it boils down to a flag and a death nearby on the battlefield.

Part (viii) brings back the concept of "transfer" that seems problematic in the content of Article 8(1)(a)(vii)—above.[108] In this context, the concept seems to be a bit clearer, largely because of additional phrase "directly or indirectly by the Occupying Power."[109] The historical paradigm is obviously Israel in the West Bank after 1967. It is true that Israel was the Occupying Power. The problem is where resettlement takes place. Until 1977, Israelis were not permitted to settle in the West Bank.[110] Then, with the election of Menachem Begin, the policy changed, and individual settlers were permitted to move in alongside their Arab neighbors. This process has made it more difficult to reach a two-state solution to the conflict.

The word that makes the Israeli reference seem more obvious is the "transfer" might be "direct or indirect."[111] The implication is that if the government tolerates the actions of the settlers, it is acting indirectly. The problem is over who is criminally liable? The settlers themselves or the agents of the "Occupying Power." There are over 350,000 settlers in the West Bank today. Some of the settlements have lasted over 40 years. Many grandchildren of the original settlers were born there. It strains credulity to think that all of these civilians would be subject to prosecution.

If this is a "leadership" crime like aggression, that too is problematic because Menachim Begin died in 1992. Arguably, the current leaders of the Israeli government are responsible for the settlements that began in 1977. But this is clearly implausible. Many of the current leaders were children in 1977. They inherited the problem as did the settlers.

107 Rome Statute, *supra* note 5, art. 8(2)(b)(vii).
108 *See id.*, art. 8(2)(b)(viii).
109 *Id.*
110 *See* Joyce Wadler, *Pioneering American Jewish Families Help to Settle West Bank*, Wash. Post. (Nov. 7, 1982), https://www.washingtonpost.com/archive/politics/1982/11/07/pioneering-american-jewish-families-help-to-settle-west-bank/19b7a23e-5cff-4a4e-8fdb-d0412efe0216/?utm_term=.47e2d9f24ffb.
111 Rome Statute, *supra* note 5, art. 8(2)(b)(viii).

Also, history has overtaken the problems generated by the beginning of the settlement on the West Bank in 1977. The Oslo Accords have legitimated the actions; there are many important legal issues that remain on the West Bank, such as choice-of-law problems in the case of accidents between settlers and Palestinian residents. These are not problems of impunity, which the Rome Statute was designed to overcome.

As we immerse ourselves in these details, we are witnessing a clear instance of over-criminalization. This is a dangerous practice in criminal law because it increases prosecutorial discretion, plea bargains, and the opportunity for discriminatory use of the powers of the ICC.

That said, when we address the latter half of part (viii), we encounter some new issues: first, the reference to both "transfer" and "deportation," and a focus on "within or without this territory."[112] It seems that the drafters of the Rome Statute want to cover all possible bases. But in the end, there are only two ways to understand the overall import of this or any other provision in the Statute. Either it represents the inheritance of some prior language from an international convention; or it has a focus on a historical paradigm, as we noted earlier in the Israeli-Palestinian conflict.

The historical precedent for transfer "within or without" the occupied territory appeals to a charge brought against Albert Speer in the Nuremberg War Crime trials. The Germans kept a vast war machine going even late into the war, and they managed to do this solely on the basis of drafted or slave labor, founded primarily in the occupied territories in France or the East.[113] Speer cooperated with the prosecutors from the Four Victories Powers and received a 20-year sentence, while many other received the death penalty.

In part (ix), we encounter the adverb "intentionally" once again.[114] It is difficult to understand why this modification of Article 30 on the "mental element" crops up in some places and not others. It seems obvious that the same mental states modify part (viii) as well. The general principles of statutory interpretation would lead us to think that the inclusion in one place should be consistent with the exclusion elsewhere. But, if we have learned anything from these meditations on war crimes, it is that we have to remain flexible and assume a variety of inputs in the drafting process.

112 *Id.*, art. 8(2)(b)(viii).

113 *See* Timothy W. Murphy & Jeff E. Whitfield, *Excerpts from the Nuremberg Trials*, 6 USAFA J. Leg. Stud. 5, 152 (1995).

114 Rome Statute, *supra* note 5, art. 8(2)(b)(ix).

It is difficult to formulate the essential nature of the war crime in part (ix). It appears to be about attacking civilian targets provided they are not a "military objective."[115] We discussed the latter issue in our above discussion of 8(2)(b)(v). A different problem arises from the listing of the specific civilian targets. The attempt to achieve a detailed list (at least eight or nine different kinds of buildings) carries negative implications about those not listed, for example, garages, stables, technological facilities. The most important targets not mentioned might be farms and water resources. No fighting force can last long without food and clean water. Yet these are no per se military objectives.

Also, there are many possible targets that are not devoted to a single use, either civilian or military. It is not uncommon for terrorists to take over churches and schools. This obviously should not create a safe harbor for them. The problem of mixed use reflects back on the interpretation of "intentionally." If oblique intentions are included, then it is easier to solve the conundrum of mixed use. If the primary purpose is to target a civilian target, then the action appears to be a war crime. I am not sure this makes sense in light of the presumption of innocence and the general principle of *nullum crimen, nulla poena sine lege.*[116] These provisions are designed to avoid defendants' guessing or relying on partisan advice about what constitutes a war crime.

Part (x) may have a historical precedent, at least in part. The Nazi doctor Josef Mengele allegedly conducted these experiments on twins in the Auschwitz death camp. And the experiments seem to satisfy the other requirements. The only possible defense would be consent—under the extreme conditions where the choice is being subject to an experiment or death. Mengele was among the Nazis who fled to Argentina (Eichmann being the other).[117]

There are other possible scenarios in the provision, one of them being "mutilation."[118] All prisoners in the Nazi death camps had their heads shaved. This presumably was not mutilation, a concept that implies permanent change to the body. The reference to the possibility of "dental" treatment implies something like pulling teeth, which the Nazis did in order in order to retrieve the gold fillings. It is puzzling, however, to group experiments and mutilation in

115 *Id.*, art. 8(b)(2)(ix).
116 *Id.*, arts. 22 & 23.
117 *See* Nick Evans, *Nazi Angel of Death Josef Mengele 'Created Twin Town in Brazil,'* TELEGRAPH (Jan. 21, 2009), https://www.telegraph.co.uk/news/worldnews/southamerica/brazil/4307262/Nazi-angel-of-death-Josef-Mengele-created-twin-town-in-Brazil.html.
118 *See* Rome State, *supra* note 5, art. 8(2)(b)(x).

the same provision. The motives are entirely different. The former is based on a pretense of scientific discovery; the latter is a form of cruelty—unless there might some perverse interest in utilizing the body parts for gain.

The only problem is that neither experimentation or mutilation satisfies the other requirement: causing death or seriously endangering the health of the victim. There is little point in raising the problematic issue of causation, which we have discussed in chapter 4.[119]

Part (xi) raises a new problem with the adverb "treacherously."[120] This is an implicit reference to a requirement of fairness in warfare—a principle honored these days in the breach.

Treachery implies trickery, as symbolized by the Trojan Horse in the war between Greece and Troy as recorded in Homer.[121] It is no longer true, if it ever was, that all is fair in love and war. Every clever maneuver in warfare requires some element of deception—although the connotation of "treacherously" is that the degree of deception is unacceptable.

It does seem odd in the provision to lump together as victims of treachery: "individuals in the hostile nation or army," that is, civilians and soldiers.[122] Attacking civilians is per se a war crime. In warfare, good generals seek a way a way to induce an enemy to a battle where they are likely to lose.

Part (xii)—declaring that no prisoners will be taken—is per se a war crime. The interesting aspect of this crime is that it must be committed collectively. Individuals do not take prisoners. It makes no sense for an individual soldier to shout out: I will give no quarter. The collective committing the crime must be a military organization capable of establishing a prison camp. This is a rather expensive operation.

An aside to this and may other crimes is the economics of warfare, the costs and benefits of committing the alleged crime. Apparently, the use of slave labor was economically necessary to maintain the German war effort. At the same time, the diverting of resources for sadistic or genocidal reasons seems economically irrational. Admittedly, neither fighting crime, not the collective analogy—fighting wars—is justified by an accurate cost/benefit analysis. Americans may care about the price of gas, but they do not care

119 *Supra* ch. IV.

120 *See* Rome Statute, *supra* note 5, art. 8(2)(b)(xi).

121 *See* Homer, Complete Works of Homer: The Iliad (Andrew Lang et al. trans., Modern Library 1950); Homer, The Odyssey of Homer 244 (Alan Mandelbaum trans., University of California Press 1990).

122 *See* Rome Statute, *supra* note 5, art. 8(2)(b)(xi).

about the costs of prisons or unnecessary military installations. Just consider the 11-million-dollar cost per prisoner that the United States paid willingly at Guantánamo Bay Prison.[123]

Part (xiii) poses at least two radically different scenarios. Let us focus on the variations of seizing property, the most likely object of seizure being valuable cultural property, primarily works of art. The difference in two stories—one about Vincent van Gogh and the other about Gustav Klimt—give us point of reference about the nature of seizure in times of war. Van Gogh's *Night Cafe* was seized by Lenin and the Communist government during the revolution. The heirs of the original owner sued to get it back.[124] At the time of the suit, the painting was owned by the Yale University Art Museum. They based their claim on a chain of title established when Stalin sold the painting. The issue in the litigation was whether the Soviet seizure was legitimate. Yale won the original case, but the dispute seems to continue to this day.[125] The painting still hangs in the Yale Museum. The deeper question is whether valuable cultural artifacts should ever be owned by private parties and not available to the public.

The other important case is posed by the Nazi seizure of art work as their armies advanced all over Europe. A work by Gustav Klimt, *Woman in Gold*, came into the hands of the Austrian government after the war. A lawyer in Los Angeles engaged in litigation to get the painting back. He won, and the work now hangs in the Neue Gallerie, a subsidiary of the Metropolitan Museum of Art in New York.[126] The story is very dramatic and inspired the namesake film based on the title of the painting.[127] For our purposes, the important question is why the Soviet seizure (the successors win) differs from the Nazi seizure (the successors lose). There are several possible answers: (1) legitimation over time, (2) revolution vs. aggressive war, (3) a general revulsion against everything associated with Hitler and his regime. I think the best answer is (2).

We have been discussing valuable cultural property, while part (xiii) is about all property. Further, the two prongs—destruction and seizure—suggest

[123] *See Wasted Opportunities: The Cost of Detention Operations at Guantanamo Bay*, ACLU (last visited Feb. 2, 2017), https://www.aclu.org/issues/national-security/detention/wasted-opportunities-cost-detention-operations-guantanamo-bay.

[124] Yale Univ. v. Konowaloff, 5 F. Supp. 3d 237, 238–39 (D.C. Con. 2014).

[125] *See* Konowaloff v. Yale Univ., 136 S. Ct. 1494 (2016).

[126] *Gustav Klimt and Adele Bloch-Bauer: The Woman in Gold*, Nueue Gallerie (Sep. 7, 2015), https://www.neuegalerie.org/gustav-klimt-and-adele-bloch-bauer-woman-gold.

[127] Woman, *supra* note 81.

that the focus should not be on cultural property at all, but on the everyday objects appropriated in the course of warfare, for example, farms, orchards, perhaps even living space such as private homes. There is an interesting precedent in the almost forgotten Third Amendment to the U.S. Constitution, which prohibits the quartering of troops in private homes without the owner's consent.[128] It is doubtful that this obscure provision—never tested in the Supreme Court—would be the basis for the Rome Statute.

The word "destruction" has an entirely different connotation—totally removed from the world of art and culture and even of the U.S. Third Amendment.[129] It brings to mind the scorched earth policies of the Soviet Union. Yet, the Soviets did this to their own territory to prevent the advancing Germans from getting the benefits of their occupation. This seems like an entirely reasonable maneuver in warfare—hardly the basis for a war crime.

It is not clear why the destruction of property should even be an issue. All acts of warfare entail the destruction of war—tanks rolling over gardens, bullets destroying windows, planes crashing into houses. These risks are omnipresent in all armed conflict. Yet the "destruction" prong of the provision seems to make sense if we take the perspective of the justification clause at the end.[130]

The possible justification for both prongs of the provision is "the necessities of war," which is not mentioned as one of the four standard grounds "for excluding criminal responsibility" in Article 31.[131] The justification would presumably be based on a cost/benefit analysis. But there is no rational way to balance the benefits to our side against the costs to their side. It is probably better to interpret "justification" in this context as a non-legal term, something like "vindicated" or "warranted."

The language of the provision tightens this element of justification. It must be "imperatively demanded."[132] This means something like "no choice"—suggesting a limited application to cases of inevitable injury like airplane crashes. Yet the provision implies that seizure would be treated the same as destruction. It is typical for advancing troops to take fruit or vegetables or simply fresh water from farmers situated on the front lines. The problem is making sense of a provision that applies to such totally different situations as

[128] U.S. Const. amend. III.
[129] *Id.*
[130] Rome Statute, *supra* note 5, art. 8(2)(b)(xiii).
[131] *See id.*, art. 31.
[132] *Id.*, art. 8(2)(b)(xiii).

the theft of valuable art works and the destruction of driving tanks through private property.

Part (xiv) is even more confusing in its wording. We gather that it has something to do with putting nationals of a hostile party on trial. The actus reus is an act of declaration, a speech act, about their rights. This is presumably a collective crime, as is declaring that no quarter be given. No single person, acting alone, could have an impact on somebody's rights in a court of law. This would be true if we take "a court of law" as something more than a dictator's deciding thumbs up or thumbs down. However, the word of law is understood, a court must consist of more than a judge. To be functional, courts require some continuity, and administrators, police, bailiffs, etc. Yet it might be true that the only the judge would be liable for his "declaration" under this provision.

What must the relevant declaration be about? This is where the provision becomes dubious. It could be about "rights" or "actions." To his credit, Michael Cottier interprets the reference to "actions" according to the German Forderungen and thus arrives at the proper term "claims." The only relevant rights at stake are, in fact, legal claims. Hohfeld famously interpreted the term "right" to mean "legal claim." As to the claim of rights of the national, we would have to inquire about relevant body of law. Presumably, it is the body of law under which the judge has legal capacity. Thus, we have to imagine the following scenario: a judge declares the defendant's claim right under his own law are (1) abolished or (2) suspended.

A declaration is a speech act, and therefore we should inquire as to whether the jurisprudence of speech acts illuminate this provision. Speech acts became famous in the philosophy of John Searle.[133] The basic principle is that X counts as Y in C. In a particular setting, saying, "I do" has the effect of effecting a marriage. Standing before a duly authorized official, a couple's saying "I do" has the effect of establishing a marriage. No, I suppose if a judge (X) says in court (C) that "your rights are abolished," they are ipso facto abolished. Yet Searle's example presupposes a binding legal background. The paradox in this situation is that without an appropriate background, the judge is just an observer, and his statement has no effect at all.

We might be taking the provision too seriously. It is not clear that a judge could ever actually declare that the rights of an enemy national suspended.

[133] *See* John Searle, *Response: Meaning, Intentionality, and Speech Acts*, *in* JOHN SEARLE AND HIS CRITICS (Ernest Lepore & Robert van Gulick eds., 1991).

What could happen is that a judge could act as these rights were suspended or abolished. For the purposes of trial in that particular judge's courtroom, the rights would not apply.

Part (xv) poses a problem of compulsory disloyalty.[134] The scenario imagined is forcing, say, a Polish national to fight in the German army against Poland. The assumption is that Polish nationals will always be loyal to Poland whether or not they have lived in Germany since childhood. This is true whether or not the Pole was in the German army prior to the war. This seems a bit odd unless, in this situation, he actually complains about the conflict of loyalties.

Perhaps the problem is resolved by invoking on the word "compelled." If the Polish soldier serves voluntarily, he is not compelled. But suppose he is drafted as is typical in military service. The Americans drafted many Japanese, Italian, and German nationals in World War II to fight against their home countries. In fact, it would be a much greater offense to their honor to prevent them from serving in the military of their adopted country.

As with so many other provisions in the Statute, the process of interpretation would be facilitated by a statutory reference to a paradigmatic case. This is done is the Restatements of various fields of American law, published by the American Law Institute.[135] It may be that the code-oriented cultures of civil law countries think that they dispose of this common law practice. But that presupposes a body of commentary and case law yet to be achieved in the international legal order.

Part (xvi) on pillaging illustrates the general problem of making the transition from the collective crimes of the preceding international conventions to individual liability under the Rome Statute.[136] Pillaging is a collective activity. Individuals may steal and destroy property, but there is some additional element in pillaging that suggests a collective animus. This is typified in Russian pillaging of Jewish villages during the late nineteenth-century pogroms.[137] Implicit is some form of state action in directing the pillaging.

The provision is qualified by the phrase, "even when taken by assault."[138] The implication of "assault" is a military attack, not a pogrom. But why would

[134] Rome Statute, *supra* note 5, art. 8(2)(b)(xv).
[135] *See, e.g.*, MODEL PENAL CODE (1962).
[136] Rome Statute, *supra* note 5, art. 8(2)(b)(xvi).
[137] David Segal, *Ancestral Enemies Meet at Olympics for a Toast to Amity*, N.Y. TIMES (Feb. 15, 2014), https://www.nytimes.com/2014/02/16/sports/olympics/ancestral-enemies-meet-at-olympics-for-a-toast-to-amity.html.
[138] *See* Rome Statute, *supra* note 5, art. 8(2)(b)(xvi).

this be qualified by the term "even when"?[139] This suggests that some random destruction—some degree of "pillaging"—is to be expected in a military assault. The problem then is twofold: the required (1) mens rea and (2) degree of destruction. It seems obvious that the random destruction would have to far exceed the normal expectations of destruction in warfare.

Part (xvii) takes me back to my experience as an expert witness in the case of the third-generation Vietnam survivors who suffered from the Agent Orange used by the United States in Vietnam.[140] This was a tort case, not a criminal proceeding, but the issue of what constitutes poison seems to be the same. The contrary view might be that a tort case poses a question of intent to injure the particular victims, which in the Agent Orange litigation were the third generation of descendants. The war crime in part (xvii) might be directed against victims in general.

This might not be an adequate reply on the ground that poison is poison regardless of intention. But is that true? In small amounts, insecticide and herbicides are not harmful; in large amounts, however, they become poisonous. Yet, the concept of poison is too ambiguous. It is something that causes death. But salt water can do that and yet it is not harmful to fish and would not constitute poison. The concept as used here seems to refer to substances (1) in sufficient amounts (2) to kill human beings. Note that this provision applies to weapons while part (xviii) to other uses of poison.[141]

Is not clear what a "weapon" is. As we have learned from terrorism in the United States and Europe in recent years, cars can easily be used as weapons.[142] Guns are typically weapons, but not always. A gun might simply be a decorative device, or an unused defensive piece. I recall a case in California where the issue was whether brass knuckles constituted a weapon.[143] Even a shoelace could be an effective means of strangulation, as is seen in prison and organized crime.[144]

The remaining point of part (xviii) is the reference to "analogous liquids, materials, or devices." Given the posture of *nullum crimen sine lege* and the general principle against interpreting criminal statutes by "analogy," this

139 *Id.*
140 *See* 517 F.3d at 104.
141 *See* Rome Statute, *supra* note 5, art. 8(2)(b)(xviii).
142 *See* Perez-Pena, *supra* note 46.
143 *See, e.g.*, People v. Deane, 259 Cal. App. 2d 82, 86 (1968).
144 *See, e.g.*, *Teen Who Strangled 13-year-old Over iPhone Sentenced*, WKBW Buff. (Dec. 10, 2015), https://www.wkbw.com/news/police-blotter/teen-who-strangled-13-year-old-over-iphone-sentenced.

clause is not well considered. Multiplying the nouns adds to the ambiguity. Again, do "brass knuckles" and simple string fall someplace in the gaps? The problem is that all criminal statutes are finding the right balance between abstractions and fair warning based on a detailed description.

Part (xix) address bullets that are conventionally called "dum-dum bullets," though there is an attempt to describe them in considerable detail.[145] In provisions like this, we arguably seeing the influence of IHL, the principle that there is a good way and a bad way to injure and kill people. One might have doubts about this. If this principle were carried out consistently, there would be prohibitions on strangulation devices. Apparently, the basis of the war crime is killing in a way that is too painful. This is a curious notion of humanitarian law, which is presumably about protecting those who are hors de combat.

In part (xx), we encounter a similar "humanitarian" effort to minimize suffering but the provision depends on an annex to the Statute, so we will skip on this provision.

Part (xxi) raises many profound jurisprudential issues. The legal interest protected here is "personal dignity." This term has an important history in the comparison of American and postwar German law. The notion of dignity does not appear in American constitutional law but is fundamental in the German Grundgesetz, which begins: Die Menschenwuerde ist unantastbar: Humanity dignity is unassailable. American lawyers put their faith in the notion of equality,[146] while the postwar German attitude is invested primarily in human dignity.

The protection of dignity leads to some paternalistic consequences that some people find undesirable. The German constitutional court held that women could not perform striptease acts because treating their sexuality in this way violated their dignity.[147] In another case, the court held a dwarf could not consent to being fired from a canon in the circus.[148] Equality and the free market, however, would certainly support their rights to earn money at the expense of their dignity.

The Rome Statute is not meant to be analogous to a provision of constitutional law, American or German, and therefore it is not clear why the

[145] *See* Rome Statute, *supra* note 5, article 8(2)(b)(xix).

[146] U.S. Const. amend. XIV.

[147] Decision of Dec. 15, 1981, 64 Entscheidungen des Bundesverwaltungsgerichts (Decisions of the Federal Supreme Administrative Court) [BVerwG] 277.

[148] *See* Deryck Beyleveld & Roger Brownsword, *Human Dignity, Human Rights and Human Genetics*, 61 MOD. L. REV. 661, 662 (1998).

violation of human dignity should be a considered a war crime. The notion of "personal" as opposed to human dignity might give us a different perspective on the provision. The term "personal" suggests a distinctive view of human dignity in particular cultures. Some cultures are more sensitive than others, say, to nudity or to barking dogs. Some allege that, after the drafting of the Rome Statute, the United States or some of its soldiers employed many of these techniques in the Abu Ghraib Prison in Iraq.[149] These well-documented incidents could provide a basis for allegations against the individuals in the U.S. military for committing this particular war crime.

The other requirements of part (xxi) seem readily satisfied by the Abu Ghraib incident. The treatment was "humiliating and degrading" to the Muslim prisoners.[150] The Triffterer Commentary (2008) mentions Abu Ghraib and quotes a *New Yorker* article in 2004 stressing the impact of forcing homosexual acts between the prisoners.[151] The interesting question for interpretation of this provision is how events after the enactment of the statute should bear on its interpretation. These events can serve as examples but should not inform the understanding in 1998. Yet, there are some provisions revised in subsequent conferences; the most important in my mind is the Kampala Conference of 2010, which defined the way "aggression" could be committed by individuals.[152]

Two important things to remember about Abu Ghraib is that officials in the military under the Bush administration committed these crimes and the victims were Muslims.[153] This is not the typical concern of the Rome Statute, as indicated in the Preamble, about the impunidad of victims, notably in Argentina. But the statute is constantly evolving and must be adapted to new circumstances. The defendants might well be American officials and the victims, Muslims.

Part (xxii) address a wide variety of sexual crimes, the central one being rape.[154] The central problem in these cases is consent, which is complicated by the power differentials between the occupying force and the local inhabitants. One might have thought of the Japanese use of Korean "comfort

[149] Ifeoma Ajunwa, *"Bad Barrels:" An Organizational-Based Analysis of the Human Rights Abuses at Abu Ghraib Prison*, 17 U. Pa. J.L. & Soc. Change 75, 75–77 (2014).

[150] *See* Rome Statute, *supra* note 5, art. 8(2)(b)(xxi).

[151] Commentary on the Rome Statute of the International Criminal Court (Otto Triffterer ed., 2d. 2018).

[152] Resolution, *supra* note 21.

[153] Seymour Hersh, *Torture at Abu Ghraib*, New Yorker (May 10, 2004), https://www.newyorker.com/magazine/2004/05/10/torture-at-abu-ghraib.

[154] Rome Statute, *supra* note 5, art. 8(2)(b)(xxii).

women" as a paradigm case. The problem is complicated by the reference to Article 7(2)(f), which shifts the focus from the sexual violence to enforced pregnancy for the purposes of "affecting the ethnic composition of a population."[155] Thus, two different moral wrongs are conflated: (1) sexual violence to women and (2) the attempt to change the ethnic composition. The latter could be accomplished by artificial insemination, which does not entail sexual violence. And the sexual violence might be based on same-sex rape, which obviously has nothing to do with unwanted pregnancies. There are two entirely different crimes, and it is unfortunate that they were interwoven in the drafting.

Part (xxiii) raises a complicated issue that seems in conflict with other crimes.[156] It is clearly unlawful to target civilians as well as other persons hors de combat. But apparently one military organization could "utilize" a civilian to prevent to prevent military attacks in the area. This could be understood as targeting by omission. The problem with all crimes of omission is determining when it occurs. This is necessary for purposes of establishing the relevant mens rea. The general principle *actus non facit reus nisi mens sit rea* means that the action must coincide with the prohibited intent. The phenomenon of failing to remove civilians or relocating them there and then failing to remove them extends over a long period of time, months, perhaps years. It is not clear when the threshold of "utilizing" would be past.

Either the crime should be defined as unlawfully targeting civilians or unlawfully permitting targeting. Perhaps the conflict is resolved by interpreting this provision to refer to one's own civilians (or perhaps the civilians of a third party), not the civilians of the opposing party. If the reference is to one's own civilians, we encounter the problem often called "voluntary human shields," whom Yoram Dinstein thinks should be labeled "unlawful combatants."[157] This has happened often in the Palestinian/Israeli conflict, that is, the problems of farmers by day, terrorists by night. But it is not clear that there is anything involuntary in this terrorist activity and whether anyone is "utilizing" their voluntary behavior. A proper emphasis on the notion of utilizing—suggesting manipulating or exploiting—should lead to a restrictive interpretation of this provision.

Two interpretative issues arise in part (xxiv). First, as to the mens rea, we encounter this word "intentionally" again.[158,159] But have never offered

[155] *Id.*, art. 7.
[156] *Id.*, art. 8(2)(b)(xxiii).
[157] Yoram Dinstein, *Unlawful Combatancy*, 32 Isr. Y.B. Hum. Rts. 247, 248 (2002)
[158] *Id.*, art. 8(2)(b)(xxiv).
[159] *Supra* notes 80–83.

a definition. In fact, there are too many aspects of intentional behavior to recommend an internationally acceptable definition. The German approach, which includes a element of desire (Wissen und Wollen), differs from the American reliance on a more strictly psychological theory of anticipation. Also, it is not clear why the term comes up in this part but not in others. Another recurrent problem is whether the adverb "intentionally" differs from the phrase "with intent" as defined in Article 30, thus coming under the proviso "unless otherwise provided."[160]

The more significant issue in part (xxiv) might be the phrase "directing attacks."[161] This begins much like part (ix) except the objects of the attacks are slightly different. The emphasis here seems to be on medical facilities signified by a religious symbol, a red cross, crescent, or Magen David. There is a slight controversy about the false uses of these symbols and how this relates to the required intention. The war crime presupposes that these are actually protected medical facilities. If they are falsely displayed, there is no actual harm and therefore we encounter serious problems about attempted liability under Article 25(3).

The theoretical problems of "impossible attempts" are more than the drafters might have bargained for. Take, for example, an attack on medical facilities bearing the Israeli symbol of the Magen David. This is not literally mentioned as on option under part (xxiv). It hardly makes sense to exclude this option, but suppose the attacking force relies upon the language of the Statute and invokes the principle *nulla poena sine lege*. That means the completed offense is legally impossible. But how about applying attempt liability? The distinction between legal and factual impossibility in the law of attempt has been a theoretical minefield.[162]

Part (xxiv) poses an intriguing conflict with the Lieber Code Article 17 (1863), which applied the Kantian principle that measures leading to the end of armed conflict are justified. Blockades leading to starvation would end the conflict quickly. In this provision, we encounter the shift in the law of war to the notion of international humanitarian conflict. Ending the conflict rapidly and returning to peaceful relations is no longer a justification for blocking a port and inducing deprivation of the inhabitants.

[160] *See* Rome Statute, *supra* note 5, art. 30(1).
[161] *Id.*, art. 8(2)(b)(xxiv).
[162] *See* GEORGE P. FLETCHER, RETHINKING CRIMINAL LAWS 139–170 (2000).

There are at least four different perspectives that generate problems in interpreting part (xxiv): 1) collective action as adapted to individual liability; 2) the humanitarian purpose of protecting civilians; and 3) the underlying purpose of the Rome Statute, which is to avoid impunidad and punish war crimes.[163] A fourth issue is the constantly changing perspective of history. These conflicting purposes might serve advocacy in the ICC. Each side picks a perspective and defends it.

As for part (xxiv), a blockade could be justified if the purpose is to achieve a military end and not to target the civilians as such. Thus, we encounter another application of the principle of double effect[164]—one of the basic theoretical considerations in interpreting the Rome Statute. The problem in the case of blockades is that they may have many purposes, as with virtually everything that happens in the fog of war. The principle of double effect requires a distinction between the dominant purpose and the side effect. In the final analysis this is a problem of evidence rather than principle.

Part (xxv) poses the problem once more of starvation and conflict with the Lieber Code as well as the recurrent issue of why "intentionally" is used here but not in other provisions.[165] What may be different here is the shift between the introductory adverb "intentionally" and the later use of "wilfully." It is obvious that there is no standard way of speaking about the mental element. Of course, Article 30 includes the clause "unless otherwise provided" but does not anticipate two different forms of mens rea in the same provision.[166] It is not easy to explain who wins and who loses from this confusion.

Part (xxv) raises a question about what is indispensable for survival. The concept is relative. In warfare, people can survive in severe cold, heat, snow, mud, floods, and landslides. Yet, the phrase "relief supplies" suggests a limited range of deprivation.[167] Fresh water is a critical element for survival, but its deprivation would not be thought of as "starvation." Medicines are in a similar category. An obvious issue is this: survival for how long? It all depends on what it is that is being deprived.

It is important to recall, however, that under the principles of jus in bello, it does not matter whether we are talking about "relief supplies" for aggressors

[163] *See* Rome Statute, *supra* note 5, pmbl.
[164] *Supra* ¶ 96.
[165] Rome Statute, *supra* note 5, art. 8(2)(b)(xxv).
[166] *Id.*, art. 30(1).
[167] *Id.*, art. 8(2)(b)(xxv).

or defenders, for Germans or Russians. Under the conditions of chemical warfare, the relief supplies might include gas masks.

With the reference to the Geneva Conventions, this provision reminds us of the "collective" origins of these supposedly individual war crimes. No one, acting alone, can induce starvation or deprive civilians of the means of survival. This is a recurrent issue under the Statute and not one easily resolved. The origins of these crimes is an international treaties between states. In some respects, it would be better if the drafters were simply making up new crimes rather than trying to adapt collective action to individual liability.

The last of these 26 offenses refers to the use of child soldiers, by conscription or enlistment. In many parts of the world, young people do not really know how old they are, and therefore it is not clear how those who conscript or enlist should be prosecuted in the case of a mistake. Assuming the commanders can know, what is the principle at stake? Is it a problem of cruelty to the youngsters themselves? If that is the issue, the minimum age should be higher than 15. A lot would depend on the minimum age in the particular society for other adult activities, such as giving valid consent to sexual relations, engaging in female circumcision or indeed male circumcision, a practice common for men in many Muslim societies.

As we have noted many times, this is one of the problematic issues in the criminal law. We should assume, however, consent is issue specific, that is, it should be higher for irreversible changes to the body than for temporary, though dangerous military service. Also, the age of consent is different for different things, for example, buying cigarettes or guns. Enlisting as a child soldier is not necessarily a life-endangering decision. It might indeed be an opportunity for village children to find a place other than a village plagued with terrorist attacks. As a result, there should be a distinction between conscription and enlistment. Only the former seems like a potential candidate for a war crime.

Now we can turn to the four crimes listed in Article 8(2)(c).[168] We have not paid attention previously to the distinction between international and non-international armed conflicts. The assumptions seem to be that there are only two kinds of armed conflicts, and the previously analyzed 26 offenses were

[168] *Id.*, article 8(2)(c) ("(I) Violence to life and person, in particular murder of all kinds, mutilation, cruel treatment and torture; (II) Committing outrages upon personal dignity, in particular humiliating and degrading treatment; (III) Taking of hostages; (IV) The passing of sentences and the carrying out of executions without previous judgement pronounced by a regularly constituted court, affording all judicial guarantees which are generally recognized as indispensable.").

about international armed conflict, even though the Statute says anything to that effect.

Assuming that Article 8(2)(c) addresses international armed conflict, what does this provision mean by "not of an international character?"[169] Several questions arise: (1) are there are only two possibilities, (A) international and (B) not international; (2) does (A) refers to conflict between states recognized under international law? The answer to this question depends, in turn, on whether we understand the notion of nation used in the Civil War and by Woodrow Wilson after World War I, namely an organic collective that seeks recognition as a state. The "nation" is a contested concept: we should interpret it in a way that situates the first set of 26 war crimes in an international armed conflict. This means that nations preexist states as Abraham Lincoln and the League of Nations claimed. This means that Jews and Gypsies are nations. If that is true, however, we have additional problems about whether the following are nations: Palestinians, Sunnies, Sheites, Navajo Indians, the Rohinga in Burma, Kurds. Recall that the word "nation" is also used in the Genocide Statutes. It is not clear whether the meaning should be the same here.

Are there are only two possibilities? The answer seems to be no because Article 8(2)(d) lists a threshold that excludes riots and sporadic acts of violence.[170] The implication seems to be that a non-international conflict must have a level organization and continuity not found in spontaneous uprising. The problem is obviously one of degree. A riot can lead to an uprising, then to a rebellion, to an insurrection, to a revolutionary war.

Why doesn't the statute simply refer to domestic rather than non-international disputes? One answer might be that it is not clear that domestic disputes should fall within the jurisdiction of the ICC, which is an "international" court. Yet impunidad is essentially a domestic problem, and nonetheless it is interpreted as international and thus a basis for the ICC's jurisdiction. The boundaries between international and domestic disputes have become blurred.

If not international is interpreted to mean not against states, we are presented with a convenient loop hole for crimes committed in the course of the current armed conflict between the United Stas and ISIS. "The Islamic State in Syria" and ISIL in Lebanon are organized military forces with a

[169] *Id.*
[170] *Id.*, art. 8(2)(d).

general ambition is to establish a Muslim Califate and impose Shariah law. There is no doubt that they have committed beheadings and other obvious war crimes.[171] Yet there in no clear way to classify ISIS and ISIL under the categories of Article 8(2).

The loophole is based on a conception of an Islamic organization that spans several conventional states in the Middle East and therefore is international in that sense. But at the same time is not inter-state or inter-nation, and therefore is not international. Yet part 8(2)(d) confuses the situation by holding that the Statute does not apply to "internal disturbances."[172] The problem is internal to what? The point of reference might be a recognized, a nation seeking to be a state or indeed a non-recognized entity like ISIS seeking to be a state. This is an area where one gets the feeling that definition by paradigms and examples would be more effective than a definition with freighted words and contested concepts.

The four specific crimes mentioned in part 8(2)(c) are intriguing in comparison to the eight war crimes in part 8(2)(a). The first two are easily subject being committed individually. The latter two are clearly collective crimes. The problem is why they should be states as four crimes in this provision, which correspond to eight crimes in part 8(2)(a). The first two rather obvious crimes are of physical violence and degrading treatment. We have also discussed part (iii), the taking of hostages.[173]

The intriguing provision here is part (iv), which raises a fine point of comparative law. Under 8(2)(a)(vi), we considered what it meant to be deprived of a fair and regular trial. Here the emphasis is on (1) sentence and execution by a (2) regularly constituted court, (3) without the guarantees generally recognized as indispensable. The obvious case is a beheading by ISIS, but a good defense lawyer has much to work with here. First, a beheading might be an execution, captured sometimes on film, but there is no preceding sentence. The latter notion is connected to some kind of court or tribunal. Thus the question becomes what kind are the judicial guarantees necessary "generally recognized as indispensable."

The second and third issues became disputed issues in the pathbreaking case of *Hamdan v. Rumsfeld* on the legitimacy of military tribunals.[174] My

[171] Sara Malm, *ISIS Release Horrific New Video of Three "Spies" Being Beheaded by Executioners on Horseback*, Daily Mail Co. (Mar. 14, 2016), https://www.dailymail.co.uk/news/article-3491571/ISIS-release-horrific-new-beheading-video-three-spies-killed-executioners-horseback.html.

[172] *See* Rome Statute, *supra* note 5, art. 8(2)(d).

[173] *Id.*, art. 8(2)(c).

[174] Hamdan v. Rumsfeld, 548 U.S. 557 (2006).

brief in the case gained four votes on the substantive vote of whether conspiracy constituted a war crime.[175] The holding of Stevens's plurality was that it does not, but the procedural issues in the commissions gained more attention. Justice Kennedy constituted the fifth vote on the procedural issue of cross-examination in the military commissions. It is not clear whether this would be a judicial guarantee "generally recognized as indispensable."

Three justices dissented on different issues. Justice Thomas addressed the issue of whether the military were regularly constituted, and they met the required judicial guarantees. So far as we know what "regularly constituted" means, the tribunals meet this standard. They are appointed by the president, though there might an argument that the president exceeded his authority.

The more interesting question pertains to the "judicial guarantees." At the time of Hamdan, the relevant issue under Common Article Three of the Geneva Conventions was whether the procedures of the commissions, notably the use of hearsay evidence, met the standard of "civilized peoples."[176] The language of the West has become sensitive to offending the Third World; in fact we do not even talk about "underdeveloped" countries or the Third World anymore in fear of offending their sensibilities or even the sensibilities of some vocal Americans.[177] Understandably, the politically correct language of the Rome Statute is "generally recognized as indispensable."[178] This is ambiguous because it is hard to know whose perspective counts.

Part of the ambiguity derives from a failure to acknowledge whether the ICC should follow the model of a common law or a civil law court. The problem is whether the attempt at a synthesis is an attempt to find the best of both systems or the lowest common denominator. I fear that the current language of the Statute appears to be the latter. Yet the word "all" modifies the required guarantees and thus suggests minimums that these courts must satisfy. The provision would be easier to interpret if it were formulated in the negative—the kind of court that would be unacceptable. After, we are discussing the terms of a war crime, and therefore the burden of arguments

[175] *Id.*

[176] *See id.* at 637.

[177] *See* Marc Silver, *If You Shouldn't Call It the Third World, What Should You Call It?*, Goats and Soda, NPR (Jan. 4, 2015), https://www.npr.org/sections/goatsandsoda/2015/01/04/372684438/if-you-shouldnt-call-it-the-third-world-what-should-you-call-it.

[178] *See* Rome Statute, *supra* note 5, art. 8(2)(c)(iv).

should not be on the defendant. But we have seen this reversal in the burden of argument several times, notably in the discussion of superior orders.[179]

Article 8(2)(e) defines war crimes committed in non-international contexts. Most of these terms have already been discussed, so I will merely point out prior references in this chapter and conclude here.

[179] *See supra* notes 62–66.

10
Accidents vs. Mistakes

There's many a slip between the cup and the lip. You can spill the milk, or you can take the wrong cup and drink the soap. One is an accident and the other a mistake.

The distinction is fairly obvious. The question concerns how it plays it out in tort and criminal law. I will improvise on J.L. Austin's classic article, "A Plea for Excuses."[1] Austin proposed a situation in which a father scalded his child. In one case, the father reaches for the cold water but slips and turns on the hot water. In the other case, the symbols are on an Italian-made tub, with the indicators C (*calde*) and F (*freddo*). He thinks the C refers to *cold*, and therefore turns it on, scalding his son. These are two ways that an actor can generate a result he does not want and for which, in the typical case, he bears no culpability—at least not for intentionally scalding the child.

We could imagine cases, however, in which the father might be liable for negligence either in the case of accidents or mistakes, and therefore we should examine how this distinction plays itself in the issues of concern to the international legal order, including both torts and under the Rome Statute.

1. Accidents

Much of the law of torts centers on negligent accidents—whether with cars, airplanes, guns, or simply walking on a slippery floor. The important feature of torts, as opposed to crime, is that there is no liability absent harm to the plaintiff.[2] For example, there is no liability for merely attempting or risking harm.

The technological age has brought on a whole new field of accidental harms. Suppose you are angrily typing the draft of a social media post

[1] J.L. Austin, *A Plea for Excuses*, Presidential Address Before the Aristotelian Society (Oct. 29, 1956), *in* 57 PROC.ARISTOTELIAN SOC'Y 1 (1957).

[2] See *Negligence*, WEX LEGAL INFORMATION INSTITUTE, https://www.law.cornell.edu/wex/negligence (last visited Dec. 6, 2018).

filled with falsehoods about a specific person, but you have no intention of sending it. Yet, you accidentally hit the send key, and it goes out to a thousand "friends" on social media. If there are falsehoods in the email, you could be liable for defamation. Note that hitting the wrong key on a computer is analogous to the father's picking the wrong faucet in the Austin hypothetical.

Something special is conveyed by the notion of "having" an accident. You could have an accident driving a car or even an electric scooter. If you are a passenger in the car, you don't have the accident, nor if you are a pedestrian hit by car. The implication of having the accident is that you are in control of the causal process. But this not a full account of English usage. You can also have an accident when you slip and fall.

There should be a coherent explanation for why one can have some accidents but not others. One account would be that one can "have an accident" only when operating a heavy piece of machinery. But that would not explain the slip-and-fall cases, once an important area of dispute about the required level of care in tort law.[3]

Accidents typically interrupt the expected causal chain. Think of Oswald's assassination of JFK on November 22, 1963. One of the shots fired in Dallas hit Governor Connally who was riding in the car with JFK.[4] He had no intention of killing Connally. This is best described as an accident. Yet the causal chain between Oswald's shooting and hitting Connally is not interrupted. Also, under the Catholic principle of double effect, one might say that Oswald had an oblique or indirect intention to kill Connally. The intriguing question is how it could be accidental and indirectly intentional at the same time.

One important question is whether these problems are language specific, or whether we have the same paradox when we think about this issue in German and French. The relevant distinction in German is between *Zufall* and *Unfall*. Both terms refer to accidents, but with different value judgments implied. *Zufall* is more typically used as adverb, as in *Wir haben uns zufallig in Berlin getroffen.*[5] The sense here is neutral. *Unfall* caries a negative connotation, for example, *Ich habe einen Unfall auf der Autobahn gehabt.*[6] In other words, a *Zufall* might be a good accident, while an *Unfall* is definitely a bad accident. (I should add that the German language relies heavily on words

[3] *See, e.g., Liability for Injury to Customer from Object Projecting into Aisle or Passageway in Store*, 40 A.L.R. 5th 135 § 16.

[4] *See* President's Commission on the Assassination of President Kennedy, Report of the President's Commission on the Assassination of President John F. Kennedy 111 (1964).

[5] We met accidentally in Berlin.

[6] I had an accident on the highway.

ending in "fall," often translated as "fall" in English. The decline and fall of the German Democratic Republic is the *Verfall* der DDR; the Christian fall based on the original sin in the Garden of Eden is called, in German, *Der Fall.*)

Another use of the word *Zufall* will illuminate our discussion of risk and negligence. I once asked a German girl to meet me for dinner. The way she said no, politely, was: *Das überlassen wir zum Zufall.* Translation: let's leave it to chance. If we happened to run into each other, we could have dinner together. Thus, another noun in the cluster related to accidents is "chance." We are familiar with this notion in "games of chance." Gambling comes closer to the accurate assessment of probability than weather or military predictions.

The complications of English appear in different grammatical forms. We have at least three distinctions: (1) doing something by accident, (2) harming someone accidentally, and (3) having an accident. The first correlated with *zufaellig* derived from *Zufall.* The second is an *Unfall.* And the third is typified by the *Unfall* on the Autobahn. Meeting someone by accident might be good. Harming someone by accident is always bad. And having an accident is typically bad, but it could wake up a driver who is asleep at the wheel, thus mitigating the risk of a more serious collision.

In domestic criminal law, accidents become relevant only in what I have called the pattern of harmful consequences, that is, where there is a causal chain between the action and the harm.[7] If the harm is incorporated in the description of the prohibited act, as in larceny, then there is no causal chain to be broken. A good example of relevance to international criminal law as well is rape. Rape requires penetration by a human being. This does not happen by accident (assuming that context or intoxicants play no sufficient role).

The causal chain we have in mind is not so easily explained. It requires an entire theory of human action to account for the way in which intentions and desires result in harm to human beings or property. In fact, there were entire schools of thought built in the German literature of the twentieth century on the theory of human action. There are many distinguished theorists of American criminal law, including Michael S. Moore, who have held that human action is defined as the will causing bodily motion. This corresponds to the German theory of *kausale Handlungslehre.* The contrary theory is called the *finale Handlungslehre.* The problem I have will all these theories is that they are circular. The will is "the ghost in the machine." How do we know that the ghost exists? Well, we observe human actions, and therefore we infer

[7] *See* GEORGE P. FLETCHER, RETHINKING CRIMINAL LAW § 5.3 (1978).

a will making these actions happen. So, what is the chicken and what is the egg? The will or recognized human action?

Back to accidents with guns. These can occur in different ways. The gun can fire accidentally. And then, the bullets can ricochet off a wall, and in addition, the shooter could hit a bystander. Note that not all of these accidents interrupt the causal chain. Some merely negate the intention. The question for tort law is where the risk begins. Is it in making the gun, selling the gun, or is it in hitting a bystander? After the Parkland shooting in February 2018, this has become a critical question—not only in the analysis of crime, but in U.S. constitutional law.

The Second Amendment was ratified in 1791 in order to protect the autonomy of the states from the federal government. It guarantees "the right of the people to keep and bear arms."[8] Many believe that the context of collective action is expressed by granting this right to the "militias" of the states, and that the notion of "bearing" implies a military style of coordination.[9] The notion of an individual's having a right to keep a firearm at home was not formally recognized until the *Heller* decision of the Supreme Court in 2008[10] and as applied to the states in *McDonald* in 2010.[11] The implications of *McDonald* as to particular aspects of "the right to bear arms" are still debated and litigated. Not long ago, retired Justice Stevens wrote an op-ed in which he argued that we should repeal the Second Amendment.[12] That is a matter of throwing the baby out with the bath water. There are many things we can do by way of interpreting the Second Amendment that are far more feasible than the nearly impossible task of amending the Constitution

In 1791, no one imagined the development of machine guns.[13] The six-shot pistol was not patented until 1836.[14] There is a whole school of conservative "originalist" interpretation—popularized by Justice Scalia,[15] who was in the majorities in both *Heller* and *McDonald*—that many believe should have looked more carefully at the language of the Second Amendment as it was

[8] U.S. CONST. amend II.

[9] *See, e.g.*, Akhil Reed Amar, *Leary Lecture: The Second Amendment: A Case Study in Constitutional Interpretation*, 2001 UTAH L. REV. 889, 891 (2001).

[10] *See* District of Columbia v. Heller, 554 U.S. 570 (2008).

[11] McDonald v. City of Chicago, 561 U.S. 742 (2010).

[12] John Paul Stevens, Opinion, *John Paul Stevens: Repeal the Second Amendment*, N.Y. Times (Mar. 27, 2018), https://www.nytimes.com/2018/03/27/opinion/john-paul-stevens-repeal-second-amendment.html.

[13] *See* United States v. Zaleski, 489 F. App'x 474, 475 (2d Cir. 2012).

[14] *See* J. BILBY, A REVOLUTION IN ARMS: A HISTORY OF THE FIRST REPEATING RIFLES 23 (2006).

[15] *See* Mary Wood, *Scalia Defends Originalism as Best Methodology for Judging Law*, U. VA. LAW (Apr. 20, 2010), https://www.law.virginia.edu/news/2010_spr/scalia.htm.

understood when it was written. These critics believe that both the interpretation and the application to handguns are inconsistent with the "original" understanding of the Second Amendment.[16]

The problem of guns in the United States is complicated by several factors—totally separate from the constitutional issues. One is the romance of the Wild West—well, at least, for the cowboys. The frequent wars against the American Indians was, to some, a great genocide in American history. The second is the recurrent violence, including the lynching of black Americans. The conflicts between the police and black Americans have the subject of intense interest in criminal law and the organization of new lobbying groups such as Black Lives Matter.[17]

The U.S. gun problem has international dimensions as well. The Mexican government arguably supported the Trump administration's extravagant idea of a wall on the southern border in order to keep U.S. guns out of their country.[18] The American gun problem is well known by all the world and either feared or exploited by foreign governments.

We are witnessing in our own time a new kind of impunity in which the victims of gun violence are unable to vindicate their rights under U.S. law. The National Rifle Association, a pro-gun lobbying organization, has enormous influence in Congress. They advertise constantly and lobby for politicians to support their agenda.[19]

The single best hope for mitigating gun deaths and injuries is tort liability. Even though the gun industry was able to secure Republican support under George W. Bush, the Protection of Lawful Commerce in Arms Act (2005) provided immunity for guns sellers, and there was an important exception called "negligent entrustment."[20] This brings us to the analysis of negligence,

[16] *See, e.g.*, Richard A. Posner, *In Defense of Looseness: The Supreme Court and Gun Control*, New Republic, Aug. 27, 2008, at 32, 33 ("The Framers and the ratifiers of the amendment probably did think that the right of militiamen to keep and bear arms entitled them to keep their weapons in their homes. . . . To use this "original' understanding to allow members of the National Guard to store military weapons (machine guns, grenades, Hummers, and so on) would be preposterous, and it is disclaimed in the majority opinion.").

[17] *See, e.g.*, Mario L. Barnes, *Criminal Justice for Those (Still) at the Margins—Addressing Hidden Forms of Bias and the Politics of Which Lives Matter*, 5 U.C. Irvine L. Rev. 711 (2015).

[18] *See* Sarah Kinosian & Eugenio Weigend, *We're Sending Guns, Crime to Mexico*, L.A. Times (Mar. 2, 2017), https://www.latimes.com/opinion/op-ed/la-oe-kinosian-weigend-guns-mexico-20170302-story.html.

[19] *See* Robert Maguire, *Audit Shows NRA Spending Surged $100 Million Amidst Pro-Trump Push in 2016*, Cntr. for Responsive Politics (Nov. 15, 2017), https://www.opensecrets.org/news/2017/11/audit-shows-nra-spending-surged-100-million-amidst-pro-trump-push-in-2016/.

[20] *See* 15 U.S.C. § 7903 (2018).

the basic form of liability in tort law and a possible, but less favored, basis of liability in criminal law.

The conventional formula for negligence is called the Learned Hand formula, essentially that conduct is negligent if the probability of damage is higher than the probably of benefit. Note that this test says nothing about the actual mental state of the actor. This leads to the classic problem called the "fault of not knowing."[21] Some scholars, notably Jerome Hall, have argued that negligence is not properly called a form of mens rea (guilty mind) because there is no conscious mind at play. In fact, all systems of criminal law recognize liability for culpa (fault) as well as dolus (intent). This does not settle the problem raised by Hall, but we should keep in mind that there is no way at trial to probe these mental states without evidence of the way the accused is, in fact, acting. In light of contributory negligence in tort law, we have to add consideration of the way the victim, too, was acting.

The interesting thing about negligence is that only human beings can act negligently. Animals can have accidents, but they cannot have mental states. They know, however, when they are victims of accidents. Oliver Wendell Homes wrote famously that "[e]ven a dog knows the difference between being kicked and being stumbled over."[22] But suppose one trains a dog to fetch a stick at the beach. Running to grab the stick, the dog stumbles and injures itself. Why do we assume that the dog could not have been negligent? The answer to the problem is that the dog could not have calculated the cost and benefits. But that presupposes that human beings actually can make this calculation, however unintelligent and uninformed they might be.

We will explore two further questions about cost/benefit analysis. First, what is the relevant time (1) of the action or (2) the moment the court decides. A good case can be made for both, for the judicial moment if there is some significant technological improvement between the action and the hearing. Suppose automatic windshield wipers are invented and become available at the time of decision. Though the driver did not have them, the goal of creating an efficient society would be better served by declaring that anyone who did not use them in the future would be considered negligent. The case for finding the driver without the innovation to be not negligent is that the purpose of the negligence or fault standard is not efficiency but

[21] For an earlier discussion, see George P. Fletcher, *The Fault of Not Knowing*, 3 THEORETICAL INQ. L. 265 (2002).

[22] O.W. HOLMES, JR., THE COMMON LAW 7 (M. Howe ed. 1963).

fairness. If someone is acting efficiently under the Learned Hand test, it is not fair to expect otherwise.

There are good arguments against both interpretations (1) and (2). Against focusing on the moment the court decides, the argument would be that everyone in the future would have to understand the facts of the case as the court did and act accordingly. This is far-fetched for several reasons, namely, that there would be inevitable distortions overtime. Some people might think that the time and place were relevant or that the brand of car was a significant variable. There is no reason to think that the court's decision would indeed have an efficient impact. In the area of deterrence in criminal law, we know this to be true. H.L.A. Hart described the factual assumption that those in the future would know the facts of the case in which punishment was imposed in the past as a "spectacular non-sequitur."[23] There is never been much evidence that punishment has much impact on future criminal behavior, except perhaps for the crimogenic effect of prison itself.

Let us suppose, then, that the relevant issue is awarding the actor for acting properly at the moment of action. The problem here is that negligence is not the only relevant standard of proper care in tort cases. As in the famous case of *Vincent v. Lake Erie Transp. Co.*, where the shipowner kept his ship tied to a dock non-negligently during a storm, the shipowner was held liable for the damage.[24] Even under economic theory, there are many reasons for holding non-negligent harm-doers liable (risk spreading, passing the costs on consumers, Calabresi's theory of the cheapest cost avoider).[25]

Even if the Learned Hand test were otherwise workable, we would have no way—that is, the judge or jury would have no way to accurately assess the probable costs and benefits. It is wrong, as a matter of physics, to speak quantitatively about risks outside of controlled situations like playing roulette or comparative aggregate statistics, for example, the likelihood of a gun death in the United States as opposed to Japan. This is possible in the courtroom because juries understand the concept of the community standard of the "reasonable person under the circumstances."

The reasonable person test always depends on the concrete situation. The test is what a reasonable person under the circumstances would do. The

[23] H.L.A. Hart, Punishment and Responsibility: Essays in the Philosophy of Law 19 (1968).

[24] 109 Minn. 456 (1910).

[25] *See, e.g.*, Guido Calabresi, *Concerning Cause and the Law of Torts: An Essay for Harry Kalven, Jr.*, 43 U. CHI. L. REV. 69 (1975).

"circumstances" vary from being awakened in the dark to being mugged on the subway. Also, the psychological "circumstances" of the actor arguably enter into the equation, for example, intelligence, strength, age, and reflexes. This was a major issue in the *Goetz* case.[26] The question was whether the following variables would be relevant to the reasonableness of the "subway vigilante:" time and location (14th Street on the Number 2 Subway during the Christmas season), racial identity of the parties (black American victims, Caucasian police shooters), and prior experience of the suspect with members of the minority race (at least two prior incidents). There are indeed more factors than this, but the more specific the "reasonable person," the less it functions as a community standard.

French and German law function quite well without reference to the word "reasonable." The French define the standard of due care (no negligence) as that of a *bon pere de famille* (Good father of the family).[27] The German Civil Code simply refers to *die im Verkehr erforderliche Sorgfalt* (Degree of care necessary in the context).[28] The term "reasonable" is, in fact, a characteristic feature of English legal discourse.

With these comparative reflections, we bring our analysis of accidents and their implications to an end. We turn now to the field of mistakes, which is more relevant than accidents in criminal law.

2. Mistakes

In general terms, mistakes negate not the causal chain but the mental state (mens rea) required for the offenses.

In defining the required mental state of intention, Article 30 of the Rome Statute distinguishes between conduct and consequences.[29] We will turn to this useful distinction later in considering relevant mistakes. Preliminarily, there are many other possible mistakes to consider that are totally irrelevant but which criminal actors might think are relevant. Take, for example, the location of the crime, which bears upon the territorial jurisdiction in domestic criminal law.

[26] *See* People v. Goetz, 497 N.E.2d 41 (N.Y. 1986).
[27] *See* Code Civil [C. CIV.] art. 1137 (Fr.).
[28] Burgerliches Gk [BGB] § 276 (Ger.).
[29] *See* Rome Statute for the International Criminal Court, July 17, 1998, 2187 U.N.T.S. 3; U.N. Diplomatic Conference of Plenipotentiaries on the Establishment of an International Court, U.N. Doc. A/Conf.183/9 [hereinafter Rome Statute]; *id.*, art. 30.

The actor thinks he is in California where smoking marijuana is legal but, in fact, he is in Arizona where it is not. This mistake is irrelevant. If the smoker is in a state where smoking weed is illegal, it does not matter what he believes. There are innumerable irrelevant mistakes of this sort—all those bear on location, time, procedure, diplomatic immunity, statute of limitations.

According to Article 31(1) of the Rome Statute, a mistake of fact is relevant only if it negates the mental element required for the crime.[30] As we have seen, however, the "unless otherwise provided" clause of Article 30 on the mental element leads us to many alternative forms of mental state, including explicit references to "willfully" and "intentionally"—not to mention the possibility of negligence under Article 28.[31] Each of these terms creates room for mistakes negating the mental state. Also, we see mention of mistake as it relates to the defenses recognized in Article 31 and the possibility of additional defenses recognized at the time of trial (Art. 31(3)).[32] Mistake, in all of these contexts, is relevant.

The recurrent desire of those drafting codes is to eliminate mistake as a relevant issue. The way to do this is to define the required culpability and then posit, as does the Article 32(1) of the Rome Statute, or simply assume, that mistakes are relevant only if they negate the required culpability—however lawyers and judges may interpret the relevant sources of law. The Model Penal Code (MPC) in the United States attempted to do the same thing, and therefore it is worth attending to its effort and the lessons it may hold for international legal order.

Much like the Rome Statute, the Model Penal Code sets out definitions of culpability, but four different levels, dividing dolus into "purposely" and "knowingly" and culpa into "recklessly" and "negligently."[33] The burden of persuasion to prove these "kinds of culpability" is on the prosecution, as many believe it should be. Indeed, one of the reasons to avoid treating mistakes as "defense" is the temptation to shift either the burden of persuasion or the burden of going forward to the defense. This has been a recurrent problem in the United States, particularly with regard to claims of justification and excuse.

One may be tempted to conclude, therefore, that mistakes are a false problem. They are simply the reverse side of culpability, as accidents are the

30 *See id.*, art. 31(1).
31 *See id.*, art. 27.
32 *Id.*, art. 31.
33 *See* Model Penal Code § 2.02 (Am. Law Inst., 1962).

reverse side of causation. Yet this perspective ignores a major philosophical issue that became acute in the famous *Goetz* case (beginning in 1984), which arose under the NY Penal Code, based on the MPC.[34] The question was whether believing, subjectively, that one was under attack was sufficient for a claim of self-defense. Goetz certainly believed he was under some attack as soon as one of the four youths who surrounded him on the subway asked him for five dollars.[35]

The ambiguity of when attacks begin highlights the problem of making a mistake about whether one is under attack. It is a bit like making a mistake about when the Civil War ended. Officially, the war ended at Appomattox Courthouse where Lee handed Grant his sword. Yet there were various skirmishes after that. That is, if the object of the mistakes is a moving object, mistakes about its location are easily made.

Note that in the discussion above, the grammar of mistakes is almost always about "making" the mistake. That is, the mistake is the direct of a transitive verb. This is true in all the relevant languages of the international legal order (French, German, and Russian). Now why should mistakes be treated as something real? Something manufactured? Perhaps the reason is that mistakes are often the basis of an apology. The way of taking responsibility for the mistake is to treat it as something done—out there, warranting an apology and forgiveness.

Of course, "mistaken" can be used as a transitive verb. The famous title that come to mind is Oliver Sacks's recount of his work as a neurologist: *The Man Who Mistook His Wife for a Hat*.[36] Interestingly, the transitive verb is almost always used in the past tense. It suggests a clinical disorder under medical investigation about an event in the past. Of course, if you confuse a $50 bill with a $20 one and then tell the recipient you made a mistake, you could use the transitive verb, but it would be more appropriate simply to say you made a mistake.

With these linguistic points out of the way, we should focus on how mistakes become relevant in assessing criminal responsibility. There are six types of relevant mistakes as indicated in the table below. We should recall that the distinction between conduct and consequences suggested by Article 30 (2).[37] If mistakes are merely negations of mens rea, the efforts to define mental element in the Rome Stature complicate the analysis of mistakes.

[34] *Goetz*, 68 N.Y.2d at 105.
[35] *Id.*
[36] Oliver Sacks, The Man Who Mistook His Wife for a Hat (1985).
[37] Rome Statute, *supra* note 29, art. 30(2).

There are already so many complexities—we leave the general problem in the Rome Statute of distinguishing between collective and individual action. Mistakes occur in cases of individual conduct. The notion of systematic mistakes is an oxymoron. A pattern of mistakes about people is often termed a prejudice. Thus, we focus on the following six types of mistakes.

MISTAKES	OF FACT	OF LAW
core elements	1	2
justification	3	4
excuse	5	6

Type 1 mistakes, those about the factual aspects of the definition of the offense, comes as close as possible to the paradigm imagined by Article 32(1), namely a mistake that negates the mental element required for the crime.[38] The assumption is that the crime is defined in the definition of the offense—excluding claims of justification and excuse.[39] A good example would be a mistake about whether an intended victim is dead or alive. The actor discharges his gun into the body of an apparent enemy that he assumes is dead. At the moment, the intended victim is still alive. The mistake negates the intention to kill.

It turns out the legal criterion of death is conflicted. Some people favor cessation of brain activity as the onset of death; the more traditional view focuses on the heart and breath. These are all disputed concepts, largely because of the factors of time and reversibility. Death on the battlefield would presumably be determined by a medic with a stethoscope.

It is hard to find a war crime that doesn't reflect these ambiguities. Consider the taking of hostages.[40] The mistake might be about the element of taking or the question of who is a hostage. Both of these issues are mixed questions of law and fact. To what extent does the "taking" occur? This requires an analysis of possession, which is a matter of degrees. The notion of a hostage implies a demand for ransom. Taking prisoners of war would not qualify—though POWs could be used as bargaining chips and therefore function like hostages.

[38] *Id.*, art. 32(1).
[39] *See, e.g., id.*, art. 31.
[40] *See id.*, art. 8(2)(a)(viii).

It would be instructive to find a type 2 mistake in the Rome Statute—one that was purely about the legality of the conduct. A good example might be Article 8(2)(a)(vi)—depriving a protected person of the "rights of fair and regular trial."[41] Mistakes about what these rights are would seem to qualify. This rule depends entirely on the perspective of the occupying power, whether it is a civil law or common law jurisdiction. Even the standard of "fairness" lends itself to mistakes. Of course, there comes a point where the standard becomes so vague that a mistake is no longer possible. If you cannot assuredly get it right, it is hard to say that you have gotten it wrong.

Analyzing types three and four mistakes about claims of justification are a challenge. First, we cannot be sure of which justifications are relevant. According to Rome Statute Article 31, claims of self-defense and duress are "grounds for excluding criminal responsibility"—the equivalent of justifications in German and U.S. law.[42] But, in addition, we have other claims that might be recognized at trial.[43] Furthermore, we have claims of consent, which would be relevant in rape cases and the classification of which is a source of dispute in the common law of rape. The classic case is *Regina v. Morgan*, which, we will see, raises several critical issues under the Rome Statute.[44]

First, note that rape is a war crime according to Art. 8(2)(b)(xxii), but the crime is not defined anywhere in the statute, thus raising a problem of *nullum crimen sine lege*.[45] The following questions arise in the definition of the offense: (1) can men as well as women be considered victims; (2) the definition of the degree and means of penetration; (3) and most seriously, the relevance and nature of consent and how it is conveyed. Let us assume that the first two questions are easily removed. Consent is more problematic. Does the definition of rape require non-consensual intercourse, or is consent the nature of a justification? Here we are torn between conflicting trends. On the one hand, the tendency is overcome by the morality of the past, and thus we treat consensual intercourse as below the threshold required for prima facie liability, that is, consensual intercourse should be no more incriminating than a handshake. On the other hand, the increasing sensitivity toward claims of

[41] *Id.*
[42] *See id.*, art.icle 31(1).
[43] *Id.*
[44] AC 182; 2 All Eng. 347 (1976).
[45] *See generally* Rome Statute, *supra* note 29, art. 8(2)(b)(xxii).

sexual misconduct should lead, some believe, to treating consent by analogy as the other grounds for excluding criminal responsibility.

Let us consider how the Morgan case bears on these issues. Morgan was an RAF officer who told three "mates" in a bar that his wife was kinky and enjoyed coerced intercourse.[46] The three came home with Morgan, and each forced intercourse while the others held her down. They claimed at trial that they honestly believed that she had consented. Of course, the word "consent" is a legal conclusion. The most we can find of them is that they had believed that she had not objected.

The House of Lords held that the officers were not guilty of rape.[47] The reasoning of the decision illustrates both the temptation and the dangers of reasoning by reference to ordinary usage. Would the man on the Clapham bus call this rape? I think it depends on the time we are asking the question? Perhaps in 1975—the days when marital rape was not a crime—the answer would be no. Today, I am inclined to think that the answer would be yes. The reason seems to be that as to the conflicting trends, the prevailing factor is the protection of women as a special category of victim.

The shift toward the protection of women has become evident in several high-profile incidents in the United States of the last two years. Allegations of sexual harassment—well below the threshold of criminal behavior—have been sufficient to end careers in entertainment and politics, for example, Harvey Weinstein, Charlie Rose, and Al Franken.[48] It is almost as though the present is seeking redemption for what they believe to be the sins of the 1970s. The politically correct tendency, therefore, is to speak of "unwanted" sex, thus introducing a victim-based theory of consent.

In reality, though, the nature of consent remains a puzzle. Is it something like a gift from the potential victim to the potential offenders, a gift that is communicated by saying "yes?" If it is a gift, can it be revoked? Can one be mistaken about the revocation? And still we don't know whether non-consent is part of the definition of rape or whether consent is a factor that functions as a justification. These issues are too important to be ignored if rape is to be treated as a war crime.

This is an area where the courts and the public repeatedly make mistakes about how to respond to our changing mores concerning sexuality. We may

[46] *Regina*, AC at 182.
[47] *Id.*
[48] *See* Daniel Hemel & Dorothy S. Lund, *Sexual Harassment and Corporate Law*, 118 COLUM. L. REV. 1583, 1585 (2018).

be in a period of overreaction, and therefore two points remain important in international criminal law: (1) we should not forget the presumption of innocence, and (2) we should not submit to the waves of political correctness that sweep across the public square.

With regard to classification of mistakes as factual (type 3) or legal (type 4), we can conclude that if mistake is a justification, then a mistake, say, about whether Morgan's wife consented, would be factual, and a mistake about third-party consent, the claims of the RAF officers, is a mistake about the legal nature of consent (type 4) and therefore irrelevant.[49] But this adds a new complication to our analysis of type 3 mistakes. Must they be reasonable? Must they be of the kind that a person on a Clapham bus would make?

The issue of subjective versus objective self-defense has been a source of great controversy in American legal history. It is easy to allege the fear of imminent attack, and in some cases, for example, the Menéndez brothers' killing of their parents in California the allegation seems implausible on its face.[50] In other cases, for example, the *Goetz* case in New York, the claim of self-defense appears more reasonable.[51] The difference between them is two-fold: (1) a context that betokens danger to ordinary people and (2) the actual harm that occurs. In the Menéndez brothers' case, there was no plausible evidence other than their claim that they feared their parents would kill them. In the Goetz case, the "subway vigilante" was surrounded and one of the youth's asked him for five dollars. As to the harm, the charge in the former case was murder; in the latter, it was seriously wounding. Of course, there are other factors, such as the compromise verdicts offered to the jury. In the end, the Menéndez were sentenced, in a second trial, to life imprisonment. Goetz served one year on the backup possession charge and was released. Both of these cases have attracted much publicity and armchair expert psychiatric assessments.

The question remains open about whether the standard for self-defense should be (A) subjective, that is, what the accused claims to have believed, or (B) objective, that is, what a reasonable person under the circumstances would believe. The former lends itself to wild self-interested claims. The latter raises endless questions about the "circumstances," which then invites an

[49] *See Regina*, AC at 182.

[50] *See* Alan Abrahamson, *Lyle Menendez Tells Court of Sexual Abuse by Mother: Trial: He says she would wash his body 'everywhere' and had him in bed with her until he was 13. He gives further testimony on violence by both parents.*, L.A. TIMES (Sept. 14, 1993), http://articles.latimes.com/1993-09-14/local/me-35149_1_lyle-menendez.

[51] *See Goetz*, 68 N.Y.2d at 105.

inquiry about the personal history of the accused(s), which is an increasingly unfashionable method of legal analysis. Neither is perfect, but the objective standard seems to be preferable simply as a constraint on self-interested testimony that might gain some support on a jury and lead, as in the first trial of the Menéndez brothers, to a hung jury.[52]

Type 5 mistakes pertain to the factual grounds for excusing conditions. Here we encounter a duplication of excuses. Let us say the alleged excusing condition is duress, and the duress is based on a bomb threat. A mistake about a bomb threat would be an excuse if it is plausible to think that the actor submitted "involuntarily" to the threat. Since the term "involuntarily" is normative, one could argue that a reasonable person would not have given in to the threat that was unlikely of realization, for example, a threat to kill the defendant's mother living halfway across the world. A mistake about where the mother was in fact living or where the country was would not distract from the central question of the "involuntariness" of the behavior. It is important to remember, however, that excuses do not negate the wrongfulness of the attack, as in the context of self-defense.

The language of Rome Statute Article 31(1)(d) creates problems of its own.[53] The structure suggests that it is about duress, but, in fact, it poses a mixed question of justification and excuse. Here are the problematic terms. (A) "[A]lleged to constitute a crime:"[54] If duress is purely an excuse, it does not negate the commission of a crime or unlawful conduct for purposes of self-defense, (B) "caused by duress:"[55] the threat does not "cause" the conduct in the same sense that conduct causes harm. An acceptable substitute in the language would be "induced" or "influenced." (C) "[I]mminent death of serious bodily harm:"[56] this implies that threats of massive destruction to property would not be included. (D) "[N]ecessarily and reasonably:"[57] the former term is proper but the notion of "reasonableness" in a situation of threats is subtle. For one, cost/benefit analysis differs from cases of self-defense. Many legal systems have had difficulty imposing a proportionality limitation on self-defense., for example, self-defense against minor assaults. In cases of duress, where the issue centers on the voluntariness of

[52] *See* Jennifer Latson, *Why It Took Three Juries to Convict the Menedez Brothers*, TIME (Apr. 17, 2015), http://time.com/3774669/menendez-brothers/.

[53] *See* Rome Statute, *supra* note 29, art. 31(1)(d).

[54] *Id.*

[55] *Id.*

[56] *Id.*

[57] *Id.*

the response, the balancing would presumably be different. A greater disproportion of harm would be acceptable in the context of duress. But it is not clear that the Statute recognizes this principle

The limitation on duress imposed by Article 31(1)(d) is that the person not intend to cause more harm avoided.[58] Note that the issue here is not what in fact happens or indeed what a reasonable personable would expect to happen. The question is not what a reasonable person would "intend." The required intent appears to be that of the actor. Here the mistake might become relevant. Since the particular actor might make a mistake, say, about where his mother is located, this mistake would be a factor in assessing the relative costs and benefits of submitting to the threat.

What is interesting about the addition d(ii) to the provision is that the threat might not conform at all to the classic pattern in cases of duress.[59] The threat might come, from "other circumstances beyond that person's control."[60] I suppose the example here is the possibility of a bomb set to go off if the threatened person does not submit. In the era of technological and cyber warfare, this kind of threat is becoming ever more plausible. The problem is that if we have a cyber attack, we might also have a computer-based defense. It would be very implausible to think about anything comparable to duress in a situation of programmer fighting programmers.

The last mistake to consider is a type 6 error about the legal aspects of an excuse. Here we encounter a plethora of issues in the context of superior orders.[61] There are many possible mistakes here about, say, the person who "was under a legal obligation to obey orders of the Government."[62] In the fog of war, one might not know who the government is. Think of the closing days of World War II. German soldiers in the field had no way of knowing who the government was. The same is obviously true in the case of genocide in Auschwitz because, in fact, Hitler was in charge until his disputed demise, but afterward, it was not clear who was alive and indeed whether government even existed.

This brings to a close our analysis of Accidents and Mistakes in the context of the International Legal Order.

58 *Id.*
59 *See id.* ("Constituted by other circumstances beyond that person's control.")
60 *Id.*
61 *Id.*, art. 33.
62 *Id.*

11

Perpetration and Complicity

Unity and Divergence

Having decided to include tort law within our assessment of the international legal order, we begin this chapter by noting the extraordinary divergence in the twenty-first-century development of these fields taking responsibility for causing harm. In tort law, both here and abroad, there is no issue of principle in holding groups jointly and severally liable for causing harm. By contrast, in international criminal law, as typified by the Rome Statute[1] Article 25, we witness a strong reaction against collective responsibility.[2] The evolution of this divergence provides an angle for understanding our current sensibilities.

In thinking about tort law, we should leave aside for the moment the controversy about the application of the Alien Tort Claims Act (ATCA). In *Kiobel*[3] and *Jesner*,[4] the courts have cut back the international application of the statute: first to transactions occurring totally abroad and second to suits against foreign corporations. But the ATCA is solely about federal jurisdiction.[5] If service of process is possible in a particular state, that is, the defendant is present and can be "tagged" with a notice to appear, the local state courts have jurisdiction and local tort law will apply.[6] Under the once fertile field of conflicts of law (called "private international law" in the international context) there might be disputes about which state law should apply, say, for example, if a driver from one state has a collision with a driver from another and the accident occurs in a third state.[7] There was initially considerable support for the lex loci delicti (the place where the tort was committed), but under the influence of Brainerd Currie and theory of governmental interests,

[1] *See* Rome Statute for the International Criminal Court, July 17, 1998, 2187 U.N.T.S. 3; U.N. Diplomatic Conference of Plenipotentiaries on the Establishment of an International Court, U.N. Doc. A/Conf.183/9 [hereinafter Rome Statute].

[2] *See* Rome Statute, *supra* note 1, art. 25.

[3] *See* Kiobel v. Royal Dutch Petro. Co., 569 U.S. 108 (2013).

[4] *See* Jesner v. Arab Bank, PLC, 138 S. Ct. 1386 (2018).

[5] *See* 28 U.S.C. § 1350 (2018).

[6] *See* Fed. R. Civ. P. 4.

[7] *See id.*

The Grammar of Criminal Law: Volume Two: International Criminal Law George P. Fletcher.

the U.S. law in this area has become complicated.[8] The law of the forum chosen might prevail over all three of the contact points just mentioned.

In interstate and international tort law, we encounter a problem of procedural impunity analogous to the question that led to the adoption of the Rome Statute. If a driver from California can cause an accident in Nevada and then return home without having been served in Nevada, an apparent injustice arises. This has led to a general practice called "long arm jurisdiction."[9] This is not about which law should apply but whether the California driver can be sued at all in Nevada. Note that the term "jurisdiction" is used in the interstate tort context to mean simply whether the state has the constitutional authority to proceed. In the Rome Statute, the usage is much broader.[10]

There are various remedies a defendant can use against being forced to appear in a suit far from home with the added inconvenience and danger of hiring a lawyer on the internet. One is called forum non conveniens, which the court will dismiss in favor of a more convenient court.[11] The other is the possibility of an injunction against suit. An additional source of protection against forum shopping is the full faith and credit clause of the Constitution,[12] which requires the recognition of one state's judgment in another state. There is nothing comparable in the international arena.

Because the topic of this chapter is complicity, we should keep in mind a scenario in which the victim is injured by, say, the supplier of dangerous commodities, like guns, to the person who uses them to injure. Preliminarily we should note that it is perfectly appropriate to use the word "victim" in this context, though we would not use the term in cases of contract disputes. Second, the example of guns raises important problems of its own because the United States government is itself morally complicit in not permitting victims to recover in the recurrent mass shootings that occur in the United States.[13] The latest legislation—the Protection of Lawful Commerce in Arms Act of 2005 (PLCAA)—provides immunity against tort suits for manufacturers and distributors of firearms.[14] The peculiarity of this kind

[8] *See* Robert A. Leflar et al., American Conflicts Law, § 92, at 270–71 (4th ed. 1986)

[9] *See, e.g.*, N.C. Gen. Stat. § 1-75.4(1)(d).

[10] *See generally* Rome Statute, *supra* note 1.

[11] *Forum Non Conveniens*, Restatement (Second) of Conflict of Laws § 84 (Am. Law Inst. 1971) ("A state will not exercise jurisdiction if it is a seriously inconvenient forum for the trial of the action provided that a more appropriate forum is available to the plaintiff.").

[12] U.S. Const. art. IV, § 1.

[13] *See, e.g.*, 15 U.S.C. § 7901 *et. seq.* (2018).

[14] *Id.*

of legislation is difficult to understand from an international perspective. It purposely creates a class of victims that can have no recovery in tort law.

Admittedly, the PLCAA of 2005 provides for one exception, namely "the negligent entrustment of a firearm" by one person to another.[15] This provision is currently being litigated with little success so far for plaintiffs.[16] One of the issues is generated by the statute's federal status and the lawsuits being formulated under state law. Thus, the question is whether the federal statute "preempts" state law and thus requires litigation in federal court.

Despite all these problems, tort law provides many incentives for victims seeking protection. The victim can select the forum, provided the service of process is feasible, and he can overcome a motion to dismiss on grounds of forum non conventions. The choice of forum influences the choice of law. Tort recovery is based on a jury trial, which can assess punitive damages. Some states are notoriously unfriendly to corporate defendants that do business and are therefore subject to suit all over the country. In an exemplary case, *BMW of N. Am. v. Gore*,[17] the claim to an Alabama jury was that the defendant's agent, BMW, sold the plaintiff Ira Gore a repaired car as though it were new.[18] The jury granted Gore $4,000 in compensatory damages and $4,000,000 in punitive damages.[19] This led to appeals that eventually went to the U.S. Supreme Court.[20] In an extraordinary opinion, the Court, with Justice Stevens writing the majority opinion, held that the punitive damages were excessive and violated the Due Process Clause of the Fourteenth Amendment to the Constitution.[21] The interesting point is that only a corporation the size of BMW would have the exposure and the funds to suffer a verdict of this size and the luck to get a hearing at the level of the Supreme Court.[22]

The takeaway from the *BMW* case is that the corporation was held liable for the behavior of a local dealer who committed a relatively minor fraud. This establishes the strength of the doctrine of complicity in tort law. There is one case comparable in criminal law. In the *Ford Pinto* case, the Ford Motor Company was charged with reckless homicide for allegedly locating

[15] *See* 15 U.S.C. § 7903(5)(a)(ii).

[16] *See, e.g.*, Soto v. Bushmaster Firearms Int'l, LLC, 139 F. Supp. 3d 560, 564 (D.C. Conn. 2015) (deciding on procedural grounds).

[17] 15 U.S. 559 (1996).

[18] *Id.*

[19] *Id.*

[20] *Id.*

[21] *Id.*

[22] *See id.* at 285.

the Pinto's fuel tank on the basis of cost/benefit analysis based on repairs costs and safety risks.[23] Many renowned writers, including Ralph Nader[24] and Gary Schwartz[25] of UCLA, provided support for the critique of the Ford Motor Company. At the trial itself, the jury was initially deadlocked but in the end returned a verdict in favor of Ford.[26] Nonetheless, the high level of publicity has undoubtedly made automobiles much safer over the years. The number of fatalities per 1000 has declined almost 50 percent since 1980.[27] The lasting message of the Ford Pinto case is that it is possible to try a corporation for complicity in the crash of one of its vehicles.

Now we turn to the theory of complicity in cases based solely on individual actors. The basic question is whether complicity is (A) a crime in and of itself or (B) a way of assisting another person to commit a crime. How should we think about this? Comparative references would be a good start. Some ancient legal systems rejected the principle of complicity. Ancient Jewish law held to the principle: *ain shlichut baverah*.[28] The motive for holding that there are only perpetrators—no accessories—would be that to deserve punishment the culprit must get his hands dirty. He must be stained. Think of Lady MacBeth in her lament: "Out damned spot."[29] This way of thinking goes well with a philosophy of punishment that holds that by punishing the perpetrator, he rid the world of the stain on nature left by the crime. Retributive thinking—punishment as a way of correcting the natural order—may appeal to common people and playwrights, but it has little traction these days among international lawyers—at least in the doctrines generally espoused.

The principle of "no agency in crime" does apply, however, and is a corner of German law called *eigenhändige delilkte*, requiring that crimes must be committed by one's own hand—meaning one's own body.[30] Incest is the paradigm example. In terms of international crimes, however, it is not clear whether we have many good examples. Here are a few possibilities: (A) the procedural offenses listed in Article 70(1), for example, perjury.[31] Also, if the

[23] State v. Ford Motor Co., No. 5234 (Ind. Super. Ct. Mar. 13, 1980).
[24] RALPH NADER, UNSAFE AT ANY SPEED (1965).
[25] Gary T. Schwartz, *The Myth of the Ford Pinto Case*, 43 RUTGERS L. REV. 1013 (1991).
[26] *See Ford Motor Co.*, No. 5234.
[27] Jim Gorzelany, *NHTSA Confirms Newer Cars Much Safer than Older Ones*, FORBES (May 11, 2018), https://www.forbes.com/sites/jimgorzelany/2018/05/11/newer-cars-much-safer-than-older-ones-nhtsa-says/#15a5a6252104.
[28] There is no agency in crime.
[29] WILLIAM SHAKESPEARE, MACBETH act 5, sc. 1 (SparkNotes 2018) (1606).
[30] *See* MICHAEL BOHLANDER, PRINCIPLES OF GERMAN CRIMINAL LAW 174 (2009).
[31] Rome Statute, *supra* note 1, art. 70(1)(a).

mens rea is defined as "corruptly" as in Article 70(1)(c), there is a good argument that only the actual perpetrator could satisfy this aggravated mental state.[32]

On the whole, the idea of complicity in the actions of another has become a standard part of modern legal and moral thought. We no longer think of individuals acting solely on their own account but of groups of people interacting to in order to produce a crime of shared responsibility. This is particularly true in the crimes of Genocide, Aggression, and Crimes Against Humanity, where the problem has been the reverse, namely reasoning from collective action to individual responsibility. Recall our previous discussion of Article 8*bis* and its importance in making sense of the mandate of the Rome Statute's insisting on individual responsibility.[33]

As for holding individual actors accountable, as Article 25 attempts to do, it would make sense to hold each liable for his or her causal role in the crime. That is, complicity should be seen not as a crime in itself but as a contribution to the crime of another. This differentiation would be expressed in the punishment imposed for the degree of contribution to the harm intended. The analogy would be to the law of attempts. But as there is a divide between retributivists and deterrence theorists about punishing attempts, there is a similar dispute about punishing relative contributions in the law of complicity. Utilitarian or deterrence advocates are likely to go further and treat complicity like a completed crime, thus permitting the conceptual possibility of attempted complicity. (The assumption is that the concept of attempt applies only to completed offenses).

The major legal systems of the world break down into two camps on the punishment of complicity. German and Russian law differentiate between the punishment of perpetrators and accessories, while French and American law support the equivalent treatment of all parties. We should say "equivalent in principle," but it is hard to believe that American judges would not consider relative causal contribution of the supplied and the killer in sentencing.

Yet American law is rendered less sensitive to the issues of complicity by the felony-murder rule, inherited from the common law, which makes every participant in a felony responsible for murder that happens, even by accident, in the course of a felony.[34] For example, if A knowingly lends his car to

[32] *Id.*, art. 70(1)(c).
[33] *Supra* ch. VI.
[34] *See* Paul H. Robinson & Tyler Scot Williams, Mapping American Criminal Law: Variations Across the 50 States (2018).

B who uses the car to commit a robbery and kills someone as a result, A is liable for murder, even subject to capital punishment.[35] The Model Penal Code has, on the whole, rejected the rule, as have many common law jurisdictions, but it survives in over 40 states as a tribute to prosecutorial power and the importance of plea bargaining in the American system.[36] That is, the felony murder rules looks draconian, but its primary function may be to intimidate defendants to plead guilty to lesser offenses.

Leaving aside the felony murder rule, let us concentrate on the possible rationales for equivalence theory, that is, treating accessories and principles as formally equivalent. Americans justify this principle by invoking a principle from private law, not of torts but rather of contracts: *qui facit per alium facit per se*.[37] This makes sense in commercial law; indeed complex business transactions would not be possible without the doctrine of agency. Introducing this principle into criminal law is subject to two possible interpretations: (1) American law cannot clearly distinguish between private law and criminal law, or (2) the inner purpose of American doctrine is to aggravate the threatened punishment in order to facilitate plea bargaining.

Despite the Fifth and Sixth Amendments and the sharp constitutional distinctions between criminal trials and private law, American lawyers perpetually pose this dichotomy of purposes. Further evidence of this persistent (and probably purposeful) confusion appears in the use of the doctrine of conspiracy as a criterion of complicity. In the eighteenth century, due to a suggestion by Lord Hawkins, the doctrine of conspiracy was solidified in criminal law.[38] Under federal law, any conspiracy—or agreement—to commit a crime is itself a crime and, in addition, renders the conspirators complicit in all the crime committed by their co-conspirators.[39]

The government's use of conspiracy as a catch-all crime became of critical importance in *Hamdan v. Rumsfeld*[40] in which the government sought to prosecute Hamdan, bin-Laden's driver on 9/11, for conspiracy as a war crime in a military tribunal.[41] In my amicus brief for Hamdan, the argument, based on a comparative study, was that conspiracy should not be treated as a war

35 *See* Tison v. Ariz., 481 U.S. 137, 158 (1987).
36 *See, e.g.*, Model Penal Code § 210.2(1)(b) (Official Draft 1980).
37 He who acts through another acts himself.
38 *See Developments in the Law: Criminal Conspiracy*, 72 Harv. L. Rev. 920, 923 (1959).
39 18 U.S.C. § 371 (2018).
40 548 U.S. 557, 566 (2006).
41 *Id.*

crime because, apart from the 1940 Rocco code in Italy, the common law was the only system that recognized conspiracy as a distinct punishable offense.

Looking at this array of arguments, many of which seem inconsistent with basic principles of culpability, one is amazed to how easily the law of complicity is twisted and manipulated by the interests at play in criminal trials. The way to guard against this in international as well as national criminal law is to recognize a bedrock of principles (the *Dogmatik* in German law) that guard against manipulation for the sake of plea bargaining. One of these principles would be to punish each offender according to his relative causal contribution to the harm.

Accessories arguably contribute less to the harm than do the principals and therefore should be punished less. The intriguing possibility of applying this contrary to our ordinary expectations came to the fore in the *Stashchynsky* case in 1963 in which a German court held that a KGB agent in Germany was merely an accomplice to the principals who had remained behind in Moscow.[42]

There are seemingly good reasons for this decision. The directors of espionage in Moscow were the ones in control. The agent was only a puppet to them. As such, it was reasonable to label him an accomplice,. But the German Bundestag was unpersuaded. There was something implausible about letting the person who actually committed the principal crime (in this case, homicide) even partially off the hook. In 1975, they adopted a provision in the new Criminal Codem which held in Section 25(1): "Any person who commits the offence himself or through another shall be liable as a principal." [43]

Stashchynsky is one of those cases that you might think are right in principle but are also too subject to manipulation. The problem is reminiscent of our discussion of superior orders. [44] As we expect soldiers to assess whether their orders are lawful, we might expect "cogs in the machine" like a KGB agent to regard themselves not as agents but as principals and to stand responsible for their actions. Nonetheless, there is reason to feel some sympathy both for soldiers and other cogs who participate in the banality of evil.

The reference to Hannah Arendt's famous book about Eichmann makes us take stock of the influence of the Holocaust on our notions of personal responsibility.[45] Germany is the site of many these of the moral conflicts. Later

[42] Bundesgerichtshof (Federal Supreme Court), judgment of 19 October 1962, in 18 Entscheidungssammlung des Bundesgerichtshofs in Strafsachen (BGHSt) (1963): 87–96.

[43] Section 25 German Criminal Code (Strafgesetzbuch, StGB).

[44] *Supra* ch. VI.

[45] *See* Hannah Arendt, Eichmann in Jerusalem: A Report on the Banality OF Evil (1963).

during the division between West and East Germany, the border guards for the East shot and killed many of the East Germans trying to escape across the wall to freedom. After the reunification in 1989, West German court tried two border guards for shooting escaping countrymen.[46] They were convicted of manslaughter and one was sentenced to several years in prison.[47] The case has generated intense analysis and criticism both under German law and international law.[48] From my perspective, the most disturbing conclusion of the West German courts is that the East German border guards could not rely on the East German law as written. The theory was that the East German statutes had to be interpreted in line with human rights law and everyone has a basic human right to leave his country.

If there is a human right of this nature, the United States clearly violated the norm as well. If a passenger in a car refused to show his papers at the border with Canada or Mexico and made a dash for the other side, there is no doubt that the police would shoot. This issue plagued the communist governments, which were generally assumed in the West to violate human rights. This is one of these issues on which your perspective determines the outcome. East thinks one way; West thinks another. In fact, from my own travels and legal representation in the Soviet Union, I can say that there many advantages to living under socialism—mainly fewer class barriers. Indeed, the Kibbutz in Israel was inspired by the socialist model. But that was another time and gradually the assumption has taken hold that life in the East was impoverished.

This assumption generated some of the intriguing highjacking cases in the late twentieth century.

In one of them, *United States v. Tiede*,[49] I served as an expert witness on German law. The following is an edited version of my experience, the full text of which can be found in *My Life in Seven Languages*.[50]

In the summer of 1978, Detlef Tiede, his friend Ingrid Ruske, and her daughter were in Gdansk, Poland, which of course was under communist rule at the time. They boarded a Polish airplane headed back to East Berlin. Jamming a toy pistol into the back of a stewardess, Tiede commanded them

[46] Stephen Kinzer, *2 East German Guards Convicted of Killing Man as He Fled West*, N.Y. Times, Jan. 21, 1992, at A1.

[47] *Id.*

[48] The issues are astutely summarized in Annemieke van Versefeld, Mistake of Law: Excusing Perpetrators of International Crimes § 2.3.2.4 (2012).

[49] United States v. Tiede, 86 F.R.D. 227, 228 (U.S. Ct. Berlin 1979).

[50] *See* George P. Fletcher, My Life in Seven Languages 40–52 (2011).

to land in Tempelhof airport in the American sector. The plane landed safely and the passengers fled to the West. Ingrid and her daughter were released but Tiede had to stand trial.[51] Under the occupation agreement between Germany and the United States, the Americans were entitled to establish a U.S. Court in Berlin. This was an Article II court under the auspices of the State Department. [52]

It is illuminating to compare the trial that Tiede received with the more political orientation of the West German courts toward the border guards. First, the United States has no real interest at stake in the case. This was before 9/11 and no one considered highjacking a major threat. Also, the preliminary procedural question in the case was whether to grant Tiede a jury trial, admittedly of politically oriented West Berliners who were going to be sympathetic to Tiede. Under the territorial principle in American approach to the conflict of laws, the applicable law was going to be German law, merged with the American system of procedure.

This is where I came into the story. The language of the trial was English and it is not easy to explain German law in English. I still struggle with the proper translation of some of the highly developed theoretical constructs of German law. The lawyer for the defense Judah Best in Washington, DC, interviewed some German experts who encountered an understandable conceptual disconnect in explaining German law in English. With the trial scheduled to begin in the summer of 1979, Judah Best sought American lawyers who had studied German criminal law. How odd that anyone would have done so, but I had, and Judah Best ended up on my doorstep in Santa Monica. I was on a plane for Berlin a few weeks later.

The Court had already appointed its own expert, a German scholar named Thomas Weigend, who would have one of the best people Judah Best could have found in Germany. One of my colleagues at Columbia, Lorrie Damrosch, an international lawyer, was then working in the State Department and could have given offered a sound opinion on the international implications of the case, but this was a criminal case. The issue for me was to win it under German criminal law.

In 1927 the German high court made an innovative decision in a seemingly unrelated field, abortion.[53] They had decided, without any backup in

[51] *Tiede*, 86 F.R.D. at 228.
[52] *Id.* at 237.
[53] *See* Entscheidungen des Reichsgerichts in Strafsachen [RGSt] 61, 242.

the criminal code, that a doctor committing an abortion could be justified under the principle of necessity, sometimes called act for the sake of the lesser evil. Was saving the life of the mother or the fetus the greater good? There was nothing in the then-applicable German code on this principle, and there is little understanding of the principle under the Model Penal Code. It is not mentioned in the catalogue of defenses listed in the Rome Statute Article 31.[54] The principle is called "extra-statutory necessity" and is now recognized in Section 34 of the German Criminal Code.[55] The question was how this principle would help Tiede on the highjacking charge.

This is where the political dimension of the case becomes relevant. Just about any argument would win the day if it was plausible, could be explained in German, and provided a good cover for letting Tiede go. The argument of necessity worked. The jury convicted Tiede of one count of highjacking. [56]

There was, however, a fallacy in the argument that worked with the politically disposed jury in the *Tiede* case. Necessity should apply as a defense only if there is a heightened risk at the moments of action. In self-defense case, this is called the requirement of imminence. There was an imminent risk of harm in the 1927 abortion case but not in *Tiede*. Whether impoverished or not, life in the German Democratic Republic in 1989 was pretty much the same as it had been in 1969.

Note that Ingrid Ruske had been passively complicit in Tiede's highjacking. As in many cases, parties benefiting from a crime are indirectly supportive. Ingrid's involvement was more serious than that of passive bystanders, for example, the other passengers on the plane who could have intervened to prevent the highjacking. The pilot, too, was complicit. Indeed, there is an analogy between the pilot and Stashchynsky.[57] The defense of the pilot would be that he had no interest in landing the plane, but nor do most cogs in the machinery of espionage.

The doctrines of German law have continued to have an enormous influence in the doctrinal thinking of complicity, even though the doctrines represent theory of collective more than individual responsibility. This is evident in an impressive book by Neha Jain, *Perpetrators and Accessories in International Criminal Law*.[58] Jain not only brings to bears doctrines like

[54] *See generally* Rome Statute, *supra* note 1, art. 30.
[55] *See* Section 34 German Criminal Code (Strafgesetzbuch, StGB).
[56] *See generally* H. Stern, Judgment in Berlin 370 (1984).
[57] *Supra* ¶ 19.
[58] Neha Jain, Perpetrators and Accessories in International Criminal Law: Individual Modes of Responsibility for Collective Crimes (2014).

Claus Roxin's *Organizationsherrschaft*[59]—organizational dominance—but endorses the continuing influence of the collective criminality basic to the regional tribunals such as the ICTY. In her book, we find a continuity from German criminal law to the regional tribunal to the ICC. This is a controversial point for two reasons: (1) the Rome Statute does not otherwise show much influence of German criminal law, and (2) the emphasis on individual criminal liability in Article 25 appears to reject the collective theories that influenced the ICTY, for example, the various doctrines of Joint Criminal Enterprise.[60]

With these background considerations in mind, we should look more closely at the details of Article 25(3)[61] and then turn to the first major cases on complicity in the ICC, those of Germain Katanga and Thomas Lubanga.[62]

Part (a) of Article 25(3)(a) punishes someone who "commits . . . a crime [as always: one of the primary four plus the administrative offences of Article 70[63]] as an individual, jointly with another or through another person, regardless of whether that other person is criminally responsible."[64] This provision contains an implied rejection of one of the common law principles of complicity, namely the idea of derivative liability from the actions of the principal. If the principle was not guilty of the crime, the accessory could be held liable. The point here is to avoid disputes in the common law about whether the principal is actually to be convicted in order to hold the accessory liable.

Part (a) poses three variations of individual acting alone: (1) acting alone, (2) jointly with another person, or (3) acting through another. The fact that number (1) is even mentioned is surprising. It is obvious that individuals acting alone can be liable. The second possibilities are not complicity either. The second is known as *Mittäterschaft* in German. An example would be an assault in which one person holds the arms of the victim and the other punches him. This doctrine become important in the first cases decided in this area by the ICC, Kutanga & Lubanga, discussed a little later.[65]

[59] Claus Roxin, Taterschaft und Tatherrschaft (8th ed. 2006) (Organizationsherrschaft is "the theory of control of the act by virtue of a hierarchical organization.").

[60] *See* Rome Statute, *supra* note 1, art. 25.

[61] *Id.*

[62] *See* Prosecutor v. Thomas Lubanga Dyilo, Case No. ICC/01/04-01/06, Pre-Trial Chamber Decision on the Confirmation of Charges (Jan. 29, 2007); Prosecutor v. Germain Katanga and Mathieu Ngudjolo Chui, Case No. ICC-01/04-01/07, Decision on the Confirmation of Charges (Sept. 30, 2008).

[63] Rome Statute, *supra* note 1, art. 70.

[64] *Id.*, art. 25(3)(a).

[65] Katanga and Lubanga, *supra* note 62.

The third possibility of part (a) is exemplified by exploiting a minor or insane person to commit the crime. The only interesting variation I can see here is using someone who has made a mistake, say, about whether the woman with whom he is having intercourse with has consented. These are the facts of the notorious *Morgan* case, discussed in chapter 10, "Accidents and Mistakes."[66] It is not exactly right, in colloquial English, to say that RAF officers misleading Morgan were committing rape "through him."

Part (b) introduces a principle of complicity in the traditional sense. The accessory is liable if the principle does one of three things: (1) orders, (2) solicits, or (3) induces the offense.[67] As to ordering, the context presumably is not one of military order where the principle is under a duty to obey but rather analogous to the second and third options. The sense of "ordering" is more like ordering a meal in a restaurant. The waiter (or principal) need not comply. The French version reads *ordonner*, which is translated back into English as "arrange" or "organize." The latter English verbs elicit the accessorial nature of the "ordering."

The second verb of part (b) "solicits" shifts the focus to the accessorial as the dominant party. The solicitor can specify the terms of the execution of the offense and typically rewards the actual perpetrator, as in a case of killing for hire. Solicitation is often associated with sexual offenses, as in soliciting prostitution.[68] The offense can also be used to trap the gullible, as in the case of a police officer in a bar pretending to be a prostitute until the offer is made.

The third verb "induces" exposes the danger of a low threshold of complicity. In a highly publicized rape case in Massachusetts in the 1980s, a crowd supposedly cheered on the rapists.[69] The connotation of encouraging would set an even lower threshold than inducing. As applied the rape case, the crowd would be complicitous for "encouraging" a rapist if even if the rapist took the initiative and the crowd cheered afterward. The danger implicit in these low thresholds of complicity is that they sweep up too many suspects and render prosecutorial discretion inevitable.

It is worth noting that in part (b), these three cases of "ordering, soliciting, and inducing" apply also to attempts. This further lowers the threshold of liability and exacerbates the problem of prosecutorial discretion.

66 Regina v. Morgan, AC 182; 2 All Eng. 347 (1976).

67 Rome Statute, *supra* note 1, art. 25(3)(b).

68 *See* Cali. Pen. Code § 647(b) (2019).

69 *See* Jonathan Friendly, *The New Bedford Rape Case: Confusion Over Accounts of Cheering at Bar*, N.Y. Times (Apr. 11, 1984), https://www.nytimes.com/1984/04/11/us/the-new-bedford-rape-case-confusion-over-accounts-of-cheering-at-bar.html.

Part (c) adds the possibility of an even lower threshold, namely by providing the "means for commission."[70] This implies that every weapons supplier become potentially liable for war crimes committed by the recipients. It also suggests liability against the directors of IG Farben for supplying Zykon B gas used in Auschwitz. The danger in driving the threshold so far back is the acts of aiding and abetting merge with the neutral activities implicit in the ordinary course of doing business. Good examples arose during Prohibition in the United States. In *Falcone*,[71] a supplier of sugar used by distillers was acquitted on the principle that even if the supplier knew the potential use, he was simply doing what all suppliers do even when they engaged in routine activities such as selling gas; providing hotel rooms; or, in my favorite example, the case of numerous civilian secretaries of Third Reich who typed the letters that, on their face, revealed knowledge of the crimes committed the Nazis.

The exception to the *Falcone* principle arose in *Direct Sales*,[72] which held a seller of morphine liable because the supplier knew that some of his customers used large quantities and the supplied had a "stake in the venture."[73] The distinction between *Falcone* and *Direct Sales* is critical for understanding complicity in international criminal law. Warfare is not possible without suppliers of deadly materials. And moderate supplies of gas and herbicides might be perfectly legitimate. When the supplier crosses the vague line between *Falcone* and *Direct Sales* and acquires "stake in the venture,"[74] he become liable for the principal's crime.

A related case arose in the Eastern District of New York under Judge Weinstein.[75] The case was bought under the Alien Tort Claims Act by the third generation of Vietnam victims of the American use of Agent Orange in Vietnam.[76] The Second Circuit affirmed a district court dismissal in the following language counter to my own testimony as an expert witness for the plaintiffs.[77]

70 Rome Statute, *supra* note 1, art. 25(3)(c).
71 United States v. Falcone, 311 U.S. 205, 210–211 (1940).
72 Direct Sales Co. v. United States, 319 U.S. 703, 713–714 (1943).
73 *Id.* at 73.
74 *Id.*
75 Nguyen Thang Loi v. Dow Chem. Co. (In re Orange Prod. Liab. Litig.), 373 F. Supp.2d (E.D.N.Y. 2005).
76 *Id.*
77 Vietnam Ass'n for Victims of Agent Orange v. Dow Chem Co., 517 F.3d 104 (2d Cir. 2008).

> In further support of their claim that the use of herbicides as "poison" violated international law, Plaintiffs rely on the opinions of their experts, Professors George P. Fletcher and Jordan Paust, as well as the works of other international law scholars, who generally contend that the use of chemical or biological warfare violates international law.
>
> In support of their claim that Defendants violated the prohibition against unnecessary suffering, Plaintiffs argue that the use of any material object that may have collateral consequences and is not necessary for military purposes is universally prohibited. In short, they contend that the use of Agent Orange was disproportionate to military necessity because it caused unnecessary human suffering. In particular, Plaintiffs assert that Articles 146 and 147 of the Fourth Geneva Convention prohibit "extensive destruction and appropriation of property, not justified by military necessity and carried out unlawfully and wantonly" if committed against protected persons or property. In addition, they argue that Article 50 of that Convention lists as a "grave breach[]" the act of "willfully causing great suffering or serious injury to body or health." Plaintiffs further contend that the 1945 Nuremberg Charter and the 1951 Nuremberg Principles prohibit "war crimes"—namely, violations of the laws and customs of war, including "murder, ill-treatment or deportation to slave labor or for any other purpose of civilian population of or in occupied territory, murder or ill-treatment of prisoners of war or persons on the seas, killing of hostages, plunder of public or private property, wanton destruction of cities, towns or villages, or devastation not justified by military necessity."[78]

There is enough in this excerpt for analysis on all the important issues in the law of war, but the part that most intrigues me is the reliance on the intention to defoliate for the purposes of facilitating combat against the Viet Cong. If the focus is on the effect rather than the intention, then Agent Orange should have been classified as a poison in violation of treaties prohibiting the use of chemical weapons. The underlying philosophical premise is the principle of double effect, which is problematic for two reasons: (1) determining the relevant intention; and (2) even if the intention is acceptable, evaluating the side effects as proportionate and therefore legitimate. Both of these arguments are subject to factual and legal manipulation.

[78] *Id.* at 119.

Part (d) is a catch-all clause that begins: "In any other way, contributes to the commission or attempted commission . . . by a group of persons acting with a common purpose."[79] This phrasing is reminiscent of the common law crime of joining a conspiracy. A good example is Hamdan driving the car used by Osama bin Laden.[80] In that case, as it was tried in the Supreme Court in 2006, the decisive factor was that conspiracy was not a war crime.[81] The analogue in the jurisprudence of the ICTY was joint criminal enterprise.[82] The point of Article 25 with its emphasis on individual criminal responsibility was arguably to overcome the collective responsibility implicit in the variations of JCE, particularly JCE III. Whether part (d) retracts on this aim is an open question.

The mens rea requirement in subparts (i) and (ii) may redeem part (d) from slipping back into a form of collective responsibility.[83] These qualifications reshape part (d) into a version of the crime of joining a conspiracy, which is a crime based on individual responsibility. The key mental element in subpart (i) is the "aim of furthering" the criminal purposes of the group. It is worth noting here the multiplication here of forms of mens rea. Now the "purpose" of the group becomes a critical element of the crime. "Purpose" generally connotes a long-range goal. It is most serious of the four mental states in the Model Penal Code.[84] The French version reads: *viser a faciliter le dessein crimine du groupe*.[85] This might be a better version of the Statute because it does not lead to confusion with concepts used in domestic law.

The mens rea requirement in subpart (ii) is simply to "be made in the knowledge of the intention of the group."[86] Thus, the overall definition of this fork of part (d) is to "contribute" to the commission of the group crime with "knowledge of the intention of the group." We don't know whether "intention" is used in the same sense as "intent" in Article 30.[87] We have seen this problem before with regard to other grammatical variations of the core word "intent." Yet, overall, this seems to be a lower threshold of complicity and thus would be presumably be the preferred charge for the prosecution.

79 Rome Statute, *supra* note 1, art. 25(3)(d).
80 *Hamdan*, 548 U.S. at 566.
81 *Id.*
82 *See, e.g.*, Prosecutor v. Tadic, Case No. IT-94-1-A, Appellate Judgement, ¶ 185 (July 15, 1999).
83 Rome Statute, *supra* note 1, art. 25(3)(d).
84 *See* Model Penal Code § 2.02 (1985).
85 *See* Rome Statute, *supra* note 1, art. 25(3)(d)(i) (Fr.).
86 *Id.*, art. 30(3)(d)(ii).
87 *Id.*

As to the application of these provisions in the ICC, we see an analysis in the pretrial chamber of complicity in the earlier stages of the charges against Katanga and Lubanga for the war crime of deploying child soldiers in the Congo. [88] It devoted something like 45 pages in the Lubanga decision to analysis of co-perpetration as a mode of liability.[89] At the time, this struck me as important as a recognition of the ICC of the relevance of theoretical considerations to the application of the law. I discuss these issues in an article in the *Journal of International Criminal Justice*.[90] The reference to *Dogmatik* means that a substructure of theoretical principles, in fact, governs the thinking of the ICC. This is obviously true and in fact underlies the conviction of Germain Katanga.[91] On his appeal, the Appellate Chamber assumed his complicity in the crime and directed its attention to procedural considerations.[92] See, even in this particular case, another principle of adjudication emerged, namely whenever possible, resolve the case on procedural considerations.[93] This is what happened in the proceeding against Katanga.[94]

Part (e) invokes the case of inciting genocide in Rwanda, the facts of which are difficult for those unfamiliar with the history of the German and Belgian occupation of Rwanda, the ensuing conflict between the two tribes or groups called the Hutus (85 percent of Rwanda)[95] and Tutsis, and the failure of the United States to intervene to prevent the slaughter of the Tutsi in the 1990s.[96] There is considerable skepticism among anthropologists whether there is any difference except one imposed by colonial powers. Some claim that Tutsis, the minority group, are taller by far, but this is obviously not a difference that could readily qualify under the Genocide NERR categories (Nationality, Ethnicity, Race, and Religion).[97] The two groups speak the same language and have the same religion. The only way to classify this slaughter as genocide is to classify the difference as ethnic—a category that is admittedly vague.

Of course, the origin of the Genocide Statute in the work of Raphael Lemkin was also based on distinctions between Germans and Jews that

[88] Katanga & Lubanga, *supra* note 62.
[89] *Id.*
[90] George P. Fletcher, *New Court, Old Dogmatik*, 9 J. INT'L CRIM. JUSTICE 179, 188 (2011).
[91] Katanga & Lubanga, *supra* note 62.
[92] *Id.*
[93] *Id.*
[94] Prosecutor v. Germain Katanga, Case No. ICC-01/04-01/07, Decision on the Confirmation of Charges (Sept. 25, 2009).
[95] *Rwanda: A Brief History of Country*, U.N. (last visited Jan. 2, 2019), http://www.un.org/en/preventgenocide/rwanda/education/rwandagenocide.shtml.
[96] *See* Rome Statute, *supra* note 1, art. 25(3)(e).
[97] Rome Statute, *supra* note 1, art. 6.

might have been totally incomprehensible to tribes of central Africa. That distinction does not fit into the NERR system either. Of course, Hitler thought that distinction was racial, but that kind of argument poses so many difficulties about cases of mixed blood as to become arbitrary. Whether one-eighth or one-sixteenth parentage should suffice is a political question. In the end the hatred of the outsider, in the words of Rogers and Hammerstein in *South Pacific*, must "be carefully taught."[98] Unfortunately, the human species is susceptible to this kind of propaganda that serves the interests of their teachers—namely governments, colonial power, political parties.

The use of the criminal law to punish those susceptible to hatred may be a cruel necessity. The orientation of the Rome Statute has been more concerned about vindicating the status and rights of victims than about the moral culpability of the offenders.[99] This may be necessary as we learned from *impunidad* in Argentina for *desaparecidos* in the late 1980s[100] and the failure of the international community to intervene and prevent the mass slaughter in Rwanda in the early 1990s.[101] At the very least, the prosecution of these offenses creates a worldwide consciousness of arbitrary discrimination.

One further point about part (e). The keywords are "directly and publicly incite[]."[102] We should generalize from the Rwandan case as the Rome Statute has developed a general aversion to impunity as expressed in the Preamble.[103] The argument should be that "directly and publicly inciting" any of the major four crimes should be punishable. Certainly, there are cases in World War II of the German leadership directly and publicly inciting aggression against Poland and the Soviet Union. We see the same phenomenon today in the Middle East, with the ongoing incitement by Hamas of Palestinians to scale the fence in Gaza and expose themselves to Israeli gunfire. There are cases of incitement to commit war crimes; indeed, any time governments preach hatred of the arbitrarily defined "other," we could make a good case for incitement.

[98] Richard Rodgers & Oscar Hammerstein, "You Have to Be Carefully Taught," SOUTH PACIFIC (1949; CBS Masterworks 1986).

[99] *See* Rome Statute, *supra* note 1, pmbl.

[100] *See* Ronald Dworkin, *Introduction* to COMISION NACIONAL SOBRE LA DESPARICION DE PERSONAS, *in* NUNCA MAS: THE REPORT OF THE AGENTINE NATIONAL COMMISSION ON THE DISAPPEARED at xi (1986).

[101] *See* SAMANTHA POWER, A PROBLEM FROM HELL: AMERICA AND THE AGE OF GENOCIDE (2002).

[102] Rome Statute, *supra* note 1, art. 25(3)(e).

[103] *Id.*, pmbl.

Looking at these issues from the viewpoint of the defense, however, the notion of "incitement" implies that the actor is subject to the influence of propaganda. He is less responsible than if he had chosen, without outside influences, to commit the offense. Incitement is often associated with riots.[104] This provision does not suggest mitigation for the actual rioters, but the term "riot" itself implies losing partial control of one's action, indeed losing factor of leadership that is necessary in organized criminality. The Los Angeles riots of 1992 in South Central Los Angeles appeared to be an uncoordinated outburst of anger after the acquittal of four police officers for beating up Rodney King, a black motorist stopped on the freeway.[105] The case is discussed in my book, *With Justice for Some: Protecting Victims' Rights in Criminal Trials*.[106]

The Rwandan case led to the establishment of the ICTR, a special tribunal comparable to the ICTY and ICTL, special tribunals for Yugoslavia and Lebanon. The long-range benefit to the international legal order may be the Rome Statute and the International Criminal Court.

This is a subject that will concern us in the next chapter on Justice. Nonetheless, the inclusion of this implicit reference in Article 25(3)(e) is important in demonstrating the responsibility of the international community to prevent this kind of mass killing in the future.

This concludes our analysis of complicity in international tort and criminal law.

[104] *See* 18 U.S.C. § 2102 (2018).

[105] *See* Koon v. United States, 518 U.S. 81, 112 (1996).

[106] *See* GEORGE P. FLETCHER, WITH JUSTICE FOR SOME: PROTECTING VICTIMS' RIGHTS IN CRIMINAL TRIALS (1996).

12

Law vs. Justice

Law and Justice express themselves in three, possibly four, intersecting and potentially confusing sets of ideas. Let's us start with the word "law," which is ambiguous in English because we use one word to express two distinction different ideas: law as principle and law as rule or regularity.

1. Two Concepts of Law

These two different ideas are expressed in European languages by a pair of words *Recht* & *Gesetz* in German, *Pravo* & *Zakon* in Russian, *Derecho* & *Ley* in Spanish.[1] We once had this distinction in English. It was called Right and Law.[2] It is not clear why we lost this distinction in English, but there is no doubt that this linguistic point has had a great influence on jurisprudential thinking and on international criminal law. To avoid and also highlight the ambiguity in English we will use the German words *Recht* and *Gesetz*.

Let us begin with the topic of this book. What kind of law is the ICC supposed to apply? Is it law as rule (*Gesetz*) or law as principle (*Recht*)? If we look at the Rome Statute[3] Article 23,[4] we find the principle *nulla poena sine lege*. The term "lege" is the Latin ablative singular for Lex—or law as rule. The principle, therefore, is there should be no punishment applied by the court without a pre-announced rule. But if we thought that the ICC was merely enforcing the Rome Statute, with no concern for justice, we should not have much respect for it.

[1] *See* James Bernard Murphy, The Philosophy of Positive Law: Foundations of Jurisprudence Table 2.1 63 (2005).

[2] *See* Georg W.F. Hegel, Hegel's Philosophy of Right 137 (T.M. Knox trans., Oxford University Press 1967) (1821).

[3] Rome Statute for the International Criminal Court, July 17, 1998, 2187 U.N.T.S. 3; U.N. Diplomatic Conference of Plenipotentiaries on the Establishment of an International Court, U.N. Doc. A/Conf.183/9 [hereinafter Rome Statute].

[4] Rome Statute, *supra* note 3, art. 23 ("A person convicted by the Court may be punished only in accordance with this Statute.").

The Grammar of Criminal Law: Volume Two: International Criminal Law George P. Fletcher.

As between *Recht* and *Gesetz*, the former is normative, and the latter is descriptive. All scientific laws are based on the word *Gesetz*. That there is any connection between man-made laws and scientific laws should intrigue us. The latter are discovered by observation. Human laws are designed to induce the kind of regularity that we observe in the solar system, but obviously they fall short. That is why we have expensive systems of law enforcement. In the hit TV series, *Law & Order*,[5] we can assume, because of the association with police-enforced order, that the reference is to *Gesetz*.

Human laws are enacted, a phenomenon that leads to philosophical questions of authority. How is a law brought into existence? How should it be interpreted written—as it is, in human and not in scientific language? The Rome Statute is written in several official languages, which exposes serious problems of translation, even as between closely related languages like English and French. Note the differences between self-defense and legitime defense. The former refers to defense just of the self; the latter includes defense of others and property.[6]

The language of human law differs entirely from scientific laws. We asked why human laws are binding, whether human laws express moral principles, and whether unjust laws are really laws. None of these questions make sense with regard to scientific law. It is a wonder that the word *Gesetz* is used commonly in Western legal systems to cover both human and scientific laws.

In this discussion, we introduced the plural form of law in the expression "enacting laws." Law as principle (*Recht, pravo*, etc.) does come in the plural form, with an interesting exception in Hebrew, which I shall take up. It is difficult to count the number of distinct laws in the Rome Statute because many provisions have multiple parts. Yet the notion clearly makes sense when we think of human-made laws as enacted laws.

The Hebrew term *mispatim* is rich in ambiguity. It is plural and therefore not likely to be an analogue to *Recht*. Yet it is not connected to scientific laws, which invoke the term *Hok*, closer in meaning to statutory law. The term *Mishpat* in the singular is closely associated with the notion of a judge, even the Divine judge. When Abraham argues with God in the classical example of the Socratic method, Abraham argues in favor of protecting the innocent in Sodom & Gomorroh and finally questions God: Will not the Judge of all the universe do justice—or more strictly, render a judgment appropriate for

[5] *Law & Order* (NBC television series).

[6] *See* George P. Fletcher & Jens David Ohlin, Defending Humanity: When Force Is Justified and Why (2008).

the supreme judge [*Shofet col haaretz lo yaaseh mishpat*].[7] This is translated in the King James Bible as: Shall not the Judge of all the earth do right?[8] We see in this problem of translation the way in which law, justice, and right are easily interwoven.

As we shall see, the name we give to faculties of law signals something important about the legal system. No law faculty would be called the faculty of *Gesetz*. There must some aim to the study of law higher than counting legislative enactments that are constantly subject to change. Even in countries with codified legal systems (France, Germany, indeed all legal systems outside the English-speaking world), the faculty of law signals a higher purpose, one that enables students to practice law even when the statutes or codes are totally different. My favorite name for a law faculty is the Italian version. *Facoltà di giurisprudenza*—Faculty of Jurisprudence.[9] Admittedly, however, some faculties are *Facoltà di legge*. The latter corresponds to the Hebrew—Faculty of Laws.

The best interpretation of the Hebrew term is that the study of law addresses many different branches of law, for example, criminal law, international law, etc. The important point in these interpretations is that the notion of law employed here is not the same as scientific law, and not the same as the forever changing laws on the books.

2. Philosophical Perspectives

The notion of enacted (or posited) law leads to the philosophical theory of legal positivism, as expressed in the work of H.L.A. Hart in English[10] and Hans Kelsen in German.[11] Presumably Hart was addressing the notion of *Gesetz*, though Kelsen wrote earlier in the positivist tradition by calling his book *Reine Rechtslehre* or Pure Theory of *Recht*.[12] The ideas behind both of these positive schools are two related ideas: (1) all laws are enacted; and (2) the validity or binding nature of a particular law depends on the process

[7] *See* Genesis 18:25.
[8] *Id.* (King James Version).
[9] *See, e.g., Facolta di Giurisprudenza*, UNIVERSITA DI TRENTO (last visited Jan. 16, 2019), https://www.giurisprudenza.unitn.it/.
[10] *See generally* H.L.A. HART, THE CONCEPT OF LAW (2d ed. 1994).
[11] *See* HANS KELSEN, REINE RECHTSLEHRE: EINLEITUNG IN DIE RECHTSWISSENSCHAFTLICHE PROBLEMATIK (1934).
[12] *See id.*

of enactment, not on its moral content. It begins with the question of why law is binding. Hart's answer is that law is binding because it is enacted by an authoritative lawgiver.[13] The question is who has the authority to enact and change particular laws. The simple answer in the United States is that Congress has the authority, but this gets complicated when we turn to laws and treaties that require ratification. This leaves aside the problem of interpretation, which is a constant struggle in the interpretation of the U.S. Constitution.

That the Constitution of 1789 is still binding in its original language is a puzzle not easily answered by any theory of law. That the Constitution was written in English even though there is no official language in the United States is also curious. Also, the Constitution is binding on all 50 states and the U.S. territories even though only 12 of the original 13 colonies sent representatives to Philadelphia to draft the document in 1787.[14] Behind every binding legal document, there are a host of customs that become apparent only when we raise questions about them.

There is an important difference between the Constitution as a document and constitutional law. The latter includes not only the 27 amendments but an entire body of case law and commentary that interprets and reinterprets both the documents and the prior case law.[15] The meaning of the original document obviously changes over time, and the relevant case law and commentary ebb and flow. One good example is the Second Amendment.[16] The United States is overflowing with guns, including semi-automatic rifles, more than can be found, per capita, in any other country on earth.[17] The brief language of the Second Amendment, which arguably only implies a collective right of the state militias to keep and bear arms, was interpreted in the last decade to imply an individual's right to own guns.[18] This is a matter of constitutional law, as interpreted by the courts.

Constitutional law is supposedly based on precedent. As of this writing, the critical precedent in doubt is *Roe v. Wade*, establishing a right to abortion

[13] *See* HART, *supra* note 10, at 102.

[14] *Rhode Island's Ratification of the Constitution*, U.S. HOUSE OF REPS. (last visited Jan. 4, 2019), https://history.house.gov/HistoricalHighlight/Detail/35264.

[15] *See generally* U.S. CONST.; Marbury v. Madison, 5 U.S. 137 (1803).

[16] U.S. CONST. amend. II.

[17] Christopher Ingraham, *There Are More Guns Than People in the United States, According to a New Study of Global Firearm Ownership*, WASH. POST (Jun. 19, 2018), https://www.washingtonpost.com/news/wonk/wp/2018/06/19/there-are-more-guns-than-people-in-the-united-states-according-to-a-new-study-of-global-firearm-ownership/?noredirect=on.

[18] *See* District of Columbia v. Heller, 554 U.S. 570 (2008).

based on a concept of privacy implicit in the Bill of Rights.[19] This is obviously a matter of opinion. So far as the issue is precedent, precedents are often overruled. The rule of stare decisis or the principle of deferring to precedent came into English law by way of judicial decision.[20] The rule itself was obviously not based on any definitive precedent. Yet the tendency in the common legal culture is to minimize the political power of the courts by creating an impression that the decisions are implicit in the binding law, even if that law is simply a matter of customary law.

In recent years, there has been a tendency in the media to label Supreme Court Justices as liberal or conservative.[21] At the moment the liberal camp consists of Justices Kagan, Ginsburg, Breyer, and Sotomayor. The conservatives are supposedly Chief Justice John Roberts and Justices Alito, Thomas, Gorsuch, and Kavanaugh, who recently replaced Justice Kennedy, who was the swing vote on many key issues.[22] The meaning of "liberal" and "conservative" in this context is not clear: on many issues, the blocks divide. The recent controversy about a successor to Justice Kennedy was whether the Court would uphold the precedent of *Roe*, granting women a right to abortion under certain circumstances.[23] There is nothing particularly liberal or conservative about this issue. A better perspective would be the originalist school, as defined by the deceased Justice Antonin Scalia, or the living constitution that led to major civil rights decisions like *Roe* and *Brown v. Board of Education*.[24]

In international matters concerning the law of war, for example, *Hamdan v. Rumsfeld*,[25] it is not clear which the political labels should imply, perhaps nationalist vs. internationalist. The vote was five to three with Justices Scalia, Alito, and Thomas in the dissent.[26] Justice Stevens wrote the majority opinion. Whatever their judicial philosophies might appear to be, the dissenting Justices favored governmental power over the rights of

[19] *See* 410 U.S. 113 (1973).
[20] *Cf.* Thomas Healy, *Stare Decisis as a Constitutional Requirement*, 104 W. VA. L. REV. 43, 56–91 (2001).
[21] *See, e.g.*, Taylor Kate Brown, *The US Supreme Court: Who Are the Justices?*, B.B.C. (Nov. 30, 2018), https://www.bbc.com/news/magazine-33103973.
[22] *See, e.g.*, Obergefell v. Hodges, 135 S. Ct. 2584 (2015).
[23] *See, e.g.*, Robert Barnes & Ann E. Marimow, *On Abortion and Other Issues, Kavanaugh's Heroes Are More Conservative than Kennedy*, WASH. POST (Jul. 15, 2018), https://www.washingtonpost.com/politics/courts_law/on-abortion-and-other-issues-kavanaughs-heroes-are-more-conservative-than-kennedy/2018/07/15/04a3975c-86ad-11e8-8553-a3ce89036c78_story.html.
[24] 347 U.S. 483 (1954).
[25] 548 U.S. 557, 566 (2006).
[26] *Id.* at 655.

individuals, nationalism over respect for foreigners (or aliens as they were once called in the Alien Tort Claims Act).[27] Justices Alito and Thomas are typically pro-government votes, but this is not necessarily the case when government seeks to provide health benefits to American citizens. In the decision upholding Obamacare, *NFIB v. Sibelius*,[28] Chief Justice Robert joined the four so-called liberals to uphold the medical plan under the taxing power of the government.[29] Justices Alito, Thomas, Kennedy, and Scalia dissented.[30] The point here is that the jurisprudential labels designed to group the Justices into political camps are not always reliable.

Politics in the international sense might be different from the domestic application. Hart's positivist theory of theory had an implicit political purpose, though the labels liberal and conservative do not fit. The issue behind Hart's masterpiece was whether Soviet law, widely regarded as manipulated by the government under what was then called "telephone justice," was really law.[31] The ambiguity of law (rules or principles) played into this debate. Hart's purpose was to defend law, regardless of its moral content, in the interests of international understanding.

The political corruption of the legal system has been a problem in virtually every regime in history. Nazi jurisprudence was notorious for taking the notion of law as principle (*Recht, droit*) and adapting it to the will of the Führer.[32] To be an analogue, a similar problem plagued the apartheid regime in South Africa.[33] The rule of law, unrestrained by principles of equality and the moral respect for others, can lead to vast injustices.

As to the binding nature of law, there are essentially two ways of approaching the issue. One is to say that law is based on morality; the alternative is a claim of the positivists, that law is binding because of some morally neutral principle, Hart's alleged sociological principle.[34] Kelsen's work is based on a logically inherent norm called the *Grundnorm* [Basic Norm], which renders the derivative norms binding.[35]

[27] *See id.*
[28] 567 U.S. 519 (2012).
[29] *Id.* at 529.
[30] *Id.* at 646 (Scalia, J., Kennedy, J., Thomas, J., Alito, J., dissenting).
[31] For a more on "telephone justice," see Cass Sunstein & Adrian Vermeule, *The Morality of Administrative Law*, 131 Harv. L. Rev. 1924, 1961 (2018).
[32] *See, e.g.*, John Wright & Steve Waugh, Hodder GCSE History for Edexcel: Weimar and Nazi Germany 8.2 (2016).
[33] *See generally* David R. Penna, *The Law and Reform in South Africa*, 37 Afr. Today 5 (1990).
[34] *See* Hart, *supra* note 10, at 102.
[35] *See* Hans Kelsen, Pure theory of Law 31 (Max Knight trans., 2d ed. 2006) (1967).

The word "derivative" above is important because it implies a principal of logical deduction of immediately binding rules from the Rule of Recognition (Hart) or the Basic Norm (Kelsen). Thus, positivism yields an implicit principle of logical validity. This is particularly interesting as we are in the realm of language and interpretation and not the language of logical deduction. The ambiguity of language should render it almost impossible to decide what "all men are created equal" means.[36] Does it refer to nations, to males, to women, to foreigners? And what does it mean for them to be "created" equal? Is this a religious claim? And the claim of equality is a bit difficult given differences in IQ, strength, genetic disposition to disease, and other factors bearing on Darwin's theory of the "survival of the fittest."[37]

In its Spanish translation, *La Teoria Pura del Derecho*, the Pure Theory of Law, has had an enormous impact in Latin America, where German literature is generally taken more seriously than the jurisprudential work in English.[38] Also, communist theories of law—loaded with value judgments—were influential in Latin America. I recall a meeting with a law professor in Cuba in the 1980s. I asked what he was teaching. He replied, Kelsen. When I inquired why, he said it was either the *La Teoria Pura* or Communism.

The American experience differs from the civilian orientation of Latin America. Hart is more influential than Kelsen. In fact, surprisingly, when Kelsen came as refugee to the United States in 1940, Lon Fuller opposed his appointment at Harvard. As we discuss later with regard to Fuller's opposition to Hart, the former insisted on a value-based conception of binding law and therefore seemingly opposed Kelsen as a scholar because he did not endorse Kelsen's theory of law (the worst kind of academic politics). Time has proven both Fuller and Harvard clearly wrong about the importance of Kelsen's early form of legal positivism.

Kelsen addressed two other questions that bear on the issues in this book. First, in the early 1930s in his home country of Austria, he advocated for a system of judicial review, not as it developed in the United States, but invested in a special constitutional court.[39] This is the model that has been

[36] The Declaration of Independence ¶ 2 (U.S. 1776).

[37] *See generally* CHARLES DARWIN, THE ORIGIN OF THE SPECIES (Random House, Inc. 1993) (1859).

[38] *See* HANS KELSEN, LA TEORÍA PURA DEL DERECHO: INTRODUCCIÓN A LA PROBLEMÁTICA CIENTÍFICA DEL DERECHO (1979).

[39] *See* Stanley L. Paulson, *Constitutional Review in the United States and in Austria: Notes on the Beginning*, 16 RATIO JURIS 229 fn. 12 (2003); RUDOLF MACHACEK, VERFAHREN VOR DEM VFGH 22 (3d ed. 1997, Vienna).

adopted in European countries. The stimulus for this theory of judicial review is the problem: Who should be the guardian of the Constitution? The National Socialist tendencies at the time supported the view that the executive should be the ultimate legal arbiter. Kelsen's proposal for a constitutional court did not succeed during the Weimar Republic but is accepted today in Germany in the *Bundesverfassungsgericht*.[40]

More significantly, Kelsen supported the war crimes trials in Nuremberg and Tokyo.[41] This is a bit difficult to reconcile with the *Pure Theory of Law* and with Kelsen's skeptical view about the coherence of justice as an ideal of the legal system. Although the *Pure Theory of Law* is Kelsen's magnum opus, his influence is felt in virtually every topic of relevance in this book. His work may resonate more with me than with others because his pattern of thought seems to be influenced by the German language and the German legal culture, which is essentially a culture of law shaped more by scholars than court decisions.

Hart's version of positivism resonates well with the Anglo-Saxon tradition of analytic philosophy. His *Concept of Law* represents a significant advance over the arguably circular theory advanced by Kelsen. Law is binding in the *Pure Theory* because of a Grundnorm, a purely hypothetical construct inherent in a binding legal culture.[42] Hart shifted the focus of positivism to a sociological—supposedly factual—Rule of Recognition as the foundation of a binding legal culture.[43] The turn toward sociology is characteristic of the tendency of Anglo-American legal culture to think of legal studies more as a branch of the social sciences than of the humanities.

The more one peels off the layers of law and justice, the more there is to explore. One question leads to another. We must constantly pay attention to implications of different languages and different philosophical traditions. At the heart of this chapter remains the attempt to clarify the distinctions among (1) law as rule, (2) law as principle, and (3) the concept of justice as the ideal of the ideal system. In addition, there are distinct schools of legal philosophy, mainly the positivists and their opponents.

It is not easy to identity the alternative to the positive legal tradition. It is not the natural law theorists, though John Finnis and other Catholic scholars

[40] *See* Court and Constitutional Organ, Bundesverfassungsgericht (last visited Jan. 6, 2019), https://www.bundesverfassungsgericht.de/EN/Das-Gericht/Gericht-und-Verfassungsorgan/gericht-und-verfassungsorgan_node.html,

[41] *See* James Larry Taulbee, War Crimes and Trials 132 (2018).

[42] *See* Kelsen, *supra* note 35, at 31.

[43] *See* Hart, *supra* note 10, at 100.

might make claims in this direction.[44] Presumably natural law is the law of nature, but as we noted earlier, human laws are unfortunately not like scientific laws (which I gather what the law of nature is). Some might believe in divine law, but that too comes in many forms, as we shall see when we turn to the biblical sources on the theory of justice.

In the debate between the positivists and their opponents, the concepts of "morals," mores, and morality come front and center. Morality is about right and wrong but not in the same sense that conventional mores dictate many issues, particularly in sexual matters. This is, of course, relevant in interpreting the war crime of rape, which depends on a conventional understanding of consent. This problem has plagued American criminal justice. "Does yes mean yes?" and "Does no mean no?" Interpersonal communication depends on the conventional understanding of certain intimate acts, such as undressing in front of another person, even accepting an invitation to private quarters.[45]

It is more difficult to argue that morality changes from time of the Greeks to the present day. If slavery is wrong now, it was wrong then. It may take a political leader like Abraham Lincoln to realize this and lead his country in doing the right thing. The universal moral truth argued by Lincoln was that all men are created equal.[46] This was, in fact, a reinterpretation of the Declaration of Independence in which the reference to "all men" referred to nations as "men."[47]

Freedom, equality, fair trial, culpability—all requirements of the international legal order retain their verbal stability by evolving over time, usually for the better, but not always. We may strive for the rule of law, but we, as George Orwell, anticipated in his book, *1984*, cannot control the language of law and justice.[48] For proof the manipulation of these respected, just note the rise of the arguably neo-fascist party "Law and Justice" in Poland.[49] Yet we have no tools to argue these issues other than the words themselves. The

[44] *See, e.g.*, JOHN FINNIS, NATURAL LAW AND NATURAL RIGHTS (1980).

[45] *See, e.g.*, Tyson v. State, 619 N.E.2d 276, 300 (Ind. Ct. App. 1993); Evan West, *The Decision: Mike Tyson's Rape Trial, 25 Years Later*, INDIANAPOLIS MONTHLY (Feb. 2017), https://www.indianapolismonthly.com/features/the-decision-mike-tysons-rape-trial-25-years-later/.

[46] *See generally* Abraham Lincoln, *The Gettysburg Address* (Nov. 19, 1863), *in* LINCOLN ON DEMOCRACY 307 (Mario M. Cuomo & Harold Holzer eds., 1990).

[47] As to the malleability of the phrase, see *supra* pt. 19.

[48] *See generally* GEORGE ORWELL, 1984 214 (Penguin Books 1977) (1949).

[49] *See* James Traub, *The Party That Wants to Make Poland Great Again*, N.Y. TIMES MAGAZINE (Nov. 2, 2016), https://www.nytimes.com/2016/11/06/magazine/the-party-that-wants-to-make-poland-great-again.html.

comparative linguistic approach followed in these pages provides some check on the manipulation of language in any single language or political regime.

The reaction against the Nazi corruption of the German concept of Recht law generated one of the landmark jurisprudential debates in American history. In the pages of the *Harvard Law Review*, H.L.A. Hart and Lon Fuller addressed whether some of the obnoxious public Nazi rules were actual law.[50] We are not talking about genocide but simply about a requirement that children report on their parents listening to foreign radio broadcasts.[51] This is arguably an unjust law because it seeks to undermine the sanctity of home and family. The question posed in 1958 therefore was whether unjust laws of this sort were nonetheless laws. The positivist Hart argued that they were laws although immoral and unjust.[52] Here we not the difficulty of translation expressed in the phrase "unjust laws." Actually, they must have been thinking, not about *Recht* but *Gesetze* (laws in plural).

For Fuller, the perceived immorality of the law was sufficient to say that the particular law was not law at all.[53] Hart's position was much easier to defend. He did not have to claim that the law was moral or that there was a duty to obey it, though the fact that it was called law would arguably create a presumptive duty to obey. Fuller devoted his career to one version or another of his view that moral considerations were inherent in binding law. This view took different forms of time. His later claim that valid legal rules had to observe certain internal requirements such as logical consistency, generality, constancy from one period to another, are entirely consistent with positivism.[54] Indeed one might say that they are necessary for the legal system to be coherent and binding.

Fuller was not a natural law theorist. There was nothing about his argument that suggests a form of law that resembles scientific laws or that could be derived from observing the patterns of human behavior. So far as I can tell, he did not claim that the values used to judge the morality of particular laws derived from nature or indeed from any identifiable sources other than tradition. It was essential, of course, that Fuller not descend into a version of

[50] *See* H.L.A. Hart, *Positivism and the Separation of Law and Morals*, 71 Harv. L. Rev. 593 (1958); Lon L. Fuller, *Positivism and Fidelity to Law—A Reply to Professor Hart*, 71 Harv. L. Rev. 630 (1958).

[51] *See* Richard Grunberger, The 12 Year Reich: A Social History Of Nazi Germany: 1933–1945 234 (1971).

[52] Hart, *supra* note 50, at 616–20.

[53] Fuller, *supra* note 50, at 655.

[54] *See* Lon L. Fuller, Morality of Law 34–79 (2d ed.1969).

subjective morality. The legal system depends on judges writing opinions that can gain a majority of the court, however political these positions may be.

There is nothing about positivism that precludes a positivist from having unacceptable moral values, such as being a serial killer or a fraudulent check casher. Positivism is simply a view about the nature of the legal system. It carries no implications about the moral evaluation of the law or conceptions of the natural order of being.

In my view, the whole debate between Hart and Fuller was a tempest in a teapot, but it does have some significant implications for international law. Let us consider first customary international law. Hart has some important insights into the distinction between custom and customary international law, which might undermine his general view about the relationship between law and morality.[55] Hart was right to underscore manners or customs such as standing up when a lady enters the room and customary law, which is based on reciprocity over time and a developed sense of obligation.

The law of the sea is the outstanding example of customary international law. The critical factors are customary behavior and *opinio juris*, namely an articulated commitment by at least some governments that they are observing the custom as a matter of legal obligation. The reason that this view introduces an element of morality in the law is that there is no objective way to decide when a pattern of behavior becomes a binding custom (there are always people who do not stand up when a lady enters the room) and customs obviously change over time. The customs we regard as "good" survive as customary laws.

The law of the sea may be morally neutral with regard to most of its rules. But there are other areas of customary international law, such as the first use of nuclear weapons, where there is an obvious moral component to the customary rule. There seems to be a consensus among the nuclear powers of the world that it is wrong to escalate from conventional to nuclear warfare.[56] The gap between powerful conventional bombs and nuclear weapons, even so-called tactical weapons, represents a moral commitment about killing civilians and creating long-lasting ecological damage.

In international criminal law, Fuller's theory of morally binding norms is foundational. We would not have begun the Nuremberg and Tokyo trials

[55] HART, *supra* note 10, at 213–37.
[56] *See* Treaty on the Non-Proliferation of Nuclear Weapons, opened for signature July 1, 1968, 21 U.S.T. 483, 729 U.N.T.S. 161 [hereinafter N.P.T.].

without a solid moral commitment to the evils of aggression, genocide, crimes against humanity, and war crimes. The entire Rome Statute is built on these moral assumptions and the necessity of moral arguments in the interpretation of these provisions.[57] But Hart's positivist theory applies in understanding how the Rome Statute became binding law. The rule of recognition of the international community is that a treaty, such as the Rome Statute, become binding upon ratification.[58] Under this principle, it is binding on countries, such as the United States, which have not ratified the treaty.

Some principles of customary international law are regarded as jus cogens, or peremptory norms. This means that they represent a set of principles higher than the rule of recognition reflected in treaties. No one agrees on what these norms are except for some, like slavery, that were once considered legally acceptable by some nation–states but are now regarded as taboo. Despite the disagreement about specific content, the idea of jus cogens provides further support for Fuller's theory on an inherent morality of international law. In all fairness to Hart, however, we should note that he was primarily concerned about domestic legal systems.

We should recognize a third position in these debates, namely that both Hart and Fuller are right in different contexts. Yet the very existence of the alternative position provides a bulwark in international criminal law against relying too much on positive law, on the one hand, or too much of a rush into vague principle of morality, on the other. A dialectic relationship between positivism and a value-based theory of law seems like the right approach.

An entirely different critique of positivism was developed by Ronald Dworkin, who was a student under Hart at Oxford. Dworkin has a sophisticated sensitivity to the English language and developed many compelling arguments by focusing on the concepts of discretion; interpretation; and for our purposes, the most significant: the theory of rights. In *Taking Rights Seriously*, Dworkin intuitively finds the unoccupied square in the systematic relationship between *Recht* and *Gesetz*, that is, law as principle and law as regularity.[59] Admittedly, Dworkin does not focus on the notion of objective Right but only individual rights as foundational in any legal system.[60]

[57] *See generally*, Rome Statute, *supra* note 3.
[58] *See* Hart, *supra* note 10, at 100.
[59] *See, e.g.*, Ronald Dworkin, Taking Rights Seriously 364 (1977) ("[A] claim of political right is a claim to a trump over the general welfare for the account of a particular individual.").
[60] *See id.*

Dworkin addressed his critique both of Hart's positivism and Bentham's utilitarianism. The latter is theory elaborated in Jeremy Bentham's famous work: *Principles of Morals and Legislation*.[61] This leading text of English jurisprudence preceded Immanuel Kant's *Foundations of the Metaphysics of Morals* by five years.[62] Kant, the reclusive Königsberg philosopher, writing in German, was the greatest legal philosopher of his time.[63] In his various work from 1785 to 1797, we encounter a systematic distinction between moral theory and legal theory.

As indicated by his title, Bentham's magnum opus addressed the intersection of utility and legislative policy.[64] He did write some things about "rights" that suggest an English preference for empiricism over abstract philosophy. Bentham's famous line, to which Dworkin would respond, at least in part, two centuries later was "Natural rights is simple nonsense: natural and imprescriptible rights, rhetorical nonsense, nonsense upon stilts."[65] Dworkin argued in favor of emphasizing rights, but that does not necessarily imply natural rights.

It seems that Dworkin was more interested in generating a critique of utilitarianism than in defending a concept of objective Right (Recht) or personal rights. There are many versions of the general principle of utilitarianism—the greatest good for the greatest number—and equally as many difficulties. The presupposition is that utility is objective, and we can just ignore the problem of "the greatest number." First, in a market economy,[66] utility is not objective but based on consumer preferences. Some people like shoes; others like hats. There is no objective basis of comparison. A free market, based on subjective preference, is the only way to determine value. The utility of paper money is that it enables those with shoes to trade with distant partners who make hats. Yet in the current neo-nationalist wave, we also find smaller countries, like Poland and Hungary, holding onto minor currencies that would seem to

[61] JEREMY BENTHAM, THE PRINCIPLES OF MORALS AND LEGISLATION (Prometheus Books 1988) (1780).

[62] *See* IMMANUEL KANT, FOUNDATIONS OF THE METAPHYSICS OF MORALS (Lewis W. Beck trans., 1959) (1785).

[63] *See* George P. Fletcher, *Why Kant*, 87 COLUM. L. REV. 421 (1987).

[64] *See generally*, BENTHAM, *supra* note 61.

[65] NONSENSE UPON STILTS: BENTHAM, BURKE and MARX ON THE RIGHTS OF MAN 53 (Jeremy Waldron ed., 1987).

[66] *See* ADAM SMITH, AN INQUIRY INTO THE NATURE AND CAUSES OF THE WEALTH OF NATIONS (R.H. Campbell et al. eds., Liberty Classics 1981) (1776).

make trading with the rest of the world more difficult.[67] Those who want to buy their goods must often first buy their paper money.

As to Bentham's thesis about the "greatest number," his claim ignores generational and international boundaries. Consider the utility of cutting down forests for the sake of building homes in the present generation. Future generations should be considered as well, but there is no logical discount factor to gauge their interests. If everyone on the planet and in the future counted as one, the entire calculus would yield infinity as the "greatest number."

The theory of personal rights was already well developed in American jurisprudence as of about 100 years ago. Wesley Hohfeld developed a theory of jural relations in the *Yale Law Journal*, ignored at the time but now regarded as a classic.[68] Essentially, personal rights are opposed to duties, that is, for every person who has a right, there is someone subject to a duty.[69] The system goes on to elaborate three other pairs of jural relations, including relations bearing on the ability to modify rights and duties. Duties are of greater interest to us in the international criminal law, in particular the duty to obey military orders.

3. Duty as the Essential Component of Legal Cultures

The notion of *Pflicht* or duty resonates more with Kantian philosophy than Benthamite utilitarianism. An act is moral, according to Kant, only if done for the sake of duty alone.[70] If I visit a sick person for reasons of personal affection, I am not acting for the sake of duty alone. If I am seeking to maximize my pleasure and avoid pain, I am not acting for the sake of duty alone. The conflict between Bentham and Kant turns on the relevance of the individual self. It seems that Bentham enthrones the personal self, and Kant emphasizes the existence of others and the disappearing self in moral conduct.

[67] *See* Jan Cienski, *Euro Push in Poland Pitched as a Peace Offering with EU*, Politico (Jan. 4, 2018), https://www.politico.eu/article/the-case-for-poland-to-join-the-euro/; *Hungary Is in No Rush to Join Euro Zone, Minister Says*, Reuters (Mar. 24, 2018), https://www.reuters.com/article/us-hungary-euro-minister/hungary-in-no-rush-to-join-euro-zone-minister-says-idUSKBN1H0085.

[68] *See* Wesley Newcomb Hohfeld, *Fundamental Legal Conceptions as Applied in Judicial Reasoning*, 26 Yale L.J. 710, 718–20 (1917).

[69] *Id.*

[70] Kant, *supra* note 62, at 9–10.

In *Rights Talk: The Impoverishment of Political Discourse*, Mary Ann Glendon argues in favor of de-emphasizing rights in favor of our duties and responsibility to other people.[71] This shift in emphasis is in sync with the Western religious tradition. The Ten Commandments do not generate rights but rather—in a series of thou shalt not's—impose duties on others.[72] The concept of Mitzvah or commandment imposing duties in the Jewish thought is fundamental. Indeed, the duties have been expanded to 613 commandments,[73] and the Bar or Bat Mitzvah (male and female) is a critical rite of passage for young adults. The ritual implies that the young adult become subject to the commandments. He or she then has a personal duty to follow the religious, ordained commandments.

The intriguing sidelight of this discussion is that there is no linguistic variation in the concept of law that enthrones the notion of duty as the label for the legal system as a whole. This is true even though the notion is relatively clear and consistent (*Pflicht*, duty, *deber*, *obyazannosti*) over legal systems of the world. Duty is the central idea of all legal systems and yet does not receive the attention it deserves in our contemporary rights-oriented, egocentric legal cultures. The term "deontology" describes philosophical theories that focus on duty.[74] Yet we do not seem to have a school of deontological legal theory. The closest may be in the work of Michael S. Moore.[75]

The duties that have received some attention in international criminal law are the duty to obey orders and the duty to obey the law. Article 33(1)(a) on superior orders requires that the person received the order be under "a legal obligation" to obey the relevant order and then goes to put the burden on subordinate to determine whether the order is lawful.[76] The Russian version of this phrase юридически обязано [juridichesky obyazano] means "judicially obligated."[77] That may be as close as we get to an explicit reference to duty in the Rome Statute.

The more general problem is the duty to obey the law. Inculcating this duty is the mission of all legal systems, however unjust they may be. The problem raised therefore is whether a general defense is available to all citizens

[71] *See* Mary Ann Glendon, Rights Talk: The Impoverishment of Political Discourse (1993).

[72] *See generally* Exodus 20:1–17.

[73] Maimonides, Mishnah Torah (The Code of Law).

[74] *Deontological Ethics*, Stan. Encyclopedia Philosophy (Oct. 17, 2016) (online).

[75] *See, e.g.*, Michael S. Moore, *Patrolling the Borders of Consequentialist Justifications: The Scope of Agent-Relative Restrictions*, 27 Law & Phil. 35 (2007).

[76] *See* Rome Statute, *supra* note 3, art. 33(1)(a).

[77] *Id.* (Rus.).

comparable to Article 33 for the military.[78] Legal philosophers—notably Hart and Fuller—have approached this question by asking whether the law is really a law.[79] There might be a non-moral sense of duty that applies even in cases of unjust laws. At least the courts would insist that there is a duty to obey the law in order to justify the punishments of offenders.

One of the most common problems in all legal systems is the duty to respond to a military draft in an apparently unjust war. American law has approached this question by asking whether the objection to the war is categorical, that is, based on a religious commitment not to take up arms.[80] In other words, the government does not trust its citizens to make the kind of judgments we expect from the military, namely to assess whether the order is "manifestly unlawful."[81]

In the extensive article on "Civil Disobedience" in the *Stanford Encyclopedia of Philosophy*, we find a detailed analysis of the conditions for disobeying particular laws to be considered legitimate.[82] There is obviously a difference between a private objection to paying taxes (to save money) and a principled objection to the government's ability to impose "taxation with representation." Yet in the article we find little attention to the preliminary, nonpolitical duty to obey the law.[83] The analogy between the military and the entire society breaks down because the military has the specific need of efficient combat. Of course, civilian authorities would like to minimize their cost of law enforcement, and inculcating a sense of duty to obey the law might be an efficient way to do this.

While we could well argue for voluntary military service, we cannot justify the voluntary compliance with the criminal law. Even the Rome Statute is binding on the citizens of countries who may not have ratified the Statute; may be entirely hostile to the ICC, for example, the United States; but still the statute is binding on all the those whose countries who meet the criteria of jurisdiction and admissibility.[84] Admittedly there is a difference between malum prohibitum and malum in se. All the offenses of the Rome Statute—except perhaps the administrative offenses in Article 70[85]—are malum in se,

[78] *See id.*
[79] *See supra* pt. 30.
[80] *See, e.g.*, 50 U.S.C. § 3806 (2018).
[81] *See* Rome Statute, *supra* note 3, art. 33(1)(c).
[82] *Civil Disobedience*, STAN. ENCYCLOPEDIA PHILOS. (Dec. 20, 2017) (online).
[83] *See id.*
[84] *See* Rome Statute, *supra* note 3, art. 12.
[85] Rome Statute, *supra* note 3, art. 70.

that is, they are morally wrong regardless of their being officially enacted and binding.

4. Justice

Having explored relevant variations of law, rights, and duties, we should turn to the second of the half of the dichotomy posed in the title of this chapter: the theory of justice. In the philosophical theory of justice, we must distinguish among relevant areas of private and criminal law. Retributive justice applies in criminal law, corrective justice in torts, and distributive justice in property law. In all of these areas, the claims of justice face challenges from utilitarian and economic considerations and based on efficiency, for example, deterrence in criminal law, searching for the cheapest cost avoider in tort law, and stability in property law. Why the latter approaches are not considered aspects of justice remains to be explained.

The leading exponent of retributive justice in criminal law was Immanuel Kant.[86] The basic idea is that if one commits a crime, presumably one malum in se, you create an imbalance in the natural order of things, one that only be corrected by punishment. Besides prescribing capital punishment for homicide, the theory does not quite work for rape and theft. One problem may be that Kant's moral theory often intersects with his legal theory. One way to justify retributivism is to ask someone in advance, what would you deserve for killing someone, stealing their bicycle, or raping their wives. The answer tells us something about the character of the person questioned. You would not have not much respect for someone who responded, "If I raped a member of your family, I would deserve a ten dollar fine."

You would have more respect for the rapists who says that he deserves serious punishment. Recall the ambiguity in Caine's response to God after killing his brother Abel. One interpretation of the Hebrew is "my punishment is more than I can bear."[87] The other view is that my "sin is more than I can bear."[88] In the latter interpretation, Caine—like Raskolnikov[89]—craves punishment to correct the evil of the crime. If he is complaining about his

[86] *See, e.g.*, IMMANUEL KANT, THE METAPHYSICS OF MORALS (Mary Gregor trans., 1991) (1797).

[87] Genesis 4:13 (New International Version).

[88] *See We Must Never Forget the Danger that Lies Beneath the Surface of the Human Heart*, THE OFFICE OF RABBI SACKS (Jun. 4, 2010), http://rabbisacks.org/thought-for-the-day-4th-june-2010-we-must-never-forget-the-danger-that-lies-beneath-the-surface-of-the-human-heart/.

[89] *See* FYODOR DOSTOYEVSKY, CRIME AND PUNISHMENT (Jessie Coulson trans., 1989) (1866).

punishment, he seems like a whiner and warrants little respect. As if in spirit with the Bible and Dostoyevsky, Kant sees the offender as willing the punishment—a position verging on "consent" to being punishment. We are confused about these issues in the twenty-first century because the process of punishment is now more complicated. In the era of imprisonment, finding a punishment that fits the crime has become complicated. The lex talionis—an eye for an eye—no longer seems compelling.[90]

In my opinion, however, retributive justice is the actual motive of all systems of punishment. True, practical people shun moral philosophy in favor of deterrence. Yet if it is hard to know whether the punishment fits the crime, it is even harder to calculate the deterrent effect of punishing one more offender. The factor of causation alone makes the rational assessment of deterrence impossible. New York now has the lowest crime rate since the 1950s.[91] Is this a consequence of having more supposed offenders in prison? How do we know? And even if we did, how would project the causal effect in the future? How long in the future and in what geographical region? The slightest attempt to calculate these imponderables should make retribution more appealing.

John Braithwaite and Philip Pettit have argued in favor of restorative justice, namely a system of mediation that brings to restore the relationship between the offender and the victim.[92] The primary example in practice has been the South African Truth and Reconciliation Commission.[93] This approach is certainly cheaper than imprisonment, but it would not work for crimes that leave lasting consequences, such as the crimes prosecuted in the ICC. The TRC was tried in South Africa after apartheid and generated many objections from those who saw the Commission as a way of circumventing the process of justice for important political leaders.[94] Though the TRC might have been more about reconciliation than about justice, it represents an important effort to find practical ways of overcoming a collective sense of guilt.

[90] *Lex Talionis*, MERRIAM-WEBSTER (2018) ("law of retribution in kind: an eye for an eye").

[91] Ashley Southall, *Crime in New York City Plunges to a Level Not Seen Since the 1950s*, N.Y. TIMES (Dec. 27, 2017), https://www.nytimes.com/2017/12/27/nyregion/new-york-city-crime-2017.html.

[92] *See generally*, JOHN BRAITHWAITE & PHILIP PETTIT, NOT JUST DESERTS: A REPUBLICAN THEORY OF CRIMINAL JUSTICE (1990).

[93] *Truth and Reconciliation Commission*, DEP'T JUST. (last visited Jan. 12, 2019), http://www.justice.gov.za/trc/.

[94] *See* Paul Pereira, *The Road Ahead May Be Rocky Indeed*, Africa News Service, Apr. 30, 1997.

Now as to why deterrence—and the other alternative to retributive justice—are not in themselves theories of justice, the answer is that these supposedly practical alternatives do not respond to Aristotle's definition of justice, namely giving every person his due.[95] Deterrence may be a useful goal, though with unquantifiable benefits. It has nothing to do with the particular offender. It is the classic example of using a person as means to an end—not respecting them as ends in themselves. Also, the idea that one could calculate the causal effect of a single incident of punishment verges on fantasy. This is not a practical theory for practical people.

Yet there is something about punishing suspected criminals that leads practical people to deceive themselves. Do we know the practical benefits in the United States of having the highest per capita prison population in the world?[96] We have no idea, and the criminogenic effects of prison might be worse than the deterrent effects. Nor we do know the practical benefits of many institutions favored by governments in the last several centuries. We think that spending money on the military deters war, but no one can even estimate this benefit at the margin. We think that torture will reveal useful military information, but there is little evidence for this.[97] The more we try to approach these issues in terms of cost/benefit analysis, the better Kant's theory of retribution begins to look.

In tort law, the conflict is between corrective justice and the search of the cheapest cost avoider, argued effectively by Guido Calabresi and his followers at the Yale Law School. There is no doubt that Calabresi's 1970 classic, *The Costs of Accidents*, defined one side of the field for generations.[98] I write "one sided" because Calabresi, a macro-economist, never effectively defended his views against the micro-economists at the University of Chicago, mostly Ronald Coase, *The Problem of Social Cost* (1960).[99] Nonetheless, good lawyers interested in tort law should know both sides of these issues.

Whatever their differences, the economic analysts of law have little to say to the advocates of corrective justice. The claim is that tort law is no more

[95] *See* Aristotle, Nicomachean Ethics 162–63 (Sarah Broadie ed., Christopher Rowe trans., Oxford University Press 2002) (c. 384 B.C.E.)

[96] *See* Roy Walmsley, *World Prison Population List*, Institute For Criminal Policy Research (11th ed.) (2016), http://prisonstudies.org/sites/default/files/resources/downloads/world_prison_population_list_11th_edition_0.pdf.

[97] *See* Matt Apuzzo, Haeyoun Park, & Larry Buchanan, *Does Torture Work? The C.I.A.'s Claims and What the Committee Found*, N.Y. Times (Dec. 9, 2014), https://www.nytimes.com/interactive/2014/12/08/world/does-torture-work-the-cias-claims-and-what-the-committee-found.html.

[98] Guido Calabresi, The Costs of Accidents: A Legal and Economic Analysis (1970).

[99] *See* Ronald Coase, *The Problem of Social Cost*, 3 J.L. & Econ. 1 (1960).

about efficiency than criminal punishment is about deterrence.[100] Corrective justice requires that the defendant compensates the victim for his loss. This requires a shift of assets from the former to the latter. The problem is that in the end if the plaintiff suffers a $500 loss and the defendant pays the victim $500, we have shifted the loss but only created a new inequality. Perhaps the right result is to shift half the loss, but the way tort responds to these issues is much more complicated. We encounter a whole range of range of issues that have bearing on the proper interpretation of the Alien Tort Claims Act: punitive damages, pain and suffering, relevance of insurance, and whether this can be disclosed to the jury. In fact, there is a lot of money in tort law both for victims and good lawyers, but it has little to do with corrective justice.

A free market in property rights should lead to a Pareto-optimal or efficient solution at the end of trading. But this presupposes many things: a clear legal definition of the property (real, personal, intellectual), a basis for establishing the validity of the transfer, and a legal regime to protect these rights against theft. Though the common law of property never satisfied these criteria as well, say, as the French definition of property that rid itself of feudal influences after the 1789 Revolution, capitalism has nonetheless prospered under the historical encumbrances of the common law.

A just system of property (real, personal, intellectual) would begin with an equal distribution to all the relevant parties (a problem about national borders we leave aside) and then permit trading. This would be rendered more efficient by having a common denominator of value, such as gold or paper money, which would also be equally distributed. To understand why an initially just distribution will not remain stable, we need only turn to the contemporary stock market.

There are two forms of value traded on the stock market: bonds and shares of ownership. The latter are called equity—a term that carries historical associations with justice. How this all bears on theories of justice requires some explanation. Recall the dispute that arose after Lord Coke's decision in *Dr. Bonham's Case*.[101] This appeared to be about "common right and reason,"[102] but King James I had a different idea of the highest value that should govern the legal system. The Chancellor of the Exchequer acquired the power to issue injunctions in equity to control legal decisions. Thus, we

[100] See the work of Ernest Weinrib in Toronto and my own *Fairness and Utility in Tort Theory*, 85 Harv. L. Rev. 537 (1972).

[101] *See* Dr. Bonham's Case, 77 Eng. Rep. 638 (C.P. 1610).

[102] *Id.* at 652.

had a battle between the courts of law and the courts of equity for supremacy of the legal system.

The common law works by imposing judgments of damages. Courts of equity operate by specific injunctions, directed to the person, to act at the risk of being held in contempt. The implications are important for our purposes. One is the coincidental blessing of distinguishing legal interests and equitable interests. The distinction has given birth to several legal institutions of great value that define the financial holdings of the modern corporation. The shareholders, who purchases their shares on the equity markets, elect the management of the corporations. One acquires control by buying shares on equity markets. For these purposes, equity is an arbitrary term that carries no implications for the theory of justice.

The historical significance of equity is evident as well in certain institutions just as the availability of a jury trial. The Seventh Amendment to the U.S. Constitution prescribes: "In Suits at common law, where the value in controversy shall exceed twenty dollars, the right of trial by jury shall be preserved, and no fact tried by a jury, shall be otherwise re-examined in any Court of the United States, than according to the rules of the common law."[103]

There are many words and phrases in the Amendment that bear on our inquiry (common law, value, right, fact), but the central point is that the guarantee of jury trials applies at law but implicitly not in equity. Oddly, there is nothing in the Constitution to inform us of the historical decision in the seventeenth century that equitable injunctions prevail against decisions of the common law courts.

The narrow issue in *Roe v. Wade*,[104] the most hotly discussed precedent of the Supreme Court in summer of 2018, was whether the Texas court should issue an injunction against the enforcement of the local abortion law. The Supreme Court refrained from issuing the injunction on the assumption that the Texas court would abide by the judgment. This is an important point: respect for the Constitution, as interpreted by the Supreme Court, implies that the remedy of a direct order to comply, namely an injunction, is not always necessary. But these were simpler times—a time when a 7-2 decision would be respected for its reasoning.

Equity has had a dual heritage. On the one hand, the institution represents the power of the crown, as expressed through Chancery, to override the decisions

[103] U.S. CONST. amend. VII.
[104] 410 U.S. 113 (1973).

of the common law court. On the other hand, the aspirations of equity point toward higher principles that warrant supremacy over the common law. These aspirations are revealed in the maxims of equity. Here are a few of the more interesting points. (A) Equity regards as done that which ought to be done, (B) Equity looks to substance rather to form.[105] These twin aspirations may be related. To achieve a solid claim to power over Coke and the law courts, the courts of equity had to appeal to higher principles, namely to principles of justice.

As we delve into the theory of justice, one might hope for less ambiguity than we found in the aforementioned concepts of law (*Recht, Gesetz,* etc.). But alas it is not true. We see this ambiguity most clearly in German as the distinction between *Gerechtigkeit* (justice as principle) and *Justiz* (the institution). So, the Justice Department in the United States is simply a bureau of law enforcement (*Justiz*). It is not necessarily the watchdog of justice as an ideal. Indeed, in some cases, it is the contrary. The president controls the Justice Department in a manner comparable to King James's use of equity to supersede the decisions of the common law. Yet there has been an evolution toward the institution's use of an independent prosecutor, such as Robert Mueller's investigation of the possible interference of the Russians in the 2016 election.[106] It is unclear whether the president can fire the special counsel.[107] With the confirmation of Brett Kavanaugh to the Supreme Court, there could be a serious danger that the president may have chosen a Justice who will protect him from numerous alleged legal violations.

In this chapter, we are not interested in *Justiz* but Justice (*Gerechtigkeit*) as an ideal. This is the idea expressed in Deuteronomy 16:20: "Follow justice and justice alone, so that you may live and possess the land the LORD your God is giving you."[108] The implication is that the Israelites would not deserve the land if they did hold justice as their ideal. This maxim is now the subject of folk songs and is often stated: *Tsdek, Tsdek tirdof.* Justice, Justice Shalt Thou Pursue. The idea is obvious: We must pursue *Gerechtigkeit*, namely justice as an ideal. We can have the criminal justice system and lock people up,

[105] For more, see GEORGE P. FLETCHER & STEVE SHEPPARD, AMERICAN LAW IN A GLOBAL CONTEXT: THE BASICS ch. 16 (2005).

[106] *See* Neal Katyal, *Trump or Congress Can Still Block Robert Mueller. I Know. I Wrote the Rules.*, WASH. POST POSTEVERYTHING (May 19, 2017), https://www.washingtonpost.com/posteverything/wp/2017/05/19/politics-could-still-block-muellers-investigation-i-know-i-wrote-the-rules/?utm_term=.c3108a252ad6.

[107] *See* Eric Columbus, *Could Trump Fire Mueller? It's Complicated.*, POLITICO (Aug. 3, 2017), https://www.politico.com/magazine/story/2017/08/03/could-trump-fire-mueller-its-complicated-215453.

[108] Deuteronomy 16:20 (New International Version).

even impose the death penalty, but without the pursuit of justice, we would be running a police state.

5. The Political Side of Justice

Judicial review in the United States was recognized for the first time in 1803 in *Marbury v. Madison*.[109] It is obviously anti-democratic and for that reason acceptable only so far as the courts are not subject to political manipulation. Nonetheless, in the United States, judicial review is limited to cases and controversies where the plaintiff has a personal interest in the dispute, that is, the plaintiff has "standing."[110] There is no abstract review of legislation as you might find in constitutional courts in Europe, for example, the Bundesverfassungsgericht in Germany. There is nothing quite like judicial review in the International Legal Order. The only way to change an interpretation of the Rome Statute is to conclude a meeting of State Parties such as the Kampala Conference of 2010, which converted the collective crimes inherited from the Geneva Conventions to cases based on identifiable individuals responsible for crimes such as aggression.[111]

It turns out to be impossible to separate politics from law. It is all a matter of degree. The necessity of writing opinions provides some check on judicial authority. Dissenting opinions in the United States ensures some oversight, and often these dissenting opinions form the basis for new precedents overruled past case law. In the final analysis, we cannot measure the objectivity of judicial decisions any more than we can gauge the influence of language on our understanding of the Rome Statute.

The principle of judicial review arguably has a precedent in the common law. As discussed earlier, *Dr. Bonham's Case* the Court of Common Pleas held that a statute was null and void for violating a principle claimed to be inherent in the common law, namely that one could be a judge in his own case.[112] The significant part of the case is Lord Coke's argument that the statute violated "common right and reason."[113] Both of these words are important in

[109] 5 U.S. 137 (1803).
[110] *See* Lujan v. Defenders of Wildlife, 504 U.S. 555, 560–62 (1992).
[111] *See* Resolution Adopting Aggression Amendments to Rome Statute, Rev. Conf. of the Rome Statute, Kampala, Uganda, May 31–June 11, 2010, Annex I, 8*bis*, 13th plen. mtg., I.C.C. Doc. RC/Res.6 (June 11, 2010).
[112] *See* 77 Eng. Rep. at 638.
[113] *Id.* at 652.

illuminating the received understanding of the common law. First, the word Right is the missing analogue to the concepts of *Recht, droit, pravo*—namely the concept of law that stands for law as principle.

Equating the common law with reason is also important because it provides an answer to the mystery of why we regard law as binding. The results of reasoned argument are binding. All claims of theoretical physics are based on reasoned argument. In law and applied physics, you can stumble upon the right answer, but the answer can survive only if backed up by reason.

6. Justice as a Humanistic Discipline

If you were planning a course on legal issues for undergraduates, you could not do better than Michael Sandel's series on *Justice: What's The Right Thing to Do?*[114] The purpose of this legal commentary on Sandel's lectures is two-fold: (1) to approach them with precedents and concepts that legal education ingrains in our minds, and (2) to use them as a basis for reviewing many of the philosophical issues were have already covered.

The first lecture, called "The Moral Side of Murder," is based on two famous factual situations, one real and other hypothetical.[115] The real case is *Dudley & Stephens*, an English case decided in 1884.[116] The assumed facts are that four starving shipwrecked sailors were lost at sea with no rescue in sight. In desperation they decided to cannibalize the weakest of the four. There are many issues such as the manner of selection of the victim, the participation of the three remaining both in the killing and the actual eating the body and drinking the blood of the victim, and the personal sense of guilt in doing what they were doing. It is worth noting the legal offense is homicide. Cannibalism as such is not an offense, and the general assumption is that this never happens except in cases of extreme necessity. If the issue is homicide on the high seas, there is a serious question about the jurisdiction of the English courts. Let us put these aside and focus on the central question of necessity as a possible justification. See our previous discussion of including necessity in the offenses officially recognized under the Rome Statute.

[114] *See* MICHAEL J. SANDEL, JUSTICE: WHAT'S THE RIGHT THING TO DO? (2010). These lectures are available on YouTube at https://www.youtube.com/watch?v=kBdfcR-8hEY&list=PL30C13C91CFFEFEA6. They are worth watching in and of themselves.

[115] *Id.*

[116] Regina v. Dudley and Stephens, 14 Q.B.D. 273 (Eng. 1884).

In the absence of a recognized defense of necessity in English law (apparently this a common problem in all legal systems), the courts were in a quandary.[117] Public sentiments were on the side of the sailors. Survival is a strong human instinct, even stronger than the aversion against eating one's own species. Yet despite the supposed flexibility of the common law, the courts lacked the ingenuity to develop a defense of necessity. In the end, they convicted with the expectation that the Crown would pardon the survivors. This is what indeed happened.[118]

Shipwreck survivor situations recur in art and legal philosophy. Géricault has the *Raft of the Medusa*, now hanging in the Louvre. The painting is based on actual incident of shipwreck of a French ship that occurred off the coast of Africa.[119] Because the *Raft of the Medusa* is thought to display an unpleasant truth, some refer to it as a metaphor for our political conflicts in the modern era.

Immanuel Kant discussed two different cases of surviving on the open sea with lifted space on a life raft. In one case, the survivors on the ship prevent someone at sea from boarding the raft and in the other, a person at sea pushes one of those on board off in order to gain a place.[120] These examples illustrate two different versions of necessity recognized in the German Civil Code. One is called defensive necessity, typified by shooting an attacking dog.[121] The other is called aggressive necessity, assessed in the book on property.[122] The famous case is *Vincent v. Lake Erie Transp. Co.*[123] The ship was tied to the dock during a storm, which was the reasonable thing to do under a cost/benefit analysis. The shipowner was s nonetheless held liable underscoring the principle that if as a matter of property law, the dock owner was not entitled to defend his property in the storm (so held in a previous case), he was entitled to compensation for the damage done. Note that under defensive necessity (shooting the dog), the dog owner is not entitled to compensation.

117 *Id.*

118 *See* Michael G. Mallin, *In Warm Blood: Some Historical and Procedural Aspects of Regina v. Dudley & Stephens*, 34 U. Chi. L. Rev. 387, 406–07 (1967) (citing Times (London), Dec. 15, 1884, at 6).

119 *See* Theodore Gericault, *The Raft of the 'Medusa'* in Musee du Louvre, Paris (1819); Moshe Carmilly-Weinberger, Fear of Art: Censorship and Freedom of Expression in Art 73 (1986).

120 *See* Kant: Political Writings 81 n. (H.S. Reiss ed.) (2d ed. 1991).

121 Burgerliches Gesetzbuch [hereinafter BGB] § 228.

122 *Id.* at § 904.

123 109 Minn. 456 (1910).

Now in the Kantian cases, we are dealing with issues of human life, so it is not clear that the same principles of defensive and aggressive necessity apply. When the German Criminal Code finally included a paragraph on necessity as a justification, the general principle was based on balancing interests with a requirement that the means be adequate to achieve the desired end.[124] Presumably, homicide is not an appropriate means (nor would be torture). There are many borderline cases such as physical restraint.

Underlying the Kantian life raft examples is the act/omission distinction, which is the second basic legal distinction in Sandel's first lecture.[125] The hypothetical of the trolley car (would you kill the fat man?) was originally developed by Philippa Foot in 1967 and then popularized by Frances Kamm. The basic situation is that an out-of-control trolley is bearing down on five people tied to the tracks. You are standing at the switch and could shunt the trolley onto another track where it would kill only one person. Of course, there are many variations in the literature and in popular philosophy. But they all boil down to a single conflict: the difference between acting and failing to act.

If we ask why this matters, there are many avenues of reply. We could focus on causation, already discussed in chapter 4.[126] We could focus on actual killing versus being a bystander on which we might impose special duties of rescue. If you shunt the trolley and kill one, you are clearly the cause. You have blood on your hands. If you are merely a bystander, you are among the many hundreds (Kitty Genovese)[127] or thousands (the Holocaust) who could have intervened and didn't. In the trolley hypothetical, there is apparently nobody else who might shunt the trolley, which makes the case more difficult. Generally, in America, we insist on special duties of rescue based on a profession (lifeguard, railroad engineer in the trolley case, medical professional). Nonetheless, the starting point for analysis is the act/omission distinction.

Sandel's second lecture begins a more formal treatment of philosophical schools. He begins by offering a general description of utilitarianism in Bentham and Mill.[128] As I have already argued, I consider these views incoherent when extrapolated over time and space. It is obvious that Sandel saw it this way as well because he begins by establishing a baseline from which he will distance himself in the course of the lectures.

[124] *See* German Criminal Code (Strafgesetzbuch, StGB) § 34.

[125] *See* Sandel, *supra* note 114.

[126] *See supra* ch. IV.

[127] Martin Gansberg, *37 Who Saw Murder Didn't Call the Police*, N.Y. Times (Mar. 27, 1964), https://www.nytimes.com/1964/03/27/37-who-saw-murder-didnt-call-the-police.html.

[128] *See* Sandel, *supra* note 114.

He could move in many directions in favor of what he calls "categorical" schools. That word suggests Kant's categorical imperative, but instead he moves toward various theories of rights, beginning with his colleague, Robert Nozick. In *Anarchy, State and Utopia*, Nozick was responding to John Rawls's *A Theory of Justice*.[129] It is obvious that there are many dimensions of this argument and Sandel chose to go from Bentham to Nozick's theory of rights.

Sandel labels Nozick's theory as Libertarianism.[130] This is only partially correct. True, Libertarians are generally opposed to the role of government in society, but perhaps leave out the point that life in a state of nature is "nasty, brutish, and short."[131] Nozick is not opposed to the legal protection of property rights, which imply inheritance and tort liability for damages to property. Property is a much more expansive concept than Nozick realized. Presumably, it would include a right to reputation, which leads to a right to privacy and tort liability for defamation.

Perhaps the most interesting issue raises by Nozick's claim of property rights is taxation, particularly progressive income taxation. As to any form of taxation (sales, income, inheritance), the arguable illegitimacy of taxation is implicit in Nozick's claim of property rights. There are some significant claims of property based on discovery, for example, Spain's claim to own all of North America, and the goldminer's claim to owning an entire vein of gold by discovering one nugget. These claims are ridiculous without some social convention about when a footprint implies control over an area too large and valuable to actually dominate. Consider claims of owning the moon. Would the United States' landing on the moon imply that we own the entire thing including the dark side, which no one could see until the Chinese landed an explorer in January 2019?[132] These claims are preposterous (or, better, lunacy).

If social conventions are necessary for claims of property by discovery, the legal regime is necessary to say that these claims have any meaningful sense. The copyright and patents clause of the Constitution provides that: "[the Congress shall have power] To promote the [p]rogress of [s]cience and useful [a]rts, by securing for limited [t]imes to [a]uthors and [i]nventors the exclusive [r]ight to their respective [w]ritings and [d]iscoveries."[133] The language

[129] *See* ROBERT NOZICK, ANARCHY, STATE, AND UTOPIA (1974); JOHN RAWLS, A THEORY OF JUSTICE (1971).

[130] *See* Sandel, *supra* note 114.

[131] THOMAS HOBBES, LEVIATHAN 186 (C.B. Macpherson ed., 1985) (1651).

[132] Ken Moritsugu, China Lunar Probe Sheds Light on the "Dark" Side of the Moon, AP (Jan. 3, 2019), https://www.apnews.com/c4dc6858a32b4b61bdbc6aebf5459a91.

[133] U.S. CONST. art. I, § 8, cl. 8.

here indicates that copyright and patents are granted to guarantee the property that appears to exist first at common law. Whatever rights are granted by U.S. legislation, the guarantee rights only apply to the United States and for a limited time. Yet underlying these claims to legal rights, there must be a moral principle that investing individual creativity in the external world should secure to an individual a governmentally protected property right. These claims are certainly more plausible than claims of ownership based on discovery.

The interesting challenge implied by Nozick's libertarianism is the legitimacy of taxation, in particular, progressive income taxation. The argument here is similar to why claims of intellectual property are limited by time and geography. The state is involved in the protection of copyright and patents and must legislate in the public interest. The same is true about the use of state power to protect basketball stars or internet entrepreneurs in their claims of ownership over all the proceeds they receive when people pay for their service. First, they pay by various means that are secured by the state. If the state secures their income, the state is entitled to a share for its services. This is called taxation.

For technical, federalist reasons, income taxation required the passage of the Sixteenth Amendment.[134] This was the first amendment after the Civil War and thus the states' rights issues were still highly contentious, as they were until the expansion of the Commerce clause under the FDR administration and remain, to some extent, today. It still takes constitutional ingenuity to approve of other nationwide measures such as Obamacare.

From an economic point of view, the most interesting feature of taxation is progressive income taxation. It appears on the surface that the rich pay proportionately more, a higher percentage based on the income bracket. The underlying principle is called the diminishing marginal utility of the dollar, for example my 200,000th dollar is worth less to me than my 2000th dollar. If this is true, then the taxation is equal across income brackets. The principle makes sense, but only up to a limit. If the money is sitting in the bank, the principle of diminishing marginal utility is right. Yet those who have money are also conditioned to enjoy things that the poor are not. They care more about diamonds and real pearls rather than fake jewelry, and some suffer when they must travel coach. Progressive income taxation and enforcement

[134] *Id.*, amend. XVI.

by the IRS are necessary to counter the enormous differential in incomes between the highest 1 percent and the lowest 50 percent.

The fourth lecture is about John Locke, whose treatises of government have had an enormous influence on American constitutional thinking.[135] I will focus on just two of these, both enunciated in the Declaration of Independence. The first is that government depends on the consent of the governed. This is obviously a fiction. No one ever lives in a state of nature and then decides to form a government. Governments exist at the family level, in tribes, monarchies, and democracies. Then philosophers try to rationalize and justify the existing institution. No one ever consented, in fact, to leaving the state of nature and then surrendering their supposed liberties to a government. The same would be true about a fantasy raised by Kant and contemporary science fiction, namely disbanding the government. These are useful thought experiments, neither history nor valid projection into the future.

The second issue, also used a justification of revolution, was that all men are created equal. This was interpreted by Lincoln in the *Gettysburg Address* to mean all individuals are created equal.[136] In drafting this phrase, Jefferson, a slave holder, was not thinking about human equality but about national equality—namely between the British and the Americans. In 1776 "all men" referred to all nations. If we understand the phrase as Lincoln did, there are still many puzzles, such as how the weak and the stronger are created equal. In context, Jefferson made sense arguing against U.S. colonial status and Lincoln was right in arguing against slavery. They chose their opponents in ways that their use of the same phrase had a compelling ring both in 1776 and 1863. The interesting word that endures is "created." This is an indication of the shared religious sensibilities of both Jefferson and Lincoln. There is no word linking "creation" and "equality" in any international document that has come to my attention.

The fifth lecture provides a bridge to the discussion of Kant by focusing on the limits of markets with attention to some high-profile legal cases. Most notable among these cases is the *Baby M* case in New Jersey.[137] The keyword that hints at the Kantian leaning is "commodification."[138] As we shall see, there is a problem in confusing Kant's moral theory and his legal theory. The moral

[135] Sandel, *supra* note 114.

[136] Abraham Lincoln, *The Gettysburg Address* (Nov. 19, 1863), *in* LINCOLN ON DEMOCRACY 307 (Mario M. Cuomo & Harold Holzer eds., 1990).

[137] In re Baby M, 537 A.2d 1227 (N.J. 1998).

[138] *See* Sandel, *supra* note 114.

prohibition against using a person as means to your private end (hiring a woman to bear your child) does not necessarily apply to contract law, which, by definition, represents a reciprocal use of the labor of others for personal profit. Still, there are limits in contract law on assigning an employer's rights to another party. I have a commitment to teach for Columbia University, but the trustees could not sell my contract to other potential employers.

The turn to Kant's moral theory takes us back to the central concept of this chapter, the concept of law. Kant recognizes that there are laws of cause and effect, which, governed out conduct, render our actions heteronomous. Freedom, he argues, is express in autonomous action, namely acting on a basis on a law that one gives oneself.[139]

The way one derives this law is by adopting a maxim of action that one can will to be a universal law. Suicide is a good illustration. If I try to will my maxim of killing myself to be a universal law, there is no human life and therefore I do not exist. Now the problem is: what we mean by law in this context. The original German tell us: *Pflicht ist die Notwendigkeit einer Handlung aus Achtung fürs Gesetz. Die Vernunft ermöglicht uns, das Sittengesetz zu erkennen*. My translation: Duty is the necessity of an action out of respect for the law. Reason enables us to recognize the moral law.

This is not autonomous action in the modern sense, which I think is basically doing what you want. This would be heteronomous action. There is all only one moral law for everyone, the assumption being that is a single concept of reason for all human beings. The problem for most people is how one can act in a moral way. For Kant, this means not acting for good reasons but acting out of duty alone. And duty he says is, "the necessity of an action out of respect for the law."[140] Autonomous action therefore is not free in any modern sense. Moral action means being subservient to a law (*Gesetz*) derived by reason. Note the choice of word, not law as principle but law as rule. The notion of the moral law is therefore analogous to a scientific law.

Sandel oversimplifies the analysis of Kant by interpreting acting out of duty alone as acting for a proper motive. This is a frequent mistake. Take the example of visiting a sick friend in the hospital. I may do this out of affection. That seems like a proper motive. No, says Kant, you have to visit your friend out a general sense of duty. The correct word in the formulation of the categorical imperative is not motive but maxim.

[139] *See generally*, *Immanuel Kant*, STAN. ENCYCLOPEDIA PHILOSOPHY (Jan. 25, 2016) (online).
[140] KANT, *supra* note 62, at 400.

Kant's sense of morality often conflicts with common sense; this is particularly true with regard to his position on lying. Lying is always immoral on the theory that if I universalize my maxim of lying, no one will believe anything I say. Therefore, I cannot have a maxim of lying anymore than I can have a maxim to commit suicide. Suppose that you know that at the door of Anne Frank's house in Amsterdam, the Gestapo will ask you where the Jews are hiding. Should you not lie? Of course, doing so represents a judgment of a particular historical situation. Kant had no interest in the relative morality of political regimes. This is an example developed by Benjamin Constant.

Sandel brings the discussion of Kant around to another interpretation of the categorical imperative, the respect for human life as an end not as a means. The reason for this view is that human beings have inherent dignity. This formulation has led, in our time, to a major difference between German and American constitutional law. The fundamental principle of American constitution is equality as expressed in the Fourteenth Amendment.[141] Dignity is not mentioned. On the other hand of the German Grundgesetz is *Die Würde des Menshcne is unantastbar. Sie zu achten und schützen und zu achten ist Verpflichtung aller statlichen Gewalt.* [Human dignity is inviolable. To respect and protect human dignity is the duty of all organs of the state.]

Note the Kantian language: dignity and duty. These terms are of minimal relevance in American political discourse, which turns toward equality and rights. There are some different implications in constitutional law. In contemporary German constitutional law, in particular, the preference for dignity represents a reaction to the National Socialist emphasis on honor. Honor is a feature of social institutions, particularly of the military. Dignity belongs to everyone. The emphasis on human dignity in the Grundgesetz is not a direct influence of Kant but rather a rediscovery and adaptation of an eighteenth-century philosopher to the contemporary political situation. The broader point here is that the meaning of these critical terms depends on context and the implicit opposite in the discussion. Dignity vs. honor is one issue. Dignity vs. equality is another.

The protection of dignity as opposed to equality can have paternalistic implications. This is particularly in the case of the German Grundgesetz, which imposes an affirmative duty on government to protect human dignity.[142] One example from the case law is preventing a dwarf from allowing

[141] U.S. Const. amend. XIV.

[142] *See* Grundgesetz [GG] [federal constitution] art. 21 (F.R.G.).

himself to be used in a circus stunt, let's say, being shot from a cannon. If the issue is equality, the dwarf has the same right as everyone else to decide how to earn a living. One can see the Kantian element reflected in any attempt to prevent someone being used as a means for the pleasure of onlookers.

In the second part of lecture 7, Sandel moves from Kant's moral theory to what he calls Kant's political theory, which leads to a theory of a social contract.[143] This move leads to the adaptation of Kant by John Rawls in his classic *Theory of Justice*.[144] Rawls argues that in the original position, where we do not know anything about our particular selves, in a state of abstract equality, we would choose two principles of justice. The important premise in Rawls's theory is that we are entitled to take risks in the original position, namely whether we would turn out to be strong or weak, good at philosophy or not.

Sandel recognizes that in the real world, contracts are not necessarily just.[145] They are protected by the legal order because they create a new form of property. They have economic value in themselves. This is notably true in the classic case of contracts based on the exchange of promise and, in the common law, a form of consideration. The expectation interest of a delivery of cotton on a certain date generates an asset that has value in itself. The discussion of contracts in a legal exchange provides the foundation of the famous fictional law school class, also at Harvard, the classic *Paper Chase*, with John Houseman.[146]

There is little relationship between contracts in real life and the hypothetical contract employed in the thought experiment of John Rawls. The beauty of Rawls's assumption about our negotiating in the original position is that we would make assumptions about a fundamental distinction between liberty, on the one hand, and social and economic inequalities on the other. The first principle of justice we should derive is the principle of Equal Liberty: each person has an equal right to the most extensive liberties compatible with similar liberties for all. The assumption is that liberty (Kant would have said: *Freiheit* or freedom) has nothing to do with our economic resources. Certainly, this is not true in the political arena. Freedom of speech, if it is to have any influence at all, must be backed by economic resources. Also note FDR's *Four Freedoms*, two of which are freedom from want and freedom from fear.[147] The distinction between liberty and social

[143] *See* Sandel, *supra* note 114.
[144] *See generally*, RAWLS, *supra* note 129.
[145] *See* Sandel, *supra* note 114.
[146] PAPER CHASE (20th Century Fox 1973).
[147] *See* SAMUEL I. ROSENMAN, WORKING WITH ROOSEVELT 263 (1952).

and economic equality is not so obvious but nonetheless Rawls's magisterial work establishes a benchmark for thinking about these issues.

The second principle, the Difference Principle, holds: social and economic inequalities should be arranged so that they are both (a) to the greatest benefit of the least advantaged persons, and (b) attached to offices and positions open to all under conditions of equality of opportunity.[148] Economic inequalities, I assume, are about the material conditions of life, that is, money and other tangible assets (which include marketable contacts). Condition (a) refers presumably to a group of persons, regardless of nationality and generation. The interesting assumption is that it does not make any difference whether the least advantaged seek to work or not. Condition (b) represents a wonderful ideal but one that hardly makes sense in the real world. Our opportunities are shaped by numerous contingent factors, including family, neighborhood, and country. Still, as an ideal, Rawls's principles of justice represent a turning point in the theory of justice.

There is undoubtedly an American influence expressed in Rawls's principle of justice as fairness. That is, if the decision procedure behind the veil of ignorance is fair, the result will be just. The principles of fair play, fair fights, fair elections, etc., all derive from the Anglo-Saxon commitment to the principle: it is does not matter whether you win or lose, it is how you play the game. This would seem strange to most of the world where winning is everything. You can see this in the problem of translation. As we have noted before, it is not easy to translate the war crime in the Rome Statute of depriving a protected person of "a fair and regular trial."[149] The French version reads: *Le fait de priver . . . te autre personne protégée de son droit d'être jugé régulièrement et impartialement.* The notion of a "regular" trial is close to the notion of a fair trial, but it is not same thing. Fairness has a special ring to the American ear. No other language, except, possibly, Hebrew, has a word that corresponds precisely to fairness. The usual translation is "just" (thus rendering Rawls's principle of "justice as fairness" tautological).

Rawls's *Theory of Justice* led to an intense debate in philosophical circles. Yet the debate morphed into a discussion of the self—the universal vs. the particular self. Nozick was first with the theory of self-possession[150] and then Sandel, in his first incarnation, took an intermediate position in favor of a

[148] *See* JOHN RAWLS, JUSTICE AS FAIRNESS: A RESTATEMENT 161 (Erin Kelly ed., 2001).
[149] *See* Rome Statute, *supra* note 3, art. 8(2)(a)(vi).
[150] *See supra* pt. 84.

situated self in *Liberalism and the Limits of Justice*.[151] The debate in the 1970s and early 1980s focused more on the contrast between individualism and communitarianism than on questions of justice. The notion of the self—(abstract in Rawls, concrete in Nozick, and intermediate in the early Sandel)—was at the center of the debate. This was premised on a closer connection between political philosophy and theories of justice.

Not to be ignored in the 1980s was the anticipated fall of Communism in Eastern Europe and the Middle East and the role of philosophers in these political transformations. Roger Scruton was recognized for his activism in Czechoslovakia, Yuli Tamir coined the concept of Liberal Nationalism in Israel, I was writing for the *New York Review of Books* from Budapest, and others were writing in Poland and East Germany. This political activism of philosophers seems to a be a matter of the past. As one astute observer of the fall of Communism noted, in the times of Samizdat and the gulag, intellectuals commanded respect, when free speech triumphs, everyone receives his 15 minutes of fame. We do not know what will happen with the combination of the internet censorship and the current trend toward neofascism in Eastern Europe.

Sandel's eighth lectures focuses on alternatives to Rawls's difference principle. He defends the difference principle against competing claims that personal effort generates a great desert to the social and economic reward. He does this by noting that the desert principle depends on a contingency of living in a society that values particular skills.[152] Depending on time and place, the rewarded skills might be speed, strength, coordination in warfare, or, in our time, intelligence and a gift in turning a phrase. About desert, it is worth noting that in criminal law, the negligent causation of harm is a precondition for deserving punishment, yet in the positive realm, for example, deserving a claim to a gold mine, an accidental discovery will suffice.

The ninth lecture addresses affirmative action, which means that the criteria for admission to academic institutions, primarily universities and graduate schools, should consciously prefer applicants from certain racial groups that have historically suffered discrimination. The primary group affected by affirmative action is African Americans. Hispanics and American Indians are also beneficiaries, but the inclusion of these groups highlights the question of who actually constitutes a member of the minority group. In the case

[151] *See* MICHAEL SANDEL, LIBERALISM AND THE LIMITS OF JUSTICE (1982).
[152] *See* Sandel, *supra* note 114.

of African Americans, it is fairly clear who is a member of the group, though there are numerous borderline cases—the offspring of mixed marriages, immigrants from Africa who may be part of the ruling tribes in their home countries, and native-born Americans, like Barack Obama, who won election after the most recent legal decisions in this area.

Those two cases, *Grutter v. Bollinger*[153] and *Gratz v. Bollinger*,[154] came to the Supreme Court in 2003 after two students were denied admission respectively to the law school and the undergraduate college when minority applicants with lower scores were admitted. In the former, the Court held, 5-4, that considering race as a factor in law school admissions was compatible with the equal protection;[155] in the latter, the decision was 5-4 that a policy resembling a quota was unacceptable.[156] Neither of these cases should be taken too seriously. The court has changed its composition, and even those decisions predicted that 25 years afterward, affirmative should not be necessary.[157] The case law being so uncertain and admission officers easily concealing their preferences, we can only consider this problem as a matter of principle.

The fallback position of those opposed to affirmative action is that equality means equality. There is no justification for any form of state-sanctioned discrimination, blacks vs. whites, men vs. women, legitimate vs. illegitimate children, gays vs. straights. At the margin, we face a difficult issue about whether we can justify discrimination between citizens and noncitizens with regard to the right to live in the United States. Most people would say that citizens have a right to live in the United States, while foreigners do not. Thus, some kind of context-based justification of inequality is justifiable.

Many African Americans who achieved success in the United States object to affirmative action because it deprives them of their well-deserved achievement. Two examples are Stephen Carter, a professor at Yale Law School; and Clarence Thomas, Justice on the Supreme Court.[158] My personal opinion is that Carter and Thomas are right. Affirmative action is not justifiable in principle on behalf of those who have not actually been forced to sit at the back of the bus. Those who do succeed are unfairly denied the recognition

[153] 539 U.S. 306 (2003).
[154] 539 U.S. 244 (2003).
[155] 539 U.S. at 306.
[156] 539 U.S. at 244.
[157] 539 U.S. at 343.
[158] *See* STEPHEN CARTER, REFLECTIONS OF AN AFFIRMATIVE ACTION BABY 62, 69 (1991); Adarand Constructors, Inc. v. Pena, 515 U.S. 200, 240 (1995).

they deserve for their personal initiative. Another reason to object is that the other categories—Hispanic and Native American—are too vague to be taken seriously. We know who is a Cherokee Indian, but we don't know whether Senator Elizabeth Warren, who argued that she was 1/16 Native American, and who was later found to be less than 1/64 Native American, counts as a minority.[159]

In the tenth lecture, Sandel turns to Aristotle's theory of virtue as an example of a philosophical theory opposed to his preference for Kant and Rawls. He considers a Supreme Court case about the nature of golf as a sport, but as for additional legal commentary, the relevant issue is the discussion of slavery in Athens.[160] Many of the things Aristotle said about slaves were also said about women before the Nineteenth amendment, namely that they had to stay home to mind home and hearth so that men could debate politics in the public sphere. This is the amendment that prohibited denying the voting franchise on the grounds of "sex."[161] Today we would probably say "gender" to make this point. Note that black men received the right to vote in 1865.[162] We have a had an African American president, but have yet to elect a female as president.

In the eleventh lecture, Sandel turns back to his earlier concerns about communitarianism by addressing the issues of loyalty and patriotism.[163] His primary citation is to Alistair MacIntyre, *After Virtue*.[164] The relevant legal issue here is the question of treason, the most basic crime of disloyalty in the American lexicon. It is the only crime defined in the Constitution, with strict evidentiary requirements (two witnesses to the overt act). It is the oldest statutorily defined crime in Anglo-American history dating back to the time of Edward III. It is defined in more or less the same way in all common law countries.

Article III, section 3 of the Constitution provides defense to the crime as either "waging war against the United States" or "adhering to the enemies of the U.S. and giving them aid and comfort."[165] The required mental state is simply adhering, an emotional disposition of sympathy. In the World Wars

[159] Maggie Astor, *Why Many Native Americans Are Angry with Elizabeth Warren*, N.Y. Times (Oct. 17, 2018), https://www.nytimes.com/2018/10/17/us/politics/elizabeth-warren-dna-test.html.

[160] *See* Sandel, *supra* note 114.

[161] U.S. Const. amend. XIX.

[162] *Id.*, amend. XV.

[163] *See* Sandel, *supra* note 114.

[164] *Id.*

[165] U.S. Const. art. III, § 3.

II cases, this threshold was satisfied by rather routine acts such as holding a money belt or finding one's son a job.[166] Cramer and Haupt were naturalized American citizens. This is important because Germans could not commit treason against the United States, as Americans could not commit treason against Germany (though the crime is defined differently in German law). This is significant because "the waging war" clause would literally apply to all of the Axis powers that declared war against the United States. The reason is that implicit in the constitutional definition is a duty of loyalty to the United States. This is made clear in the federal statute defining crime and requiring a duty of allegiance to the United States. The only case of an actual trial under the "waging war" clause was against Aaron Burr, vice president under Thomas Jefferson.[167] In a trial supervised by John Marshall, Chief Justice of the United States Supreme Court, Aaron Burr was charged under the waging war clause but acquitted.

In the twelfth and final lecture, Sandel begins by discussing issues related to human sexuality. There are many different issues lumped together—masturbation, polygamy, same sex marriage, divorce, abortion. They are recurrent issues but about different questions and treated differently in different societies. Religious institutions, such as the Catholic Church, seek to regulate many of these issues by preaching positions on the nature, the beginning and the end of human life. They are also affected by federalism and the role of the U.S. Constitution. Let us sort them out. Male masturbation is condemned in Genesis 38 as spilling one's seed, which is not wrong per se but because it violated the duty of Onan to provide an heir to Tamar.[168] This is a peculiar religious issue and, arguably, should have no influence on civil society. Female masturbation raised no comparable biblical issue.

Polygamy has a tortured history in the United States. The Mormons (Church of Jesus Christ of Latter Day Saints) favored polygamy, allowing one male and up to four wives. As a result of these views, Mormons were driven out of New York State when they began and settled in Utah, where they are still a collective force in politics. The Mormons have been influential in comparative law largely because the required obligation of every male Mormon to go on a mission abroad, and thus many of them are fluent in various foreign languages. Though polygamy is illegal in the United States, it is

[166] *See, e.g.*, Cramer v. United States, 325 U.S. 1 (1945).
[167] United States v. Burr, 25 F. Cas. 2, 13 (Marshall, Circuit Justice, C.C.D. Va. 1807) (No. 14,692a).
[168] *See* Genesis 38.

acceptable in a large number of Muslim states. Polyandry (one woman and several husbands) is illegal in most, if not all, places. This correlation suggests that the prohibition of polygamy carries an implicit bias against women. This bias should not be tolerated in the United States under interpretations of the equal protection clause, but it is.

As for same sex marriage, there is a good argument for keeping the state out of marriage altogether. Yet, marriage is a social as well as a private institution. Many insurance plans depend on it. Inheritance may depend on it. Also, many people might simply wish to appear as a married couple. Gay marriage generated enough public controversy for the Supreme Court to intervene in state law: *Obergefell v Hodges*.[169] It is hard to avoid state-supported discrimination on these issues, either against women or against men who are required to pay alimony or even "palimony" in cases of a dependent spouse not married. The implicit problem is not marriage but divorce and its consequences. Under American law, two people over the local age of consent (and with no incest issues) can go to the civil hall and take their vows. Divorce is different because once the couple is married, the state has an interest in maintaining the marriage. Thus, divorce requires residence in the state granting the divorce, and it once required rather demanding grounds such as adultery.

Abortion is an entirely different problem, and after *Roe v. Wade* it was thought to be settled law.[170] The argument in favor of a woman's right to decide to bear the child or terminate it (called the pro-choice position) is based on a constitutional right to privacy implicit in the Bill of Rights. Unfortunately, precedent controls this issue only so long as the appointments to the Supreme Court are apolitical. As of the moment, some believe that the issue may soon become controversial again.

Having reached this grand number, in Hebrew: *Meah esrim* (the life span wished upon everyone), and as Sandel winds up his class, I should close by praising his lectures and endorse his parting message that in view of all the conflicting theories, the only way to proceed is to rely upon engagement and reasoned argument. This is the proper calling of both philosophers and lawyers.

[169] 135 S. Ct. at 2584.
[170] 410 U.S. at 113.

Index

For the benefit of digital users, indexed terms that span two pages (e.g., 52–53) may, on occasion, appear on only one of those pages.

The Grammar of Criminal Law: Volume Two: International Criminal Law. George P. Fletcher.

www.ingramcontent.com/pod-product-compliance
Ingram Content Group UK Ltd.
Pitfield, Milton Keynes, MK11 3LW, UK
UKHW020849150926
475595UK00003B/89

9 780190 903572